John Laughland's last book, ~~described~~ described by one reviewer as 'the ~~...~~ ~~...~~ ~~...~~ of the year' in 1994. Renowned as a commentator on European affairs for the *Wall Street Journal Europe*, the *Spectator*, the *Sunday Telegraph* and other papers, John Laughland taught politics and philosophy in Paris for five years, first at the Sorbonne and then at the Institute of Political Science. He studied at Oxford and Munich universities, and has been a visiting lecturer at the University of Bucharest. He is a trustee of the British Helsinki Human Rights Group in Oxford, and European Director of the European Foundation in London. John Laughland now lives in Brussels.

'*The Tainted Source* is one of the most important books ever written about European integration. The chapter on European ideology should be compulsory reading for everyone interested in the European debate. It explains why Europe is an important constitutional issue and why the creation of a European state is unworkable, and in the end will destroy parliamentary democracy'

NORMAN LAMONT

'Preposterous . . . A hideous distortion of both past and present'

SIR EDWARD HEATH in the *Observer*

'*The Tainted Source* shows just how far removed are ideas of European integration, which go back to fascism and even Napoleon, from the Atlantic world of liberty. No commentator – including me – can rival John Laughland for the depth, width and linguistic power with which he conveys this truth'

PROFESSOR NORMAN STONE

'A hundred years ago, Lord Acton noted that "few discoveries are more irritating than those which expose the pedigree of ideas". To judge from outraged reviews of this book by Europhiles, John Laughland has hit a bull's eye'

MARK ALMOND in the *Yorkshire Post*

'I don't know if Laughland is right, or how far he's right, but he certainly makes you think'

EUGEN WEBER in the *National Review*

'This is an insidious and invidious book'

MARTIN WESTLAKE in the
Times Higher Educational Supplement

'Political dynamite'

BRIAN DENNY in the *Morning Star*

'Laughland's views will find few admirers among Europhiles . . . But he is passionate in his view that sovereignty and nationhood are eternal concepts not to be dismissed lightly'

HELEN GIBSON in *Time*

'This latest work is less a spotlight than a ton of plastique . . . Once Laughland's explosive has done its work, the Union's true foundations are exposed'

DAN ATKINSON in the *Catholic Herald*

'Laughland presents a forceful and compelling argument'

MICHAEL MERTES and NORBERT PRILL
(advisers to Chancellor Kohl) in *Prospect*

'A sick view of Europe. Laughland is scholarly, mostly sober, and hopelessly trapped in the kind of intellectual spiral that occurs when you try to apply rigorous logic to a selective view of history'

IAN BELL in the *Scotsman*

'John Laughland has long been one of the Eurosceptics' most effective thinkers . . . No one reading this book could doubt that Laughland is a serious scholar'

ALASTAIR BRUTON in the *European*

'Nothing is what it seems, and it is a merit of John Laughland's book that it reminds us of that painful fact'

MAX BELOFF in the *Times Literary Supplement*

'John Laughland, who has first-hand knowledge of how "Europe" works, explores the myths and half-truths that underlie the EU . . . Three cheers for Laughland, the man who saw the Emperor as he really was: naked'

Contemporary Review

'This work may well be destined for status as a classic anti-European text'

MICHAEL FRY in the *Glasgow Herald*

THE TAINTED SOURCE

SOURCE

The Undemocratic Origins
of the European Idea

JOHN LAUGHLAND

WARNER BOOKS

A *Warner* Book

First published in Great Britain in 1997
by Little, Brown and Company
This edition published in 1998 by Warner Books

Copyright © 1997, 1998 by John Laughland

ILLUSTRATION CREDITS
p. 10: Lapi-Viollet
p. 82: E. T. Archive, National Gallery (Richelieu), and *Zeitschrift für
Geopolitik*, August–September 1939 (Haushofer)
p. 154: *L'Espresso*, 27 December 1992, *France–Allemagne. Parlons franc* by
J.-P. Chevènement (Plon, Paris, 1996); map © HarperCollins Cartographic
p. 158: Palazzo Pubblico, Siena
p. 230: Brian Reading, 'Economic Realities Facing Europe' in *Visions of
Europe*, ed. Stephen Hill (Duckworth, London, 1993)
p. 260: Ullstein-Photoline

The moral right of the author has been asserted.

A CIP catalogue record for this book is
available from the British Library.

ISBN: 0 7515 2324 0

Typeset in Goudy by M Rules
Printed and bound in Great Britain by
Clays Ltd, St Ives plc

Warner Books
A Division of
Little, Brown and Company (UK)
Brettenham House
Lancaster Place
London WC2E 7EN

For M., M., and O., with love

CONTENTS

ACKNOWLEDGEMENTS

Over the last six years, I have profited immensely from conversations and discussions on European questions with many friends and colleagues. During the preparation of this book, many of them have helped to find documents, have read early versions of the text, and have been the source of ideas. I am especially in debt to Mark Almond, Bill Cash, Bernard Cherlonneix, Marie-France Garaud, Edouard Husson, Russell Lewis, John London, Michael Neal, Christine Stone, Johnathan Sunley, Radu Portocala and Eugen Weber. I would also like to thank the editor of this book, Alan Samson, for his friendship, encouragement and professionalism.

'Since the past has ceased to throw its light upon the future, the mind of man wanders in obscurity'

ALEXIS DE TOCQUEVILLE

I

THE WITHERING STATE

*'A brave people will certainly prefer liberty, accompanied with a
virtuous poverty, to a depraved and wealthy servitude'*
EDMUND BURKE, *REFLECTIONS ON THE REVOLUTION IN FRANCE*

In recent years, European politics has resounded to a dull, repeti-
tive thud: that of nails being driven into the coffin of democracy.
The most recent blow came in June 1997, when the French
President called elections early in order to refresh his government's mandate for preparing the country for monetary union:
when the French people denied him this mandate, both the goal
and all its associated policies remained in place nonetheless. In
Britain, it was only as a result of the chance intervention by an
outside force – in the form of the late lamented Sir James Goldsmith – that the two main parties were forced to allow a
referendum on the single currency. Most notoriously, when the
Danes voted 'No' in the 1992 referendum, they were told to vote
again on the same text until they got the answer right.

In July 1996, Belgium effectively suspended parliamentary rule.
The host country of the main European Union institutions
granted its government special powers to rule by decree for a year
and a half on the two most important political questions facing the
state: the budget and the reform of the social security system. The
government awarded itself this *carte blanche* in spite of the fact that
the constitution allows such powers to be granted only in times of
national emergency.

The purpose of the step was to allow the government to tackle the budget deficit, in order to make the country qualify for European monetary union. It is commonly accepted that Belgium has a chance of so qualifying, even though its state debt is over twice what the Maastricht Treaty says it should be: by some strange political alchemy, a country on the verge of bankruptcy can evidently glitter in European eyes as a paragon of financial prudence. But quite why the national legislature was considered otiose was never explained. The Prime Minister just seemed to think that the country could do without its parliament. 'The important thing is that the social partners are in agreement,' he said.

Belgium is a microcosm of Europe. The previous December, the newly elected French government had also obtained the power to rule by decree in order to reform the social security system and reduce the budget deficit. The French Fifth Republic has a notoriously weak parliament, which plays little role in the nation's political life, and this was reflected in the fact that, unlike the Belgian government, the French government did not *ask* for its special powers. Instead, it forced them out of the National Assembly, using the most authoritarian article in the French constitution. The notorious Article 49.3 allows a bill to become law immediately and without debate if the government declares it a matter of confidence, and is not voted out of office within twenty-four hours.

Having thus muzzled the national legislatures, both governments invited the trade unions to discuss a wide range of government policies, including the most important ones. On the one hand, therefore, the elected parliaments were sidelined, and on the other, the governments invited people with no mandate to make laws, and who do not represent the nation, to decide policy with them.

France and Belgium thus put themselves into a similar constitutional position to that from which Britain began to suffocate in the 1970s, when in the name of a 'social contract' trade union leaders and other non-elected people came to be recognised as part of the machinery of government, entitled to share in the general formulation of economic policy. It was only when it was understood by reformers in Britain that, in the words of one of them, 'This was an almost unbelievably blatant violation of the Constitution' (quite apart from being an economic handicap) that they were able to lay the conceptual groundwork for the restoration of a liberal political, and hence economic, order in the country. A liberal economy requires a liberal state.

The idea that national parliamentary rule is useless for dealing with the great political questions of the day is part of a world-wide trend towards supranational administration. According to the view peddled by European federalists, prophets of world government, and technocratic liberals alike, the nation is too small and anachronistic a form of social arrangement to be capable of meeting the challenges of the modern world and its economy. Few of these people have the courage to say that they will abolish the nation-state entirely. But all their other theories in fact support its dislocation. They argue variously that, with modern mass transport, communications, technology, and an increasingly interdependent international economy, 'sovereignty' is meaningless; that the 'region-state' will replace the nation-state; that multinational companies are now more powerful than states, and that they will soon take over many of their functions; or that we are evolving towards governmental structures for the whole planet.

Like the Marxists, such people believe that the structures of the state depend on those of the economy: that the one is a 'super-structure' of the other. Having a primarily economist, rather than political, understanding of the state and law, they believe that the state must adapt to changes in economy. Theirs is a determinist view of history, as of human nature, and they believe that both are governed by the laws of economics, rather than by intelligence and free choice. In fact, the boot is on the other foot: the state, and especially its law, creates the market by ensuring that freely concluded contracts are respected and enforced by a legal framework.

This error flows in part from the stranglehold of economist thinking over modern government. Over recent years, modern politicians have become increasingly in hock to an approach to economics and politics which, by concentrating obsessively on global quantitative analysis, risks undermining the very bases of the liberal order. Excessive reliance on macro-economic data as the principal lode-star for policy-making encourages the illusion that everybody's (economic) interests are the same, and that the only question is how to organise society rationally for their realisation. It also encourages the belief that a country should be managed like a commercial enterprise.

In fact, the modern international economy changes little in the traditional liberal understanding of statehood, which has always understood that the state's role is political and juridical, not primarily economic. The liberal nation-state was precisely never an autarkic economic unit (it is the antithesis of it), and allegiance to a liberal state was never considered incompatible with travelling outside it. Sovereignty never meant isolation. Furthermore, modern trade has been multilateral – and not national or even regional – for several centuries now. International electronic communications are also old: the first transatlantic telegraph cable was laid over 100 years ago, and the first transatlantic steamer crossed the ocean in 1818.

Moreover, government is not – or should not be – mere macro-economic book-keeping. Politics should be based on the recognition that the state is a public entity based on law, not an enterprise run by managerial decisions made in private. Government is a public activity which requires leadership, and the taking of clear choices, in order to carry the people with it. The view that government is only about producing certain material results, and that politicians should be chosen on the extent to which they can 'deliver the goods', is but an illusion built on a debased notion of political legitimacy. In its worst forms, it approaches a sort of feudalism, in which allegiance is bought with protection.

As such, it is corrosive of the sense of citizenship and community. For much of continental Europe, the welfare state is explicitly seen as the glue which holds the state together. This view is especially strong in France, Germany, the Benelux countries,

Scandinavia and Austria. Attractive though these systems can appear from the outside, they encourage citizens to think that their country – and by extension their fellow citizens – owes them a living, and that their allegiance to it depends on what they get out of it materially. This undermines the generous sense of public duty and responsibility which should properly be the hallmark of the citizen, and replaces it with a grasping, selfish mentality instead. Political tensions are thus exacerbated, especially as the honey-pot begins to run dry. It also renders political life sclerotic: although most Continental countries' health and pension systems are bankrupt, no government is truly prepared to grasp the nettle of reform.

Such systems are by definition *dirigiste*. *Dirigisme* is the system of government in which discretionary executive policy-making by governments predominates over neutral law-making by parliaments. It is a managerial or administrative system of rule, in which the government sees itself as issuing commands to society in pursuit of a certain goal, rather than a primarily law-based regime in which the government's principal goal is to maintain an ongoing legal order (the rule of law) by adapting it to the changing contingencies of time and place.

In foreign policy, the replacement of government by administration encourages the proliferation of international bodies, and the illusion that the world can be controlled from on high. It also encourages the view that international negotiation is an end in itself, in which no difficult choices between clashing interests have to be made. But choice implies difference: because a politically independent nation must choose how to interact with the rest of the world, and how to govern its own citizens, the decisions it takes on its own interests will inevitably be different from those of another nation.

Nations, indeed, are considered to be the problem. Just as, in internal affairs, this unpolitical vision regards the free individual choices of citizens as a potential for discord and conflict (rather than realising that properly expressed, such conflict is the stuff of human life), so free nations are held to be a threat to stability and rational economic planning. At worst, the nation – with its supposedly inevitable corollary, nationalism – is considered to bear war within it as the storm-cloud bears the storm. To prevent such wars, runs the argument, it is necessary to subsume nations in supranational ensembles, so that in the 'post-national' future, all political differences evaporate.

Nowhere is a post-national future being pursued with greater vigour than in Europe. It is no coincidence that the consignment of national parliaments to the oubliettes of history is being under-taken in preparation for European monetary union. For that technocratic programme is unpolitical and anti-national. In con-stitutional terms, it goes way beyond and is qualitatively different from the project of creating a single market – even though it may use the language of free exchange between nations to disguise its project of establishing central control over them. Its supporters regard with suspicion the natural conflict between persons, parties, nations, and between their values and goals, which – man being a political animal – are the definitive elements of human society. According to the European ideology, multiplicity implies disorder, and order requires uniformity.

This, the Christian Democrat view of history, holds that nation-states are an obsolete form of political organisation. 'The nation-state . . . cannot solve the great problems of the twenty-first century,' says Chancellor Kohl.[1] To be sure, the ideologues of a post-national Europe never say that nations as such are threat-ened by a post-national Europe. They believe instead that nations need not be constituted in states in order to exist: 'Nation and nation-state are not identical.'[2] But a nation's 'cul-tural identity' – whatever that is – is no more a compensation for its political identity and independence than the kitschy glow of an electric log heater is a satisfactory substitute for the blaze of a real fire.

An independent nation-state is the political expression of a people taking up the challenge of running its own affairs, and throw-ing off the torpor of empire. An independent nation-state is one in which decisions are taken politically, in virtue of public debate and opposition. Being a political form of human association – that is, one in which conflict is recognised and even institutionalised as a healthy constituent of the body politic – it is one which generates law, not directives. To believe that constitutional independence or sovereignty are irrelevant as concepts is to believe that political liberties and the rule of law can exist without the state.

The Vichy government thought that France's identity and nationhood could be preserved even in the absence of national sovereignty: it thereby destroyed the *political* bases of the French nation, and thus of French citizenship. Quite apart from reducing the noble, democratic and challenging concept of political nationhood to the level of contemptible and imbecile folklore – while De Gaulle was leading the Resistance, Marshal Pétain was asking all French children to send him a drawing of their village – this left Vichy France no other notion of citizenship to fall back on except a racial one. The result was buses to Auschwitz.

Finally, to believe that borders – those delineations of jurisdiction which must be clearly drawn in order to exist – can be disposed of or made irrelevant, is to hold that the clarity and rigour of the law, and the public activity of politics, can be dispensed with in favour of the obscurity of bureaucratic regulation and the power of the corridor.

The project of European monetary union is an example of the latter choice. It proposes to place the parliamentary regimes in each European member state (such as they are) under the economic control of a single independent central bank. It is, furthermore, proposed that the overall framework of economic policy (especially the budget) will be decided by the European Council of Ministers, or some sub-grouping of it, even though this body is not accountable to any parliament or electorate. In such a Europe, all essential executive and legislative powers will be divided between three equally unaccountable and unelected institutions: the Central Bank, the Council of Ministers, and the European Commission.

European federalists lyricise the Utopian idea that all European states have the same interests with the term 'community of destiny', but in fact this beatific vision is nothing but their unitarian vision of domestic arrangements raised to the international level: if the interests of all citizens are held to be the same, then why should not the interests of different nations be identical?

Laced with the soporific language of inevitability and determinism, this administrative approach to government evacuates the notion of political choice and leadership. It thereby makes government anonymous, and befogs the lines of responsibility which are the very sinews of democracy. It leaves no room for the notion which is at the heart of the doctrine of the 'rule of law': that citizens interact intelligently with one another within the framework of the law, on the basis of their understanding of the situation in which they find themselves. By ignoring or downplaying this, the basic fabric of a free society – by failing to see that the very unpredictability of individual economic behaviour is a strength – this plannificatory vision also risks destroying the sources of prosperity.

The belief that parliamentary rule is anarchic, that the market is disorganised, and that the free interaction between nations leads to war, is an old one. It is time to look at the pedigree of these ideas, and to ask what are the political, constitutional and economic implications of following them.

'The Waffen SS is fighting for Europe' reads the slogan at an
exhibition organised by the French Waffen SS in Paris, January
1944. Just over a year later, it was soldiers from the French Waffen
SS division 'Charlemagne' who were to be among the last to defend
the Reichstag in Berlin from Soviet attack.

II

Fascists and Federalists

*'I am convinced that, in fifty years' time, people will no longer
think in terms of countries'*

JOSEPH GOEBBELS, 1940[1]

According to the administrative understanding of government,
nationhood leads to nationalism which leads to war. The German
Chancellor famously warned of this in a speech at Louvain in
Belgium in February 1996, when he said that European integration
was 'a question of war and peace in the twenty-first century'.[2] The
leader of the German Greens has expressed the same thought
more provocatively, saying that, after Auschwitz, it is no longer
permissible to be 'against Europe'. Pro-Europeanism, it seems, is
the litmus test of political respectability.

It is similarly claimed that the project of European integration
was born out of the aftermath of the Second World War, and as an
antidote to it. During that conflict, runs the argument, nationalism had reached its most hideous excesses, and so pro-Europeans
realised that the states of Europe had to be bound together by
supranational institutions in order that war might never wreak
destruction in Europe again. Thus, a member of the Bundesbank
directorate declared in November 1995 that monetary union was
to be seen as 'the last step in a process of integration, which was
begun only a few years after the Second World War, in order to
bring Europe peace and prosperity, and which found its first clear
expression in the Treaty of Rome'.[3]

According to this version of history, the belief in supranationalism has its origins in the thinking of Resistance circles during the Second World War. In 1943, the *Political Theses and General Directives* of the 'Movimento Federalista Europeo' declared that nations should no longer possess the right to make war and to conclude peace. Its authors thought that if a post-war world was established in which each state retained its national sovereignty, the basis for a third world war would still exist. 'Militarism, despotism and wars,' they wrote, 'can be abolished only through the creation of a European Federation to which sovereign rights are transferred which concern the interests of all Europeans: rights which are today in the hands of national states bring about death and destruction.'[4] The argument is that, if free, states will fight each other, and that therefore their freedom must be restricted, and their sovereign powers placed under supranational control. The idea that populations might themselves restrict irresponsible action by rulers does not seem to enter into the equation.

However, the pedigree of these theories is much less politically correct than its proponents like to believe. In particular, it is false to say that the ideology of European unification of Europe postdates the Second World War, or even that it was only ever conceived in opposition to its worst excesses. On the contrary, not only the Nazis, but fascists and collaborators from many European countries, made very widespread use of European ideology to justify their aggression. Nazis, Vichyites, Italian Fascists and others spent many of the war years – as they or their spiritual fathers had done in the 1930s – developing sophisticated programmes for European economic and political integration.

Meanwhile, German propaganda in occupied countries devoted huge effort to convincing the rest of Europe that the working conditions of German workers, their social security system and housing, the transport infrastructure, and the economy generally, were far superior than elsewhere in Europe, and that, therefore, Europe should be integrated on the German model. Hitler's desire to establish a single political entity in the whole of Europe, his need to curry support in occupied countries, and indeed many of the central elements in Nazi philosophy (including a fascination with the planned economy), all combined, therefore, to produce what can only be described as a coherent body of Nazi pro-European thought.

When its existence is admitted, Nazi European thought is some-times dismissed as simply a hypocritical invention, produced in 1940 as a fig-leaf for German aggression. But the chronology does not bear this out. Hitler made regular references to Europe throughout his entire time in office, including before the war. (They are collected in, among other places, a lavishly illustrated coffee-table book entitled simply *Europa*, for which Ribbentrop wrote the Introduction.[5]) In 1937, for instance, he told the Nazi Party rally in Nuremberg that, 'We are perhaps more interested in Europe than other countries need to be. Our country, our people, our culture and our economy have grown out of general European conditions. We must therefore be the enemy of any attempt to introduce elements of discord and destruction into this European family of peoples.'[6] Similarly, in 1938, Rudolf Hess organised an exhibition at the National Socialist Party Congress called 'Europe's Struggle of Destiny in the East', which explained why German colonisation of Russia would bring European civilisation to the barbaric Slavs.[7] Indeed, even before the Nazis came to power, in 1932, Alfred Rosenberg, the prominent Nazi, attended a 'Europe Congress' in Rome.[8]

Nor can Nazi European propaganda be dismissed as mere pro-paganda. It was too sophisticated for that, as we shall see when we study it more closely. Not only do the various themes interlock to form a coherent philosophy; one might even say that the Nazis' conviction that they were selflessly fighting for a new Europe precisely oiled the wheels of German aggression.

The purpose of drawing attention to the detail of Nazi propa-ganda about Europe is not to imply that modern pro-Europeans are fascists. That would be absurd. Modern pro-Europeans are obvi-ously neither racialist nor militarily aggressive. The purpose, instead, is four-fold. Firstly, it is a matter of straightforward histor-ical interest, which has not been adequately examined, that these ideas were being discussed during the war years by Europe's most gruesome fiends. Secondly, it is to refute the argument that those opposed to European integration are somehow supping with the devil in supporting nationhood. As we shall see, the boot is on the other foot. Thirdly, it is to show how easy it is to slip into hypocritical positions: by pretending that one is doing everything for 'Europe', a lot of self-serving actions can be easily covered up. But fourthly, and most sensitively, it is to argue that there are anti-liberal implications in the rejection of the nation-state as a viable political and economic unit. This thought will be developed further elsewhere in the book; but this chapter concludes with some modern pro-European writers who have explicitly said that the works of some Nazi theoreticians do nourish modern pro-European thinking. It also draws attention to some personal links between the wartime period in France and Belgium, and the post-war European construction. With these points in mind, the reader is now invited to look in depth at what the Nazis and their allies were actually saying.

The fascist contempt for the sovereign nation-state

The normal view is that fascists, as hysterical nationalists, exalted the nation-state and all its doings. But this is not so. Firstly, it is obvious that Hitler cared little for the national sovereignty of the countries he conquered. Secondly, and more profoundly, it is important to grasp that, far from exalting the nation-state, fascists generally hated it. To see this is to realise an important point about the nature of fascism itself, and the dangerously unpolitical mentality which inspired it.

It is beyond the scope of this book to give a critical account of the ideological roots of Nazism and fascism. However, it is clear that they were fundamentally anti-individualist, anti-liberal, anti-parliamentarian and anti-capitalist movements. (Indeed, as the French fascist writer Pierre Drieu La Rochelle said, 'We are against everything. We fight everybody. That is fascism.'[9]) Above all, fascists hated the idea of little nations, or individuals, making up their own minds and taking their own decisions. As becomes clear when one looks closely at what Nazis and other fascists actually said, they were convinced that big was beautiful, and they had only contempt for pluralism. Multiplicity implied disorder.

Racialism, moreover, as a form of materialist determinism, is a non-national concept. Race transcends the boundaries of the nation and of the state, and racialist theory is thus, by definition, an international doctrine. It is also non-political, because it was predicated on the view that polities and political behaviour are determined by biological forces, not by free choice or intelligible public behaviour. Indeed, racialism often regards choice and freedom as irrational, in comparison with the 'science' it pretends to be. But if individuals are not or should not be free, then there is no reason why groups of people, or nations, should be either.

Certainly no Nazi or pro-Nazi writers dismissed the principle of nationhood outright. Like the German Institute for Foreign Policy Research, they generally claimed that the 'Europe idea' was 'the idea of a spiritual and political co-operation which would gather together to a higher unity, but not destroy national differences'.[10] A Spanish Nazi supporter was typical when he wrote that the new European order could not be created without its feet on the firm ground of national spirit; but he, like the others, also argued that Europe in the past had been unable to assert itself because it was divided up into national groups.[11] An Italian Fascist wrote of the need for the creation of an organic European unity and the preservation of the national and political individualities of the European peoples.[12] And the president of the German Institute for Foreign Affairs, Karl-Heinz Pfeffer, argued in 1944 that 'European nationalism', while necessary, must not destroy the nationalism of European peoples, 'but must sublimate it in the Hegelian sense, so that it continues to exist but becomes a living element in a larger unity . . . What we offer is not so much a programme as an idea – the idea of Europe itself.'[13]

On the other hand, the rejection of the sovereign nation-state as a viable political and economic entity on its own was explicit in Nazi and fascist thought. Werner Daitz, the prominent Nazi economist, attacked the very concepts of national sovereignty and statehood: in 1938, he argued that Nazi *völkisch** thinking dissolved the primacy of the state, an idea whose origins lay in British political thought and the French revolution. 'If the biological, life-based process by which the European family of peoples grows back together demands a certain dismantling of the state sovereignties of individual peoples, which have been exaggerated by English political and legal philosophy over the last four hundred years, then this necessary dismantling of state sovereignty will be balanced out by an increase in *völkisch* sovereignty.'[14]

Völkisch thought, Daitz made clear, was the opposite of liberalism, capitalism and parliamentarianism, each of which were themselves mere aspects of the same thing. State sovereignty, he explained, should never be primary or even an end in itself. 'Through this false English political philosophy the biological togetherness, the biological totality of the European family of peoples, is cut up and dissolved into state sovereignties which have no connection with one another.'[15] Daitz held that the nation was small and selfish by comparison with the great common undertaking which was Europe. 'This new morality within the European family of nations . . . must likewise presuppose, or bring about, an attitude of mutual preference among the nations of Europe as far as political and cultural matters are concerned. The common interests of Europe take precedence over the selfish interests of nations.'[16]

It was thus a common diagnosis that, in the nineteenth century, Europe had lacked any sense of community, and was instead divided by selfish rivalry and competition. This thought is common in modern pro-European discourse, which distinguishes the idea of 'community', which it believes it defends, from that of selfish national self-interest, which it holds to be self-defeating and chaotic. A pro-Nazi work written in 1944, entitled *German Deeds for Europe*, wrote that before Bismarck 'Europe was painfully sliding apart, its states smashing against each other. It

---

* The word '*völkisch*' cannot be adequately translated into English. Derived from '*Volk*' (people) it was a central Nazi concept with strong racialist and reactionary connotations which the nearest English equivalent, 'national', does not capture.

had long since lost all binding sense of community. Its individual parts had developed into sharply delineated zones of interest which were cluttered together in a narrow space. The inhabitants of each zone regarded the other zones with envy and distrust and watched ambitiously over the others' advantages. Indeed, they often strove for their own aggrandisement at the expense of weaker neighbours.'[17] In a similar vein, a Swede wrote, 'We must learn to become Europeans. We must understand that the time of European civil wars must end, and that the time of co-operation must begin.'[18]

Arthur Seyss-Inquart, the Austrian Minister for Security and the Interior in 1938, who later became Commissioner for the Occupied Netherlands, also held that the nation-state was small and puny in comparison with the great ensemble Germany was creating in Europe. Addressing his Dutch subjects, he said:

Above and beyond the concept of the nation-state, the idea of a new community will transform the living space given us all by history into a new spiritual realm . . . The new Europe of solidarity and co-operation among all its people, a Europe without unemployment, economic and monetary crises, a Europe of planning and the division of labour, having at its disposal the most modern production techniques and a continent-wide system of trade and communications developed on a joint basis, will find an assured foundation and rapidly increasing prosperity once national economic barriers are removed.

No doubt with his audience's preoccupations in mind, he went on, 'Talents become stunted when they are confined to small national political and geographical boundaries. In a larger sphere it is possible even for small countries and their nationals fully to develop their cultural, economic and human potentialities. Nations and human beings only develop to the full when they participate actively in a great common destiny.'[19]

Walther Funk, the Nazi Finance Minister, agreed that common interests had to take precedence over particular ones. 'There must

be a readiness to subordinate one's own interests in certain cases to
that of the European Community,' he wrote.[20] Similarly, the
Vichyite economist Francis Delaisi argued that the war aims of
Germany and her allies included not only the destruction of liberalism, but also overcoming the division of the world into
nation-states: 'For the men of the Axis, the universe is too vast . . .
the nation is too small: the world must be divided up into "vital
spaces".'[21]

Like modern pro-Europeans, the Nazis believed that the nation-
state system encouraged division and war in Europe, and that, if it
could be overcome, wars in Europe would end. One Nazi propagandist insisted that the New Order in Europe would remove the
causes that have led to internal European wars in the past. The
nations of Europe would no longer be one another's enemies, and
the age of European particularism would be gone for ever. 'In a
peaceful Europe organised as a higher unity all European nations
will find a rightful and worthy place.'[22] Similarly, Vidkun Quisling,
the Norwegian collaborationist leader, argued that Europe would
be strong and peaceful only if united: 'We must create a Europe
that does not squander its blood and strength in internecine conflict, but forms a compact unity. In this way it will become richer,
stronger and more civilised, and will recover its old place in the
world.'[23] An official in the Nazi Foreign Ministry similarly wrote
that it would be the purpose of the New European Order to
remove the causes that had in the past given rise to wars in
Europe, to end the period of intestine wars and to 'overcome
European particularism'. 'Europe has become too small for feuding
and self-contained sovereignties. A fragmented Europe is too weak
to preserve its individual nature and keep the peace while maintaining itself as a force in the world.'[24] Another Nazi official
concurred: 'National tensions and petty jealousies will lose their
meaning in a Europe freely organised on a federal basis. World
political development consists inevitably in the formation of larger
political and economic spheres.'[25]

Even Hitler, who was less interested in the European idea than
his propaganda chief, Joseph Goebbels, or his foreign minister,
Joachim von Ribbentrop, expressed the view that a European

system based on independent nation-states was anarchic. In August 1941, he and Mussolini issued a joint communiqué which said that the New European Order which would follow the Axis victory should remove the causes which have led to European wars in the past. 'The destruction of the Bolshevik danger and of plutocratic exploitation will create the possibility for a peaceful, harmonious and fruitful co-operation between all the peoples of the European continent, in the political as in the economic and cultural domains.'[26]

In a similar vein, Hitler insisted in 1943 that 'the clutter of small nations' (for which he used the contemptuous word 'Kleinstaatengerümpel') must be liquidated. (The word 'Kleinstaaterei' is used by modern Germans to dismiss as anachronistic the division of Europe into individual states.) The aim of the Nazi struggle was to create a unified Europe instead.[27] After the invasion of the Soviet Union, Hitler spoke warmly about this 'feeling of European solidarity' to Count Ciano, the Italian ambassador.[28] He was reported as saying that the future 'did not belong to the ridiculous half-civilised America, but to the newly arisen Europe that would also definitely prevail with its people, its economy, and its intellectual and cultural values, on condition that the East was made to serve the European idea and not work against Europe . . . The older culture and the higher intellectual level of Europe would in the end be victorious.'[29]

Because the fascists believed that they were the harbingers of a New Order (much fascist thought was overtly futuristic) they argued that the concept of national sovereignty was simply out of date – a view which is peddled vigorously by pro-Europeans today. In Vichy France, the senior Vichyite minister and admirer of Hitler, Jacques Benoist-Méchin, who was a Secretary of State in the Vichy government in charge of Franco-German relations from June 1941 until September 1942, declared that France's policy of collaboration required 'the abandonment of old illusions'. France would be able to join the new Europe, he asserted, 'only when she abandons all crumbling forms of nationalism – which was itself in reality only an anachronistic particularism – and when she takes her place in the European community with honour . . .'[30]

The Italian Fascists held similar views. Aldo Bertele, in his essay 'On the Principle of Nationality: The Origins, Life and Overcoming of Nationalities', argued that international anarchy resulted from the primacy of the nation-state as the basis of the world order.[31] Another Italian commentator affirmed that the principle of nationality itself conflicted with the economic life of modern states.[32] Indeed, one of the most prominent and intelligent of Mussolini's collaborators, Giuseppe Bottai, Mussolini's Minister of Education, who edited the journal *Critica Fascista* (and whose name got into the papers in 1995 when the Mayor of Rome wanted to name a street after him), wrote in 1943:

> Nationalism can be looked on either as an inescapable part of the human outlook, or as the ossification of a political principle that has served its time. In the latter aspect there comes a time when it acts as a hindrance to the general advance of civilisation. It may do so either accidentally, by exacerbating vital problems to which it offers no solution, so that there is no escape but in the direction of Communism; or else by its intrinsic property of stunting the development of the most sublime products of the human spirit, whether in the field of culture or that of industry, and frustrating its supreme demands.[33]

Or again, Alberto de Stefani, a lecturer on finance and political economy, who was Minister of Finance from the March on Rome (October 1922) to 1925 – and who was associated with a deflationist policy of balancing the budget and restricting government expenditure – wrote (with explicit deference to the Nazi economics minister, Walther Funk, whose public declarations were constant reference points for Italian Fascist formulations of an economic New Order[34]):

> Nationalities do not form a sound basis for the planned new order, because of their multiplicity and their traditional intransigence . . . History shows that incompatibilities due to nationalist intransigence and an exaggerated spirit of

autonomy are sources of friction and war . . . It is plain to all
that the continuance of intransigent nationalism, blind to
the need for a continental policy, has finally turned Europe
against itself . . . If we can overcome the nationalist principle
in the sense of reconciling it with the principle of unity, this
solution should find its own guarantee and its proper counterpart in the form of respect for certain spiritual autonomies
and for the interests of individual peoples in due proportion
to those of the continent as a whole. If the new order is to be
stable and fruitful it must be based on this principle. The
results of excessive nationalism and territorial dismember-
ment are within the experience of all. Thus there is only
hope for peace by means of a process which on the one hand
respects the inalienable, fundamental patrimony of every
nation but, on the other, moderates these and subordinates
them to a continental policy . . . A European union could
not be subject to the variations of internal policy that are
characteristic of liberal regimes.[35]

Another eloquent fascist opponent of the nation-state was
Camillo Pellizi, the editor of the magazine *Civiltà Fascista*. In an
article entitled 'The Idea of Europe',[36] Pellizi argued that the New
Europe would not destroy nationhood: 'A *new* Europe: that is the
point, and that is the task before us. It does not mean that Italians,
Germans and all the other nations of the European family are to
change their spots and become unrecognisable to themselves or to
one another, from one day or one year to the next. It will be a new
Europe because of the new inspiration and determining principle
that will spring up among all these peoples.' On the other hand,
the fascist principle would overcome the 'particularism' of Europe's
nation-states: 'The Axis is, or can be, the first definite step towards
surmounting, or expressing in a higher form, that typically
European phenomenon which we call the nation, with its
inevitable, one might say physiological corollary of nationalism . . .
One cannot "create Europe" without the nations or against them:
we must create it from the different nations, while subduing
national particularism as far as may be necessary.'[37]

Pellizi concluded his account with some junk metaphysical justifications for his desire to amalgamate the nations of Europe into
a higher unity. 'The important thing is to get away from particular
and parochial unity, from the windowless monad of the single
nation which finds itself the be-all and end-all of its acts and moti-
vations. The two of us must become one, while at the same time
remaining different entities, so that this two-in-one may develop
the many-in-one that must constitute the new Europe if it is ever
to come into being.'[38]

It is perhaps not surprising that in August 1943, that is, after the
Allied landings in Italy, Pellizi was contacted by the 'Movimento
Federalista Europeo' because of his work on European integration
under Mussolini. Although the federalists seemed to have broken
off contact with him almost immediately, he did not abandon his
fundamental convictions. Indeed, his writings after the Allied
landings in Italy sound like a plan of action for the kind of
'behind-the-scenes' integration which Jean Monnet was to make
his hallmark in the European Economic Community: 'The problem of the hierarchy of states will no longer arise, at least in its
usual form, once we have cut off the dragon's head, that is, the
notion of state sovereignty. Moreover, this does not have to be
done outright, but can be achieved indirectly, e.g. by creating
interstate European bodies to look after certain common interests
(exchange rates, communications, foreign trade etc., then defence
and colonies and so on).'[39]

Post-war fascists continued to realise that the multiplicity of the
nation-state system was an obstacle to their grand designs for the
continent. The former leader of the British Union of Fascists, Sir
Oswald Mosley, devoted considerable effort to working for
European integration after the war. In 1953 he founded a magazine
called *The European*, and in 1958 he published a book, *Europe:
Faith and Plan – A Way Out from the Coming Crises and an
Introduction to Thinking as a European*.[40] There he wrote, 'We need
the swing and idealism of the people to break through the maze of
diplomacy and haggling which today obstructs European union.
The statesmen of divided nations are lost in the detail of their
search for small individual advantage, and the whole which alone

can serve the real advantage of all is forgotten.'[41] Without unity, Europe was doomed to weakness: 'Can these relatively small, isolated, individual nations of Western Europe face for fifteen years on world markets the competition of America's normal production surplus, plus the deliberate market-breaking dumping of the Soviets at below European production costs?'[42] No, for 'small, individual nations are dependent on external supplies of raw materials for their industries . . . they are forced to pay for these necessities by exports sold in open competition in world markets, under conditions where they have no influence whatever'.[43] He concluded: 'We require a closed system to the extent of being independent of the world cost system, but within the necessary area it can be a free economy.'[44]*

The obsession with modern technology and economic interdependence

One of the main reasons why fascists were convinced that the nation-state was at an end was because of technological development. They felt that notions of national sovereignty were simply anachronistic in a modern world with an interdependent economy, international transport, and electronic telecommunications. It is worth looking closely at just what they said.

Camillo Pellizi, for instance, argued:

---

* When this author published an article in the *Sunday Telegraph* on 22 September 1996 drawing attention to Sir Oswald Mosley's pro-European ideology, the article caused outrage in pro-European circles. But Mosley's widow, Lady Diana Mosley, sent a letter to the editor of the newspaper in support of the article, which was published on 6 October. 'Mosley's pre-war economic policy was based entirely upon our Empire,' she wrote. 'In 1945, the Empire lost, he decided the only acceptable and profitable role for Britain was in European union. For the rest of his life, in speeches and writings, he emphasised this. Britain astonished Europe by its laggard tactics, every opportunity missed. Now, with ever-increasing relative weakness, union has become essential. We have signed on the dotted line, and must not allow diehard Tories to wreck a prosperous future for our country.'

No single European nation can hope even now, still less in
the future, to compete in military, economic or cultural matters with the great forces that are coming to birth or are
already in being outside Europe . . . Modern technology
requires huge space and vast resources to achieve its utmost
efficiency, and outside Europe these huge areas and concen-
trations of resources now exist or are in the process of being
formed. If only for elementary reasons of defence Europe must
either become a 'concentration' (an ugly but expressive term)
on a similar scale, or else resign itself to becoming, sooner or
later, a mere appendage of the Asiatic continent . . . Too
many old-fashioned national interests, of an outmoded and
particularist kind, whether conscious or unconscious, led to
the outbreak of the present war and are still influencing its
course.[45]

The Nazis typically believed that 'the development towards
larger units' was economically inevitable. A Nazi Foreign Ministry
official in charge of information briefed the press that 'the division
of Europe into small or tiny national economies and systems of
communication is out of date. No more passports and visas.
General European prosperity will bring about prosperity and economic security of all members . . . The unification of Europe . . .
was already showing itself to be an inevitable development in
accordance with the iron laws of history.'[46] The leader of the
Dutch Nazis, Anton Adriaan Mussert, also argued that technological development was bringing the peoples of the world closer
together. 'In economics and communications,' he claimed, 'the
development is towards larger units. After centuries of separatism
and decentralisation there has again come a time when the
European peoples are conscious of their need for solidarity.'[47]

Joseph Goebbels, Hitler's propaganda wizard, was also persuaded
that technology brought peoples together and made borders
anachronistic – a thought which is common among modern pro-
Europeans and others who speak of the demise of the nation-state.
In a speech entitled 'Das Europa der Zukunft' (The Europe of the
Future), Goebbels claimed that technology 'has brought not only

tribes but whole peoples closer together than was once imaginable. Whereas formerly it took twenty-four hours to talk from Berlin to Prague indirectly via the press, today it does not take me an extra second . . . Whereas it once took twelve hours to travel to Prague by rail, today I can fly there in an hour . . . As these technical achievements are put to use, so the continents are inevitably brought closer together. Meanwhile European peoples are realising more and more clearly that many of the issues between us are mere family quarrels compared to the great problems that today require to be solved as between continents.'[48]

Goebbels even used the metaphor of 'bringing down borders' which is so central to the modern European ideology. 'What it means for you is that you are already members of a great Reich which is preparing to reorganise Europe, tearing down the barriers that still separate the European peoples and making it easier for them to come together.'[49] He also advanced the argument which one hears frequently from German pro-Europeans today that the history of German unification was a model for that of Europe. Like many other Nazis and their supporters, he assumed that political entities should correspond to supposed economic 'spaces', and that Europe's division into nation-states was thus analogous to, and as nonsensical as, Germany's division into micro-states after the Treaty of Westphalia in 1648. Speaking of the European unification Germany had brought about, Goebbels wrote in 1940, 'About a hundred years ago our German Reich went through a similar process. At that time it was fragmented into just as many larger and smaller parts as Europe is today. This medley of small states was endurable so long as technical facilities, especially those of communications, were not yet so developed that it took too short a time to travel from one small country to another. But the invention of steam power made the old conditions intolerable.'[50]

Perhaps Goebbels' most striking assertion is that, 'in fifty years' time' people would no longer 'think in terms of countries'. 'I am firmly convinced,' he said, 'that just as today we smile when we look back at the parochial quarrels that divided the German peoples in the '40s and '50s of the last century, so . . . future generations will be no less amused at the political disputes that are

now going on in Europe . . .'[51] Many modern German politicians
also stress that it is no longer appropriate to *think* in terms of
nations – as if reality depended on the mind. The veteran foreign
minister, Hans-Dietrich Genscher, often used to speak of the need
for European 'consciousness' as if it matters more what people
think than what they do.

*Großraumwirtschaft** and the Nazi 'European Economic Community'

The Nazis proposed to use economic integration to do away with
European particularism once the war had ended. Here, indeed,
are the most striking similarities between Nazi thought and the
pro-Europeanism of our own day. An early Nazi plan for European
integration said that the most important precondition was to do
away with 'the economic Balkanisation of Europe':

> A new large economic area will come into being, in which
> the economy can develop with only basic direction from the
> state . . . This creation of an economic area on a European
> scale was arbitrarily prevented after the World War by the
> dictated peace of Versailles and associated treaties. The result
> was to set up 35 independent European states, 16 of which
> had less than 10 million inhabitants, and to create 7,000 kilo-
> metres of new customs frontiers. Attempts at unification, e.g.
> the Anschluss of the former state of Austria to Germany, were
> frustrated, and the regime of small economic units was artifi-
> cially encouraged.[52]

In other words, the hatred of the nation-state and the desire to
create a great European economic space were two sides of the
same coin. Indeed, it was an understatement for Vidkun Quisling
to say that there was no opposition between European economic
co-operation and National Socialism.[53] This was not least because

* 'Great Space Economy' or 'Large Area Economy'.

of the geo-economic aims of the war which Hitler started. The Nazis were convinced that they needed to ensure economic autarky against the British blockade. Independence, they held, was increased if the Europeans could provide for themselves. What they really meant was that state power was threatened by free trade: as one ideologist limpidly put it, 'The creation of a world economy would have meant the destruction of the economic sovereignty of Europe.'[54]

The history of the Nazis' planning for a new European economic order began on 22 June 1940, when Göring gave orders which gave rise to a project for 'the large-scale economic unification of Europe'[55] or 'Central European Economic Community'[56] submitted to the Reich Chancellery on 9 July 1940. It mentioned the establishment of fixed exchange rates between the currencies of other countries and the Reichsmark; the abolition of customs barriers in Europe and the creation of a 'customs-free marketing area'; the need for 'increased leverage in trade negotiations and relations with other countries'; and the protection of agriculture. Shortly afterwards, two officials in the Foreign Ministry, Carl Clodius (the Deputy Director of the Economic Policy Department, who later became the Minister responsible for economic relations with Italy and the Balkan countries) and Ambassador Ritter, drew up plans for a future 'continental economy' for which preferential tariffs, a customs union, a customs and monetary union, or an economic union, were all suggested as possibilities.[57]

The Nazis' notion of Großraumwirtschaft or 'large area economy', which they intended Europe to become, was predicated on the idea that economic activity and interaction could and should be confined mainly to a certain area. One of the most influential theoreticians of this view was Werner Daitz, the head of Germany's Central Research Institute for National Economic Order and Large Area Economics. Daitz spent most of the war writing and speaking on the notion of Großraumwirtschaft. Like other Nazis, he saw the development of an economically and politically integrated Europe as part of a historical anti-liberal process: 'The ideologies of a world economy, democracy and parliamentarianism, invented by Britain during the past century to justify and prolong this unnatural form of European life, are losing ground and disappearing along with the equally unnatural phenomenon of British hegemony.'[58]

Daitz argued that the development towards *Großraumwirtschaft* was dictated by impersonal factors like population growth. This had introduced a 'tension between living space and political space'. He held that the concepts of *Volkstum* ('nationhood') and *völkischer Lebensraum* ('national living-space') should have been recognised after the First World War as being superior to the idea of the territorial state (*Staatsraum*). Because the Versailles system did not do this, the constructed territorial units were incompatible with the needs of economics.

Indeed, Daitz's writing helps us to understand just how central to Nazi philosophy the drive towards European integration really was. With a simple Malthusianism, the Nazis believed that their populations did not have enough 'space'. As early as 1936, Hitler had told the Reichstag:

> How much trouble would humanity and especially the European peoples have been spared if natural and obvious living conditions had been respected when the European living space and economic co-operation were being politically fashioned . . . The European peoples represent a family in this world . . . It is not very intelligent to imagine that in such a cramped house like that of Europe, a community of peoples can maintain different legal systems and different concepts of law for long.[59]

'More space' was also obviously a necessary prerequisite for the autarkic and monopolistic control of the entire European continent which the Nazis intended to establish.

Thus, the concept of *Großraumwirtschaft* was intimately linked with that more famous Nazi concept, *Lebensraum* ('living-space') and the theoreticians of the *Großraumwirtschaft* certainly often made this link clear.[60] One ideologist lectured on 'The Concept of "Reich" and the European Economy', while a prominent German Nazi ideologue of Scottish extraction, Colin Ross, said in a lecture entitled 'The Coming of a New Europe Within the Framework of a New World Order' that 'National Socialism is a regional idea. On this planet, which has become small and narrow, there are no longer individual destinies of single peoples. It is a law that the vital space of communities becomes ever more vast, and thus the European peoples find themselves obliged to constitute together a greater community. And thus the first step to take henceforth is the creation of Europe.'[61]

Daitz believed the first *Großraumwirtschaft* to have existed before 1500, when the Hanseatic league had been the focal point of trade between Central Europe and Russia. The discovery of America (a new space or *Raum*) had caused this integrated economic system to collapse, and the 'so-called free economy' had destroyed 'the natural order, bonds and arrangements' of the original European economy.[62] Now the world economy had in turn collapsed itself, and things were returning to their original order. The world was dividing up into great economic zones, and the stability which had been regained was based on the Nazis' recognition that agriculture was the basis of all economies. Daitz added that *Großraumwirtschaft* was needed to shield Europe against monetary dumping by the United States and Britain. 'The *Großraumwirtschaften* are thus showing themselves to be components of a new world economic order, which will give it more stability in future,'[63] he explained.

Daitz thus advocated 'spatial–political unity' from Gibraltar to the Urals, and from the North Cape to Cyprus. Unlike the liberal world economy, the *Großraumwirtschaft* would give Europe more independence in the world. He was also convinced that what was good for Germany was good for Europe. 'From its very inception, the Reich has always been a Germanic and also European idea. A strong Reich was always necessary for a strong Europe, and conversely a strong Europe is inconceivable without a strong Reich. This is Europe's political law.'[64]

Another theoretician of *Großraumwirtschaft*, Alfred Oesterheld, also emphasised the political implications of economic integration. He distinguished trade from economy, arguing that the first can orient itself anywhere, but that a fixed economic area was necessary to ensure the unity of production in the latter. 'Großraumwirtschaft,' he argued, 'is not just an economic construction, but rather the economic aspect of a political concept.'[65] The 'organisation of area' (Raumgestaltung) was 'a European idea'.[66]

But the most detailed Nazi reflection of the future economic integration of Europe came in 1942, when the Berlin Union of Businessmen and Industrialists, together with the Economics University in Berlin, convened a high-level conference entitled 'Europäische Wirtschaftsgemeinschaft' (European Economic Community), at which numerous ministers and leading industrialists spoke.[67] It is striking that, even in otherwise detailed post-war accounts of Nazi Euro-propaganda, mention is almost never made of this conference. The omission is strange, not only because of the conference's high profile, but also because the lectures were printed up in a book which went into two editions. Perhaps it is simply too close to the bone.

The titles of the lectures delivered at this conference are eerily reminiscent of modern pro-European discourse: 'The Economic Face of the New Europe', 'The Development Towards the European Economic Community', 'European Agriculture', 'The European Industrial Economy', 'Employment in Europe', 'European Transport Issues', 'European Currency Matters', 'European Trade and Economic Treaties', 'The Fundamental Question: Is Europe a Geographical Concept or a Political Fact?' The introduction was written by Professor Heinrich Hunke, the economics adviser for the NSDAP Gau of Berlin, who was also President of the Berlin Union of Businessmen and Industrialists.

Hunke argued that the European continent had banished the English conception of the economy in 1940, and that the age-old English doctrine of the balance of power had been militarily smashed. He emphasised the link between the concept of 'Reich', the European economy and the notion of political union in Europe, using phrases like 'the historical, cultural and economic significance of the German economic order' and 'the essence of the European Economic Community'.[68] He claimed that 'the peoples of Europe have long since recognised that they belong to a "community of destiny"'.[69] Hunke also wrote a postface to the published version of the conference, in which he expressed his admiration for Friedrich List, whose theories he contrasted point by point with the liberal vision of Adam Smith.[70]

The head of the economics department of I. G. Farben, Dr Anton Reithinger, was especially exercised by the threat posed to European industry by economic growth in countries peripheral to it. The old industrial states were threatened by cheap competition and rapid industrialisation in developing countries such as Japan, India and the Soviet Union. Southern Europe was growing while Central and Northern Europe were declining. Because England had not realised her 'continental task' – as a result of her numerous overseas interests – the continental European peoples would have to address it themselves.[71]

Walther Funk, Reichsminister for Economics and President of the Reichsbank, held that the construction of economic areas followed 'a natural law of development'.[72] He evoked the backward age when a traveller in Germany had to cross hundreds of borders between Germany's myriad micro-states, each with its own currency and laws, and divided by thousands of toll barriers, and pointed out that political leaders of the time did not understand that France and England were far more advanced than Germany then because they had large unified economies.[73] He attacked the liberal theory of economics which was predicated on the autonomous search by individuals of their own self-interest. By contrast, economics should serve social aims: 'This economic mentality demands a social conscience.'[74]

Like Hunke, Funk believed that this sorry state of affairs had been overcome thanks to the theories of Friedrich List, and thanks also to the development of technology and transport. For Funk, the economic integration of Europe was to follow the same pattern as that of Germany: the increased speed of train travel, the extension of the network across the entire continent, 'all this has brought borders nearer to each other'.[75] 'In her own interest,' he went on, 'Europe cannot stay behind in the backward romanticism of the stage coach era. It is true that the economic integration of Europe will prove more difficult to overcome than those of the

German *Zollverein* [Customs Union]. Even the methods will be different and more complicated, and they will not be able to be mastered with a customs union. *Nevertheless, European economic unity will come, for its time is here.*'[76]

Although Funk could not promise the immediate abolition of all border controls, he did promise full employment and strong growth. 'The word "unemployment" will disappear from the European dictionary,' he announced.[77] His description of how the economy should work was a typically Keynesian mixture of socialist euphemism and lip-service paid to the market: he accepted the 'importance of the entrepreneur' and of private capital, but also emphasised the need for 'the rational organisation of the economy'.

Architects of the New Europe

But Nazi plans for European integration were as political as they were economic. As Heinrich Hunke said, 'The necessity of a political order for the economic co-operation of peoples is recognised.'[78] From the middle of 1941, therefore, Goebbels began to take a stronger hand in the 'European question' and he devoted numerous speeches, meetings and newspaper articles to it. He filled the pages of his weekly newspaper *Das Reich* with European slogans: 'the New Europe', 'the new European order', 'Europe's *Lebensraum*', 'the vision of a new Europe' and so on. Meanwhile, Ribbentrop insisted that the fight against Bolshevism, which united many peoples in the East of Europe, was evidence of 'a constantly growing moral unity of Europe within the New Order that our great leaders have proclaimed and prepared for the future of civilised nations. Herein lies the deep meaning of the war against Bolshevism. It is the sign of Europe's spiritual regeneration.'[79]

Within the Foreign Ministry, interest in 'Europe' culminated with the creation of a 'Europe committee' in the autumn of 1942. The committee contained officials from the Foreign Ministry, and senior officials from the Institute for the Study of Foreign

Countries. The leading lights were Alfred Six, the head of the Foreign Affairs Institute – which organised a conference in 1941 called 'The New Europe' for 303 students from 38 countries – and Werner Daitz. By March 1943, formal plans for a European confederation had been drafted.

These took the form of constitutions or treaties, laying out the competencies and structure of the future European confederation. A note written by Ribbentrop on 21 March 1943 begins, 'I am of the opinion that, as already proposed to the Führer in my previous minutes, we should at the earliest possible date, as soon as we have scored a significant military success, proclaim the European Confederation in quite a specific form.'[80] Ribbentrop proposed inviting all the heads of state concerned (Germany, Italy, France, Denmark, Norway, Finland, Slovakia, Hungary, Romania, Bulgaria, Croatia, Serbia, Greece and Spain) to sign the instrument bringing the Confederation into being. Annexed to the memorandum was a draft document, which spoke of the 'common destiny of European peoples', and of the aim 'to ensure that wars never break out among them'. It also foresaw the abolition of customs barriers between the participating states.

In June 1943, an official submitted the 'Basic Elements of a Plan for the New Europe' to one of the members of the Europe Committee. Peppered with all the usual mantras about 'the nations' longing for peace', the section entitled 'The Economic Organisation of Europe' foresaw trade based on the principle of European preference *vis-à-vis* non-European countries, with the eventual objective of a European customs union; a European clearing centre and stable currency rates in Europe, with the eventual objective of a European monetary union; and the 'harmonisation of labour conditions and social welfare, in the direction of improving standards'.[81] It foresaw 'Conferences' in each area (Labour, Agriculture, and so on) deciding policy for the whole Confederation.

This document was followed up in August 1943 with a 'Note on the Establishment of a European Confederation'. Its author, Cecile von Renthe-Fink, who held the diplomatic rank of minister, wrote:

In the tremendous struggle for the future of Europe we Germans are champions of a new, better order in which all European peoples will find a rightful and worthy place. Up to now we have avoided coming forward with a concrete proposal regarding the European question . . . If we were now to put forward the idea of a confederal solution based on free co-operation among independent nations, it would certainly confirm the European peoples' confidence in our policy and increase their willingness to follow our lead and work for our victory.[82]

Although the 'principles embodied in the constituent act of the European Confederation', which were appended to the memorandum, specified that the European Confederation was a community of sovereign states which mutually guaranteed one another's freedom and independence, it is clear that, in fact, the confederation was to have near-total control over the internal affairs of its member states. 'The European economy will be planned jointly by the member states on the basis of their common and national interests,' the document said. 'The aim will be to increase material prosperity, social justice and social security in the individual states, and to develop the material and labour resources of Europe . . . to protect the European economy against crises and economic threats from outside . . .' It suggested that 'the customs barriers which stand in the way of increasing trade between individual members of the Confederation shall be progressively eliminated,' and that 'the intra-Europe system of communications by rail, *Autobahn*, waterways and airlines will be developed in accordance with a unified plan'.[83]

The document also, typically, expressed the view that the integration of Europe was inevitable because of technological developments. It held that European nations had a common destiny. It added that Germany wished to unite Europe 'on a federal basis', and although it insisted that there was no intention of interfering in other countries' internal affairs, it added the catch-all caveat that 'all that is required of European states is that they be loyal, pro-European members of the community and co-operate

willingly in its tasks . . . The object of European co-operation will
be to promote the peace, security and welfare of all European
states and their population.' It was not a question of one state or
group of states dominating the other but rather 'a mutual relationship of trust and loyalty instead of the imperial methods of the
former era'.[84] In a similar – and equally preposterous – vein,
Werner Daitz declared that 'Europe cannot be administered in
centralised way: it must be led in a decentralised fashion'.[85]

It is striking how unaggressive the bulk of Nazi Euro-propaganda is, and therefore how self-deceptive. Goebbels had the gall
to claim that 'it has never been our intention that this new order
or reorganisation of Europe should be brought about by force. You
must on no account think that when we Germans bring about a
certain order in Europe we do so for the purpose of stifling individual peoples.'[86] He trotted out the well-worn argument that
European integration was only realistic: 'In my view a nation's
conception of its own freedom must be harmonised with present-
day facts and simple questions of efficiency and purpose. Just as no
member of a family has the right to disturb the peace for selfish
purposes, in the same way no single European nation can in the
long run be allowed to stand in the way of the general process of
organisation.'[87] In the same vein, an official in the Nazi ministry of
employment declared that Germany could claim that she was not
fighting for herself, but for Europe.[88]

The thought was often stressed that states would join the new
Europe on a voluntary basis. 'Leadership does not mean domination but external protection and internal responsibility,' declared
one propagandist. Germany and Italy did not want subjection but
only sincere co-operation. 'All European peoples that have
proved themselves historically are welcome as members of the
new Europe. Their national and cultural development in freedom and independence is guaranteed.' He argued very implausibly
that the examples of Finland, Hungary, Bulgaria, Romania,
Croatia and Slovakia proved that there was no intention to interfere in the internal affairs of other states: 'Our only requirement of
European states is that they be sincere and enthusiastic members
of Europe.'[89] Germany had found a new way of running Europe

without dominating her: 'The idea of leadership, which will be the dominant conception of the new international life of Europe, is the negation of the imperialist methods of a bygone age: it signifies recognition of the confident co-operation of the independent smaller states in tackling the new communal tasks.'[90]

In a similar vein, Arthur Seyss-Inquart wrote that no one wanted to see a Europe dominated by Germany. 'Our only wish is that a Europe shall arise that is truly European and conscious of its European mission.'[91] After the invasion of the Soviet Union, the mass circulation periodical, *Signal*, also wrote that there would not be a German Europe: 'In reality the soldiers of the Reich are not just defending the cause of their own homeland so much as protecting every European nation worthy of that name.'[92]

Indeed, it was a staple element of German self-delusion to talk about her 'partners and neighbours', and to peddle the idea that the mutual pursuit of common interests had replaced inimical competition. Much propaganda was devoted to related matters, such as 'the European sense of community'.[93] Dr Anton Reithinger of I. G. Farben, speaking at the 1942 'European Economic Community' conference, spoke of the balance between the different interests of the individual partners of the European economic space, on the one hand, and of the common interests of all European peoples on the other: 'To put these interests into practice requires . . . a belief in the European idea and in Germany's European task . . .'[94]

Like many modern Germans, Goebbels believed that German regionalism could be a model for Europe because the sensitive absorption of the German states into the German Empire had worked. European states could thus be integrated harmoniously without infringing their identity: 'If we with our Greater German outlook have no interest in infringing the economic, cultural or social peculiarities of, say, the Bavarians or the Saxons, so it is equally not in our interest to infringe the economic, social or cultural individuality of, say, the Czech people.'[95] His mistake – shared by modern pro-Europeans – was obviously to assume that the nations of Europe were just 'regions' of it. But his lackeys around Europe also agreed that Germany was a model: Vidkun

Quisling declared that 'a Germanic Confederation' could serve as a model for co-operation with other European states.[96] Indeed, a later version of the note on the European Confederation claimed that Germany's role in Europe was 'to reconcile the particular interests of the European states with the interests of Europe as a whole'. To this already rather Genscherite sentiment, it added the view that 'the interests and needs of Germany are essentially and inseparably linked with those of Europe'.[97]

The document also returned to the theme of federalism, hoping to find within it the solution to the contradiction between multiplicity and unity. It argued that the special feature of the European problem was that a multiplicity of peoples had to live in a comparatively small area in a combination of unity and independence.

> Their unity must be so firm that there can never again be war between them and that Europe's external interests can be jointly safeguarded. At the same time, the European states must retain their freedom and independence so as to act in accordance with their very different situations and national tasks, and to fulfil their particular functions within the larger framework in a joyful and creative spirit. The strength and security of Europe depends not on the compelled or demanded subordination of one European power to another, but on the union of all . . . The European problem can only be solved on a federal basis, whereby European states resolve of their own free will, based on a recognition of necessity, to unite in a community of sovereign states. This community may be designated a European confederation.[98]

As in the first document, it insisted that all member states had to be 'pro-European', and that they ensure that no acts were committed on their territory which were incompatible with 'European solidarity and European obligations'.[99]

As has been seen, it was common for Nazi theoreticians of European integration to say that their plans envisaged maintaining the national sovereignty of Europe's member states intact.[100] But the same theoreticians just as often added riders which effectively eradicated any pretence at that maintenance. One draft constitution for 'The New Europe' called for 'the right of each country to organise its national life as it thinks fit, provided it respects its obligations towards the European community'.[101] Other documents repeated the same thought: 'The present war is also a war for the unity and freedom of Europe,' wrote the deputy head of the second department of the Foreign Ministry.

> Its aims are to bring about and guarantee lasting peace for European countries . . . removal of causes of European wars, especially the 'balance of power' system . . . overcoming European particularism by free peaceful co-operation among European peoples. Loyalty to Europe does not mean subjection but honest co-operation based on equal rights. Every European people must take part in the new Europe in its own fashion. The only requirement is that European states be honestly loyal to Europe, of which they are members.[102]

Or again, 'Every continental state must remain conscious of its responsibility towards the European Economic Community.'[103]

Although the author of these plans claimed not to want a 'supranational bureaucracy' nor a conference system, he did foresee the need for an 'Economic Council', composed of representatives of member states, which would be divided up into committees for trade, industry and navigation; finance and currency matters; labour and social questions; food, agriculture and forestry.[104] The document repeated the ultimate aims of the Confederation:

> The solution of economic problems with a view to immunity from blockade, the regulation of trade on the basis of European preference *vis-à-vis* the rest of the world, with the eventual object of a European customs union and a free European market, a European central clearing system and stable exchange rates in Europe, looking towards a European currency union. Objectives would include the standardisation and improvement of conditions of employment and social

security, as well as long-term production planning in the field of industry, agriculture and forestry.[105]

(Agriculture, indeed, often figured prominently in the Nazis' policy papers on Europe.[106])

Such documents often claimed that the fragmentation of economic resources in Europe was a serious obstacle to prosperity and social progress in the different countries.[107] Economic planning and 'purposeful co-ordination' were therefore necessary. 'In order to encourage mutual trade and create a large European market, the customs and other barriers between countries will be progressively eliminated.'[108] European agriculture had to be made self-sufficient.[109] Labour instead of capital had to be the economic and social yardstick. Care would be taken to protect certain industries and to maintain high living standards.

There was also said to be a need to develop what, fifty years later, Jacques Delors was to call 'trans-European networks': 'Experience has shown that Europe's present system of communications is inadequate to the increased demand. The internal network of railways, roads and airlines will be developed in accordance with a common plan.'[110] This was a favourite Nazi theme: it pleased the fascist sense of being on the cutting edge of modernity. Just as the Vichyite minister, Jacques Benoist-Méchin, bewailed the centralisation of the French transport system ('as if Paris were the only centre of the world'[111]) and called for new arteries to link up with the German and Italian motorways in order to give France's transport infrastructure 'a genuinely European character',[112] so a speaker at the European Economic Community conference proclaimed that 'the future belongs to motor transport'.[113]

Currency as an instrument of state power: the fascist hatred of gold

As Germany expanded into Western and Eastern Europe, questions of foreign exchange began to arise, especially in relation to German plans for the future reorganisation of the continent. Like many of his colleagues, Walther Funk placed importance on having a 'central clearing system', to replace the old multilateral clearing system. He had already broached this issue in one of the earliest Nazi statements on the European economy, in 1940, when he had argued in favour of stable exchange rates between the European currencies and the dominant Reichsmark, and an integrated European clearing system.[114] He thought that talk of currency union was premature. Indeed, it is amusing that when Dr Horst Jecht, a Professor at the Economics University in Berlin, addressed the conference on the European Economic Community in 1942, he said that monetary union was undesirable because it would infringe respect for the independence of the states concerned.[115]

In fact, these so-called 'clearing' (or 'compensation') arrangements were to become one of the Nazis' main instruments of domination. The idea was that states would buy and sell to and from each other without payment, until a specific date, when the net value of imports and exports was calculated and net payments made. If a Frenchman sold a good to someone in Germany, he was paid by a *caisse de compensation* ('compensation office') in Paris. Meanwhile, the German purchaser paid the sum he owed to the Frenchman to a Franco-German compensation office in Berlin. But this sum remained in Berlin until the day when the accounts were calculated. The system was supposed to function both ways, but in fact the Reich bought far more from its partners than it sold to them (while making them pay very high prices for what it sold, because of the artificially high exchange rate for the Reichsmark). Thus goods arrived in Germany immediately after purchase, whereas the money itself stayed in Germany.

In 1942, Funk was still defending the need for state control of foreign exchange by saying that it would prevent uncontrollable capital flows from disturbing the planning of the economy. The Germans, of course, maintained price stability through price controls, and Funk saw this as the only alternative to inflation.[116] But the control of prices was not the only way of stabilising the economy: wages had to be kept under control too. Public spending had to be controlled, as did money, credit and consumption.[117] Funk explained that no one need fear for the stability of the Reichsmark, and he believed that economic convergence was necessary to achieve stabilisation of exchange rates.

The extent of state control which the Nazis exercised on both domestic and international monetary arrangements explains their universal hostility to the gold standard. Funk, like all fascists, realised that the gold standard – especially the right of the holder of a banknote to redeem it on demand for gold cash – was at the very heart of the liberal system he was determined to destroy. Instead of allowing people and companies to trade freely with a commodity currency controlled by no state, totalitarians of all sorts preferred to control the economy centrally. As one commentator reminds us, the Axis powers rejected gold partly because they did not have much.

> But the rejection of gold also had an emblematic and ideological significance in Axis economic propaganda, since it marked the transformation from the materialist, liberal capitalist economy to the totalitarian, corporatively organised economy of the European New Order. Gold was irrelevant once prices were determined not by the free market, but by governments which regulated all economic activity and once trade was managed through clearing arrangements. The underlying strength of the 'fascistised' European economy and of its dominant currencies, the lira and the mark, would correspond not to the arbitrary possession of gold but to the state's political will and to the capacity and potential for labour and production.[118]

The Nazis were determined to replace a market-based monetary system with a state-controlled one. Werner Daitz wrote, 'In future, gold will play no role as a basis for the European currencies, because a currency does not depend on what it is covered by, but rather it is dependent on the value which is given it by the state, or in this case by the economic order which is controlled by the state.'[119] Joachim Radler, in a paper subtitled 'Can one already speak of a European economic community?', wrote, 'Since we abandoned the gold cover, there is only "state money" which has a purchasing power only in the economic space ruled by the state.'[120]

Walther Funk realised that in order to establish the greatest possible degree of economic and political autarky, a monetary regime would have to be set up to protect Europe from outside influences. 'We in Germany,' he declared, 'will under no circumstances ever try the so-called gold currency again ... which would deliver our economy to uncontrollable international influences, and could be used as an instrument for power-political attempts to suppress us.'[121] Because the free world market was in reality 'an Anglo-American world hegemony' the whole purpose of the continental economy was to protect the European 'living and economic space' against manipulation by foreign powers.[122] Elsewhere, he repeated that 'we certainly refuse to hand our economy over to the automatism of gold, and thus to swings in the international economy which are out of our control'.[123]

Indeed, the speaker on 'European Currency Questions' at the 'European Economic Community' conference in 1942, Dr Bernhard Benning, the head of the Reich Credit Company, was also hostile to the gold standard – even if he emphasised the importance of the goal of price stability in currency management.[124] He praised the nineteenth-century German economist, Georg Friedrich Knapp, for having destroyed the philosophical bases of the gold standard in his book *The State Theory of Money*.[125] Benning claimed that gold subjected countries to swings and influences from abroad, because it accorded primacy to the exchange rate. He was thus in favour of a system of fixed but flexible exchange rates, with the Reichsmark as the leading currency. He held that full employment and purchasing power stability should be the primary goals of currency management, and that exchange rate stability should be secondary. He was proud of the fact that German monetary policy had been directed towards price stability since 1936, for whose success price controls were responsible.

Benning did address the question of European Monetary Union. He spoke of different 'phases' by which currency unity could be achieved in Europe (for which he believed price equivalence was a necessary prerequisite) but believed that a single currency was impossible and undesirable in the immediate future. Instead, he thought that the Reichsmark should assume a leading role in European currency management, and that Berlin would replace London as the centre of financial and commercial transactions.[126] After the war, incidentally, Benning became a member of the Directorate of the *Bank deutscher Länder*, the new central bank which became the Bundesbank in 1958. He remained on the Bundesbank's directorate until his retirement in 1972, when his place was taken by the future President of the Bundesbank, Helmut Schlesinger.

Similar views were held by Professor Ferdinand Fried. He was a prominent journalist and professor of economics, who worked in the office of the Nazi Minister of Agriculture, Walter Darré, and wrote such edifying tracts of Nazi economic theory as *The End of Capitalism* (1931), *Autarky* (1932), *The Ascent of the Jews* (1936), *The Change in the World Economy* (1937) and *The Future of World Trade* (1941). He agreed that gold money was incompatible with total state power. In his lecture 'Social Problems in the New Europe', delivered to the Groupe 'Collaboration' in Paris in 1941, he explained that money was, by its very nature, wandering and international. 'When the state was weak – when money dominated – money had to be covered by real gold. But when the state became strong again, the gold cover had no role any longer: the money in circulation is covered by the authority of the state . . . Money is covered by the fact that it is no longer anything but a function of the state and its forces. This means that prices are no longer the regulator of all economic phenomena. Instead, prices are regulated by the state according to the needs of the collectivity.'[127]

Other speakers who addressed the meetings of the Groupe 'Collaboration' also attacked gold. Introducing Jean Maillot's lecture on 'The Technical Revolution and its Consequences', Jacques Duboin explicitly rejected the gold standard as an integral part of economic liberalism. He said that there was no question of having recourse to the pundits of liberalism and the gold standard in order to find a solution to economic and social problems. 'The socialism of abundance can only be realised within a united Europe, within which each people will have become conscious of the solidarity which binds it to all the others.'[128]

In general, fascists and Nazis formulated plans for a 'labour-standard' as opposed to a gold standard.[129] Daitz certainly proposed that labour, not capital, be the monetary standard.[130] After the war, Sir Oswald Mosley was to advocate economic theories almost identical to those of the Nazis – such as the creation of large trading blocs and a common agricultural policy – and he, too, took pride in something called 'the wage-price mechanism'. This involved fixing the levels of wages and of prices to one another.[131] He also advocated 'planned investment and development policy'.

This was because the Nazis thought of themselves as champions of social policy. 'Special collective efforts must be made to develop the backward economies of Europe,' said one memorandum. 'The living standards of the broad masses of Europe . . . must be systematically improved, and far-seeing provision must be made for social stability.'[132] In the words of another:

> Germany offers her contribution in the social field: integration of broad masses in the national community, social welfare, equality of rights, recognition of dignity of labour and achievement, responsibility of the individual to the nation and vice-versa, provision of necessities, starting with basic needs and from the bottom upwards, a fair day's pay, social solidarity, restoration of the family and joy in child-bearing – all these have been displayed by the German people in peace and war. Application of these ideas to mutual relations of European peoples will guarantee a greater measure of social justice as between nations.

The memorandum concluded fantastically, 'The struggle is for restoration of the concept of personality, private property and freedom of religious belief.'[133]

One of the most accomplished theoreticians of fascist monetary theory – and of hostility to gold – was the Frenchman Francis Delaisi. Before the war, Delaisi had been a trade unionist, and a long-time believer in European integration. He had first called for it in his book *Les Contradictions du monde moderne* (The Contradictions of the Modern World) in 1925, and was subsequently active (as a member of the Committee of Honour) in an aggressively federalist magazine called *Jeune Europe*, published in Brussels and Geneva. After the fall of France, Delaisi became a prominent Nazi apologist – notably for economic reasons – and he explained why in his book *La Révolution européenne* (1942).

The 'European Revolution' to which the title referred was the definitive abandonment of economic liberalism and internationalism – especially of that which Delaisi considered to be its heart, the gold standard – and their replacement by rationing, price-fixing, and the creation of a unified European economy. Delaisi was convinced that the economic history of Europe after 1918 had shown the capitalist system to be on the verge of collapse. He argued (correctly) that the explosion of credit between 1919 to 1929 in the United States had led to the crash of 1929, and that the consequent depression had brought massive unemployment in the Anglo-Saxon economies. This threatened to destroy the entire social structure of Europe. But Delaisi was determined to throw the baby out with the bath-water by condemning the very principle of the gold standard, when in fact it was certain arrangements within the perverted post-First World War Gold Exchange Standard which were to blame.

Like Marshal Pétain, Delaisi hated 'the reign of money', but he also recognised the evils of inflation. He wrote that the primary condition for social peace was monetary stability. Germany had created monetary stability without gold, and based its calculations of monetary stability on the housewife's weekly 'basket of goods' instead.[134] Thus, he said, was the Retail Price Index invented. He argued that this was a direct way of controlling prices, much better than the indirect method which the gold standard represented. Thus had the Reichsmark become the most stable currency in Europe.[135]

The abandonment of gold was no incidental matter of monetary policy, according to Delaisi: it was an integral part of totalitarian economics. He showed that Hitler wanted to abolish the price mechanism (which liberal philosophers understand to be the numerical expression of the rights enjoyed by the holders of money) and that he did this by price-fixing and rationing. There is no ambiguity in Delaisi's writing about the totalitarian nature of the economic controls he advocated: 'How can one effectively survey even the smallest transactions in distant villages, and how can one suppress fraud about which buyers obviously never complain? This is where the National Socialist Party has intervened.'[136]

Delaisi held that the gold standard restricted social progress because, being a world currency, it opened labour markets to world competition and thereby forced down wages. He held the gold standard to be an instrument of inhumane competition.[137] It was important to liberate producers from the competition of exotic countries whose standard of living was too low.[138] Instead of a monetary standard, therefore, he proposed a standard based on labour: 'It is man, not gold, which is the measure of all things.'[139] He believed that the Reich's social policy was its 'most beautiful success'.[140] Hitler had needed to get 6 million people back to work, and so he had had to abolish the effects of foreign competition: it was therefore essential to abolish the gold standard, which he did on coming to power in 1933.[141] The European Revolution, Delaisi argued, protected salaries from low wage competition elsewhere.[142] Instead of 'the yoke of trade and of competition from exotic countries',[143] he proposed 'a single economic vital area with a single currency'.[144] With a charming solicitude for the well-being of people living under National Socialism, he pointed out that rationing may have reduced the choice available to consumers (there was no more coffee or bananas, for instance) but this made life much more simple. Because of price controls and rationing, he explained, the worker could not spend all his salary anyway. 'Moreover,' he concluded, 'the state thinks for him.'[145]

Fascist Italy: corporatism at the supranational level

Fascist thinking about the future of Europe was not limited to Germany. Indeed, Italian reflection on Europe during the war was largely concerned with ways to limit future German economic hegemony. Giuseppe Bottai resented the arguments of Carl Clodius which implied relegating Italy to the status of an agrarian client state,[146] and the inadequacies of the Italian state in comparison to Germany played a significant role in the development of Bottai's Europeanism. He wrote to Mussolini on 20 July 1940 that Italy faced the problem of economic dependence on Germany after the war. For these reasons, he urged the Duce to set up groups to study the problem of European integration. This led to frequent discussions of the European problem in Bottai's reviews. Many journals gave close attention to the cultural and institutional problems involved in European integration, and the subject was frequently discussed in editorials in *Primato* and *Critica Fascista*.[147]

As in Germany, Italian Fascist pro-Europeanism had a strongly moralistic or spiritualistic element. Fascism was the bearer of a 'new civilisation' based on the antithesis of the principles of 1789: it offered a spiritual and moral transformation of Europeans corrupted by the materialism and individualism of liberal-democratic values. As Mussolini told the National Council of Corporations on 14 November 1933, 'Europe may once again grasp the helm of world civilisation if it can develop a modicum of political unity.'[148] And in keeping with the trilateral vision of the world which was so dear to fascists and Nazis alike, Mussolini never tired of conjuring up the picture of a Europe threatened by US imperialism in the West and Japanese advance in the East: one historian of Euro-fascism considers that the idea of a 'European community opposed to both capitalism and Communism' was the essence of Mussolini's Europeanism, and that it transcended such earlier Fascist notions as 'sacred egoism' and the primacy of the Italian spirit.[149]

Italian Fascists held that Western decadence was due to the triumph of a materialist way of life, and a political system based on class interests, over those of the community as a whole. This decadence could be cured only by the triumph of a political philosophy inspired by higher spiritual values. The economic component of this reflection was important. As R. Riccardi, the Minister for Exchange and Currency, wrote in 'The Economy at the Basis of

the New European Civilisation',[150] the permanence and success of
the new European economic order depended on a changed consciousness and the implanting of Fascism's spiritual and moral
values. This is why, despite occasional rhetoric about preserving
national sovereignty in the new Europe, those publicising the new
European economic order insisted on a harmonisation of internal
political and social systems as a prerequisite for the economic reorganisation of Europe.

For the Italians, corporatism was at the heart of European
fascism (as it was of Vichy France). One of the most prolific theoreticians of corporatism was Bottai. He described the new
European economic order, indeed, as 'the projection of the corpo-
rative regime on to relations between nations'.[151] Like the Nazis,
the Italians Fascists were convinced that, if left to their own
devices, nation-states would anarchically pursue their own indi-
vidualistic self-interest. Just as it is unacceptable for individuals to
pursue their own interest, so state control at the supranational
level was a more rational way of arranging the European economy.

Corporatism, as first formulated by Mussolini, held that,
because people are not politically articulate, their interests could
be consulted only through institutions related directly to their
occupations. A small ruling elite placed in charge of those institutions would be both the guide of, and guided by, the people. In
Vichy France, for instance, the Charter of Labour was announced
as one of the main pillars of the National Revolution: by replacing
a single and obligatory syndicalist system and social committees, it
was supposed to put an end to the class struggle. Like the Nazis,
the Italian Fascists were in favour of economic planning. Indeed,
as in Vichy France, Italian Fascism's twin main impulses came
from, firstly, theoreticians of the 'new civilisation' and, secondly,
technocrats. Thus, many Italians thought that economic planning required the creation of a European supranational political
authority.[152]

Corporatists, like contemporary anti-capitalists, wanted to
replace what they thought were the conflict-ridden relationships
of the capitalist regime, and the 'anonymous power' they associated with it, with 'socialisation in the sense of self-government on

a syndical basis'.[153] This is why corporatist Fascists in Italy – again like the Nazis – believed they could 'harmonise the interests of member states, uniting both victors and vanquished in a collaborative European "community" framework and hence ensuring justice and peace among nations . . . Corporations would be the basis for a social unity within nations and, by extension, also for unity and reconciliation between nations; a system applied nationally to bring about inter-class harmony would, when applied internationally, make for collaboration among nations.'[154] Therefore, corporatists thought that they were creating a new form of international solidarity in which individual nations might preserve their identity, but not their political and economic independence. But it is, of course, precisely the difference between the liberal conception of nationhood on the one hand, and the European ideology on the other, that nations should in general have a *political* existence. Merely preserving 'culture' or 'identity' will not do.

The Franco-German couple, fascist-style

As in Italy, much pro-European thinking in wartime France was the natural continuation of currents of thought which had been prevalent in the 1930s. The ideology of Marshal Pétain's National Revolution was predicated on a pro-German, anti-British, pro-communitarian and anti-liberal view of economics and politics. Pro-European thinking was also a central element. Indeed, when Marshal Pétain proclaimed the policy of collaboration after his meeting with Hitler at Montoire in June 1941, he explicitly mentioned the New European Order as a central justification for it. 'It is with honour and in order to maintain French unity, a unity which is ten centuries old,' he told the French, 'and within the context of a constructive activity of the New European Order, that I am today embarking on the path of collaboration.'

Much Vichyite propaganda was therefore European. When French workers were encouraged to go and work in German factories, posters exhorted them to 'work for Europe'.[155] An Easter card in 1942 showed a mother hen with 'Europe, Our Mother' written on her breast: she gathers around her brood of chicks, each of which bears the flag of a country allied to Nazi Germany – Vichy France, Fascist Italy, Nazi Germany herself and so on. Two chicks are hesitating, Denmark and Switzerland. (Fifty years later, Denmark was to vote against 'Europe' in the Maastricht referendum of June 1992, while Switzerland voted against joining the European Economic Area. In 1993, indeed, the European Commission used the slogan 'Mother Europe Must Protect Her Children' in its propaganda.) A last chick, bearing the Union Flag, is seen storming off into a Judeo-Bolshevik-American box.[156]

Even more sinister was the explicitly pro-European propaganda which accompanied the creation of a French SS Brigade in July 1943. (The brigade's most famous division, 'Charlemagne', was one of the last units to defend the Reichstag in Berlin against Soviet attack in May 1945.) One poster of the period showed the serried ranks of the SS, with the slogan, 'With your European comrades, under the sign SS, you will win.'[157] Another call-up poster said that the purpose of the SS was to 'preserve the existence of the West and to maintain the spiritual culture of France and Europe'.[158] Finally, the monthly magazine of the French SS, called *Devenir* (Becoming), whose first edition in February 1944 was adorned with a swastika and a portrait of Hitler in heroic pose, was subtitled 'Journal of Combat of the European Community'.[159]

Meanwhile, the pro-Nazi writer Alphonse de Châteaubriant, who thought Hitler was hand in hand with God, expounded in newsreels on the necessity for France, like other nations, to submerge herself in the vast new geo-economic and geopolitical ensembles which technological progress were making inevitable. Similarly, the overtly fascist leader, Jacques Doriot, who dreamed of becoming the Führer of a fully fascist France, had the rallies he addressed adorned with banners saying, '*L'Europe Unie*' (Europe United).[160]

In general, a distinction has to be made between the government of Vichy, which imagined it was holding the fort against the excesses of Nazi Germany, and the Paris collaborators who were engaged in wholehearted support for the Nazi cause and all it entailed.[161] For the most part, the Paris collaborators were convinced fascists and Europeans, while the most typical Vichyites were reactionary, narrowly patriotic and, above all, defeatist.

On the other hand, as with Italy, an important motive behind Vichy's policy of collaboration with Nazi Germany – especially where the Prime Minister, Pierre Laval, was concerned – was the fear of being left out. Much of the impetus behind collaboration was undertaken with a view to ensuring France's place in Germany's New Europe. Robert Paxton, the great American historian of Vichy, has written of 'a broadly shared and concerted Vichy policy of preparing to step beyond the armistice to an accommodation with Hitler's Europe'.[162] For instance, Laval's Matignon declaration of 31 October 1940 said, 'In all domains, and especially in the economic and colonial spheres, we have discussed and we will continue to examine in what practical form our collaboration can serve the interests of France, Germany and Europe.'[163] A full-blooded collaborationist ideologue said, in 1941, that Marshal Pétain had understood that France's destiny could not be separated from that of the world which was 'forming itself under our eyes'.[164] Another declared that, 'Our actions will prove to Germany, before it is too late, that there are many people here in France for whom the word "collaboration" is not a dead letter, and who do not want Europe to be built without France.'[165]

Even in their relations with the Vichy government, the Germans pandered to this French urge. Joachim von Ribbentrop reassured Admiral Darlan at their meeting on 11 May 1941 that (in the words of the minutes of the meeting) it was essential for France to realise that Germany had no intention of depriving France of her life, or the French people of their means of existence. 'No one in Germany wanted that.'

'Just in the last few days,' the memo continued, 'the Führer had made reference to French culture, which had achieved so much in the past and must be preserved as a positive factor. In the Europe of the future the German and French cultures must enrich each other and create new values through this interchange.'[166] This was, of course, to assume that the maintenance of a nation's 'culture' and 'identity' (whatever that means) is sufficient for the nation to exist in any meaningful sense.

Ribbentrop continued to soothe French fears that they were going to be dominated by Germany. He insisted that, while the union of the German nation with the states related to it would make Germany the preponderant centre of power in the new Europe, the other nations would nevertheless be guaranteed the honourable places to which they were entitled. He said that the Führer believed that on this basis a real and sincere collaboration between France and Germany in the course of future developments could be assured. The decisive question was whether France was genuinely desirous of carrying out this collaboration. Ribbentrop said he was aware that there were circles in France which were toying with the idea of a new coalition against Germany. 'This attitude was, of course, incompatible with the large concept of Europe . . . A confederation of European nations would arise. Collaboration in absolute harmony would rule out the possibility of any internal war in Europe.'[167] And then the assertion – common to pro-European ideology in our own day – that the process of integration was inevitable: 'Whether one liked it or not, it would be impossible to stop this trend of development, and it would be well for the peoples if those governing them had a clear realisation of this.' The next day, Darlan went to see Hitler in Berchtesgaden. On his return, he wrote happily to the Führer about 'first steps toward a happier future for our two lands, and the future of "European co-operation" '.[168] For French consumption, he announced that a 'new Europe' was in preparation which could survive 'only if France has her honourable place'.[169]

Le Groupe 'Collaboration' and its circle

It was in order to propagate a policy of whole-hearted support for Nazi European integration that a group called Le Groupe 'Collaboration' – its full title was 'Collaboration, a Grouping of Energies for European Unity' – was founded in Paris on 24 September 1940 by the aristocratic essayist and admirer of Hitler, Alphonse de Châteaubriant. Châteaubriant had gained notoriety in 1937 as a pro-German and pro-Nazi with the publication of his book *La Gerbe des forces* (The Wreath of Power).[170] Although not openly fascist, the Group was inspired by a positive interest in Germany and, above all, by the belief that it was in Germany that answers could be found to French problems.

The people who frequented it were largely drawn from the pro-German circles which had existed in France before the war, and who drifted into pro-Nazi positions during it. These, the most extreme elements in occupied France, were the most pro-European. They included the 'Comité France–Allemagne', the Franco-German reconciliation committee established in 1935, which was headed by Georges Scapini, a veteran blinded in the First World War, who under Vichy became a French representative to Berlin for prisoners of war and played a major role as an advocate of collaboration. Other members of the Group, and of its associated circles, on the other hand, were not active collaborators even though they may have held pro-Nazi or pro-German positions in the period leading up to the war, and even at the beginning of it.

The Comité France–Allemagne was an important element in pre-war Nazi strategy to woo France. It was set up under German impetus, concomitantly with the creation of a sister organisation in Germany, the 'Deutsch–Französische Gesellschaft' (German–French Society). The latter organisation was created by one of the key figures in Nazi advocacy of a 'Franco-German *rapprochement*', the man who was to become German ambassador to Paris, Otto Abetz. (The original Deutsch–Französische Gesellschaft, which had been founded in 1926, had been dissolved by the Nazis.) Its opening ceremony was held in the presence of Von Ribbentrop and the French Ambassador to Berlin, André François-Poncet (whose son, Jean, became French Foreign Minister under Giscard, and who remains a prominent French spokesman for European integration to this day). The Deutsch–Französische Gesellschaft included, as collective members, the Nazi organisations 'Strength Through Joy', 'The League of National-

Socialist Women', and 'The National-Socialist Mutual Help Association'.[171]

Abetz's role in engineering reconciliation between France and Nazi Germany in the inter-war period was crucial. He was promoted to the rank of subaltern of the Reich Youth Leadership in 1934, as its expert on French affairs, and given the task of setting up a Franco-German liaison organisation. He built contacts between senior Nazi officials responsible for propaganda (Baldur von Schirach, Johannes Maas) and French opinion-makers (Bertrand de Jouvenel and Jean Luchaire of the pro-Briand magazine *Notre Temps*; Denis de Rougemont and others from the review *Ordre Nouveau*; and Thierry Maulnier of *L'Action française*).

These efforts culminated in the creation of the Deutsch–Französische Gesellschaft and the Comité France–Allemagne in 1935. The members of the Comité France–Allemagne were nearly all to become leading lights in French collaboration with the Nazis after 1940. They included Fernand de Brinon as one of the vice-presidents, who became Vichy France's Ambassador to Germany; Jacques Benoist-Méchin, a member of the group's political bureau, who became a senior Vichy minister; and Jean Weiland, on the administrative council, who became a leading light in the Groupe 'Collaboration' in Paris. Brinon, indeed, having been pro-German before the war, became explicitly pro-Nazi during it, and even tried to establish a Nazi-style government when in exile with Marshal Pétain in Sigmaringen in 1944. He declared at his trial after the war that any talk of a clever 'double game' being played by Marshal Pétain was nonsense: the old marshal had been, Brinon said, a thorough-going and genuine supporter of collaboration.[172]

Thus the Comité became, in Abetz's words, an important 'short-circuit' during the numerous Franco-German crises of the 1930s. It was recognised and subsidised by the French government, and had representatives all over France. Jean Weiland, indeed, boasted that the Comité had contributed to the 'success' of the Munich conference in 1938. Its magazine, the *Cahiers franco-allemands*, founded in 1935, grew out of the *Cahiers du Sohlberg* ('*Sohlbergkreis*' in German), which in turn grew out of meetings between friends who first met in Sohlberg in the summer of 1930 under Abetz's patronage.

The group debated such themes as 'French and German Youth Before the European Union' and 'The European Tasks of French and German Youth'.[173] It brought together many of the great pro-Europeans of the period from France, Germany and Belgium, including Henri de Man, the future leader of the Belgian socialists; Moeller van den Bruck, the star of the Young Conservative movement in Germany; Bertrand de Jouvenel, Jean Luchaire, numerous sympathisers of French fascism, *L'Action française*, and the French Romantic nationalist movement inspired by Maurice Barrès.[174] Abetz presented himself as a peace-loving democrat, but in fact he wrote regular reports for the German foreign office on the group's meetings, which he began to sign '*Mit Hitlerheil*' in 1934.[175]

The *Cahiers franco-allemands / Deutsch-Französische Monatshefte*, run by Abetz and published in both French and German, is a great monument to Nazi pro-Europeanism. It preached Franco-German reconciliation and the notion of 'the Franco-German couple'.[176] The titles of the articles speak for themselves: 'Europe Will Be' (Marcel Déat); 'How Did Napoleon Conceive of Europe?' (Hans Friedrich); 'Marshal Pétain's Policy of Co-operation Examined from an Economic Perspective' (Dr Wilhelm Grotkoop); 'The New Europe' (Dr Karl Megerle); 'For a Renaissance of Europe' (Reichsleiter Alfred Rosenberg); 'The German Conception of Vital Space' (Professor Dr Ludwig Schmitt); 'The Destiny of Europe from a Historical Point of View' (Professor Wilhelm Weber);[177] 'The Close Cultural Relationship Between France and Germany' (J. Noulens); 'German Youth and Happiness' (Otto Abetz); 'Frenchmen and Germans' (Henri de Montherlant); 'On *Mein Kampf*' (unsigned, in the literary section); 'The Documentary Film as a Work of Art' (Leni Riefenstahl);[178] 'The Greater Europe';[179] 'Charlemagne, the First Unifier of Europe';[180] and 'England Against Europe'.[181]

The magazine would also carry folksy photographs of peasant life in the two countries; pictures of Franco-German meetings; and lavish photographs of Nazi rallies at Nuremberg.[182] Its editorials contained the customary denunciation of the liberal Anglo-Saxon order which we have encountered elsewhere in Nazi propaganda. In the November–December 1940 issue, for instance, the editorial – entitled 'The Year of Europe' – claimed: 'The liberal system has collapsed on our continent this year with such astonishing speed that even its former supporters have accorded it only formal mourning.' It said that 'good Europeans' would ask themselves what England has to offer Europe: a balance of power? Economic liberty? A world system based on the gold standard? All these it rejected, concluding that France would be able to stand up to these challenges all the more calmly and effectively, the more she integrated herself firmly into European solidarity.[183]

All this was ultimately thanks to Abetz. His efforts were rewarded in 1938 when his mentor, Joachim von Ribbentrop, the Nazi Ambassador to London, became German Foreign Minister. After the fall of France, Ribbentrop appointed Abetz German Ambassador to Paris. He wrote to Hitler on 30 July 1940 that Germany should continue with her strategy of weakening France in order to integrate her into a German Europe: 'Just as National-Socialist Germany has usurped the idea of peace, which caused the moral weakening of France without suppressing the combative spirit of Germany, so in the same way can the Reich henceforth usurp the European idea, without prejudicing the will for a continental hegemony which National Socialism has anchored in the German people.'[184]

Another character who prepared the ground for Franco-German reconciliation in 1940 was Friedrich Grimm. Grimm joined the Nazi party in April 1933, and published 'Hitler and Europe' in 1936. In 1937, he accepted a mandate from Ribbentrop to become the vice-president of the Deutsch-Französische Gesellschaft. He wrote forewords to the works of the French historian, Jacques Bainville, which he published in 1939, the purpose of which was both to show the undoubted greatness of Bainville (and thus to woo the French nationalist Right) but also to demonstrate the futility of France's traditional policy of weakening Germany.

From the beginning of the war, Grimm became semi-officially in charge of Nazi propaganda in France. He particularly tried to capture the most anti-Bolshevik and anti-Semitic sections of the French Right, trying to convince them that only a Franco-German accord would save Europe from the Bolsheviks and the Jews. He helped to set up the Groupe 'Collaboration', and he spent the rest of the war calling for a 'new European order' to stand up to 'the Judeo-English domination' and 'Jewish Bolshevism'.[185] It is rather surprising to find a modern pro-European commentator describing him as 'a German patriot and a convinced European'.[186]

The culmination of all this was the foundation of the Groupe 'Collaboration'. From 1940 onwards, the Group held a series of conferences with a distinctly pro-European flavour; it organised public discussions of collaborationist themes; and it showed films produced in Axis countries, and sponsored lectures by visiting Germans.[187] It promoted 'French renewal, Franco-German reconciliation, and European Solidarity'[188] and the expression 'European community' was used at its first session.[189]

One of the Group's earlier lectures, 'Towards a New Europe' was delivered by a German diplomat and parliamentarian, Baron Werner von Rheinbaben, who had been German Ambassador to the League of Nations and Vice-President of the Reichstag's Franco-German parliamentary group in the 1920s. Like nearly all pro-Europeans before and since, Rheinbaben fancied that all conflict and tension between European nations could be abolished. Hostile to the proposals of the Disarmament Conference, he said that the wounds caused by the last war had to be healed. The division of Europe must disappear, and the tensions between nations had to be overcome. 'A new system of life together among peoples must be created.'[190] It was necessary, he said, to avoid the balance-of-power system, according to which countries grouped together in coalitions against one another.

Rheinbaben made a plea in his speech for France to contribute to the New Europe through Franco-German collaboration.[191] Franco-German collaboration was the essential condition for the construction of the new Europe, he said.[192] 'The only path which will lead France today towards a new Europe is close collaboration with Germany.'[193] According to Marshal Pétain's well-known phrase, he went on, France's collaboration with the new Europe should become the determining and decisive directive in the future of France.[194]

Warming to a common German theme, Rheinbaben excoriated the 'English policy of maintaining the balance of power'. He said that this policy consisted in opposing European powers against one another in order to achieve their mutual weakening and England's domination in the world.[195] 'In the period of constructing the new Europe,' he went on, 'there cannot be any half-measures, and no possibility of ulterior motives.' The question of Franco-German collaboration was becoming more and more pressing. Rheinbaben dismissed suggestions that German talk about the 'new Europe' was just a smokescreen for German domination of Europe. France could only gain politically and economically from the new Europe. Did France not want access to German markets? The English had to be evicted from the continent once and for all, and the new Europe had to keep its distances from the United States. It was necessary, he said, to build 'the new European home' without American help.[196]

Dr Colin Ross also addressed the Group. Ross's meeting was chaired by René Pichard du Page, who described Ross as a partisan of 'the Franco-German understanding, the solid and only possible basis for this *patrie européenne* which must be created – or rather resuscitated, for as he will remind you, Charlemagne's empire was the first outline of it . . .'[197] Ross did not disappoint his listeners, and he terminated his speech by saying, 'We must return in some form or another to the empire of Charlemagne, which means that we must rediscover what unites us, beyond that which divides us . . . It is this kind of community that must be re-created, and we will re-create it in spite of everything. I do not believe only in a *rapprochement* between France and Germany. I believe in Europe, in OUR EUROPE, in the New Europe, which will be *the great common Fatherland of the French and the Germans*.'[198]

In a speech entitled 'Our European Role' Jacques de Lesdain spoke of 'the resurrection of France within Europe'.[199] 'A guest has arrived on our doorstep,' he went on rather improbably. 'That guest's name is "Europe". France has to open the door to Europe or risk greater calamities even than those which had just befallen her.

France's long-term security and prosperity depend on Europe . . . Our prosperity and the prosperity of our neighbours are in a direct relation of cause and effect with the decisions which we will take voluntarily – I insist on the adverb *voluntarily* – whether or not to collaborate with Europe; in a word, whether or not France will accept wholeheartedly to become *European France*.' But France was not the only nation which had to become European: the Reich itself, Italy and Spain, also had to prove themselves as European as France.[200]

Lesdain's analysis of the need for European unification employed all the themes encountered earlier. Europe was too small for feuding little countries to compete against one another. 'Look at the map of Europe and the twenty nations which compose it. These twenty peoples, instead of extending a hand to one another, instead of maintaining a spirit of good neighbourliness and helping one another out, have got the habit – under financial influences from outside Europe – of turning their backs on one another, of being jealous of one another, and of buying from far away that which they could exchange with each other for evident benefit.'[201] Denouncing the power of 'trusts' in London, New York and Amsterdam, De Lesdain argued that the theory of 'vital space' was nothing but a self-evident necessity. Once they had been put into practice, these living spaces consisted simply in establishing those rational relations which should have existed between neighbourly peoples for centuries, he argued.[202] Using the metaphor of a 'construction', De Lesdain simply argued that the European economy needed to be planned more rationally, with each country doing what it did best. Similarly, another speaker, addressing the question of agriculture, insisted that, without Europe, French agriculture could be neither secure nor prosperous. 'Europe is the vital space of French agriculture . . . Our market, our vital space, we have it at our doorstep: it is Europe.'[203] He concluded: 'Joining the European Community implies an immediate programme of action which we must realise.'[204]

Lesdain was also the initiator of an exhibition which opened at the Grand Palais in Paris on 31 May 1941, entitled *La France européenne*, whose purpose was to 'show France's role in the New

Europe'.[205] A magazine of the same name was issued. Lesdain himself said that the exhibition was 'above all an act of faith' which was intended to restore the confidence of the French in themselves after the defeat. The prospect of 'France's integration in Europe'[206] required much discipline as well as enthusiasm. There was no future for France outside Europe, and France's national industries had to integrate themselves into European industry in order to prosper. The exhibition, which was inaugurated by Fernand de Brinon, accompanied by General von Stülpnagel, the German military commander in France, was a kind of grandiose *son et lumière* show about France's European destiny: the spirits of France's history were all there – Sainte Geneviève, Charlemagne, Louis XIV, Sully, Colbert, Napoleon, Victor Hugo, the unknown soldier. There were pictures of French life – a peasant village, an artisan's workshop, a village in an African colony. The final apotheosis showed France and Europe sealing their union. An orchestra played a hymn to 'European France' as a vibrant end to each session.[207]

The Groupe 'Collaboration' continued in operation throughout the war. Financed by the Germans to the tune of 2 million francs a year, by 1943 it claimed a membership of over one hundred thousand, with some estimates running as high as twice that.[208] It established an office in Vichy in 1943. On 4 March 1944, the Group was addressed by none other than Werner Daitz, on the theme 'The Continental Policy of Napoleon, Anticipation of the European Policy of the Reich'.[209] His French editors later said that Daitz was the first man to throw light on 'the future of our continent, and the role that France can play in it'. But Daitz was not, in fact, the first to draw an explicit comparison between Napoleon's economic policies and those of the Nazis. The geopolitician Kurt Vowinkel had done so in 1941.[210]

Interest in the subject had also been expressed by Bertrand de Jouvenel in 1938. De Jouvenel was a leading intellectual in France in the 1930s, and some of his books on political philosophy – *Du pouvoir* (On Power), for instance – remain legitimate classics to this day. But before and during the war, Jouvenel was very close to the anti-capitalist and corporatist thinking which characterised the French, Belgian, Italian and German fascists and proto-fascists. At a Franco-German meeting in Berlin in 1934, Jouvenel had famously expressed admiration for the planned economy in Germany.[211] It was in this spirit that, at the very height of the implementation of the Nazi economy in 1942, he wrote *Napoleon, or The Directed Economy: The Continental Bloc*, published by the pro-fascist publisher Les Editions de la Toison d'Or in Brussels.

Not surprisingly, Jouvenel's views on economic planning inevitably led him to be pro-European and even one-worldist. He had written *Europe's Awakening* in 1938 and *Towards the United States of Europe* in 1930. In 1931, he published *From European Economic Unity to the World Directed Economy*. Jouvenel was also notorious for having written a very laudatory interview with Hitler in 1936[212] – even though, to his credit, he resigned from the Comité France–Allemagne over Munich in 1938.

The Groupe 'Collaboration' also sponsored a youth movement, the 'Jeunesse de l'Europe Nouvelle' (Youth of the New Europe). It took a year to set up, from May 1941 until its establishment in both occupied and unoccupied France in June 1942. Although it did not maintain contacts with Vichy's paramilitary youth movements – 'Les Chantiers de la Jeunesse', or 'Les Compagnons de France' (of which the youthful Jacques Delors was a member, and which Marshal Pétain declared to be 'the avant-garde of the National Revolution'[213]) – like them, the Jeunesse de l'Europe Nouvelle adopted a runic symbol and its members wore uniforms. At the peak of its influence, in 1943, it claimed about 4,000 members. They gradually dispersed into other groups like the National Socialist Trucking Corps, the Anti-Bolshevik Legion and the Waffen SS. The leader of the Jeunesse de l'Europe Nouvelle, Jacques Schweizer, told the group's congress in January 1944 that the National Revolution meant 'a European France and National Socialism'.[214] By 1944, indeed, the Jeunesse de l'Europe Nouvelle had acquired the rudimentary organs of a totalitarian movement: protection squads to serve as guards at the meetings of the Groupe 'Collaboration' and at its own meetings, cadets for children aged eleven to fourteen, and a women's auxiliary.[215]

Personalism

Probably the most intriguing direct link between pre-war, wartime
and post-war Europeanism is personalism. Personalism is a nebu-
lous philosophy, which despite (or perhaps because of) its
vagueness has exerted great influence in post-war continental
Europe. It is an anti-liberal, left-wing, Catholic-ecumenical, federalist, pro-European, Third Way, anti-individualist creed. During
the 1930s, it was associated with virulent anti-parliamentarianism
and anti-capitalism.

Its most famous adherent is Jacques Delors, who declares the
doctrine's most prominent proponent, Emmanuel Mounier, to be
one of his spiritual godfathers. Mounier is not well-known in
Britain, but his influence in France and elsewhere on the continent is very great. A lifelong supporter of a federal Europe,
Mounier's thought was also an important driving force behind the
social philosophy and humanist theology which imposed itself on
the Catholic Church at the Second Vatican Council.

The two principal personalist reviews in the 1930s were *Esprit*,
founded and edited by Emmanuel Mounier, and *Ordre Nouveau*,
founded by Alexandre Marc. Both circles were united by a deep
hatred of the nation-state. A third figure, the Swiss philosopher
Denis de Rougemont, belonged to both groups. He was a lifelong
European federalist and a fervent supporter of the notion of 'revolution' throughout the 1930s. Like many others confronted with
the economic turbulence of the period and with the endemic
weakness of France's parliamentary system, Denis de Rougemont
was profoundly anti-liberal, anti-capitalist and anti-parliamentarian. He was also the link between the two magazines, being the
only person to write for both of them over a sustained period.

De Rougemont, indeed, unites with a rare clarity the link
between personalism, federalism, pro-Europeanism and the hatred
of politics. He wrote: 'A political consequence of personalism is
federalism. Laws founded on the person are obliged to take
account in the first place of personal, local and regional diversities.'[216] He felt that the 'European revolution' for which he was
struggling had to bring political life 'to the centre of man himself,

to the person', and not to the nation-state.[217] His vision was Utopian and holistic: he thought that, once the right structures had been put in place, all conflict between persons – and hence all politics – would evaporate into general harmony and bonhomie: 'I am involved in politics so that there will not be any politics any more,' he declared.[218]

Unlike some of his colleagues, De Rougemont never compromised with Nazism, even if he observed it from close quarters. He was a lecturer at the University of Frankfurt for a year (1935–36) and, as we shall see, took Emmanuel Mounier to a Nazi rally. Exasperated with Swiss neutralism, he founded a Resistance group called The League of Gothard, although it never actually entered into combat with Nazi Germany. Strangely enough, it was while looking at trains that De Rougemont had his deepest conversion to Europeanism: he described how he watched international express trains crossing occupied Europe, and wrote, 'I could read on the long brown carriages "Amsterdam, Basel, Milan, Zagreb, Bucharest". For the first time, I felt Europe.'[219] From 1937 onwards, he became convinced that Swiss federalism was a model for Europe.[220]

His hatred of the nation-state, of parliamentary rule, and of liberalism were all part of the same thought. He believed that the parliamentary regime only took account of people's interests, and not of their needs. He felt that cosy small-scale communitarianism could produce harmony based on spiritual togetherness and a teleological view of society. He thought that liberalism and the parliamentary regime based on the nation-state were nothing but crass materialisms.

There is some agreement with fascism in these theories. Indeed, there is even evidence that personalism may have influenced fascism. According to De Rougemont, Joachim von Ribbentrop and Otto Abetz actually took the phrase 'New Order', which they used to describe the Nazi vision of Europe, from the title of Marc's magazine, *Ordre Nouveau*.[221] *Ordre Nouveau* was indeed often pro-Nazi and pro-Mussolini, even though it criticised their movements here and there. What its contributors particularly liked about Nazism was its hostility to liberalism, communism and parliamentary democracy. In November 1933 the magazine published a 'Letter to Adolf Hitler, Chancellor of the Reich'. Signed *Ordre Nouveau*, it wrote, 'Your work is courageous; it has grandeur.' It spoke of Nazism's 'heroism', 'sacrifice', 'abnegation', and its 'protest against contemporary materialism'.[222] 'You have put an end to a lie,' said the magazine, 'the lie of liberal democracy.'[223] Indeed, the article finished by saying that Hitler had not gone far enough.

The founder of *Ordre Nouveau*, Alexandre Marc, was, like De Rougemont, a federalist. Born in Russia in 1904, he had admired Trotsky in 1917.[224] He wrote a book in 1933 called *Jeune Europe*, in which he asserted that the Nazi regime would dissolve itself in 'despair, chaos, mud and blood' if it did not 'transcend itself', 'surpass itself' by adopting some of the ideas of the elite of German youth, 'the primacy of the human person, federalism, and regional corporatism'.[225]

Marc was central to the personalist link between Emmanuel Mounier's *Esprit* and the Nazi Left – those 'dissident' National Socialists dissatisfied with Hitler's leadership of the Workers' Party Movement in the early 1930s. Before founding *Ordre Nouveau* he had collaborated on a magazine called *Plans*, launched in 1931 by a young lawyer, Philippe Lamour. Lamour had been a militant Blue Shirt in Georges Valois' fascist 'Faisceau' party, before he tried to found his own 'Revolutionary Fascist Party'. Interested in the planism of the Belgian socialist and future Nazi collaborator Henri de Man (who was to write in 1943 in a German magazine that 'the sovereignty of nation-states in customs and trade matters is economic nonsense'[226]), *Plans* had collected assorted scientists and artists, including Le Corbusier, and published romantic pictures of Hitler and Mussolini. Jacques Maritain, who was otherwise Emmanuel Mounier's spiritual godfather, was to reproach Mounier for having anything to do with the 'goose-stepping philosophy' of Marc and his friends.[227]

Marc had attended meetings with young Germans at the Sohlberg camp in the summer of 1930, where he met Otto Abetz. Although then only a design teacher, Abetz was already taking a lead in promoting contacts between German and French youth. Marc's friend, René Dupuis, with whom he co-authored *Jeune*

Europe in 1933, wrote a Manifesto for a 'Single Front of European Youth', which called for a common revolutionary struggle of the youth of France and Germany, 'a return to the real man', 'federalism', and the 'elaboration of a European plan'.[228]

Philippe Lamour declared that the people who gravitated around *Ordre Nouveau* and *Plans* were all 'anti-individualists' because they were all 'personalists'.[229] At the Franco-German Youth Conference in 1932, held in Frankfurt, a German version of *Plans* was created, called *Planen*: Otto Strasser and Otto Abetz appointed a left-wing National Socialist friend of Marc's to run it. 'Friends of *Plans*' were set up all over Europe.

Ordre Nouveau also inspired the foundation of *Esprit*: Mounier told Marc in the summer of 1930 that he wanted to found a Catholic version of *Plans*.[230] This, indeed, is what *Esprit* became, and remains to this day: a Catholic, communitarian, left-of-centre, pro-European paper which commands great influence. Marc wanted to merge *Esprit* and *Plans*, and make the former the literary organ of the latter, because Marc and his friends were developing 'personalism' in their Single Front of European Youth.

Mounier eventually set up *Esprit* independently, but Marc was a contributor to it. Like *Ordre Nouveau*, *Esprit* professed a hatred of liberal democracy and a deep conviction in the sickness and weakness of France. In the second number of Mounier's review, Marc called for a 'revolutionary federalism'. In February 1933, *Esprit* published an attack on Hitler for being weak and indecisive, a man who was not sufficiently revolutionary.[231] Indeed, some of the early editions of *Esprit* ran long articles by Otto Strasser. Meanwhile, Otto Abetz published Emmanuel Mounier in the *Cahiers franco-allemands / Deutsch-Französische Monatshefte* in 1936, because he was always on the lookout for 'signs of health' in decadent, 'capitalist and liberal' Europe.[232]

Thus the personalists enjoyed a fascist reputation in the 1930s.[233] Jacques Bartoli described *Esprit* as 'pre-fascist' not 'fascist', and predicted that many of the group would quickly pass to an 'acknowledged fascism'.[234] Indeed, even within the *Esprit* group, Mounier was criticised for attending a conference in Rome from 21–25 May 1935, organised by the Institute for Fascist

Culture to study the corporatist state, after which Mounier paid 'homage of our youth to the men we met there'. He mentioned 'their youth, their fervour, their combative spirit . . . Even those in the French delegation who had been brought up as sworn enemies of fascism spoke publicly of the deep kinship which they felt between themselves and the constructive elan of these new generations.'[235]

Esprit was indeed unique among French reviews in the number of its collaborators who had German philosophical roots. Many *Esprit* partisans betrayed admiration for the German National Socialists' spirit of 'community', because it was on the same wavelength as their own communitarian ideals. Indeed, it was the very ties with the *völkisch* or 'Europeanist' national socialism of Otto Strasser, and the 'social democratic' national socialism of Otto Abetz, which encouraged *Esprit*'s disdain for the more militaristic elements of Hitlerism. As John Hellman says, 'The kind of national socialism favoured by the personalist movement was revolutionary, spearheaded by youth, and involved in European federalism.'[236]

The Berlin–Paris–Brussels triangle

Mounier and *Esprit* were active in Brussels as well as Paris. By May 1934, the friends of *Esprit* in Brussels had become numerous. They were particularly interested in the planist socialism of the future Belgian collaborator, Henri de Man, as well as in the initiatives of a young leader of Catholic Action, Raymond de Becker, who was the great inspiration of *Esprit*-Belgium. Mounier declared that De Becker's new review, *Esprit Nouveau*, was remarkably similar to his own. De Becker, meanwhile, was himself impressed with Léon Degrelle, the future leader of the Belgian fascist movement, the Rexists. In 1934, De Becker became director of *L'Avant Garde*, the Louvain student newspaper which Degrelle had made influential among Belgian youth.

Mounier went to Belgium frequently. In 1936, he attended a summer camp with the Hitler Youth, organised by Edouard Didier at the Belgian coastal resort of Zoute from 11–19 July. He expressed understanding for the 'historical reason' of the German movement, but felt that its nationalism was suffocating its socialism. Nonetheless, 'on international affairs, everyone remarked an almost complete agreement and real possibilities for collaboration'.[237] By December of that year, Mounier was able to write that 'communitarian feeling was one of the most exciting psychological aspects of the Nazi vision of the world'.[238] He thought that Nazism, like Russian Communism, might be stages towards integral personalism. Although he usually found some reason or other to distance himself from Nazism and fascism, he always seemed to find important positive elements within it. It was especially the notion of community which fascinated him. 'Fascism and communism,' he asserted, 'are the first starts of an immense communitarian wave which is beginning to break over Europe.'[239] Generally, indeed, *Esprit* took a very gentle line on Nazism before the outbreak of the war. Although it occasionally published articles critical of German policy (such as after the invasion of Czechoslovakia in 1939) there seems no doubt that Mounier was fascinated by Nazism. After his trip in 1936 to see Denis de Rougemont in Frankfurt, Mounier wrote of the 'authentic spiritual vigour' which he had felt the Nazis to possess.[240]

Belgium, indeed, was also a place where Abetz concentrated his energies. The *Cahiers franco-allemands / Deutsch-Französische Monatshefte* urged reconciliation between nationalists and socialists in both Belgium and France. Abetz had fused his own strong Catholic upbringing and youthful social democratic leanings into a personal brand of Nazism, and seemed to want to project his personal synthesis on to both countries by transforming Belgian and French youth within a new social order. Both countries proved ripe for his influence: they had the right combination of authoritarian leaders (King Leopold III, Marshal Pétain) and planist traditions (Henri de Man in Belgium – Mounier's idol – and François Perroux, the prominent corporatist economist in France). They also both had a plethora of youth movements keen to establish a 'spiritual revolution': *Esprit, Communauté, Jeune Europe, Ordre Nouveau*, and the Rexist groups in Belgium. When Abetz was banned from France in 1939, he continued to work for Franco-German reconciliation through his contacts in Brussels.

Edouard Didier, who organised the Zoute camp in 1936, was one of the main men through whom Otto Abetz exerted ideological influence in Belgium. He was the delegate for Belgium of the Central Committee of the movement 'Young Europe: League for the United States of Europe', whose magazine, *Jeune Europe*, was published in Brussels and Geneva. Otto Abetz spoke at meetings organised under *Jeune Europe*'s auspices. (It is ironic that, from 1952 to 1967, a federalist magazine called *Jeune Europe* was also published by the 'Mouvement Jeune Europe'.) Didier was later to set up a publishing house, Les Editions de la Toison d'Or, which published, among many other things, Francis Delaisi's *La Révolution européenne* in 1942, as well as the visions of the pro-Nazi Belgian Raymond de Becker and of Henri de Man, the great theoretician of planist socialism. Indeed, Von Ribbentrop also provided secret funds to Les Editions de la Toison d'Or.[241]

Not surprisingly, *Jeune Europe* favoured *rapprochement* with Germany. Its programme for European federalism had been reported in Abetz's magazine *Sohlbergkreis* as well as in *Esprit*, as offering new hope for Belgium. It included, predictably enough, 'the abandonment of the principle of the absolute sovereignty of states' and plans for European economic integration.[242] (Oddly enough, this document is not to be found in the official bibliography of Mounier's writings, one of the many instances in which Mounier doctored his own war and pre-war record.) It was rare for Abetz's review to discuss ideologies other than Henri de Man's planism, or the 'fascist socialism' of Marcel Déat and the novelist Pierre Drieu La Rochelle. But in this issue it returned to an analysis of Mounier and De Rougemont. Mounier had, in *Jeune Europe*, called for a revision of the Treaty of Versailles in Germany's favour, and also for European federalism.[243]

Abetz also selected Raymond de Becker's *Communauté* movement as being especially promising in Belgium, for, like other groups including those around Henri de Man's planism, *Esprit* and *Terre Wallonne*, he felt that they were struggling 'against Versailles and for a new understanding with Germany'.[244] Abetz's interest in these groups contrasts with the Nazi disdain for the overtly fascist movement in Belgium, Léon Degrelle's Rexists.[245]

In July 1936, De Becker went to Hamburg for the International Congress on Workers' Vacations, then to Berlin and Bavaria. He was particularly impressed by the evening he spent with Joachim von Ribbentrop, where he noted the 'democratic origins' of the men around him. On his return, he organised the first visit of the National Socialist press to Belgium, and explained to the *Cahiers franco-allemands / Deutsch-Französische Monatshefte* the differences between the Rexist and *Communauté* currents of Belgian nationalism. In December his personalist colleagues went skiing with Max Liebe, Abetz's Belgian expert, and the Hitler Youth.

Another important *Esprit* contact in Belgium was Paul-Henri Spaak, one of the future founding fathers of the European Community: the conclusions of the Intergovernmental Conference, chaired by Spaak, published in April 1956 and known as 'The Spaak Report', recommended the creation of the Common Market and Euratom, which duly occurred two years later. Before the war, Spaak was a member of the Belgian Workers' Party, of which De Man was vice-president. Spaak described himself as 'a national socialist', and Mounier supported him in Belgium. Like De Becker, Spaak had an admiration for 'some of Hitler's magnificent achievements', but Spaak 'thought the price of importing them into Belgium too high'. In the autumn of 1936, both men were interested in a 'personalist socialism', but in De Becker's words, as time went on, their dogma became 'for us, more and more, a national socialism'.[246]

Paul-Henri Spaak declared in February 1937 that 'the hour of Belgian national socialism has come'. By March 1938, he and Henri de Man began urging Belgian neutrality after the German Anschluss of Austria. In March 1938, Mounier endorsed the De Becker–Spaak cabal in Belgium. Even if an essay in *Esprit* in November 1938 criticised Spaak for working with pro-Nazi groups, and recommended that France take steps before Belgium was irretrievably pro-Nazi, the following issue (in December) ran a defence of Spaak. Meanwhile, Raymond de Becker drew ever closer to Nazism, and felt himself 'liberated' when he left the Catholic Church at the end of the year.[247]

In May 1939, Henri de Man was elected president of the Belgian Workers' Party with the support of Spaak. His programme was that of a 'national socialism', the struggle against capitalism, and an authoritarian system based on a reinforcement of the state through strengthened executive power. The following summer, Otto Abetz was refused entry to France, because he was thought to be directing a spy-ring there and financing lavish publications, but he was able to visit Belgium. There he encouraged the Didier salon's core of young intellectuals around Spaak and De Man to prevent Belgium from entering the war on the side of the allies. When the war broke out, Spaak was instrumental in helping De Man to found a weekly newspaper, *Ouest*, which reinforced neu-tralist sentiment. In the spring of 1940, it received a substantial contribution from Abetz's deputy, Max Liebe. Perhaps under De Man's influence, on the day German troops invaded Belgium, the Belgian trains went on strike, which prevented allied troops from getting to the front lines. Spaak and other Belgian ministers sought an armistice with the Germans (as Marshal Pétain was to do successfully in France) but the Germans refused.[248]

When De Becker opted for Belgian national socialism in early 1938, the fears of Jacques Maritain and others were confirmed: Mounier's personalism had become a crypto-Nazism, although of course Mounier himself cannot be held directly responsible for the actions of his friend. During the war, Raymond de Becker edited the leading Brussels daily, *Le Soir*, which Abetz secretly funded, and, aided by the talented Rexist author of *L'Europe aux européens* (Europe for the Europeans),[249] Pierre Daye, he was soon publishing 25,000 copies a day. As John Hellman says, 'Personalism had transcended the world of small-circulation reviews and become, in the imaginations of De Becker and Spaak, the future orientation of the whole of Belgian society . . . De Becker, enthralled by the vision of a dawning European golden age which came to him at the Ordensburg in Bavaria, soon called for a Europe dominated by Adolf Hitler.'[250] Mounier never disowned or even commented on his friend's option, even though he lost many followers in Belgium to Spaak's national socialism from the autumn of 1938 onwards.

Uriage: the crucible of post-war pro-Europeanism

After the fall of France, Emmanuel Mounier became actively involved in the Vichyite 'National Revolution'. Indeed, it was under Vichy that *Esprit* achieved the kind of prominence in France which it enjoyed under Raymond de Becker in Belgium: before 1940, it had been a rather obscure outsiders' review with a readership of left-wing Catholics, spiritualist socialists, authoritarian educational reformers, unemployed intellectuals, adventurous priests and schoolteachers in the provinces. By the end of 1940, the review became the key publication in an effort to transform the whole of French youth. Some of its contributors were advisers to Marshal Pétain, aides to his chief ministers, leaders of the youth movement or leading lights in the new Higher National School for Officers at Uriage, where Mounier was to teach.

In particular, *Esprit*'s appeal for a spiritual revolution among youth which was neither 'Right' nor 'Left' was very close to the rhetoric of the National Revolution. According to a well-known historian of Vichy, the three bases of the national revolution included the anti-democratic nationalism of the *Action française*, the personalism of young Catholics, and corporatist economics – whose purpose of corporatist economics was to shield the person against overweening state power by setting up intermediate corporate bodies.[251] Vichy's youth movements – 'Les Compagnons de France', 'Les Chantiers de la Jeunesse' – were also strongly influenced by the kind of youthful optimism and left-wing Catholicism of *Esprit*.

Marshal Pétain, like Mounier, attributed France's defeat to spiritual and moral causes which the school system should remedy. Using vocabulary indistinguishable from that of Mounier, Pétain wrote: 'Individualism is what almost killed us . . . Individualism has nothing in common with respect for the human person . . . The French school of tomorrow will teach respect of the human person, the family, society, *la patrie*.'[252] This similarity between *Esprit*'s pre-war aspirations and some of the rhetoric of Vichy could be explained in large part by the fact that Pétain's initial statements on the National Revolution were written by old supporters of *Ordre Nouveau* and *Esprit*.[253] Vichy's Labour Charter, the centre-piece of the National Revolution's social policy, drew heavily on the corporatist economic theories of *Esprit*'s François Perroux. (After the war, Perroux continued to publish prominently on economics, notably a book explaining why states could no longer be considered independent in a modern, interdependent economy.[254])

Indeed, Mounier himself became a lecturer at the Higher National School for Officers at Uriage, which was the intellectual think-tank and chief educational establishment for the National Revolution. *Esprit*'s personalism became its unofficial doctrine. Mounier's influence on the National Revolution grew through the spring and summer of 1941, even though he, like many others at Uriage, no doubt deceived himself that he was organising some kind of 'inner resistance' against the enemy. *Esprit* prospered for the first year under Pétain: the ministry for foreign affairs took 250 subscriptions for its embassies and consulates throughout the world. In February 1941, Mounier received congratulations from the Minister for Youth for his youth programme. *Esprit* was recommended by the national bulletin of 'Les Chantiers de la Jeunesse'.

Mounier fell from favour, however, in 1942, when an anti-Catholic purge occurred within Vichy's power-structures. He was eventually arrested as a resistant: he was indignant at the time, and protested that he had never had any contacts with the resistance. But, after the war, this event enabled him to present his lectures at Uriage as a clever double-game of inner resistance, and his modern supporters presumably believe this version of events. But Mounier also did not lose his fascination for authoritarian regimes: his hatred of 'capitalism' was so great that, after the war, he became one of France's leading apologists for the Stalinist Communist take-over of Eastern Europe.[255]

Mounier's ambiguous role gave rise to a heated Parisian quarrel in the early 1990s when one historian called the founder of Esprit 'the minister of Culture of Vichy'.[256] He also referred to him as 'the French Heidegger'. Other historians agreed that Mounier saw positive elements in the 'fascist élan'.[257] Mounier's friends and followers replied with shock and outrage, one of them replying to the accusations of the Canadian historian, John Hellman, by delivering the following *coup de grâce*: 'How can a historian with an Anglo-Saxon education possibly understand what happened in France between 1930 and 1950?'[258] Most recently, one historian has attempted to prove that Mounier was at all times vehemently anti-Nazi and anti-Vichyite by showing that his involvement as an officer in the youth movement, Jeune France, an organisation run by the Vichy Youth Ministry, and thus a key element in the regime's cultural policy, did not compromise his principles.[259]

Another figure at Uriage, who was to achieve very great influence after the war, was Hubert Beuve-Méry, the future editor of the French paper of record, *Le Monde*.[260] Beuve-Méry, who had been directly involved in a militant right-wing, even proto-fascist youth movement in the mid-1920s,[261] became a leading ideologist of Uriage: he had a fairly clear idea of an authoritarian, but newly Christian, France that could be created in a Europe dominated by Hitler's Germany. In February 1939, in his book *Vers la plus grande Allemagne* (Towards a Greater Germany), he wrote that despite the elements of disorder and violence, 'the elements of a new synthesis remained . . . And it is not too late to prepare, beyond the . . . dreams of Chancellor Hitler, the coming of a more united and more just Europe.' Because the book caught the attention of political and diplomatic circles, Beuve-Méry was invited to a dinner in Berlin in 1939, where he was seated opposite Goebbels and Himmler.[262]

In March 1941, Beuve-Méry published an article in *Esprit* entitled 'National Revolutions, Human Revolutions'. He foresaw a more authoritarian and Germanised Europe, in which a France reconstructed along the lines of Salazar's Portugal would find its place. Rejecting the Versailles settlement, Beuve-Méry dealt with a theme which, as we have already seen, preoccupied many pro-Europeans of the period: 'The principles that were the bases of Europe for a long time – the absolute sovereignty of small or large states, the European equilibrium (that is, the balance of power), the right of neutrality – must cede their place to a more orderly arrangement of the continent.'[263]

Like many of his ilk, Beuve-Méry hated the 'anarchic individualism' of liberalism and capitalism, and 'the reign of money'. He wanted instead a more authoritarian state, offset by intermediary bodies. In this, he was influenced by the corporatism of François Perroux (himself an admirer of Germany's conservative revolution) and the planism of Henri de Man. John Hellman writes, 'He endorsed the idea of a Europe-wide return to the ancient provinces, on the Swiss model, as an antidote to tyranny. At Uriage, a sort of *völkisch* federalism, similar to that nurtured in groups like the *Ordre Nouveau* circle before the war, shone in contrast to the concern for the fundamental liberal and democratic values which others considered essential to the resistance against world totalitarianism and fascism.'[264] Indeed, as one of the other main historians of Uriage has commented, 'It was perhaps on the European question that the importance of the Uriage spirit for *Le Monde* was most clearly seen.'[265]

Meanwhile Alexandre Marc, and many of his collaborators on *Ordre Nouveau* including Denis de Rougemont, also continued to work for European federalism after the war. Having run a magazine with pro-German sympathies before the war, Marc had supported De Gaulle during it. But he broke with Gaullism over Europe in 1958, having become the First Secretary-General of the European Union of Federalists in 1946. This grouped together about fifty federalist groups, and included people like Altiero Spinelli and Henri Brugmans. The founding congress took place at Montreux from 27–31 August 1947: Denis de Rougemont was charged with writing the initial report, entitled 'The Federalist Attitude'. Less than a year later, in May 1948, the Council of Europe met at The Hague, chaired by Churchill. Denis de Rougemont and Alexandre Marc were co-rapporteurs of the Council of Europe's cultural commission. In the manifesto published by De Rougemont, 'Message to the Europeans', the Council of Europe and the European Community are prefigured. Rougemont also had the idea of setting up a European Court for Human Rights. Spaak, meanwhile – as we

have seen – played a determining role in the creation of the
European Economic Community.

Robert Schuman and Jean Monnet

However, perhaps the most intriguing link between Vichy France
and the European Community is Robert Schuman. Robert
Schuman was the French Foreign Minister, who, together with
Jean Monnet, is considered one of the two grand founding fathers
of the European Community because they created the European
Coal and Steel Community in 1951.[266] Indeed, the European
Commission in Brussels is situated on a roundabout named after
Schuman.

Schuman was born in Luxembourg in 1870 of a French father
and a Luxembourgish mother. His father fought against the Prussians in 1870 and refused to return to his native Lorraine, which
they subsequently occupied. Robert Schuman, by contrast, had
no such scruples, and he established himself in the Reichsland
Lothringen, in Metz, at the end of his school career, thus taking
German nationality. He studied German – rather than French –
law at Bonn, Munich, Berlin and (German) Strasbourg. In 1911
he became a lawyer at the Metz bar where, after his mother's death
in a car crash, he nearly became a priest.

During the First World War, Schuman was called up into the
German army. At first he was stationed with a non-fighting unit in
Metz, and then, in 1915, he was transferred to civilian service in
the administration of the Kreis of Boulay, some thirty kilometres
east of Metz. By 1919, when Alsace and Lorraine returned to
France, Schuman was elected to the French National Assembly,
where he was to remain for over forty years. In other words, his primary attachment was always to Lorraine – whether it was French
or German.

In 1938, Schuman played an important role in the Munich
agreement. In an article in *Le Lorrain* on 11 September 1938, he
supported the Munich agreement, arguing that Germany would
not attack France without provocation, and so it was better not to

offer her one. Returning to the subject in the German language paper, *Elsässer*, on 25 September 1938, he used a jurist's analysis of the Franco-Czech treaty of 16 October 1925 in order to minimise French obligations to Czechoslovakia, saying that France should under no circumstances take any steps which might destabilise 'peace'.

He went even further on 27 September, when a group of Alsatian deputies met in Strasbourg and called on Pope Pius XI to persuade Mussolini to intercede with Hitler. Schuman then led a delegation of deputies from Alsace and Lorraine which went to see the French premier, Edouard Daladier, on 28 September, to stress their constituents' profound desire for peace. Schuman's biographer even suggests that he may have threatened to vote against the necessary military credits.[267] This meeting occurred on the day before Daladier's departure for Munich, and on 29 September, Schuman's party voted a new motion of confidence to Daladier 'to save peace in honour and dignity'. It is worth emphasising that pro-Municheers were in fact in a minority in Schuman's party, but his stance evidently prevailed. Indeed, while the Alsatians were overwhelmingly pro-German and pro-Munich – the Alsatian party organised meetings to support Munich and to call for Franco-German *rapprochement* – the feeling was different in Schuman's native Lorraine, where the press attacked Schuman's support for an agreement which it saw as a defeat.

Moving on to the Vichy period itself, Paul Reynaud replaced Daladier on 21 March 1940. Schuman became a minister for the first time, when he was appointed Under-Secretary of State for Refugees in the government which Reynaud presented to parliament the next day. Schuman remained in his ministerial post when Reynaud himself was replaced by Philippe Pétain on 16 June 1940. In other words, one of the founding fathers of the European Community was a minister in the first government led by Marshal Pétain.

The armistice was signed on 22 June. Schuman made his way to Vichy, still a government minister. On 10 July 1940, he was one of the 569 parliamentarians who voted the death of the Third Republic in France – or for that matter, of the republic *tout court* – when the

French National Assembly voted a series of constitutional laws which put an end to the Third Republic, and thus to French democracy, by transferring constituent powers to Marshal Pétain. The next day, Pétain proclaimed the 'French state' (*État français*) to replace the Republic, and henceforth all state authority flowed from his own person. It was this delegation of national sovereignty by a body which was its mere trustee, not its owner, which De Gaulle always insisted made Vichy null, void and illegitimate, and which the great historian of France, Eugen Weber, has accurately described as the 'gang-rape of Republic, constitution, parliament, democracy, liberty'.

In an interesting parallel, Jean Monnet was at the same time also waging a small private battle against De Gaulle in Britain. Immediately De Gaulle arrived in London, he asked Churchill's permission to speak on the BBC. It was granted, and De Gaulle delivered his seminal '*appel*' on 18 June 1940, where he called on the French to continue the war even though the Battle of France had been lost. The next day, De Gaulle went to see the man who had spirited him out of Bordeaux, Major-General Sir Edward Spears. 'Will you be speaking again today, *mon général?*' asked Spears. 'I speak every day,' replied De Gaulle. However, he had reckoned without Jean Monnet, who had been in London since being sent there in 1939 by Edouard Daladier to purchase arms for France, and who had been given a post in the Foreign Office when the Reynaud government was dissolved. Monnet persuaded Lord Halifax, the Foreign Secretary and onetime architect of appeasement, that De Gaulle should not be allowed to speak, and on 20 and 21 June De Gaulle was indeed prevented from making a broadcast. It was only when Spears and Duff Cooper telephoned Churchill at Chequers on 22 June that the Prime Minister, horrified to learn of this decision, overturned it. De Gaulle's speeches on the BBC resumed that very night.[268]

Schuman, meanwhile, left the old Pétain government when the '*pleins pouvoirs*' were voted, and went to Metz at the end of August, where he had the privilege of being the first French politician to be imprisoned by the Germans, on 17 September 1940. He remained in Metz prison, reading Mommsen's *History of the Popes*, until 12 April 1942. He was then detained in the Rhineland Palatinate, but escaped and made his way to Lyon. After his escape, he was determined to obtain a private audience with Marshal Pétain because he was convinced that Germany would lose the war, and wanted to tell him so. He met the Marshal at a lunch and spoke to him of his belief, and of the condition of men from Alsace and Lorraine press-ganged into the German army, but Pétain, it seems, was not interested.

When the southern zone of France was occupied in November 1942, Schuman had to hide, so he wandered from monastery to monastery for two years, reading Shakespeare and Thomas Aquinas. After Liberation, Marshal de Lattre appointed him as an adviser on Alsace-Lorraine questions in August 1944. But Schuman remained in this post for only three weeks because the Minister of War, André Diethelm, ordered De Lattre to 'get rid of this product of Vichy'. On his return to Metz, the Liberation authorities also treated him with contempt, as a former minister of Pétain and as a deputy who had voted the *pleins pouvoirs* in 1940.

Schuman was thus declared ineligible for public office for several months. A warrant was issued against him, but Schuman managed to work his way on to a Liberation Committee in February 1945. It was finally only as a result of the intervention of De Gaulle himself that the case against Schuman was dropped, on the grounds that he had left Pétain's government on 17 July 1940 and that he had supported the Resistance since then – even if the sum total of his Resistance activity seems to have been listening to the BBC. His ineligibility for election was thus overturned, and he was subsequently elected to the new constituent Assembly in October 1945. Apparently, he retained for the rest of his life a bitter memory of the 'humiliation' he had to undergo to clear his name at that time.[269]

Conclusion

There are, therefore, some links between Nazi, Vichyite and fascist thought, and the ideology of European integration in our own day.

One contemporary pro-European even writes of the 'achievements' of the Nazis' *Großraum* (great space) economic policy, and to say that the European solutions formulated after the victories of 1940 were 'almost practical'.[270] The same commentator adds that the idea of *Mitteleuropa* (central Europe) was based on 'hard facts of economic policy'. He goes on, 'It was no accident that all attempts to integrate Europe originated in economic concepts, and it is no surprise that Germany took the lead in planning for Europe: as early as 1940 far-reaching plans of economic transformation and integration were evolved not by politicians but by industrial managers.'[271] In a similar vein, another pro-European commentator has drawn attention to the influence of the theories of Friedrich List (whom many Nazi economists admired) on the economic integration of the post-war European Community – in a book published by the College of Europe in Bruges.[272]

Furthermore, in the following chapter, where the science of geopolitics is discussed, much reference will be made to a book recently published in Germany on Karl Haushofer, the leading Nazi geopolitician.[273] The book is a determined attempt to rehabilitate the man who provided so much ideological inspiration to Hitler, and the author insists at every turn that Haushofer did not condone military aggression or racism. The argument seems improbable, and the political motives behind it are perhaps revealed by the fact that the book is published under the aegis of an institute whose chairman joined the Nazi party in 1932, and with whom there is an interview at the end.

But it is interesting that the author tries to defend Haushofer's reputation principally by *emphasising* the ideological links between his theories and those of modern European integrationists. The author claims that many of Haushofer's themes are now being openly discussed in German debates on Europe – for example, in a conference on Europe held in Germany in 1991 – especially the concepts of *Mittellage* (Germany's central location in Europe), *Mitteleuropa*, and of the way that the 'regions' in Europe will 'overcome anachronistic ideas about borders'.[274] He writes that Haushofer's geopolitical theories – which only fifty years ago were being excoriated as having excused the most hideous aggression of all time – can be considered 'a fruitful basis' on which to build European thinking. And the science of geopolitics, as elaborated by Haushofer, is said to be 'a necessary component of political pragmatism and European thinking at an important stage of European integration'.[275]

In all this, the point is not to suggest that the European idea was directly inspired by Nazis or their allies (even though there is a book to be written on the continuity of official elites in France and Germany spanning the wartime and post-war periods). It is rather to show that there is a certain overlap between two currents of thought – Nazi and modern pro-Europeanism – whose antecedents (the 'tainted source' of this book's title) reach back in European intellectual and geopolitical history to well before the outbreak of the Second World War – as we shall see in the next two chapters.

Two opposing theoreticians of European geopolitics: Cardinal Richelieu (TOP), Louis XIII's Prime Minister, from a portrait by Philippe de Champagne; and Karl Haushofer, the man who tried to give scientific respectability to the Nazi doctrine of *Lebensraum*.

III

HOLDING THE CENTRE

'*The idea of the law of nations presupposes the distinction between independent states. Although this is a state of war . . . it is still, according to reason, better than the fusion of those states by means of a hierarchy of power culminating in a universal monarchy. Laws which are passed for a large area lose their vigour, and such a soulless despotism, after it has hollowed out the kernel of goodness, ultimately collapses into anarchy*'

IMMANUEL KANT[1]

John of Salisbury was angry. 'Who made the Germans the judges of nations? Who gave this brutish and impetuous people the authority to determine at their discretion who is to be the prince over the heads of the sons of men?' The English-born Bishop of Chartres was writing in 1160 to his friend, Randulf of Sarre, to protest against the manoeuvres by the Holy Roman Emperor, Friedrich I Barbarossa. At the Council of Pavia, the Emperor had succeeded in getting his man elected as Pope Victor IV.

The issue was control of the Church, to which the whole of medieval Europe belonged. What John objected to was the way in which the German emperor had managed to hijack the Church, and thus augment his own power in Europe. He objected, in other words, to the way in which a supranational organisation could increase – rather than mitigate – the power of its most powerful member. The sentiment John expressed about the Germans was not new. Odo de Deuil, a chronicler of the Crusades, had also attacked the Germans as *importabiles Alemmani* – the unbearable Germans – who minded everybody else's business and, as a result, 'disturb everything'.[2]

John of Salisbury had been productive the previous year. He had published his great political tract – the work for which he is principally remembered – 'Policraticus: Of the Frivolities of Courtiers and the Footprints of Philosophers'. Although he was not a jurist by training, he showed great talent in handling existing jurisprudence, especially that of Rome. His greatest contribution to the development of medieval jurisprudence – and, by extension, to medieval political theology – was his description of the role of the King as being the image of Equity, or Justice. This was an old image, and not one invented by John.[3] What was novel was the new nuance which John gave it. He stressed the legal aspect of the King's role, rather than merely his liturgical functions. In particular, he tried to square the apparent circle between the King's absolute power on the one hand, and his absolute limitation by law on the other. He wrote: 'That the Prince, although he is not bound by the ties of Law, is yet the Law's servant as well as that of Equity; that he bears a public person, and that he sheds blood without guilt.'[4]

In other words, John of Salisbury's political thought is an important landmark in the development of a theory which we now know as the rule of law. John argued that the prince, although not limited by civil law, was not permitted to do wrong. On the contrary, he was expected to act on the basis of his innate sense of justice. He was bound *ex officio* to venerate law and equity. He acted as a public person (*persona publica*) for the good of the commonwealth (*res publica*) and not with regard to his private will. The king as a public person was both free from the law and beholden to the law.

John was not merely drawing a distinction between the man and his office; he was, rather, drawing attention to the curious duality of kingship itself. Government is both mortal and eternal: it continues through time even though its individual members change. Although the king is a person, the King never dies. Like

Christ, who both died and is immortal, the King is at once father and son of the law. Being the very image of Justice, the King is the incarnation of it on earth. Being real, kingly personal rule was therefore not understood as the direct or scientific application of universal principles to earthly affairs, but rather as a kind of ministry. The king, being human, tries to *realise* – make real – justice on earth. But being human, that attempt to raise earthly affairs up to those universal standards is necessarily fallible.

John of Salisbury's influence was very great, especially on another English medieval jurist, Henry Bracton. What had most influence was the doctrine of the 'king's two bodies' which his theories reinforced, namely the insight that the king had both a private and a public self, and that kingship is by nature partly human and partly divine, partly mortal and partly eternal. It was thanks to these theories that the notion of corporation sprang up: it was only by being able to formulate the idea that a body could live on while its individual members died, that the medieval mind was able to conceive of, say, 'Bologna' as an legal entity which persisted in time, even if particular citizens were constantly dying and being born. As Tocqueville showed, it was the strength of the notion of corporation in Anglo-Saxon law, and the real strength of real corporations in England and America, which were crucial elements in the constitution of liberal orders there.

Indeed, the theory of the king's two bodies gained less acceptance on the Continent than it did in England. In Germany, the development of the theory under the Holy Roman Emperor Frederick II tended to justify *raison d'état* rather than the 'right reason' which the medieval mind considered to be the means by which we (fallibly) apprehend justice. In France, the doctrine of the king's two bodies was given the *coup de grâce* by Louis XIV's assimilation of the state to his own self. 'Whereas Continental jurisprudence might easily attain to a concept of the "State" in the abstract, or identify the Prince with that State, it never arrived at conceiving of the Prince as a "corporation sole" . . . from which the body politic as represented by Parliament could never be ruled out.'[5]

In England, the theory inspired some seminal legal cases which were to constitute the British legal system as we know it. One of these was Calvin's Case in 1608, at which the great jurist, Sir Edward Coke, defined the limits and meaning of political allegiance and juridical space, and the concomitant duties and rights of sovereigns and subjects.[6] Ultimately, the theory of the king's two bodies led to the legal fiction which enabled the king, Charles I, to be executed as a private person in the name of the King (or the Monarchy) as an institution. The king's body natural was killed without affecting or doing serious harm to the body politic – unlike France in 1793. In other words, it enabled the English Revolution to be essentially conservative – it was intended to restore old rights which had been recently abused – rather than destructive of the past, as the French Revolution was to be. The theory which John of Salisbury helped to develop, in other words, is the very basis for our notions of law and parliamentary rule.

In the light of this, it is significant that John of Salisbury was also interested in the question of the balance of power in Europe. The attitude which other countries – Germany, for instance – took to the rule of law and to the Church could influence decisions which had an effect on other people. To adopt a maximalist position which John of Salisbury does not make explicit, one might say that the question of the balance of power in Europe is intimately connected with the question of the rule of law there. It is worth taking a look at the sweep of German history to see why this is so.

*

'Man is limited by his nature but infinite in his desires. The world is thus full of opposing forces. Of course, human wisdom has often succeeded in preventing these rivalries from degenerating into murderous conflicts. But the competition of efforts is the condition of life. In the last analysis, and as always, it is only in equilibrium that the world will find peace'

CHARLES DE GAULLE[7]

The theme of the balance of power crops up frequently in modern European ideology, especially in Germany. It is nearly always rejected there as a viable international system for Europe. Its rejection goes hand in hand with the rejection of something to which Germans rather clumsily refer to as 'the nineteenth-century nation-state'.[8] It is held that supranational and economic integration is the only alternative to such anarchy and war: the German President of the European Parliament, Klaus Hänsch, has argued for European monetary and political union by saying that, 'Never again must a state be so sovereign that it can decide between weal and woe, between war and peace.'[9] In other words, the danger from nations is held to come not only from 'nationalism', but also from 'the rivalries of nation-states on a nineteenth-century model' which it is official German government policy to prevent.[10]

German politicians often address their remarks on the balance of power specifically to the British. The Foreign Policy Spokesman of the ruling Christian Democrat/Christian Social Union parliamentary party in Germany, Karl Lamers, on a tour of foreign capitals to promote his party's vision of a Europe of concentric circles directed by a strong 'hard core' at the centre, made a point of making an explicit additional reference to the balance of power when he spoke in London in 1994. 'Britain's glorious history in past centuries,' said Mr Lamers, 'was determined not least by its insular position, which allowed the country thoroughly to distance itself from the bloody conflicts on the continent through a policy of the "balance of power", and never to be a theatre of war. Today, however, an insular position is certainly not a decisive objective, and not even properly a strategic factor any more . . . "Fog over the channel, continent isolated" does not seem to me to be a realistic description of reality any more.' Having listed various reasons why this is so, Lamers concluded that the British attempts to break the Franco-German axis were nothing but 'a rather faint echo of the glorious "balance of power" of previous centuries'.[11] The implication, in other words, was that the balance of power was a hegemonic policy to which Britain should say goodbye for ever.

In a similar vein, Lamers' boss, the Chairman of the CDU/CSU parliamentary party Wolfgang Schäuble (one of the men tipped to be Chancellor Kohl's successor), addressed the British Chamber of Commerce in Cologne in 1993 thus: 'For centuries, Britain was one of the major powers which ensured order in Europe. Since the Treaty of Utrecht [1713], Great Britain repeatedly intervened as the arbiter of Europe and exercised a balancing force in European affairs. But today it is no longer a question of ideas about the balance of power, or about old ideas of balance or hegemony.'[12]

The idea which underlies these statements is that European integration has replaced power politics with a more structured, law-based framework for interaction between states. In a solemn speech to mark the fiftieth anniversary of the Second World War, the German President, Roman Herzog, declared that, 'Western Europeans . . . have learned that one can continue to live in nations without preserving the national state of the nineteenth century for ever, and that co-operation is cleverer than insistence on ideas of sovereignty which belong to past generations.'[13] In such a structure, the policy of the balance of power is irrelevant.

Indeed, European federalists tend to believe that it was precisely the unstructured nature of the balance of power which 'broke down' in 1914 and 1939. They believe that the lack of structures led to anarchy. The completion of monetary union, and the creation of a Europe of concentric circles with a hard core, are thus held to be the only protection against states jockeying for position among each other, and eventually perhaps fighting one another.

In propagating these views, European federalists are merely repeating one of the principles which the founding father of the European Coal and Steel Community, Jean Monnet, saw as his most important achievement. Monnet never tired of stressing that he wanted anarchic and potentially destabilising power politics to be replaced by a legal order for governing the relationships between European states. Believing that he had succeeded in 'civilianising' relationships between European states, Monnet used to daydream in later life about writing a book in two parts – 'Yesterday, Power', and 'Today, the Law'.[14] He believed that economic integration was the way to achieve this.

This sentiment was not unreasonable after the convulsions of the first half of the twentieth century. That period had seen classical European diplomacy in 1914 overwhelmed by the horrors of modern warfare. It had seen an unworkable settlement imposed on Europe after the First World War which itself also broke down. Surely, thought many in 1945 (and before), now was the time to replace power-play with a legal order, especially as the old 'balance of power' system had proved unsafe.

Much of this theory is valuable. There is no doubt that relations between the states of Western Europe have been transformed beyond recognition in the half century since 1945. On the other hand, that transformation took place under the exceptional circumstances of the Cold War, when the states of Western Europe were forced together by the presence of Soviet troops on their very doorstep. The *pax Americana* also helped. In other words, the creation of the EC, and of the law which now governs intra-Community relations, was itself the result of a balance of power between the chief protagonists, France and Germany, and guaranteed by the United States. It was the natural outgrowth of an equilibrium, without which it could not have existed. Indeed, any state of law – whether domestic or international – is usually the result of just such a prior balance.

The reunification of Germany has undeniably changed that equilibrium. In addition, a power-political vacuum has arisen in East Central Europe. The Franco-German reconciliation took place when the two countries were in equilibrium: that the Germans now say that further European integration is more necessary than ever implies that they think that the balance has now been overturned. It implies that a reunited Germany has a different geopolitical role from the old Western Federal Republic. And the proposal to restructure Europe from a system in which European law and policies applied equally to all states, to one in which a hard core leads the whole continent, implies that the old legal order which arose out of that previous balance needs to be abandoned too.

It is also difficult to see how this proclaimed renunciation of power-politics is compatible with the equally proclaimed aim that

a 'strong united Europe' will be able to assert herself more powerfully in the world. This thought, which for better or worse seems to
derive from classic power-political thinking, is frequently adduced
as a reason for supporting European integration. In a typical
remark, Chancellor Kohl indicated that he conceived the world as
composed of three blocks – Europe, North America and the Far
East – in competition with the last two of which a united Europe
had to 'assert itself'.[15]

Nations and empires

Modern German attacks on the 'balance of power' as a hegemonic
British policy are historical nonsense. *Pace* Wolfgang Schäuble's
identification of the two concepts, the balance of power is
customarily opposed to hegemony. The title of a book published in
1948 neatly sums up the antithesis: *Balance of Power or Hegemony*.[16] This is because the doctrine of the balance of power is
precisely the doctrine which *opposes* the establishment of any
hegemonic power on the continent of Europe.

On the other hand, German attacks on the balance of power
are nothing new, as we shall see. Indeed, the opposition between
the balance of power and hegemony characterises precisely the
eternal see-saw in European history between the strength of the
Empire at the middle of Europe, and the strength of the peripheral
European powers. The clash between the two options especially
characterises the German question throughout the nineteenth
century and up to the end of the Second World War. But it also
characterises much European diplomacy for centuries before 'the
German question' was formulated in those terms.

Just as Germans foolishly equate 'the nation-state' with 'the
nineteenth century', so they are inadvertently speaking only about
their own country when they associate 'the nineteenth century'
with the kind of power-politics they say they now wish to avoid.
For, like the nation-state, the policy of maintaining a balance of
power in Europe, and an approach to diplomacy based on considerations of state power (rather than ideology or religion), do not

date from the nineteenth century. On the contrary, it was precisely in the nineteenth and early twentieth centuries that this kind of diplomacy was destroyed.

In its modern form, the policy of the balance of power dates not from the nineteenth century but rather from the seventeenth, when the old medieval dream of universal empire was decisively displaced by the rise of secularism and the modern state. Indeed, the two concepts – of statehood and empire – are antithetical. As the great nineteenth-century German jurist, Otto Gierke, argued, 'The thought of a concentration at a single point of the whole life of the Community . . . was opposed in theory to . . . the medieval thought of a harmoniously articulated Universal Community whose structure from top to bottom was of a federalistic kind.'[17]

Ultimately, however – again like the nation-state – the concept of balance of power pre-dates the seventeenth century. In a different, but substantially unaltered form, it informs much European diplomacy throughout the thirteenth and fourteenth centuries. (Indeed, some historians argue that the ancient Greek city-states understood the principles of the balance of power perfectly well.[18]) When the Capetian dynasty began to rule in France (Hugues Capet ascended the throne in 987), the French king was small-fry in comparison with the Holy Roman Emperor himself. The sheer extent of the latter's domain, the imperial and divine sources of his authority, and his status as the inheritor of Charlemagne, all combined to make him extremely powerful.

Like all power, that of the Holy Roman Emperor met with opposing forces. In particular, the Popes were usually keen to maintain the power of the Emperors within certain limits. Because the French king also had an interest in preventing the creation of a powerful centralised monarchy to the East, there grew up a natural alliance between the Holy See and the young French monarchy, in opposition to the growth in power of the Holy Roman Emperor of the German Nation. From at least the time of Philippe Auguste (crowned in 1180) and Innocent III, therefore, and despite the numerous quarrels which opposed the king of France to the Pope in Rome, the principle of what the French call 'the European equilibrium' was born. Despite the

inevitable vicissitudes of history, this remained a constant in
European diplomacy for centuries.

France allied with Rome because the latter's power was supranational. It represented a constraint on the Empire, imposed from
above. But there was a second instrument which France and Rome
traditionally exploited to constrain the power of the Empire: internal decentralisation. Because the Emperor was chosen by the
princes, imperial power was subject to internal constraints. Indeed,
the prime opponents of the Emperor's attempts to shake off the
shackles of election by establishing a hereditary imperial line were
the princes themselves, who suspected him of seeking absolute
power in Germany and the world. Princes, dukes, margraves –
what the great French historian, Jacques Bainville, called 'all that
dust of German dynasties in the Middle Ages'[19] – hated the idea of
a single dynasty which would have limited their own sovereign
rights. They were supported in this by the various ecclesiastical
princes, the Hanse towns, the free cities and the peasant com-
munes (of which the Swiss cantons are the modern remainder).
All of them realised that a prerequisite for the development of a
centralised state was a hereditary monarchy.

The Popes realised that these two constraints – supranational
and internal – were inseparable. If ever the Emperors escaped from
the constraint of election, they would attempt to liberate themselves from the second, the Pope's spiritual tutelage. The Popes
thus regarded the maintenance of the power of the Princes, who
wanted to protect their local privileges against the centralising
tendencies of the Emperor, as an essential internal counterweight
to the Emperor's power. They therefore opposed the creation of a
hereditary Hohenstaufen imperial system. In other words, from
the Middle Ages, there grew a natural alliance between foreign
powers afraid of German strength, especially France, and those
elements within the Empire who resisted the development of a
strong centralising power in their country. Jacques Bainville was
convinced that he could detect a pattern to Franco-German relations. 'There is antagonism and violent conflict every time
Germany is a large political construction, as she was under Otto
the Great, Charles V and the Hohenzollerns . . . By contrast, every

time Germany has been divided up into various independent states, being linked only by more or less coherent federal links, wars are rare, localised and free from that national character which makes them pitiless . . .'[20]

It is perhaps not too fanciful to see in this early alliance between the French kings and the spiritual (supranational) power of Rome a precursor of the post-war use by Paris of the supranational powers of the 1957 Treaty of Rome (which created the EEC) to keep Germany in check. The parallel is especially close because these supranational powers could be imposed only because Germany was then divided internally: not only were there two German states, but also West German federalism was set up as an important check on the emergence of a strong central power in Bonn. Charles de Gaulle well understood the symbiosis between these two constraints on German power: he used to interrupt meetings of the French Council of Ministers whenever anyone said '*l'Allemagne*' and insist that people say '*les Allemagnes*' instead.

These constants in French foreign policy reached their apogee at the end of the Thirty Years' War with the Treaties of Westphalia in 1648. Germany had been bled white by thirty years of fighting between Protestants and Catholics on her soil, aggravated by the intervention of peripheral European powers. She had lost a third of her population. The treaty which put an end to the war entrenched the mosaic of Germany's internal political arrangements: there were some three hundred statelets on the territory of the Holy Roman Empire, and nearly two thousand political subdivisions in total.

For France, indeed, her interest in a weak and divided Empire was very direct. Her capital, Paris, was not far from territories which belonged to the Emperor. In the sixteenth and seventeenth centuries, France was actually encircled by imperial possessions – from Spain in the South to the Spanish Netherlands in the North, with the Empire itself to the East including Burgundy, Franche-Comté, Luxembourg and Savoy. It was at this point that Louis XIII's First Minister, Cardinal Richelieu, despite being a prince of the Church, invented a novel idea, *raison d'État*.

Richelieu is usually portrayed as the worst kind of Machi-
avellian cynic because, in apparent contradiction with the dictates
of religion, he concluded alliances with the Protestants in northern Germany and the King of Sweden against the Catholic
Habsburg Emperor. Although Henry Kissinger is himself one of the
foremost modern proponents of the theory of the balance of power,
he argues that Richelieu's policy (which shaped French diplomacy
for three centuries) was ultimately self-defeating: 'For all the glory
raison d'état brought France, it amounted to a treadmill, a never-
ending effort to push France's boundaries outward to become the
arbiter of the conflicts among the German states and thereby to
dominate Central Europe, until France was drained by the effort
and progressively lost the ability to shape Europe according to its
design.'[21] In other words, the sheer cold-blooded pursuit of power,
unaided by any moral vision of politics, was not enough. It often
made France aggressive rather than defensive (the policy might
perhaps have been defended in the latter case) such as under Louis
XIV or Napoleon.

However, it has been left to a German historian to show that
this view of Richelieu, which is widely held in Germany, is false.
Richelieu was certainly the first great practitioner of the balance of
power, but he was neither a cold-blooded pursuer of French
national interest nor someone who wanted to banish morality
from international affairs. On the contrary, he cared deeply for
peace in Europe and for the future of the Church. Indeed, he was
convinced that the Emperor's proclaimed role as the protector of
Catholicism would endanger both. In fact, Richelieu saw it as a
mere pretext for the Emperor's own aspirations to universal monarchy. In a cutting phrase, the Cardinal accused the Spanish, the
self-appointed defenders of a religiously united Europe, of nothing
but sheer hypocrisy. 'They have God and the Virgin Mary on their
lips, a religious appearance, a rosary in their hand – and nothing
but temporal interests in their heart,' he wrote.[22]

Far from being cynical, Richelieu was deeply imbued with
Catholic natural law theory. He drew heavily on the thought of
the late Spanish Scholastics, especially those in Salamanca, who
used traditional Thomist legal philosophy to elaborate a modern

theory of international law, a development which had been given new urgency by the establishment of colonies in the New World. A key element in the political ethics of one of the greatest Salamancans, Francisco de Vitoria, a contemporary of Luther, was the idea of a universal natural law which applied not just to Christendom but to the whole of humanity. This notion – which is in some respects an antecedent of modern phenomena like the Universal Declaration of Human Rights – was an important intellectual weapon in the fight in Spain against the absolutist pretentions of the Habsburgs, and against Charles V's aspirations to universal monarchy in Europe.

Richelieu, in other words, thought that people's natural rights could be preserved only if there was a balance of power or equilibrium between states, and that these rights would be threatened if one state became too powerful and dominated the whole of Europe. Like John of Salisbury before him, Richelieu understood the organic link between the rule of law in Europe, peace and the balance of power. He knew that all of these would be destroyed if one European state exercised hegemony over the whole continent, in the name of whatever ideology or religion.

It is for this reason that the actions of countries keen to counterbalance centralised German state power were not necessarily incompatible with the interests or wishes of the Germans themselves. The Treaty of Westphalia suited German tastes for what Madame de Stael was approvingly to call 'a gentle anarchy' a century and a half later.[23] Indeed, the French presented themselves as the protectors of German liberties by pursuing this policy. They were the guardians against the Empire's unification under a despotic and centralising king. This attitude was not entirely hypocritical. Just as the German princes were opposed to centralism, so too in post-war West Germany, the federal system (the decentralisation of power) was widely held to be the very bedrock of German liberties and of peace in Europe, and the essential bulwark against any return of the kind of tyrannical centralism which Hitler had introduced. Modern Germans, indeed, tend to use the word 'centralism' as a synonym for 'authoritarianism' (even if they invariably exaggerate the degree to which their own country is still decentralised). This is why another great practitioner of the balance of power, Winston Churchill, could quite legitimately say that, as preserver of the balance, Britain had preserved the liberties of Europe.

Moreover, the pursuit of the European equilibrium did provide the basis for a policy whose effects were largely beneficial. Richelieu's diplomatic manipulation and intrigue, for which he seemed to have had an insatiable appetite, was itself a means of preventing war: he did not fight until the resources of diplomacy had been exhausted. Westphalia itself introduced a century and a half during which Europe was free of major conflagrations.

Above all, France established the principle – even if she did not apply it to herself – that Europe as a whole would suffer if one state became too powerful. Independent statehood itself was guaranteed by that balance: a powerful state was not allowed to bully weak ones. Indeed, as the above quotation from Immanuel Kant indicates, the very principle of European equilibrium and the law of nations *presupposes* the existence of numerous different states in Europe. As Henry Kissinger puts it, 'Empires have no interest in operating within an international system: they aspire to *be* the international system.'[24] The kind of law-based relationship of which Monnet used to boast, therefore, can only grow out of a prior balance of power; and the notion of balance of power is by definition antithetical to that of universal government.

The European equilibrium and the empire of the middle

The concepts of independent nation statehood and of the balance of power are thus two sides of one coin. They are both the opposite of imperial power. Any attempt to direct the affairs of the European continent by superstructures – rather than by allowing interests to be reconciled harmoniously according to an agreed procedure – is, at best, an attempt to replace the free interplay between states with a system of international corporatism, and, at worst, evidence of a nostalgia for the days of empire. In the words of one eighteenth-century commentator, 'The continual negotiations that take place make modern Europe a sort of republic, whose members – each independent, but all bound together by a common interest – unite for the maintenance of order and the preservation of liberty. This is what has given rise to the principle of the balance of power, by which is meant an arrangement of affairs that no state shall be in a position to have absolute mastery and dominate over others.'[25]

Like all such systems, the balance of power emerged spontaneously. In general, when its protagonists formed a coalition against a resurgent power, they did not do so in the name of a theory of international relations, but rather because of their perceived short-term self-interest. However, a sort of equilibrium did emerge out of this seeming anarchy. Thus, international relations were analogous to the relations between free citizens in a liberal republic: a long-term balance of interests could be achieved by the interplay and conflict between the pursuit of short-term individual ones.

Although many other states supported the balance of power – Russia, for instance, was to become an extremely important player – the state which formulated the principle of the balance of power most clearly, and which did explicitly act by it, was Britain. Indeed, the British preoccupation with the European equilibrium constituted an important addition to, or development of, Richelieu's policies. Britain differed from France precisely because – *pace* Schäuble, once again – she never entertained any hegemonic ambitions on the Continent. She was therefore genuinely in a position to act as disinterested arbiter by siding with one country or another, according to which power threatened to upset the balance. Indeed, Palmerston's oft-quoted but much misunderstood remark – 'We have no eternal allies and we have no perpetual enemies. Our interests are eternal and perpetual, and those interests it is our duty to follow'[26] – is not so much a defence of amoral *Realpolitik*, or an admission of hard-headed perfidy, but rather an explanation that Britain's interest in maintaining the balance of power *by definition* excluded perpetual alliances with, or enmity against, any one particular country.

Under British leadership, therefore, the policy of maintaining the balance of power on the European continent became more morally defensible than it had been under France. Of course, Britain pursued this policy not least in order to be able to maintain her hegemony on the seas, undisturbed by any too-powerful European competitor, and in that respect the policy was not especially moral in its ultimate origins. Nevertheless, it generally meant protecting the weak against the strong, and it is therefore disappointing to see this principle ridiculed as quaint and anachronistic by modern German politicians.

In truth, the practice of the balance of power has always been resented in Germany. Traditionally pushed down by the countries on the periphery of Europe in the name of it, German leaders have very often been resentful of the geopolitical vulnerability of their country's position in the middle of Europe. They have traditionally responded to this vulnerability by trying to push the influence of the peripheral states back out again, thereby giving rise to a concept of national freedom which Thomas Mann once called *Ellenbogenfreiheit*, elbow-room freedom. Surrounded on all sides, self-assertion has always been self-aggrandisement. Indeed, of few countries is Napoleon's remark that 'each country pursues the politics of its geography' truer than of Germany. The essence of that geography – for both Prussia and for the Greater Germany which Prussia was to fashion in her own image – was to be in the middle of Europe.

As early as the seventeenth century, the Grand Elector Friedrich Wilhelm of Prussia and Brandenburg advised his successors, in his political testament, to give Prussia's enemies no cause to unite against her, and to maintain good and peaceful relations with all of them. The need for this was imperative, he said, because Prussia was surrounded by states which envied her possessions. Eternal vigilance was essential, 'For it is certain, if you sit still and think that the fire still lies far from your borders, then your land will soon become the theatre upon which tragedies will be played out.'[27] Friedrich I similarly warned his successor in 1705 that the future King in Prussia and Margrave of Brandenburg 'should maintain his state in peace and tranquillity' by 'keeping war and unrest away as much as possible'.[28] He wrote: 'Our Kingdom, our Electorate, and our other lands have many powerful neighbours who mostly stand in opposition to us, and who display no little jealousy towards the growth of our House. It is easy, if the King in Prussia enters a war with another party, that one or more of such neighbours side with the enemy, and that the power of our house is thus so distracted that the said war could only be won with extreme difficulty.'[29]

In principle, therefore, German policy was defensive. But the self-appointed victim quickly became the aggressor. As the outside world was to realise, there was something hypocritical in the insistence by successive Prussian and German leaders that the central principle of their policy was the ensurance of peace. Frederick the Great used his proclaimed desire for peace to counter potential opposition to his conquest of Silesia in 1752, for instance. The position of Berlin, close to enemy states, was also an excuse: Frederick the Great said he wanted 'to push the frontiers of the state as far away as possible and protect Berlin'.[30] Conquest was thus one of the main means which Prussian kings employed to remove the problem of envious neighbouring states. The other main means was to inherit them instead.

But this expansionism was only a vicious circle, which did not solve the original dilemma. The more the state grew in power and size to rid itself of hostile neighbours, the more hostile the new neighbours became. The same problem always remained, and it continued to vex Brandenburgish, Prussian and ultimately German history for 300 years from 1648 onwards: the existence of a state in the middle of the continent, with territories covering very large areas, led ineluctably to attempts by other states to prevent the further strengthening of this state, and even to destroy it.

At the height of her powers, Prussian lands extended from the Netherlands to the north-eastern Baltic coast – 'Von der Maas bis an die Memel', in the words of the old German national anthem. Consequently, Frederick the Great, Bismarck, Kaiser Wilhelm II, and even Hitler, were all preoccupied with the problem of what Bismarck was to call 'the nightmare of coalitions'. The desire to

dissipate conflict away from Prussia – away from the centre of
Europe to the periphery – was therefore a constant preoccupation
in Prussian foreign policy thinking from the time of the Grand
Elector, through Frederick the Great to Bismarck, up to and
including our own day and Chancellor Kohl. The danger of hostile
coalitions was aggravated by a feature of the Germans which they
themselves have sometimes admitted: nobody likes them. In 1912,
the German Chancellor, Theobald von Bethmann-Hollweg wrote
that no one 'loved' the German empire: 'We are too strong for
that, too *parvenu*, and just too repulsive.'[31]

Consciousness of the *Mittellage* and its attendant dangers thus
animated German foreign policy thinking consistently from the
time of the Grand Elector to the First World War. Prussians and
Germans learned from bitter experience that they could not afford
to be isolated in the middle of Europe: when the peripheral powers
of Europe (England, Russia, Turkey, the Scandinavian states, the
Church, even France) were weak, then the central power,
Germany, was strong and vice-versa. Prussia-Germany understood
that alliances were thus a prerequisite for her strength and expansion. It was therefore precisely the aim of Prussian-German
diplomacy to allow the state to expand by cultivating good relations with her neighbours, or at least by preventing them from ever
all entering a coalition against her. Far from being the opposite of
expansionism, therefore, the cultivation by Prussia- Germany of
good relations with her neighbours – or even their absorption into
its orbit – was the very precondition for it.

Expansionism by the back door: economic union and the *Zollverein*[*]

The balance of power system reached its pinnacle after the defeat
of Napoleon, when the Congress of Vienna set up a system for
continental conflict resolution, buttressed by basic agreement on
the common values of stability and co-operation. But the Congress

[*] Customs Union.

of Vienna also opened two new problems which were decisively to influence the history of the nineteenth century. The first was the rise of national liberation movements, which were to sweep Europe in 1848: however stable an international system may appear from the top, it will eventually be rejected if it is felt to be unjust by the people to whom it applies. The second was the continuing rise of Prussia and Germany, itself facilitated by the weakening of France which the Congress had intended to ensure.

Prussia responded to the political challenge of escaping the constraints imposed by the balance of power by seeking hegemony through economic integration. In 1834, Prussia stimulated the creation of a customs union (Zollverein) between herself and eighteen other states. By taking the lead in economic integration, Prussia was obviously promoting her hegemony within the German confederation. She was thereby asserting herself as a powerful force in the traditionally vulnerable middle of Europe, and thus transforming that centre from a zone of weakness into one of strength. And yet she was doing so in a way which did not represent an explicit challenge to the international political system.

The desire to make Germany into the powerful centre of Europe by means of economic integration was perhaps also stimulated by an old German historical memory. In the first two decades of the sixteenth century, Germany had been wealthy and assertively self-confident. Trade from all Europe poured from Venice into the Rhine, and then out again from the great Hanseatic towns along the coast of the Baltic Sea. The cities on the Rhine and in the North produced the great burgher culture which made Germany a standard-bearer of the Renaissance.

But suddenly the Cape route to India was opened, and the bottom fell out of Germany's trade. From being the centre of world commerce, the country became an economic backwater: her great towns dwindled, and the wealth of her burghers collapsed. As A. J. P. Taylor says, 'No trading community in Europe has ever experienced such a profound and lasting disaster as did the German middle classes just at the moment when their financial power was at its greatest.'[32] From that date on, perhaps, Germany has resented the primacy which world-wide free trade has enjoyed, and longed for the restitution of a continental economy in which she can prosper.

Anyone who doubts that such terrestrial thought-processes continue to be the driving force behind making the EU into a land-based economic bloc, symbolically cut off from the sea with which free trade is associated, need only consult the Amsterdam treaty, signed in the summer of 1997. The text contains a 'Declaration on Island Regions' which reads as follows: 'The Conference recognises that island regions suffer from structural handicaps linked to their island status, the permanence of which impairs their economic and social development. The Conference accordingly acknowledges that Community legislation must take account of these handicaps and that specific measures may be taken, where justified, in favour of these regions in order to integrate them better to the internal market on fair conditions.'

That a British government could sign such a text is unbelievable. You may consider, like John of Gaunt in Shakespeare's *Richard II*, that the sea 'serve[s England] in the office of a wall, / Or as a moat defensive to a house, / Against the envy of less happier lands,' and that it makes the British isles 'a fortress built by Nature for herself / Against infection and the hand of war.'[33] Or you may also consider the sea to be an exceptional means of communication to the outside world: this is, after all, exactly the role which British naval power and economic expansion has made it play since at least the reign of Elizabeth I. Either way, the idea that, in the age of mass air transport, island status is a handicap to economic development, is only an indication of how dangerously anachronistic modern European ideology is. It is also piquant irony that this text should have been signed in Amsterdam, the 'Venice of the North', the city which more than any other epitomises sea-based commerce. Voltaire's description of Amsterdam as seeming to float in the sea, when the dykes were breached to defend the city against the French in 1672, is an unforgettable image which captures more powerfully than any other the deep congruence between thalassocracy and free trade.[34]

Anyway, the purpose of the *Zollverein* was to abolish the myriad little states, and especially their individual customs and tax regimes, which made up the German mosaic. It was established under the influence of the economic theories of Friedrich List. List was the German answer to Adam Smith, and he countered him on all the essential points. Where free trade was concerned, he argued that states should protect their nascent industries against foreign competition by the imposition of protective tariffs. Such artificial measures were necessary, in his view, because the industrial revolution had made it possible for one state completely to 'capture' the internal market for manufactured goods in another state. By means of the peaceful penetration of foreign manufacturers, a state that possessed all the outward, *political* attributes of independence and power might be robbed of the internal, material, *politico-economic* bases of such independence and power.

List defended the idea that the European continent was threatened in the long run by a double hegemony: that of Russia in the East and that of the Anglo-Saxons in the West. In order to face up to this double hegemony, the continent had to be organised in such a way as to emancipate itself from the need to import products from external powers. Thus united in one single economic ensemble, Europe would not only escape the risk of pressure from outside powers, but could also compete with them properly in world markets. According to List, it was the vocation of the Germans to organise the whole of the continent economically.

List had a profoundly economist understanding of the state. His views, indeed, were not foreign to Colbertist France. According to this view, economic unity and power are the definitive elements of the state. 'Economic unity and political unity,' List wrote, 'are twins: one cannot be born without the other following.'[35] Elsewhere he wrote, 'It is the task of the national economy to accomplish *the economical development of the nation*, and to prepare it for admission into the universal society of the future.'[36] As one (perhaps disappointed) liberal politician from Brunswick commented in 1844, 'The *Zollverein* has become . . . in fact the nourishing ground of the idea of unity . . . We will have to get used to foreigners believing Germany to be principally the customs union.'[37]

List intended to apply his theories to the European continent as a whole. He advocated the establishment of a Continental alliance between France and Germany against Great Britain, in order to force Britain into a European coalition against the supremacy of America. Britain would thereby be compelled to seek and find protection, security and compensation in the leadership of the united powers of Europe. 'It is therefore good for England,' List mused, 'that she should practise resignation betimes; that she should by timely renunciation gain the friendship of European Continental powers; and that she should accustom herself to the idea of being only the first among equals.'[38]

Indeed, List believed that the whole world could be integrated economically as Germany had been. Although this gave his theories a liberal flavour, and although he may have shared some aims with a free-marketeer like Adam Smith, his view of the state was incompatible with a truly liberal one. He was convinced that economic power and an extensive internal market were prerequisites for statehood itself. He held that small nations were by definition unable to be complete states because 'small states lie everywhere at the boundary'.[39] Without economic power, a state could be taken over by foreign manufacturers. He wrote: 'Only through alliances with more powerful nations, through the partial sacrifice of the advantages of nationality (that is, complete statehood) and through an exceptional straining of its powers, can a small state assert its independence.'[40]

This is a point of view which any classical liberal will immediately reject. Statehood is a matter of the authority to make laws and to adjudicate individual cases. It is not a matter of economic power. But for List, the essence of the Zollverein 'lay in the internal freedom of exchange and the common external representation *that was inherent in the concept of nationality.*'[41] List's doctrine, in other words, was emphatically not a technique for liberalising the external trade of states. As one commentator explains:

> It was, rather, the transformation by mutual agreement of external trade into internal trade. Through union, trade between states or nations was enclosed and subjected to

uniform laws passed by a common power. It was qualitatively altered. Thus out of several external markets, with all the uncertainties, discontinuities and dependencies external markets implied, one internal market was created, that is to say a market united, guaranteed and governed by a joint authority which simultaneously watched over the external trade of the new totality.[42]

It is not surprising if List has been identified as one of the authors of the economic theories which underlay the creation of the Common Market,[43] and if parallels are often drawn, especially by Germans, between the creation of the *Zollverein* and the present project of European integration.

The difference between a Listian view of the state and the economy, and a Smithian one, has been elucidated by Ralf Dahrendorf. Developing an argument first used by Max Weber, Dahrendorf distinguished between market rationality and plan rationality. The latter is based on industrial discipline, the 'discipline of rigid organisation, the habit of subordination and obedience' which had been the principle behind the 'military training of the Prussian pattern'. It requires a bureaucracy to design lines of action and to control their execution. The former brings about an optimal result through competition between the interests involved: it requires the game to have rules, and neutral referees to apply them.

It is easy to see that these two concepts of industrialism are incompatible. As one commentator puts it, 'In terms of market rationality, plan rationality is not rational: all plans may err, and reliance on them may lead to vast and expensive losses. In terms of plan rationality, market rationality is not rational: competition means a considerable waste of resources.'[44] Dahrendorf concludes that Adam Smith's theory of political economy is market rational, while List's is plan rational. The political theory and practice of liberalism imply an attitude of market rationality; authoritarian and totalitarian states, by contrast, are based on an attitude of plan rationality.[45] To put it another way: Listians are no more capable of conceiving free trade between states in the liberal

manner than they are capable of conceiving the operation of the
free market between citizens within a state. This explains why the
Zollverein, which was originally designed by well-meaning free-
trading bureaucrats, was not an arrangement for free trade between
independent (German) states, but instead an instrument for the
promotion of a unified and exclusive central Europe.[46] The pedigree of these ideas thus emphasises the conceptual difference
between a free trade zone between independent states – which the
British thought they joined in 1972 – from what the EC really is,
namely a customs union intended to create an integrated politico-
economic space.

The main *Zollverein* treaty, signed on 23 March 1833, provided
for common tariff and common administrative regulations, proportional sharing of revenues, and standardisation of tolls,
measures, weights and coinage. Although the *Zollverein* did not
include several German states (the Free City of Bremen was not
brought into the imperial customs area until 1885), 'it formed' –
in the words of one nineteenth-century historian, 'a core'.[47]
Therefore, the greatest architect of the Congress of Vienna
system, and arch-defender of the balance of power, the Austrian
Chancellor Metternich, immediately realised the true political
implications of Prussia's apparently innocuous plan for the economic integration of the member states of the German
Confederation. (The German Confederation included Austria,
but the *Zollverein* excluded her.) As the treaties between the
Zollverein states were being negotiated in 1833, Metternich wrote
to the Austrian Emperor:

> Within the great Confederation, a smaller union is being
> formed, a *status in statu* in the full sense of the term, which
> will only too soon accustom itself to achieving its ends by its
> own machinery and will pay attention to the objectives and
> machinery of the Confederation only when convenient. Little
> by little, under the active encouragement of Prussia and in
> the light of common interests which must inevitably emerge,
> the states composing this union will form a more or less
> coherent bloc which, on every question that comes before the

Diet (and not only in commercial affairs) will act and vote as one according to prior arrangement. Then there will no longer be any useful discussion in the Diet; debates will be replaced by votes agreed in advance and inspired not by the interests of the Confederation but by the exclusive interest of Prussia . . . Even now it is unfortunately easy to determine in advance how these votes will be cast on all the questions where the interest of Prussia conflicts with that of the federal body.[48]

He was right: Prussia fashioned the *Zollverein* in her own image, and exerted pressure on other states to integrate their economies with hers. The further strengthening of the *Zollverein*, from North German Federation in 1866 to German Empire in 1871, only enabled Prussian influence to grow even more. At each stage, Prussia convinced the other German states to enter into the new arrangements by insisting that it would be better for themselves: outside it, they would just react passively to what Prussia decided, inside they would be able to influence affairs themselves. Thus Prussia established a classical hegemonic relationship with the other German states. Even though the German Empire was supposed to contain Prussia, therefore, it did the opposite.

This was reflected in the Empire's constitutional development. Its constitution contained federal and unitary elements, and yet it was invariably the latter which won out. Early guarantees of decentralisation were rapidly swept away in a wave of new laws, industrial standards, and other forms of integration, most of them emanating from Prussian ministries, and imposing harmonisation with existing Prussian legislation.[49]

Paradoxically, indeed, the so-called 'unique character' of the German Empire – its relative looseness, the preservation of the identities of its constituent states – encouraged, rather than discouraged, Prussian hegemony. As the great German constitutionalist, Heinrich Triepel, observed – on the basis of what he knew about Prussia's position within the German Empire – 'A looser association of states encourages hegemony more than a tight one . . . the more unitary elements predominate in a federation, the more inner firmness there is, and the greater are the obstacles to the creation of a hegemony.'[50]

This is because the truly unitary elements in a confederation *prevent* one state from dominating the others, because federal or confederal law treats all states alike. Conversely, a looser arrangement – or one in which unitary and decentralised elements co-exist – can facilitate the creation of a hegemony, because whenever centralisation takes place, it is invariably on the terms of the most powerful state. Whenever that state is opposed to a certain measure, it invokes the principle of decentralisation and prevents it being adopted. This is exactly how Prussia behaved from 1871 to 1914 within the German Empire. She even used to threaten to leave the *Zollverein* if small states were recalcitrant in adopting her measures. On that threat, they always gave in. Thus she was able to take control of what were then supranational institutions from the inside, and force her imprint on them by causing a 'hard core' to arise within the larger federation (the *Zollverein* within the German Confederation, and then the North German Federation within the *Zollverein*).

A state which wishes to establish hegemony within a federation will therefore usually attempt to weaken the central institutions of the federation, or at least to control them, and it may well use the language of decentralisation to do this. This does not mean that the state might not become centralised anyway, but only that this process will occur on the most powerful state's terms. Strong supra-national or central institutions, independent of the most powerful state, are a bar to such hegemony.

Triepel also saw that hegemony developed particularly when the agreements between the states were of a political, rather than a merely technical, nature. This, he argued, was the case with the *Zollverein*, which had a more political aim than the mere creation of a free trade zone. Above all, he showed that Metternich had been right about the occult way in which such hegemony would be exercised. In 1871, Prussia had only 17 votes out of 58 in the Bundesrat (Federal Council) which ruled the Empire. 'This number,' Triepel explained, 'could easily be raised – even to a majority – by the inclusion of votes of countries which were in the

Prussian zone of influence, or of states which had special relationships and alliances with Prussia.'[51]

The upshot of all this was that, while the Congress of Vienna
may have established some important elements of the balance of
power, it also led to its own undoing. By regarding France as the
eternal enemy – the notion of an eternal enemy was, as we have
seen, antithetical to the pure doctrine of the balance of power – it
allowed a unitary German state to arise. By 1914 the German
state was aggressive, dangerous and centralised. Therefore, by failing to keep Germany decentralised, both European and German
liberties were fatally jeopardised. The old truth, which the French
had first understood, that the balance of power and peace in
Europe depended on liberty and decentralisation in Germany, was
confirmed.

The First World War

Bismarck made explicit reference to Frederick the Great when he
spoke to the Reichstag just after the foundation of the new Empire,
in November 1871. 'For a country in such a central position in
Europe, which has three or four borders on which it can be
attacked, it is very useful to follow the example of Frederick the
Great.' He attacked 'those who reckon with a simplistic and irresponsible policy, who assume that the German Empire . . . can
simply wait for an attack which might be planned by one country
or by a powerful coalition' before seeing it off.[52] Pro-active policy
was required instead: diplomacy first, and war if absolutely
necessary.

The acuteness of the old dilemma was aggravated when
Germany was united in 1871. She became simply too big, too self-
conscious and too arrogant to be easily integrated into the
European balance. Ever since Westphalia and the emergence of
the modern state system, the powers on the edge of Europe had
been exerting pressure on the centre. Now, for the first time, the
centre was becoming sufficiently powerful to press on the periphery. On the other hand, Germany was still too small to achieve

hegemony on her own. Thus Bismarck had to practice the tactful and sensitive diplomacy for which he was to gain renown. For twenty years, indeed, the Iron Chancellor practised *Realpolitik* with such moderation and subtlety that the balance of power did not break down.

One of Bismarck's main preoccupations was directly related to the perceived weakness of the *Mittellage*. Ever fearful of what he thought was Germany's precarious position, he attempted always to direct tensions away from the centre of Europe and towards the periphery. This involved allowing disputes – such as ones over colonial territory, or that between Russia and Turkey over Constantinople – to distract attention from disagreements at the centre of Europe.

Unfortunately, although Bismarck's own genius was sufficient to steer the huge bulk of the ship of the state he had created through the rocks and stormy seas of European diplomacy, that of his successors was not. Once the novelty of Bismarck's tactics had worn off, his successors and rivals sought safety in the arms race, as a simplistic way of reducing their reliance on the baffling political challenges of diplomacy.

The late-nineteenth-century Prussian-Germans attributed great importance to military and political planning: this was the heyday of politics by the instruction book. The military planners never tired of observing the constellation of foreign powers as minutely as possible, and developing plans for different scenarios, in order to be able to be the first to act and to put other states on the defensive. Their 'defensive' plans quickly evolved into precisely the contrary as security was sought in ever greater expansion. But once the button was pushed on these military plans, the great machine operated as if automatically. It was a technocratic war.

It is therefore wrong to think that the Kaiser and his lieutenants just crashed accidentally, like adolescents who foolishly take charge of a fast car. The problem was not that Germany was too big to be contained, or that the balance of power proved precarious. It was rather that, fearful of encirclement as ever, the Germans started their preventative war in 1914 precisely in order to escape the perceived constraints of the balance of power and to destroy the system itself. When the British Lord Chancellor, Lord Haldane, tried to try to make it clear to the German ambassador in London on 3 December 1912 that Britain would not tolerate 'a unified Continental Group under the leadership of one single power', the Kaiser, on reading the report of the conversation, covered it with the most violent marginal comments. In a characteristic attack of anger, he declared the English principle of the 'balance of power' to be an 'idiocy', which would turn England 'eternally into our enemy'. The principle of the balance of power was nothing more than an attempt by that 'nation of shopkeepers' to prevent other powers from defending their interests with the sword.[53]

Instead of a European system based on the balance of power, Kaiser Wilhelm wanted to unite Europe under German leadership. He insisted that the balance of power policy had been revealed 'in all its naked shamelessness' as the 'playing off of the Great Powers against each other to England's advantage'. He wrote to his brother Heinrich that Haldane's statement that England 'could not tolerate our becoming the strongest power on the Continent and that the latter should be united under our leadership!!!' amounted to a moral declaration of war on Germany.[54]

It is therefore hardly surprising to learn that the Kaiser was later greatly to admire Hitler, and in 1940 looked on in wonder as the Führer put into effect the goals for which he, Wilhelm, had striven in his own reign. Always a virulent anti-Semite – he advocated gassing the Jews in 1929,[55] and blamed Jews and Freemasons for unleashing war on Germany in 1914 and 1939 – the Kaiser wrote that the Continent 'was consolidating and closing itself off from the British influences after the elimination of the British and the Jews!'[56] The result would be 'a U.S. of Europe!' he cried in triumph. To his sister he wrote in jubilation, 'The hand of God is creating a new World & working miracles. We are becoming a U.S. *of Europe* under German leadership, a united European continent, nobody ever hoped to see.'[57]

The fact that German troops arrived in Flanders before the Austrians had attacked Serbia (a desire to punish Serbia had been the original *casus belli* in 1914) suggests that Germany did have clearly defined aims for which the war was just an excuse. Germany invaded Belgium because Belgium is the very fulcrum of the balance of power in Europe: the United Kingdom of the Netherlands was created in 1815 after the Battle of Waterloo as a buffer between France and Germany (then Prussia), and the successor state of Belgium continued to fulfil the same function. Thus, all attempts to overturn the balance of power in Europe have been met with fighting in Belgium: the Battle of Waterloo took place there; the battles of 1914–18 raged there; the Germans invaded Belgium to get to France in 1940; and they invaded again during the Battle of the Ardennes in 1944, when they were trying to reach Antwerp. The British are not the only ones to know that the maintenance of Belgium as an independent entity was crucial to the balance of power: one of Napoleon's first visits abroad was to Belgium in 1804, when he went to Antwerp. He refurbished what became the Bonaparte docks there from 1807–12, in preparation for an invasion of Britain, and declared that Antwerp was 'a pistol pointed at the heart of England'.

In sum, therefore, the balance of power was deliberately destroyed by German leaders after Bismarck's departure in 1890, and replaced by a mindless armaments race. The German word *Realpolitik* came to embody sheer cynical power-play. Friedrich von Hayek, the great Austrian liberal economist and philosopher, used to argue that it was in Germany that the belief that the state should act morally had been destroyed most thoroughly. Although he was referring to the positivist legal theories of Hans Kelsen, which mainly concerned the domestic legal structure, it is not difficult to see that similar beliefs infected the German practice of foreign policy as well. In other words, *Realpolitik* denoted a very different concept from the realistic policy of trying pragmatically to apply a worthy principle, which had characterised British balance of power policy up to that point.

For, as Henry Kissinger never tires of pointing out, there are two necessary conditions for the balance of power to work. Firstly, states must have flexibility ('the major players must be free to adjust their relations in accordance with changing circumstances').

Secondly, they must be 'restrained by a system of shared values'.[58]
He goes on:

> The reason German statesmen were obsessed with naked
> power was that, in contrast to other nation-states, Germany
> did not possess any integrating philosophical framework.
> Bismarck's Reich was not a nation-state, it was an artifice,
> being foremost a greater Prussia whose principal purpose was
> to increase its own power . . . The absence of intellectual
> roots was a principal cause of the aimlessness of German
> policy. It was as if Germany had expended so much energy on
> achieving nationhood that it had not had time to think
> through what purpose the new state should serve. Imperial
> Germany never managed to develop a concept of its own
> national interest . . . The Kaiser wanted to conduct *Weltpolitik*
> without ever defining the term or its relationship to the
> German national interest.[59]

The economics of hegemony

As with Prussia in the 1830s, Germany's plans for establishing
hegemony in Europe in 1914 had a crucially important economic
component. The programme went under the name of
'*Mitteleuropa*', and it involved the creation of a vast unitary economic space extending to Central Europe and beyond under
German direction. The northern, southern and western fringes of
the continent would gravitate around the hard core of continental
Europe.

The groups which propagated the *Mitteleuropa* idea drew
explicit inspiration from Friedrich List. Their hand was strengthened around the turn of the century when Germany's head-on
competition with Britain for naval supremacy was obviously lost.
They argued that the creation of an informal economic empire was
preferable to a formal empire composed of colonial possessions. In
February 1913, Gustav Stresemann, the Secretary General of the
Alliance of Industrialists who was to become Foreign Minister

after the war, and be famous for his policy of *rapprochement* with France, spoke of 'a closed economic area to secure our need for raw materials and our exports'.[60]

The key document in the creation of *Mitteleuropa* was the 'September economic programme' of 1914, written by the Chancellor, Theobald von Bethmann-Hollweg. The objective was to create a customs union including France, Belgium, Holland, Denmark, Austria-Hungary, Poland and perhaps Italy, Sweden and Norway. This design recalls that of Napoleon's continental economic bloc, which was also to inspire Nazi leaders and Vichyites during the Second World War. It is also noteworthy that Bethmann-Hollweg envisaged formally integrating Northern France into the Reich, an interesting anticipation of what happened after 1940.

It is hardly surprising that this economic method of achieving political domination should have been devised, for its authors grew up imbued with the historical experiences of the Prussia which had managed to snatch domination of Germany away from under the nose of Austria by means of the *Zollverein*. By 1890, indeed, once Prussian leadership had been secured, the Germans were even contemplating a customs union with Austria. Their plans – like much modern European thinking – assumed that it was right to divide the world into vast geopolitical and geo-economic ensembles.

It remains a matter of debate between historians as to exactly what status these German plans had in 1914. According to the historical school founded by Fritz Fischer, the German author of *The Grasp for World Power* (1961), Germany bears the primary responsibility for declaring the First World War, because that war attempted to realise geopolitical aims which had been nurtured for a very long time. Other historians disagree, arguing that plans to establish hegemony were merely produced to order as a *post hoc* justification.

Whichever is true, it is clear that certain patterns of thought were prevalent in economic matters, and that, at least by September 1914, Bethmann-Hollweg was convinced that the economic union was a means of achieving German security.[61] He was also convinced that Britain was determined to smash Germany's economic imperialism on the continent. Bethmann-Hollweg's programme was designed to create a zone of security around Germany, composed of countries which Germany would dominate economically, but not formally annex. The programme was developed during August 1914, and by the end of the month the Chancellor had decided that economic union was the right instrument with which to ensure German security. The use of the economy was regarded as more subtle than outright annexation, which, it was feared, might create unnecessary resentment and thus prove unstable.

The aim therefore was not to abandon the world economy totally, but rather to put in place a regime of protection as a complementary and preliminary strategy to winning world markets. Domination of Europe was the springboard to domination of the world, and the concept of *Großraumwirtschaft* ('Great Space Economy' or 'Large Area Economy') was by no means incompatible with Germany's playing a meaningful role in world trade. Indeed, much of the strategy of economic integration was supported by German industrial interests for this very reason. Germany's large chemical and electrical companies wanted to continue to trade internationally, from a basis of politically secured strength in Europe.

Bethmann-Hollweg was not the only one to advance the idea of an economic union in Europe. The industrialist Walther Rathenau, chairman of the Allgemeine Electricitäts-Gesellschaft (AEG), was convinced that it would be 'civilisation's greatest conquest'. Although he called for the creation of a larger Central European trading space, he never thought in terms of autarkic blocs. He saw the matter as a goal in itself, whereas Bethmann-Hollweg considered it to be the essential goal of the war, but only as a means to ensuring German security. Rathenau was also convinced that the greatest threat to it was 'the rise of Anglo-Saxon and Russian economic spaces'. He wrote that only the victory of the Reich could ensure the realisation of *Mitteleuropa* and that, by 'merging Europe together through practical common interest', it would enable Germany to accept her dominant role within it.[62]

In particular, Bethmann-Hollweg was convinced that economic union was the only way out for Germany from the contradictions with which Bismarck had saddled the country. As one historian writes, 'The problem [for the Chancellor] was how to get out of the contradiction in which the Reich had been trapped since Bismarck: how could German security be ensured, if she – considered in principle as encircled – was not to proceed with direct annexations which would only aggravate internal and external political problems?'[63] For a second time, therefore, the solution of economic union was proposed as a solution to the problem of the *Mittellage*.

But, as with the previous expansionism of the Prussian kings, Bethmann-Hollweg's plans only raised Germany's problems to a higher power. A policy which was intended to be defensive ended up being offensive. Georges-Henri Soutou writes, 'The German position was contradictory: a policy conceived largely in terms of the nineteenth-century balance of power was to lead ineluctably to a permanent destabilisation of international life, and it was to bring about just that which most of the Reich's leaders wanted to avoid, the end of liberalism and the constitution of antagonistic economic blocs.'[64]

In other words, whereas previous German rulers had generally played the European diplomatic game in order to further their expansionist aims, the German leaders in 1914, especially the Kaiser himself, elaborated plans whose very purpose was to overthrow it. Far from representing the inevitable outcome of the pursuit of the balance of power – as modern Germans are wont to say – the First World War represents its definitive and deliberate destruction. Indeed, if the balance of power system had operated properly, and if there had been a clear coalition of states against Germany in 1914, then – according to Henry Kissinger at least[65] – the First World War could have been prevented. Not only was there no coalition – far from being alone, Germany was allied with Austria – but also Britain had failed to make it clear that retaliation would ensue if Germany attacked Belgium. The Germans were literally astonished when British troops were despatched to Flanders.

From this, and from much other German history besides, we can conclude that Germany is precisely at her strongest when she has allies. Conversely, as the outcome of two world wars shows, and as the Prussian kings had realised for centuries, Germany is at her weakest and most vulnerable when surrounded by enemies. In other words, when modern Germans claim that Germany will never again 'go it alone', but will always co-operate with her European allies, this is the most traditional German policy imaginable. It is not even clear that Germany did 'go it alone' in 1914 or 1939, for on both occasions she made sure that she had allies – Austria in the First World War, Italy and the Soviet Union in the Second – before undertaking aggression. It is for this reason that the very pro-European *Le Monde*, in a very pro-German article, could conclude: 'At bottom, Chancellor Kohl has succeeded in obtaining peacefully what others have attempted to obtain by conquest since Bismarck: a zone of peace and of prosperity all around Germany.'[66]

Versailles

Ever since Keynes, the Treaty of Versailles has been generally understood as a rapacious and self-defeating act of vengeance. Recalled are the reparations payments and the ensuing hyper-inflation in Germany. As such, it is often denounced as an extreme example of the balance of power principle in operation, and one which rebounded with the worst imaginable consequences.

But in fact, the Versailles settlement represented the decisive abandonment of the balance of power principle in international relations. Although an important element in the treaty was obviously the desire to punish and suppress Germany – and to this extent, it embodied some traditional aims associated with balance of power politics – the fundamental purpose of the treaty was in fact to replace balance of power politics with something else, the self-determination of peoples. The author of this idea, the American president Woodrow Wilson, was convinced that it was balance of power politics themselves which caused wars rather than preventing them.

He therefore arrived in Paris with his famous fourteen points, of which the most important was that the Austro-Hungarian empire should be formally dismantled and replaced by nation-states. It is not difficult to see that it was this abolition of the only counterweight to German power in Central Europe, and its replacement by new, weak states, which was later to encourage and permit German aggression in that geopolitically weak part of the world which lies between Germany and Russia.

The fault of the Versailles treaty, in other words, was as much political as economic. Whatever the economic chaos in Europe after 1918, it was the fundamental political disequilibrium which was to prove fatal in the end. Indeed, the failure of Versailles was precisely that it was too technocratic. Its technical provisions were elaborated with particular care: rules about trade, customs duties, railways fares, river navigation, and so on. There was even a provision in it forbidding the Germans from calling their sparkling wine 'Champagne' – probably the only part of the treaty still in force. This was all in addition to the later technical provisions about reparations payments, and the provisions for harnessing German industry for the benefit of the victors.

Above all, the new borders were principally the work of technicians, especially cartographers and demographers. Minute attention to technical detail combined with massive ignorance of political principles to produce absurd political contradictions. For instance, although the treaty was supposed to have been propelled by a desire to replace the multi-ethnic Habsburg empire with nation-states, it ended up by creating a state – Czechoslovakia – which was supposed to be the jewel in the treaty's crown but which had nearly as many nationalities in it as the old Empire had had. By Balkanising Central Europe, it deprived Europe of the only credible counterweight to German power in the region, and the support given to Czechoslovakia by the Western Allies proved its worth in 1938. Meanwhile, the treaty specifically denied to Germany the self-determination which it pretended to accord to other states, by preventing the union with rump Austria and by driving the Polish corridor between the main part of Germany and East Prussia. Thus it can be said that the details of the treaty were written by experts, and the basic principles by amateurs.

Above all, the treaty's most intriguing failure lies in this. As Jacques Bainville argued in *Les Conséquences politiques de la paix*, published in 1920, the treaty's main fault was to have reinforced German centralism. 'All the measures which the Allies took had as a consequence the centralisation of the German state and the consolidation of Prussia's old victories. If there were any aspirations to autonomy or federalişm among the German populations, these were snuffed out.'[67] This was because the treaty allowed the Germans to think of themselves as victims. The debt itself, which obviously fell uniformly on the entire nation, also made the Germans feel greater solidarity with one another: they became united in their common protest. It made Bavarians and Saxons feel for the territorial losses of Prussia, whereas fifty years previously, such losses would have concerned only Prussians. The tribute which the Germans had to pay to the French thus united them in common resentment. With Germany bordered to the East with nothing but new weak states, this was a fatal combination. As Bainville says, 'At no point did the authors of the treaty of Versailles think about balance.'[68]

The Treaty of Versailles was thus politically incoherent because it failed to achieve an equilibrium in Europe. It deliberately flouted the old policy of the balance of power, instead proposing national self-determination as the only principle. But instead of creating structures which would have enabled such national self-determination to be truly realised (such as by encouraging a reformed Austrian empire) it created the very conditions which were to destroy it utterly, especially in Central Europe. Its political incoherence introduced tensions and imbalances, in Germany and in Central Europe, which took less than a generation to collapse.

Briand and Stresemann

After the war came the first serious attempt to create European unity. Indeed, it was precisely the collapse of the European system in the First World War which encouraged an intensive discussion of ways in which peace might be institutionally safeguarded by a supranational legal system. Plans to create 'The United States of Europe' were conceived.[69] Inspired by the conviction that multiplicity implies disorder, while only uniformity creates order, many came to believe that the numerous nation-states of the continent risked falling back into the national rivalry of the pre-war period unless they become ever more closely integrated with one another.

Several organisations during the inter-war period promoted European integration. These included a 'European Customs Union', founded as a grouping of those who believed that a European economic and customs union was an urgent and attainable objective; the Heidelberg programme of the German SPD which contained the following commitment: 'The SPD supports the creation of a European economic unity, which has become urgent for economic reasons, and the creation of a United States of Europe . . .';[70] and the Pan-European Union set up by Count Coudenhouve-Kalergi in 1923.

Such ideas assumed central importance in the foreign policy objectives of France and Germany with the process of reconciliation undertaken by the French and German foreign ministers, Aristide Briand and Gustav Stresemann. Briand proposed a project of European Federal Union to the Assembly of the League of Nations in 1929. One historian writes, 'It seems Briand initiated this new course in order to put a brake on the renewed trend towards German hegemony. It is probable that he picked up the idea of European and political unification because he felt that the rise of Germany could not be held in check by France alone . . . By entwining Germany in a broad European web, she could perhaps be domesticated.' Stresemann, for his part, had even fewer European feelings than Briand:

> Rather, he was inclined to embrace Briand's plan because he
> foresaw that in the not-too-distant future it might give
> Germany an outstanding opportunity to establish at least an
> economic predominance in East-Central Europe. He may also
> have calculated, as some German diplomats did, that the

desired customs union with Austria, which had been forbidden by the Treaty of Versailles, could be attained under the
cover of Briand's plan for European unity.[71]

A. J. P. Taylor famously argued that there was a fundamental
continuity between Stresemann's foreign policy and Hitler's. He
allowed that there were differences in method, but did not see
these as having the same significance as the fundamental agreement of goals and broad strategy. At any rate, it seems fair to say of
Stresemann that he was convinced that German hegemony in
Europe had to be attained by way of dominance in East and
Central Europe, and that the necessary condition for the achievement of this was the pacification of France. As Kissinger
concludes, 'Stresemann was not a "good European" but rather a
ruthless practitioner of *Realpolitik* who pursued traditional national
German interests with ruthless persistence. For Stresemann those
interests were straightforward: to restore Germany to its pre-1914
status, to dispose of the financial burdens of reparations, to attain
military parity with France and Great Britain, and to achieve the
Anschluss of Austria and Germany.'[72] Stresemann died prema-
turely in 1929: perhaps if he had lived as long as Adenauer, then
Germany might have attained by the quiet and seemingly concil-
iatory methods of Stresemann what was in fact destroyed by the
hectic impatience of the man who came to power in 1933.

The 'science' of geopolitics

It was in reaction to the Versailles settlement that the science (or
pseudo-science) of geopolitics underwent significant development
in the inter-war years, especially in Germany. Geopolitics is the
discipline which conceives geographical location as an important
and perhaps major component of political thought, identity and
action.

The two most prominent names associated with geopolitics are
those of the Swede, Rudolf Kjellén (1864–1922), and the German,
Karl Haushofer (1869–1946). Haushofer was a leading figure in

German intellectual life under the Nazis. He taught Rudolf Hess, and it was through Hess that he influenced Hitler. Indeed, he spent time with Hitler himself while the latter was imprisoned in Landsberg, acquainting him with his ideas. He continued to frequent the highest Nazi circles throughout the war – even though his wife was half Jewish – and he was arrested by the Americans in 1945. At that time, he was paraded as having had a major intellectual influence on the development of Nazi aggression, in particular because his theories were linked to the concept of *Lebensraum*. In fact, he was never tried at Nuremberg; he committed suicide in 1946.

The starting-point for geopolitics was that the kind of conflagration from which the Old World emerged in 1918 should never happen again. This was not least because the geopoliticians believed that the world was dividing up into blocs of mutually antagonistic ideologies: if they were ever to clash, the wars would obviously be massive, and there was thus no longer any room for the small-scale wars which had preceded the Great War. The European 'space' was one such block, and therefore it had to be managed in the right way. The geopoliticians, in other words, wanted a new world order to prevent war.

Above all, the geopoliticians were very pro-European. They believed that Europe was a *Raum* – a space – and that it should unite to defend itself against the other spaces with which it might compete or by which it might be threatened. The Young Conservative movement of which geopolitics was an outgrowth realised that Germany could not exist without Europe. In particular, the geopoliticians, like the Nazis they were to serve, regarded their country as Europe's watchman against the barbarous East. Versailles had made Germany incapable of fulfilling her role as defender of Europe, and thus the return of Germany to strength was an act of European common sense. Karl Haushofer wanted Europe to become 'a part of the world which counts for itself'.[73] He was convinced that the division of Europe into little states would bring about the decline of the continent. Indeed, he thought that the 'enemy' was not any particular country, but rather the principle of power-politics itself, which, in its historical form, contradicted the higher interests of the community. The geopoliticians wanted to avoid any further division between the brother nations of Europe.

The realisation of this aim required the subordination of particular interests under a European 'common good'. Haushofer tried to transfer the basic principle of national 'order', the regulation of the freedom of the individual, to the supranational level. With the concept of an amalgamation of the nations (of Europe) Haushofer aimed to overcome the present conflict-ridden order in Europe through the creation of a single 'common European idea and meaning'.[74]

Unless Europe came together in this way, the geopoliticians feared, it would be squeezed out by the other giants of geographical space, the USA, the British Empire, and the Soviet Union. Geopoliticians were convinced that Europe was threatened by extra-European powers, and that it was thus in danger of splitting down the middle.

The concept of the 'middle' was central to geopolitical thinking. The middle of Europe was, obviously, Germany. The geopoliticians conceived Germany's central position in Europe not merely as a spatial phenomenon, but also as a spiritual one. Europe, and above all Germany, were hemmed in between the liberal powers to the West, and the Socialist Empire to the East. The 'core space' of Europe was thus subject to great psychological pressure.

It was to escape from this predicament that Haushofer formulated his theories. A central proposal was that Germany should ally herself with the Soviet Union in order to create a single Eurasiatic continental bloc. The geopolitical implications of this had been recognised by the man generally credited with being the founder of geopolitics, the Briton Halford Mackinder:

> The oversetting of the balance of power in favour of the pivot state, resulting in its expansion over the marginal lands of Euro-Asia, would permit the use of the vast continental resources for fleet-building, and the empire of the world would then be in sight. This might happen if Germany were to ally herself with Russia.[75]

Haushofer was, of course, rewarded in 1939 when Hitler and Stalin signed their non-aggression pact. He and his crew were convinced that this would enable the balance of power to be overthrown. This was obviously an anti-British policy: one of their number coined the phrase, 'Anglosaxia contra mundum'[76] and England was reviled as the grave-digger of the European idea.[77] By rigorously pursuing its own interests according to the selfish theory of liberalism, England was only engaging in an Anglo-Saxon plot to keep the continent weak and divided.[78] By contrast, Germany was the bearer of the true European idea. Writing in 1941, one geopolitician insisted that Germany should therefore operate as the pace-maker of European unification:

> If we Germans call ourselves the actual people of Europe, that means that we take a heavy duty upon ourselves. It is now clear what Germany lacked in the last century: the European task, to find justice, and to be a pace-maker for better conditions in this part of the world, which is still so fateful for humanity. A struggle for justice, that is what it must be, not any attempt to trick people. A struggle for justice is a German task, it is a European task, it is a task for humanity . . . Let us unfurl the banner of the struggle for true peace in Europe.[79]

Thus it was necessary to develop the idea of 'community' in order to get out of the selfish fight between the interests of different nations, and thus to establish an 'order' in which all could live together.[80] Germany was the link between East and West, and the geopoliticians thought that Germany's position and history gave her a special role in the leadership of Europe. Therefore, the idea of German resurgence and that of a new order in Europe became inextricably linked. This gave Germany a clear sense of mission, which became highly developed in the inter-war and war years, just as it had been in the nineteenth century. The geopoliticians believed that the political unity of Europe was a natural and moral state, and that Germany had a special duty to realise it. In the words of the prominent geopolitician, Karl-Richard Ganzer, 'For there is simply nothing else in the 300-year history of the medieval empire than a powerful striving to organise unformed Europe from the German core space.'[81] Some prominent members of the Young Conservative movement even began to believe that the Germans, being the core of Europe, were the core of humanity.[82]

Those who supported the unification of Europe in this way generally ruled out the use of force, claiming that Germany's natural leadership over the continent had always been peaceful. Ganzer thus was able to write of what were, in fact, hegemonic theories in highly moral terms. He thought that the Germans had a moral right to lead Europe. In quasi-religious terms, he wrote, 'The Reich is, ethically considered, carried by a special force, which allows the *Reichsvolk* ['the people of the empire'] to become the protectors of Europe.'[83]

The Reich as the model for European integration

The geopoliticians, indeed, ascribed precisely to the Reich the role of the bearer and realisor of European unity. They used the term 'Europe' specifically to describe the concept of the great space in which the different nations of Europe would live together in unity and diversity. *Großräume* (great geographical spaces) were, indeed, for the geopoliticians, the appropriate modern form of economic and political order. They thought that the concept of limitedness was an integral part of the concept of 'nation', and that the nation was too small for the modern interdependent world and economy.

As such, their idea of the Reich – and, *ipso facto*, of Europe – was in direct and explicit contradiction to the liberal concept of the state, which is predicated on territorial clarity. It was precisely their fantasy that interests could be harmonised, and that the natural conflict between them somehow subsumed in a greater whole. This enabled the geopoliticians to excuse and ignore Nazi aggression. Their Reich theories, which accorded a greater role to the non-political factor of space than to the political arrangements which nations had in fact chosen, were explicitly predicated on the idea that the notion of sovereignty itself should be abandoned

in favour of the higher interests of the 'community'.[84] This mentality led the geopoliticians to make the kind of explicit excuse for
Hitler's aggression for which they were to become so notorious:

> Any objective observers must see that the greater German
> army has achieved its calling to lead Europe to unity with
> greatest possible circumspection, in the knowledge of the
> common greater home of all Europeans. For it is not a matter
> of an imperial dream or of German hubris, but rather of the
> fulfilment of an epochal task.[85]

Or again:

> Every European knows quite clearly that without the victory
> of German weapons, Europe will not continue to exist, and
> that it will lose all its values. The power of the Reich and of
> its allies guarantees European order.[86]

One geopolitician even explained how the German concept of
empire was more modest and limited in its aims that the
universalist British concept of empire:

> The simple fact that the British empire is geographically dis-
> persed and spread over the entire earth, has caused British
> imperialism to sabotage and defame the spatially defined idea
> of order, the concept of a certain *Lebensraum*, that honest,
> limited and modest great-space-idea.[87]

Geopoliticians considered that the Reich was the appropriate
political form for the modern world. In their eyes, only the Reich
could solve Germany's and Europe's contradictions. Although they
did not accept the European system of Versailles, the geopoliticians were aware that Germany was inextricably a part of Europe.
The Reich was a supranational organisation, composed of many
different peoples, which would accord them the greatest possible
degree of internal freedom while guaranteeing their external
security. Thus the Reich would unite Europe. Once again, in other

words, the Germans were proposing non-national solutions to Europe's problems.

Indeed, the geopoliticians often used the concepts 'Reich', 'Europe' and '*Großraum*' interchangeably. As Frank Ebeling, Haushofer's rehabilitator, comments, 'All the concepts of "Reich", despite the intrinsic vagueness of their content, longed for the supranational union of the peoples of Europe: there were also positive Utopias among them. Such positive ideas about European integration and European identity actually existed.'[88]

The greatest and most famous theoretician of the Reich was the conservative jurist Carl Schmitt. Although Schmitt's theories are still considered respectable by some modern philosophers of law, he was the Nazis' court jurist throughout the war. Having written numerous brilliant books on constitutional law throughout the 1920s and 1930s, Schmitt turned his talents to the juridical defence of the Nazi concept of the Reich.

In 1941, he published *Constitutional Great-Space-Order, Forbidding the Intervention of Powers Exterior to the Space*. With this work, Schmitt tried to provide a theoretical, geopolitical and juridical basis for Hitlerian anti-liberalism. Schmitt held that the world was divided up into *Reiche* or *Großräume*. A Reich was a nation which was strong enough to organise others beyond its borders. Drawing on the Monroe doctrine ('America for the Americans') Schmitt suggested that the same 'spatial' thought should be applied to the whole planet, and the world should be divided up into great zones in which other *Großräume* would be forbidden from interfering.

The purpose of this idea was to overcome constitutional theory as it had existed up to that point. Schmitt held it unrealistic to think that individual states could remain independent in the modern world. (This is perhaps why Schmitt has been called an early theoretician of European integration by modern German commentators.[89]) The true actors of the day were the great powers, whose zones of influence went beyond their borders. Schmitt thought that constitutional theory had in the past been a mere ruse to hide the reality of domination of little states by big ones. He therefore proposed that the principle of the equality of states in international law be replaced by one which recognised the reality and importance of regional groupings, and which indeed was based on them. It is fairly clear that these theories were intended to legitimise Nazi aggression and hegemony in Central Europe: other powers would, according to his theory, not have the right to intervene in the European space.

The Nazis and the balance of power

It is therefore not surprising that the Nazis hated the policy of the balance of power. Because this theme is so central to Nazi thought, it is worth returning to the Nazi Europeanism discussed in the previous chapter, and concentrating on the Nazis' geopolitical theories here.

The Nazis explicitly blamed the British policy of the balance of power for the division of Europe which they wanted to overcome. They argued that, together with 'European particularism', this was the cause of Europe's many 'civil wars', and that Germany should put an end to them by eradicating their causes. An official on Von Ribbentrop's staff drafted guidelines on the theme of 'Europe' in September 1941 for use by the media: Nazi Germany's goal was 'a federal Europe . . . the fight against England is a fight for European unity'.[90] Hitler's policy was to 'overcome the balance-of-power policy and the playing off of one European power against another by forces from outside the area. This aim will be secured by the elimination of Britain, destruction of Bolshevism, and voluntary adherence of France to the policy of European solidarity.'[91] A document prepared by a colleague warmed to the same theme: 'If Europe has been plagued by wars for centuries it is above all the fault of Britain's policy of playing off one European state against another.'[92]

Goebbels expanded on the same theme in articles in his weekly newspaper *Das Reich*. He especially linked the Nazi notion of 'Europe' with a definitive rejection of the balance of power.[93] Instead of suffering from the domination of extra-European powers (Britain, America, the Soviet Union), the Nazi geopolitical aim was to establish Germany as the strong centre of a strong Europe. Von Ribbentrop himself agreed: 'Too long have the British made mischief on the continent, playing off one power against another, intriguing and fomenting wars which they nearly always caused to be fought with others' blood. Today every child knows this, and Europe is determined once and for all to be rid of this English policy. Even France is beginning to develop a European conscience on this subject . . .'[94] As for France, speaking to the Groupe 'Collaboration' in Paris, Friedrich Grimm attacked the 'eternal Richelieu, the eternal treaty of Westphalia'.[95]

Indeed, hostility to the British policy of the balance of power was so central to Nazi thinking that there was even a propaganda sheet devoted entirely to it. Entitled *The New Europe: A Magazine of Struggle Against the English-American World and Historical View* and edited by Walther Körber, it is a veritable monument to Nazi European propaganda. Calling itself 'a press service', it was inspired by the geopolitical theories which Karl Haushofer had developed. It published article after article about England's determination to divide the continent. It attacked England's 'insular mentality';[96] its 'enmity towards Europe';[97] its 'particularism';[98] and American 'Dollar imperialism'.[99] It carried articles with titles like 'Europe is Fighting for Unity';[100] 'England, Victim of its Own European Policy';[101] 'Germany, the Heart of Europe';[102] 'European Tasks in the East';[103] 'Jewish Attempts to Establish World Domination Against Europe';[104] '*Völkisch* Economy in the New Europe';[105] 'The Co-operation of European Science';[106] 'The Enemies of the European Construction' (about British hostility to the continent);[107] 'The New Europe: A Victory Over Anglo-Saxon Hostility to the Reich and to Europe';[108] 'Youth Ensures Europe's Future';[109] 'The Economic Unity of Europe';[110] 'European Economic Community';[111] and 'Building Blocks of the New Europe' (a chronology of political events which had led to European unity).[112] It attacked things like 'The World Lodge of Jewry against Europe's New Order.'[113] It extolled 'the birth of European solidarity'[114] and of 'the European spirit'[115] or 'European consciousness';[116] reported on books which were 'fighting for a new Europe', and on 'Voices of the New Europe' from publications across the continent. It reported with glee, for instance, the publication of a magazine called *The New Europe* in Britain, which called, with Mackinder, for Britain to take a 'positive interest' in Europe in order to be able to influence it.[117]

In contrast to Britain's peripheral, cynical and anti-European geopolitical agenda, Germany was at the centre of Europe: she therefore represented the real Europe. One of the foremost ideologues of Nazi Europeanism, Friedrich Stieve, explained how, from Charlemagne's day onwards, the unity of Europe had always been advanced from '*die deutsche Mitte*', by the German middle (that is, of Europe). 'The middle never lost its longing for European unity,' he wrote.[118]

He also emphasised the idea of the 'resurgence of the middle', explaining that Hitler had extended the 'source of energy of the middle'[119] – from which Frederick the Great and Bismarck had fashioned the Prussian-German empire – further and further afield, to Austria, Bohemia and Moravia. 'What a resurgence of the middle! What a European reversal!' he gasped. 'The backbone of this part of the earth, which had been deliberately broken, was not only more firmly welded together than ever before, but thanks to the magnetic force of its new construction, it began to draw towards it deliberately separated parts and thus ineluctably to increase in size.'[120]

He contrasted this European policy with that of the peripheral states – Portugal, Spain, France, Holland, England – which had expanded into extra-European 'spaces', and then attempted to dominate the European continent. Only England put a stop to this in the name of the balance of power, but that meant 'the suppression of European peoples'.[121] Thus, it was always the 'middle' of Europe (that is, Germany) which asserted 'the freedom and autonomous development' of the whole. Just as the Germans had resisted Napoleon, so, under Bismarck's leadership, Germany had selflessly and successfully worked towards European peace.

Indeed, Stieve criticised Bismarck's successors for attempting to grab world power by developing colonies in the extra-European spaces. They should have learned the lessons of centuries of history, and devoted their attentions only to Europe instead: their sin was to have driven Germany off her European path. Having explained how Poland attacked Germany, Stieve argued that Hitler had begun to 'think in terms of continents' as early as 1914. He 'saw the great areas which had constituted themselves: the French, the English, the Russian, the American, and understood that Europe too had to become such a great area if it wanted to achieve freedom'.[122] Hitler had then realised that he had to defend Europe from Bolshevism.[123]

The idea was thus widespread that Germany, being geographically at the centre of Europe, was its very heart or essence. 'Our Reich is at the heart of Europe,' declared Werner Frauendienst, a leading historian at the Friedrich Wilhelm University in Berlin, in 1942.[124] Another Nazi theoretician, Dr Hans Pflug, stressed that Germany's geopolitical fate was to be 'the heart of Europe'. This heart, he argued, should be linked to the rest of the body by a developed transport infrastructure. It was from the 'heart of Europe' that the old medieval notion of empire had gone out, 'the embodiment of a European state order . . . In political, economic, social and spiritual matters, this war has made the country of the European middle the centre-point of affairs.' Germany had always been aware of its 'over-national duty'.[125]

Walther Darré, the Nazi minister of agriculture and prominent advocate of green policies, also spoke eloquently on the *central* role which Germany was to assume in Europe. 'If Greater Germany achieved this task of creating order, then other states will crystallise around this central European block of order of their own accord, in balanced and constant economic relationships. Thus will the foundation for a true European order be created.'[126] Once again, therefore, just as the Customs Union had created a 'core' around which other states gravitated, so, according to Darré, Germany should become the hard core of a Europe of concentric circles.

Indeed, because it was at the geopolitical centre of Europe, Germany – according to another Nazi thinker – had a special role to play in protecting and uniting Europe: 'Can Europe be organised without Germany or against Germany?' he asked. 'The central position directs the Germans towards Europe more than all other peoples on this continent . . . Because of this fate, Germany has lived and thought European questions more deeply than those countries who knew themselves to be in safety on the edge or who linked themselves to other spaces beyond the borders of Europe.'[127]

It was often emphasised that Germany was not acting alone in Europe. The metaphors of 'axis' and 'core' were commonly used to show this. Hitler himself spoke of the need for a 'core as hard as steel' composed of Germany, Austria, Czechoslovakia and Western Poland 'forged to unbreakable unity'.[128] His lackeys underlined that an 'axis' is that around which things turn – Werner Daitz explained that Germany was Europe's centre of gravity: 'As the planets revolve around the sun without being absorbed into it, in the same way the European powers will order themselves around their natural centre.'[129] Another declared, 'The Berlin–Rome axis is today the central nucleus of radiation and power for Europe. The entire regulation of political and social conditions proceeds from it . . . Thus the axis had become the natural political law of European history in our century, vanquishing and superseding the British principle of the "balance of power".'[130] Similarly, the author of one of the plans to create a European federation, Cecile von Renthe-Fink, noted that the New Europe could not be built without France: 'France's attitude will be decisive,' he wrote.[131]

Indeed, in this context, it is amusing to find the Nazis using metaphors of transport to illustrate the inevitability of European integration. 'As the strength of a chariot resides in its axis,' wrote R. Höhn in *Reich, Great Area, Great Power*,[132] 'so the strength of the Reich depends on its continental situation in accordance with the laws of life.'

Finally, Martin Heidegger, the prominent philosopher who belonged to the Nazi party from May 1933 to May 1945,[133] similarly believed that the necessary reaction against the technical revolution coming from America and Russia had to come from the 'real' Europe, from Central Europe – that is, from Germany. In 1953, he still subscribed to the view, espoused by the Nazi geopoliticians who saw the world divided up into 'great areas', that 'This Europe, which in its state of incurable blindness is always on the point of stabbing itself in the back, lies today in the great pincer between Russia on one side and America on the other. Russia and America are both, from a metaphysical point of view, the same: the same desolate madness of technology and rootless organisation of the normalised man.'[134]

Post-war Germany

After the defeat of 1945, Germany's position straddling the East–West divide contained some elements which were novel, and others which were very traditionally German. Her position was novel because a fundamentally Western orientation was imposed on the larger of the two German states, the Federal Republic. This was epitomised by the choice of a new capital, Bonn, in the extreme West of the country. Adenauer made commitment to the West the cornerstone of his domestic and foreign policy, and he rejected attempts – such as that by Stalin in 1952 – to detach Germany from the West in return for reunification. Never before had a German state, now on the front-line of the West, turned so unambiguously Westwards, and towards its erstwhile enemies as their new friend.

The Western orientation was not simply geographical; it was moral as well. If Germany had been culturally torn between East and West at different times during her history and according to political taste, the West had generally been associated with rationalism (such as of the French Revolution), liberalism (such as that of the British Empire) or individualism (such as that of the United States of America). The East, by contrast, stood for communitarianism, authority, and culture.[135] The geographically Western orientation imposed by the presence of hostile Soviet troops in Berlin and in the Soviet occupation zone in the East forced a culturally and politically Western orientation on the new German state.

On the other hand, the post-war settlement also encouraged Germans once again to identify their fate with that of Europe. After all, the new Germany epitomised Europe itself. Like Europe,

she was divided between East and West, and just as throughout
history she had resembled Europe – with her unclear borders, her
division into different states and religions, her lack of a single
political identity – so now she embodied in her own predicament
the drama of the entire continent.

The acuteness of this division naturally encouraged Germans to
want to overcome it. It also fixed in the German mind the idea
that all borders were barriers like the Berlin Wall, rather than
domains of jurisdiction. This gave rise to lazy calls for the 'barriers
in Europe to be lowered', as if the Franco-German border was
comparable to the German–German one. This desire chimed in
neatly with a very German yearning for synthesis and harmony,
and a fear of conflict. In the words of one commentator, Germany
went from wanting to be the hammer of international politics to
wanting to achieve a political world in which there were simply no
hammers at all. 'In the public presentation of West German foreign policy, it was further suggested that the harmony could extend
not only to the interests of other Western states, but to those of
the Soviet Union and Eastern European states as well. In the
rhetoric of *Ostpolitik** it was almost implied that the great work of
reconciliation, *détente* and co-operation, the seamless web of ever-
closer ties, cultural, economic, human and political, would bring
benefits equally to all. There would be . . . all winners and no
losers.'[136]

It was therefore inevitable that ideas of pan-European reunification should resurface, yet again, in Germany after the war.
While the architects of *Ostpolitik*, Willy Brandt and Walter Scheel,
were always at pains to insist that their efforts would not be
allowed to compromise the coherence of the Western alliance and
Germany's commitment to it, they persisted in thinking that
East–West relations could be harmonised. The great ideologue of
Ostpolitik, Egon Bahr, produced a working paper in June 1968
which defined the goal of the Federal Republic as 'the overcoming
of the status quo through a European peace order' at the centre of

---

* West German foreign policy towards the Eastern bloc, particularly East
Germany and East Berlin.

which it clearly placed 'the overcoming of the division of Germany'. It concluded that the best way to do this was via the creation of a pan-European security system replacing NATO and the Warsaw Pact. It headquarters were to be in . . . Berlin.[137]

So even after the war, the Germans resumed their old habit of believing their own interests and needs to be identical to those of Europe. In December 1966, Willy Brandt said to De Gaulle, 'The trench that divides my country also divides Europe. Anyone who fills that trench also helps my country. We have no other prospect than to overcome the division of Europe.' Twenty years later, Wolfgang Schäuble – Chancellor Kohl's heir apparent – declared, perhaps a little more frankly, 'Our chance lies in the fact that the division of Germany is simultaneously the division of Europe.'[138] Policy papers produced by Helmut Schmidt's office used the expression 'the Federal Republic/Europe' on two occasions (e.g. 'more autonomy for the Federal Republic/Europe') as if the two were really the same thing.[139] By 1989, Chancellor Kohl was using the metaphor of the Rhine ('it carries on flowing however much you try to dam it') to describe the inevitability of German and European unification indifferently. During his appearance on a television broadcast with François Mitterrand to campaign in favour of the Maastricht Treaty in September 1992, Kohl repeated what he had by now made into a cliché: that German and European unification were two sides of the same coin.

As the Soviet empire in Eastern Europe began to break up, Germans contemplated what life might be like in a Europe which was no longer divided by the Berlin Wall. They elaborated intelligent plans for the future Europe, their mature reflection on this topic contrasting strongly with the panicky reaction in Britain and France when the plan for German reunification was announced in December 1989: those two great European powers had no contingency plans for such an event, and seemed indeed not really to have thought about it even as an eventuality.

The plans which were developed then and over the following six years were animated by the two classic German fears: the fear of the Mittellage, and the fear of balance of power-politics. The Germans knew that if their country was ever reunited, it would find herself back in the position in which Bismarck had left it: large, united, in the middle of an ambiguous European system, and at permanent risk of instability and encirclement. European integration was the only solution to these problems. As the senior German negotiator of the Maastricht Treaty wrote in 1996, 'There is no alternative to European integration. Any other choice could cause the other countries of the continent, one day, to unite against us.'[140] Chancellor Kohl explained: 'We Germans have specific reasons why we need a united Europe. Germany has more neighbours than any other country in Europe . . . Germany has an elementary national interest in all of her neighbours becoming members of the European Union.'[141]

Kohl, in other words, had exactly the same foreign policy preoccupations as Bismarck: the desire to dissipate all conflict as far away as possible from the vulnerable middle of Europe. He wants a zone of stability on his country's borders. There is nothing the Germans fear more than a re-run of the process by which Bismarck's subtle diplomacy degenerated into brutal war-mongering in 1914, by people unable to master the complexities of the situation. This is not least because they know – after two failed tries – that any attempt by Germany to dominate Europe on her own is doomed.

Not only is the dilemma traditional: Chancellor Kohl's response to it is very traditional too. Perhaps this is why his policy has been subject to such broad agreement across the political spectrum in Germany, and why Germany's European policy has such clarity, strength and purpose. His plan is to restructure Europe, especially the European Union, according to a model of 'concentric circles' with Germany and her allies forming a so-called 'hard core'.

The earliest formulation of the 'concentric circles' model was published by two senior advisers in Helmut Kohl's office, Michael Mertes and Norbert Prill, in July 1989.[142] Before examining its content, it is important to consider the timing of this piece: June 1989 was the occasion of a seminal visit by Mikhail Gorbachev to Bonn. Gorbachev had made the slogan 'The Common European Home' the key to his policy (even though the phrase had originally been coined by Leonid Brezhnev on a visit to Bonn in 1981). Gorbachev's aim was to play down the tensions between the two blocs in Europe, and he had been received with wild adulation from the German public. His message chimed in well with their innate desire for harmony and their hatred of division. The European question – in the widest sense of the word – was very much on everyone's minds. It was not just a matter of integrating Western Europe, but of bringing the entire continent closer together. It seemed that the old Genscherite dream of universal reconciliation and harmony, which Chancellor Kohl shared, was about to come true.

Moreover, a crucial event had taken place during Gorbachev's visit which casts important light on the atmosphere in which the paper was produced. Gorbachev had all but told Helmut Kohl outright that the Soviet Union would not oppose German reunification. During a moonlit talk at the bottom of the Chancellery garden overlooking the Rhine, Kohl had compared the unification of Germany to the flowing of the river. Both, he said, were unstoppable. Gorbachev did not contradict him. Kohl has since said on various occasions that this was the moment when he realised that German reunification had become possible. In other words, the paper produced by two senior advisers in the Chancellor's office was prepared with German reunification in mind. They probably knew what Gorbachev had said.

The paper argued that European integration should not be conceived in contradiction to German political integration, but rather that it should be the model for it. It should extend convergence to the entire continent. 'The European Community is proving to be a centre of gravity with an unmistakable attraction for the Eastern half of our continent,' it stated. 'This will sooner or later raise the question of whether it would not be better for the sake of European progress if only the truly convinced members were to head for the shores of a European federal state – provided that the other members of the European community are cordially invited to do likewise at a later stage.' The Europe of 'variable geometry' – or the 'hard core' and 'concentric circles' – had been born.

The paper called for 'a federal nucleus' to become 'the focal point and centre of gravity for an ever expanding community'. 'This model can be seen as a system of concentric circles or as "dolls within a doll",' it went on. Such a Europe was to replace the current 'confusing diversity' of Europe's overlapping structures – EC, WEU, the Council of Europe, EFTA, and CSCE – with 'a single consistent structure'. That structure was to consist of a 'European federal state', the 'United States of Europe' as its 'centrepiece'. It would comprise the original six members plus any others who wanted to join. It would have a common federal constitution, a federal army and common foreign and defence policy. The second circle would be 'the European Community' including the 'United States of Europe' and the other seven EC states. The third concentric circle would be comprised of an 'Association of European States', perhaps modelled on EFTA, which would be open to the Eastern European states, the Scandinavian countries, and Switzerland. The final concentric circle was 'the common European home' itself, corresponding to the OCSE (CSCE as it then was) states, that is, all of Europe plus the Soviet Union, Canada, and the USA. The authors never understated the breadth of their vision. They envisaged the Baltic States joining, and even Mediterranean countries like the Maghreb states and Israel.

The document concluded with what sounded like a threat. It was to become a cliché. 'Western integration, in other words the preservation of freedom, is the prerequisite of unity, and must not be the price paid for unity. Anyone who questions this consensus that has existed for decades is striking at the very foundations of democracy and the rule of law in Germany.' In other words, the paper ended with a fatally confused thought which continues to stymie clear German understanding of what is at stake in Europe. Germany's Western orientation – her alliances with France and the United States, as well as her commitment to Western-style parliamentary government and federalism – is confused with something completely different, the continued integration of the states of Europe into a federal-type union.

France and the German influence on EMU

'Before Prussia had actually beaten France, Bismarck treated her carefully, made a fuss of her – and tricked her'

JACQUES BAINVILLE[143]

These geopolitical reflections help us to understand the evolution of the single currency project, and the roles of France and Germany. When Chancellor Kohl announced his 'ten-point programme to overcome the division of Germany and Europe', the French President and the British Prime Minister reacted with hostility. Jacques Attali, Mitterrand's faithful adviser, has documented Mitterrand's fury at Kohl's announcement. He was convinced that the Soviet Union should and would prevent German reunification. Having failed to convince Mrs Thatcher to intercede with Gorbachev to prevent unification, Mitterrand went to see the Soviet leader in Kiev on 6 December to try to persuade him face to face. On 20–21 December, Mitterrand also paid a state visit to East Germany, which was by then in a state of collapse, and reassured the tottering Communist regime of France's continuing support for the existence of East Germany as an independent state – that is, that France was opposed to reunification.

These actions by Mitterrand infuriated the Germans. Many articles were written at the time, saying that the Franco-German relationship had suffered a mortal blow from which it could not recover. And yet, by April 1990 – less than four months later – Messrs Kohl and Mitterrand had signed a joint letter to the President of the European Council saying that it was time to transform the nature of the relationships between the EEC states, and to undertake further steps towards European Union. This joint letter set in motion the process which was to become the Maastricht Treaty eighteen months later. The only possible explanation for why the Germans agreed to work together with the country which had just tried to prevent their national reunification is that, however angry they may have been, their determination not to lose France was overriding.

The French had made few bones about the fact that their intention in proposing EMU was to escape from the diktats of the German Bundesbank. They have never renounced this aim: as late as 1996, the French minister for Europe said that France was committed to the single currency because 'we have had enough of being subject to the domination or the sovereignty of others',[144] a clear reference to Germany. Given Mitterrand's own behaviour during the last weeks of December 1989, there could be no reason for doubting that France's aim in embracing European unification was to mitigate or sublimate the power of Germany in Europe. Why, then, did Germany accept this plan?

It is possible that the Germans proceeded with European unification because they knew that the French were afraid of them. The French had made that very clear in their declarations and actions. Above all, they had accepted the German scenario according to which Germany was in danger of abandoning her Western orientation if monetary union and European integration did not succeed – a fear which continues to animate much French pro-European thinking. Armed with this knowledge, the Germans were able to exploit French fears. Those fears, indeed, turned the tables completely, because if Germany had not detected that France was frightened that Germany might leave or weaken the alliance, then she, Germany, would have had cause to fear that France might leave or weaken it herself.

Germany would have been afraid of France leaving or weakening the Franco-German axis precisely because that could only imply a return to the politics of the balance of power. As we have seen, Britain is usually attacked for having pursued the balance of power – for having been the 'balancing needle', as the Germans say. But in fact the author of the policy is France, not Britain. If France were ever to decide that she had priorities other than the Franco-German axis, then there would only be one alternative for her: to return to the policy of the balance of power. This could take the form of a *rapprochement* with Britain, the United States, or Russia. There is nothing that Germany would fear more than the possibility of France abandoning her in the middle of Europe, the potential victim of coalitions against her.

Conversely, Germany knows what potential the axis with France offers her. Without France at her side, then the creation of a monetary union including only the D-Mark zone countries (Belgium, the Netherlands, Luxembourg, Austria, perhaps some Eastern Europe states) would appear, very simply, as what it would, in fact, be: a new German Reich. With France in the picture, by contrast, German hegemony is disguised. German power is increased by the alliance with France, not decreased. It is not for nothing that the two countries refer to themselves as 'the motor of European integration'. France, indeed, bought into the relationship with Germany partly for this reason, and partly because European integration was an escalator she was too frightened to get off.

Because France never exploited these potential German fears, and instead demonstrated only her own, the Germans felt able to accept the French proposal and turn it to their own advantage. Rather than playing hard to get, the French put themselves in the position of suitor, and thereby handed Germany the role of being hard to get instead. Germany was to play this role to perfection over the next six years, and a series of moves successfully consolidated German hegemony over the monetary union project.

The first was to insist that German monetary policy was the best in Europe. Once this was accepted, it followed that Europe should adopt German institutions and practices. That the new European currency had to be as strong as the D-Mark soon became a shibboleth for all German political pronouncements on monetary union, and it was rapidly accepted as a sacred principle by the whole European political class. It conveniently ignored the fact that the D-Mark is not the strongest currency in Europe: it is the Swiss franc, and, because of a constitutional link to gold, the Swiss central bank has far less discretionary political power than the Bundesbank.

But it was argued that the new central bank had to be independent, federal in structure, and committed to the (undefined) goal of price stability – in other words, a copy of the Bundesbank. When the Delors Report on monetary union was published in

April 1989, the influence of the then Bundesbank president, Karl-Otto Pöhl, was there for all to see.

The next step was presumably unforeseen by the German government. A disgruntled former official of the European Commission, exasperated at the authoritarianism and *dirigisme* of the EC, took the German government to the country's constitutional court and alleged that the treaty infringed German sovereignty. This, he said, was contrary to the constitution. By then, moreover, a popular newspaper campaign was under way to 'save the D-Mark', and public opinion in Germany was afraid that 'our lovely money' was about to be taken away.

The court ruled that the treaty did not infringe German sovereignty. In keeping with this assertion, the court proclaimed itself responsible, in the last resort, for the protection of basic rights in Germany, and for the interpretation of the terms in which the treaty was binding on Germany. This was a direct challenge to forty years of European jurisprudence, which had always been based on the primacy of Community law over national law.

The consequence of this is a very strange constitutional position. All the member states of the European Union (as it became when Maastricht came into force in November 1993) are subject equally to EU law. Only Germany has declared that her own law, in a case of conflict, will prevail. All other similar cases of conflict (such as the Factortame case in the United Kingdom) have resulted in a clear victory for the primacy of Community law. This puts Germany into a position *vis-à-vis* the rest of Europe which is not dissimilar to that of Prussia within the German Empire after 1871.

This constitutional lopsidedness has been reinforced by political practice and widespread acceptance. It passes now as an accepted truth – proclaimed as official policy by leading politicians in Germany and elsewhere – that monetary union makes no sense if it does not include France and Germany. As the President of the Bundesbank, Hans Tietmeyer, said, 'I cannot imagine a monetary union without France and Germany. Not without Germany, because presumably the other countries have no interest [in EMU] without the participation of the country which has hitherto been the anchor in the European monetary system. Not without France, because France is a core country of European integration. A monetary union between Germany and some other small countries could quickly lead to problematic and divisive tendencies in Europe.'[145] France and Germany, in other words, constitute the core of European integration and, according to this official declaration, a treaty and a Community which purports to treat all states equally is, in fact, run by the two states at its centre.

Further examples of German influence over the monetary union project included the important choice of Frankfurt as the seat. The German argument had been that only in Frankfurt was there a sufficient 'culture of stability' – proof, if any was needed, that the central bank there would not be 'independent' of its surroundings. Chancellor Kohl was jubilant, declaring afterwards that the choice of Frankfurt meant that 'European monetary policy will be German monetary policy'.

Then came the change of name from 'ecu' to 'Euro'. This was decided in December 1995, and represented a break with an important French symbol. The ecu had been an old French gold coin, and ECU was also an acronym in English. By christening the new currency Euro, the Germans were also making it clear that monetary union represented a break with the previous European Monetary System, and not a continuation of it. The EMS had been set up in 1979 by Valéry Giscard d'Estaing and Helmut Schmidt and, according to the Maastricht Treaty, it was supposed to evolve and harden until its centrepiece, the (basket currency) ecu, became a currency in its own right. Instead, as the Germans took pleasure in reminding people, the ecu had never ceased to devalue against the D-Mark since its invention. The change of name thus symbolised that Europe's new monetary arrangements, the monetary union, would be based on a clean break with the previous one, in which all of Europe's currencies had been represented. Henceforth it would be the German model and German influence alone which would be decisive. Thus it was not surprising that, in December 1995, the *Frankfurter Allgemeine Zeitung* referred to 'the process of Germanisation in Europe'.

By 1996, European officials were saying as explicitly as they could that the Euro was nothing but the D-Mark in disguise. It was not just a matter of German politicians like Theo Waigel speaking of the 'Euro-Mark' or 'Europa-Mark', as he has done on various occasions.[146] It was more subtle and more profound. The president of the European Monetary Institute, Alexandre Lamfalussy, told a German newspaper that, 'We must convince the Germans that changing the currency does not mean that there will be a monetary reform.'[147] He added that the Germans did not perhaps need the Euro, but that they did need monetary union. On the face of it, these two remarks make no sense: the introduction of the Euro *is* monetary union, and changing a currency *is* a monetary reform. They are intelligible only if one assumes two things: first, that the Euro is the D-Mark under another name, in which case the Germans can be said to be continuing with the same currency and thus not undergoing a monetary reform; and second, that EMU implies the adoption of the D-Mark by other countries, in which case the Germans could be said to need monetary union (that is, the attachment of other countries to their monetary zone) but not the introduction of a new currency.

After all these victories, German pressure continued to try to ensure that the monetary instruments used by the future European central bank would be the same as those used by the Bundesbank. In particular, the President of the Bundesbank, Hans Tietmeyer, stressed the need for monetary targets (instead of inflation targets) as the primary instrument of monetary control.[148] As Bernard Connolly has shown, the Bundesbank does not like the precision of inflation targets, for it compromises its discretionary room for manoeuvre.[149] Secondly, he emphasised the need for minimum reserve requirements, a favourite instrument of the Bundesbank. Minimum reserve requirements oblige the clearing banks to make non-interest bearing deposits with the central bank. The central bank uses these funds to release money into the market when liquidity is required, and take it out when there is too much: it is an added means by which the central bank can maintain its control over the financial marketplace, especially over the big banks which themselves control German industry.

Der feste Kern ist unser Gott[*]

Meanwhile, the 'concentric circles' plan never left German policy-makers' heads. In November 1995, for instance, the head of the Bavarian Central Bank, Franz-Christoph Zeitler, said, 'The image of a Europe of concentric circles contains a lot of realism. To make sure that it remains a valid concept, attention must be devoted to the question of monetary policy co-operation between those EU states which participate in the monetary union right from the start, and those which do not.'[150] By this he meant that the creation of a new European Monetary System linking the non-EMU currencies to the Euro corresponded to the model of a hard core of united states, with the others orbiting around it.

The term 'hard core' itself was used for the first time in a policy document produced by the ruling Christian Democrat Party, published in September 1994. The document attracted a great deal of attention at the time because it contained the following sentence: 'Without such further development of [Western] European integration, Germany could be required, or tempted for its own security needs, to stabilise Eastern Europe alone and in the traditional way.'[151] This was widely understood as a threat that military action might be necessary in Eastern Europe if political means proved unsatisfactory in ensuring German security. It seemed as if Europe were back in 1912.

The document also shocked some because the Germans named the countries they foresaw joining the hard core: France, Germany and the Benelux countries. Italy, a founder member of the European Economic Community, was insulted, and the Iberian states felt sidelined. But the fact that the hard-core plan was deliberately designed to overcome the 'balance of power' in Europe was illustrated by the fact that the Germans were determined to get Belgium into it, even though the Belgian state debt is over twice what the Maastricht convergence criteria allow.

---

[*] 'The hard core is our God.' An old Lutheran hymn begins, 'Eine feste Burg ist unser Gott' – 'Our God is a solid fortress.'

But the most crucial aspect of the paper was its suggestion that Europe's old institutions could no longer work with numerous new members. The paper affirmed that fifteen or twenty members would cause institutional blockage, and that more flexible arrangements were needed instead. The document therefore proposed that a politically, economically and monetarily united 'hard core' of five states be formed, which would enable a Europe of 'various speeds' or 'variable geometry' to be institutionalised.

The essential point sounded reasonable enough: 'Those countries which are ready, willing and able to go further in co-operation and integration, should not be able to be blocked by the veto rights of other members.'[152] But in fact, the Germans were displaying their customary muddy thinking in constitutional and European matters. (Unfortunately, other countries, notably Britain, also failed to think clearly on this subject as well.) Of course other states have no right to prevent other countries integrating or co-operating as much as they liked; but other member states of the European Union obviously do have a right to veto attempts to do so within the institutional structure of the treaties, for that structure belongs to, and must accommodate, all its members and their interests.

This becomes clear when one studies the effect which these proposals are intended to have on the functioning of the European Union. They are intended to control those institutions from the inside. This was explicit when the document proposed that France and Germany have a right of veto over all European policy-making. In a striking affirmation of the absolute primacy of the Franco-German axis which the document proposed institutionalising, it said, 'No essential action of foreign or of European policy should be able to be undertaken without the prior agreement of France and Germany.'[153]

In accordance with the geopolitical analysis proposed above, it added that the Franco-German axis had become 'even more important' since the end of the Cold War. France, flattered, bought the idea. In early 1996, the French Prime Minister gave the idea the government's official seal of approval when he called for 'a Europe of two levels . . . a Union of common law, including the present fifteen members and those who are going to accede; and at the heart of this union, of this first circle, a second and more limited circle, composed of a small number of states around France and Germany, of nations who are willing and able to go further or more quickly than others on subjects like the single currency and defence'.[154]

One of the authors of this document, the CDU's foreign policy spokesman, Karl Lamers, elaborated on the leadership role which he foresaw for the hard core. In a series of lectures and articles delivered all over Europe, he explained that the hard core required full political integration, and that it would exercise 'a centripetal or magnetic effect on the other countries. Any country which tried to evade the influence of the [European Central] Bank would marginalise itself. It would be impossible.' He called for a Europe of 'variable geometry *and* hard core'; he rejected those who opposed his plans as 'national ideologues'; he called the concept of national sovereignty 'an illusion'; and he insisted that countries which tried to escape from the influence of the Central Bank would be 'self-centred and ultimately irrational'.[155] In a typical expression of German Utopianism and urge for harmony, he added, 'The vital interests of all Europeans are identical.'[156]

Lamers' colleague, Wolfgang Schäuble, also dwelt on the force which the hard core is supposed to exert on other states. 'If we are to keep European integration on course, then the slowest state must not be able to determine the speed. We need the dynamics of member states pushing forward, willing and able to integrate. They are the core of a magnetic field: thus is our concept of a hard core to be understood.'[157] Europe, in other words, can only hold together if it is led. The identical thought was also been stressed by the President of the Bundesbank. He used the image of concentric circles to endorse the concept of a multi-speed Europe:

A single speed for all would reduce progress in monetary and political integration to the lowest common denominator and thus probably hinder greater European unification. A Europe which wants to go forward can develop better on a model of

concentric circles. The members of the tighter community of
stability will have to bind themselves more quickly and more
thoroughly together. The other EU member states, the partic-
ipants in the European Economic Area, and the associated
states of central and Eastern Europe, can at first be satisfied
with lesser conditions.[158]

When the suggestion is made that the hard core will enable
Germany to establish a hegemony, it is important that hegemony
is understood in the true sense of the term. Hegemony does not
denote a relationship between dominator and dominated, but
rather between leader and led. Isokrates' call for a 'hegemon' for
Hellas, and Philip of Macedonia's success in fulfilling the role,
was not a matter of his superior weaponry or even fighting skills. It
depended rather on the willingness of the Greek states to unite
behind him in the fight with the Persians. Indeed, hegemony is
usually accepted by the states which are led precisely because their
loyalty to the hegemon is given in return for his forbearing to
dominate them completely. Prussia argued precisely that its aim
was to bind itself in, which, Triepel says, is the hallmark of all
hegemons.[159] Modern Germans similarly say that Germany wants
to 'bind herself in' to Europe.

Properly speaking, European statesmen were wrong in 1871 to
say that Germany had established or wanted to establish a
European hegemony: there is no hegemon without followers. The
struggle against 'hegemonic' powers in nineteenth-century Europe
was in fact always and only a struggle against the most powerful
state. It was a struggle to maintain the balance of power: it was
never the struggle against a truly leading state in Europe.

Hegemony, therefore, does not mean 'domination'. The
Germans, who always insist that they do not want to dominate
Europe – or, more intriguingly, admit that they cannot do so on
their own – usually fail to make the distinction between hegemony and domination. The following quotation from the Chief
Economist of the Bundesbank illustrates the confusion: 'The economic weight of Germany and its political role have nothing to
do with a "bid for hegemony". Rather the size and position of

Germany give us the task of fashioning the growing together of the entire continent in an orderly political way, and fitting ourselves into this order.'[160] But if a country pushes for integration along its own national model, thereby extending that model to other states, this is classic hegemony. In Triepel's words, and as the example of Prussia's hegemonic role in promoting the unification of Germany shows, 'Hegemony is always a means of "integration". All hegemony presupposes a certain measure of federalism . . . The fact that Prussia exercised hegemony [within the German Empire] did not undermine [German] unity, it strengthened it.'[161]

The hard core is therefore an instrument which will enable Germany to escape from the present constrictions of European law and institutions (and from the vetoes of other states), and to fashion Europe's institutions in her own image instead. In geopolitical terms, it bears a passing resemblance to the *Los von Rom* ('Free From Rome') movement, the *Kulturkampf* ('war of culture'), or even the Reformation itself, in which that traditionally protestatory nation sought to wriggle out from the constricting power of the universal Church based in the eternal city. By replacing a multilateral system of fifteen states which are equal before the law with a system of concentric circles gravitating around a hard core, of which Germany represents 50 per cent in terms of population, Germany will transform institutions which used to control her into ones by means of which she can exert decisive influence over other states.

In other words, the institutionalisation of the hard core turns the tables on forty years of Community law, completing the work of reversal begun by the Karlsruhe judgement. It is consistent with this aim that some German politicians (the Finance Minister, Theo Waigel, for instance) have called for the Commission's monopoly on legislative proposition to be ended, and for that right to be given to governments as well: a hegemonic power will, as Triepel showed, always try to weaken the central institutions it cannot control. This hegemony can be established whether Germany becomes weak or remains strong: in the former case, she may well drag other states economically down with her.

European integration and the centralisation of Germany

> *'Doch – alles, was mich dazu trieb,*
> *Gott! war so gut, ach war so lieb'**
> GRETCHEN, IN GOETHE'S FAUST[162]

This chapter began with reflections about the link between the balance of power in Europe and decentralisation in Germany, and it ends with the same thought. The process of European integration will not only centralise a large area around Germany, it will also centralise Germany herself. German federalism cannot survive in an integrated Europe. Therefore that which the Germans say will save them from themselves, European integration, will in fact remove the very bedrock of their post-war liberties, their federal system. As such, European integration is neither good for Europe nor good for Germany.

This is because European integration will inevitably strengthen the power of the central government *vis-à-vis* that of the federated states, the *Länder*. Like other states, Germany is represented in the Council of Ministers by a government minister. That body is responsible for making European law, which applies equally and directly throughout the EU, and supersedes national law. The more legislative and political power is transferred to the EU, the more power will be centralised in the hands of the federal German government, represented in the Council of Ministers, at the expense of that of the *Länder*. In monetary matters, for instance, the Maastricht rules on state debt, which apply to the whole state, significantly curtail the freedom of the *Länder* to manage their own budgets.

As a senior official in the German Federal Finance Ministry has pointed out:

> The levelling – or rather the reform – of the federative
> structure of competencies [in Germany] cannot be reversed
> unless Germany leaves the European Union, even though it

---

* 'But everything which drove me to it, oh God, was so good and so lovely.'

represents a considerable reduction in the statehood of the *Länder*. The *Länder* are compensated only by new co-operation rights in taking account of the membership rights of the Federal Republic in the organs of the European Union, and by the creation of a Committee of the Regions. But this compensation, brought about by a change to the Basic Law, is inadequate.[163]

It is no coincidence if this perspicacious commentator has also noticed the hegemonic implications of the hard core, for internal centralisation and external hegemony are, in reality, only two sides of the same coin. In the same paper, he writes: 'Germany's European policy, which foresees closer frameworks for member states who are willing and able to integrate, easily arouses the suspicion that Germany is trying to build up a hegemonic position for herself. The special relationship with France, which is increasingly seen abroad as being dominated by Germany, does not neutralise this suspicion.' But such suspicion can hardly be good for anyone, least of all for Europe's most economically powerful state. Germany's current leaders may be enticed by the vision of a leading role for Germany in Europe, as their predecessors have done in the past. But, also as in the past, that it not necessarily what is right for the German people themselves.

German conceptions of the state

A further danger is that Germany's leading role will repose on economics rather than politics. From the *Zollverein* to the European Union, Germany has used economic means to escape from the political weakness of the *Mittellage*. Just as Prussia used the *Zollverein* to wriggle out of the constraints imposed by the German Confederation, so the reunited Germany is trying to consolidate her power in the middle of Europe by reinforcing economic integration there. It is no coincidence, given this long economist heritage, that the German-led push for monetary union is based around economic management, and not around explicitly political leadership: Karl Lamers has called monetary union 'the highest and purest form of integration'.[164]

This tradition has had a profound effect on the German conception of the state. Germany has traditionally been an unpolitical country. The sources of national identity in Germany have generally not tended to be political, but rather cultural or economic. When the intellectual movement for German unity got under way in the late eighteenth and early nineteenth centuries, the ideologues of national unity, such as Fichte and Herder, concentrated on the unpolitical phenomena of culture, language and even music as being the definitive marks of the German nation. Statehood was not an appropriate pole around which to unite the German nation, because it represented no reality in German history. In those parts of Germany where the state was strong, the concept of the state was illiberal: in Prussia, for instance, the army was obviously the main reference point. Statehood, inasmuch as it existed, was not identified with a body of law which permitted free action, but rather with a structure of command and obedience.

Later, as Germany industrialised, the economy became a national reference point – the new industrialists produced light-bulbs called Wotan, for instance. A properly *political* identity was still avoided.[165] Similarly, in post-war Germany, the principal national symbol has been the D-Mark. Indeed, the contemporary German unease with the newly reunited nation-state of Germany, and the desire immediately to sublimate that state into Europe, is also symptomatic of this unpolitical German tradition. Furthermore, German citizenship laws are essentially racial – *jus sanguinis* means that you are German if your parents were German – rather than political, as they are in countries with a tradition of *jus solis* like France or Britain, where you are British or French if born in the country. Indeed, the political existence of both France and Britain has always transcended ethnicity: the French are, in reality, many different ethnic groups (Breton Celts, Scandinavian Normans, Germans from Alsace, Flemings, Basques, Provençaux) while the United Kingdom is composed of four nations. In both countries, a member of the nation is a subject (of the law, as of the

Crown) or a citizen. According to German law, by contrast, the German nation is composed of people with blood ties to one another.

At no time in German history have the borders of the German state or states corresponded to the boundaries of the German nation. Either those borders have left Germans outside, or those borders extended well beyond, into foreign territory and including non-Germans. Consequently, German nationalism has never successfully identified itself with the territorially defined concept of the nation-state after the liberal-national movement failed to unite Germany in 1848.

Instead, the old medieval dream of a universal empire has never quite left the Germans' fantasy. This is why modern Euro-federalists evoke Charlemagne: the Holy Roman Empire was the very archetype of universal monarchy. (Charlemagne's empire was also very highly regulated: 'in capitulary after capitulary, Charlemagne and his successors laid down detailed regulations for every aspect of economic, political and religious life throughout the empire'.[166]) Germany's fluid frontiers; the special role of the Holy Roman Emperor as the secular half of a bicephalous universal empire; the country's tardiness or even failure to achieve political existence as a nation; the unpolitical mentality which accompanied this – all these encouraged the Germans to think of their country as an embodiment of universal sovereignty.

Therefore, it is significant that 'thinking in terms of *Raum*' ('space' or 'area') has become common again in modern German reflection on Europe, albeit in a primarily economic context. It is common to refer to a 'common currency *Raum*', 'the European Economy *Raum*', or to say that 'Germany has now returned to the middle of the whole European economic *Raum*'.[167] It is also common for commentators to dream that the world will be divided up into great economic zones (usually USA, a D-Mark-dominated Europe and a yen-dominated Far East). 'Hence,' it was argued in one such case, 'Germany will become one of the world's power-centres.'[168] The most striking example of *Raum* thinking is Hans-Dietrich Genscher's map of Europe, reproduced overleaf, which hubristically re-draws the frontiers of Europe along supposedly

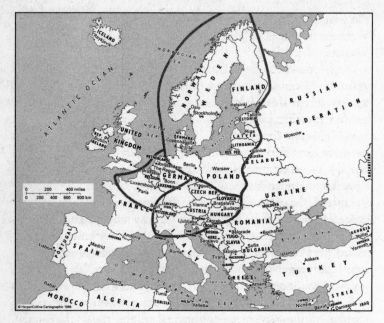

Europe according to Hans-Dietrich Genscher, the former German
foreign minister.

economic lines. In fact, this kind of 'economic' *Raum* thinking is
quite obviously bunk: why exclude Britain and yet include Poland,
Königsberg/Kaliningrad and the Baltic States, for instance? The
only explanation is that it owes more to political design and imperial nostalgia than to anything remotely approaching analysis of the
realities of economic interaction. Although 'divided' between zones,
Genscher's Germany is the nodal point of the entire continent's
economy.

Some historians of German thought have argued that this kind
of thinking, and especially the German dream of universal sovereignty, is the key to German aggression in two world wars.[169]
Precisely because the German nation was unified as an *Empire* –
that is, as an entity which has pretensions to universal sovereignty,
and not as a nation-state – the Germans tended to associate the

self-assertion of the state with Messianism and aggression. Thomas Mann, who supported German expansionism in the First World War, identified the German push for *Weltpolitik* (the desire to assume a world role) with the philosophical school of idealism, which, predominant in Germany, believes that the only reality is universal. 'The world people of the mind,' he wrote, '. . . wanted to become a world people . . . *the* world people of reality.'[170]

Certainly, he then added '. . . if necessary by means of a violent breakthrough'. That is certainly not on the cards now. But, as this chapter has sought to show, it is a false dichotomy between a 'European Germany' on the one hand and a 'German Europe' on the other. It is a false dichotomy because German interests are realised precisely by making other states abandon their nation-hood, and adopting the unpolitical, German, administrative model instead. For just as Germany has traditionally sought to assert her power by economic means, against the political attempts to dilute it by France and other states, so the construc-tion of a supranational Europe implies the abolition of the one thing which has traditionally counter-balanced German power – politics.

Germany thus has every interest in the dismantling of Europe's political structures and their replacement by economic ones. The German nation can exist – indeed usually has existed – without a state. The dislocation of statehood would not prevent the Germans from weighing heavily on European economic policy-making. By contrast, the French, British and other nations would not exist unless constituted in a state, because they are political nations. A 'post-national' Europe would therefore be a German Europe, in which Germany would dominate Europe by *principle* as much as by size.[171]

In pursuing her own perceived interests, the German govern-ment is behaving just like the government of any other state. Indeed, it is strange to claim, as defenders of Germany's European policy implicitly do, that she is unique in acting for altruistic motives alone – as if the Germans were somehow different from everyone else after all. Being normal, legitimate practice, there is absolutely nothing wrong with them behaving in this way. The danger is rather that when Germans say that the concept of national sovereignty is an empty shell, that the balance of power should be abandoned, and that borders are irrelevant, they are in fact propagating an old, and not necessarily liberal, German dream – while pretending, or deluding themselves, otherwise.

Prudence and Fortitude, among others, are the courtiers of The Common Good in Lorenzetti's *Allegory of Good Government*. Beneath them are cavaliers, soldiers, and a line of citizens in concord.

IV

THE EUROPEAN IDEOLOGY

'We, on our parts, have learned to speak only the primitive language of the law, and not the confusing jargon of their Babylonian pulpits'
EDMUND BURKE, *REFLECTIONS ON THE REVOLUTION IN FRANCE*

Two central themes emerge from the previous chapters, which have analysed wartime European propaganda and the history of Germany's place in Europe. The first is hostility towards the concepts of sovereignty and the nation-state. The second is what one might call 'economism', that is, the view that politics consists essentially of the administration of the economy and society.

These two themes are deeply connected. As has been seen, it is one of the principal arguments of the contemporary European ideology that sovereignty and the nation-state are anachronistic concepts. It is also commonplace to argue that modern Europe co-operates, while states in previous centuries were determined to live in autarky and isolation from one another because they thought of themselves as sovereign.

Because the 'absolute power' of individual states is anachronistic nonsense, goes the argument, the future belongs to great geo-economic ensembles. A German central banker has argued that 'a multiplicity of small states [*Kleinstaaterei*] is not suitable for the world economy of today'.[1] Individual states are said to be no longer able to run their affairs 'in isolation', and therefore they must band together in order to become more powerful and more 'sovereign'. Technology, air transport, the money markets, the globalisation of trade, and the development of mass communications are usually adduced as reasons why states can no longer live in autarky – which, according to the European ideology, is what sovereignty is.

Some even argue that the state itself is an anachronistic concept, outdated in an economically interdependent world, where the power of markets appears greater than that of individual states themselves. They are joined by those, like Kenichi Ohmae, who, fascinated with the power of multinational companies, write of the 'region-state' replacing the nation-state, as the economies of 'regions' become more integrated.[2] Others claim that multinational companies are now richer and more powerful than states, and that they will therefore replace them as the primary human groupings. There is, then, a strange political alliance between antinational free marketeers (people one might call liberal technocrats) and plannificatory *dirigistes* on this score: both find national sovereignty inexplicable and irrelevant. Some sections of big business share this view.

These beliefs are held by one-worldists and European federalists alike. Both camps are in fact in alliance against the nation-state. To be sure, few European federalists say that they want to get rid of the nation-state altogether. In fact, however, all their theories display an ignorance of its political *raison d'être*. They always claim that supranational government is compatible with national identity, or even that it ensures the continued existence of nations, because they are not capable of solving their 'existential problems' alone.[3] At the same time, they often dismiss the very concept of sovereignty as incomprehensible – Wolfgang Schäuble has rejected the 'academic debate over whether Europe is a federation or an alliance of states', for instance[4] – and display an economist or unpolitical concept of nationhood which grants nations everything except political independence.

The German federal system is an important model for such people. In their parlance, Germany is a 'post-national state'. It is said to be modern and laudable precisely because it has evacuated the question of sovereignty (which they consider unanswerable and even unintelligible) by ensuring the diffusion of power at different levels. (It is curious that European federalists never refer to the American model, where the separation of powers is much stronger. It is also curious that the Germans themselves tend to be less dismissive of their own sovereignty when it comes to things they really care about, like the removal of Soviet troops from their territory, or the transformation of the D-Mark into the Euro.) This clever German way of ensuring permanent harmony and consensus, it is argued, has resolved both Germany's domestic and international problems: her peaceful nature, indeed, is said to rest on the dilution of centralised power within the country and, internationally, on her institutionalised political interdependence with other states. As such, Germany is said to be a model for Europe and the world.

At bottom, this attitude aims to abolish political life completely. This is why the European construction is so fundamentally undemocratic. For the 'war' which pro-Europeans say they want to eradicate is not just military combat. As the foreign policy spokesman of the CDU/CSU parliamentary group, Karl Lamers, has made clear, European integration is intended to overcome all forms of rivalry between nations: 'If the great nations of Europe,' he said, 'do not develop a system which institutionally excludes war, then they will perhaps wage different kinds of wars from those they have waged in the past.'[5] Ultimately, however, this means overcoming human action altogether.

Both Mr Lamers and his boss, Chancellor Kohl, speak as disciples of Clausewitz when they equate free nationhood with war. If war is the continuation of politics by other means, then the only way to eradicate war – whether by 'war' one means military combat or economic competition – is to eradicate politics itself. In reality, of course, Clausewitz was wrong: war is not the continuation of politics, but rather the consequence of its utter failure.

Yet the view that war is inevitable for as long as Europe is structured on the basis of free nation-states, and for as long as those nations compete with one another, is an old German view, as we saw in the previous chapter. The German Chancellor in the First

World War, Theobald von Bethmann-Hollweg, used the argument to excuse his own country's responsibility for starting it: 'The imperialism, nationalism and economic materialism, which during the last generation determined the outlines of every nation's policy, set goals which could only be pursued at the cost of a general conflagration.'[6] Like all other theories of historical inevitability, this one has the advantage of exculpating the real authors of political decisions.

The desire to overcome politics is based on the assumption that, if not subject to structures imposed from on high, free human action – whether in international affairs or domestic politics – is unstable and dangerous. People who think in this way cannot conceive of there being an order which they have not consciously designed: they cannot imagine that people and states themselves might be able to develop rules, perhaps unspoken ones, to foster peaceful free commerce. Politics, the very quintessence of such free human action, is perceived as a threat – and the only antidote to this, the very buzz of human life itself, is to drug people with the soporific certainties of anonymous economic planning instead.

This is why this hostility to sovereignty and the state is destructive of democracy and the rule of law. This does not mean that no supporter of the European ideology is liberal in the broad sense. It means, instead, that the arguments between a supporter of the European ideology and an opponent of it are not arguments about different foreign policy options or economic priorities, but rather very profound disagreements between two different notions of the role of the state and law. As with many such disputes, the argument is often between people who care about something, and those who are ignorant of its importance. If one does not have a liberal heritage, it is easy to slip into illiberal positions without realising it, because many of our political choices and reactions are determined by instinct or habit and not by conscious reflection. As Churchill once said, 'We fashion our institutions, and our institutions fashion us.' To allow an entire super-state to be built on illiberal foundations is likely to only further entrench and amplify that heritage.

Democracy eclipsed by economism

> *'Liberalism has been, and still is, the major source of the*
> *Community's weakness'*
> FRENCH TEXTBOOK ON THE EUROPEAN UNION[7]

The unpolitical nature of the process of European integration
belongs to its very roots. From its inception Europe has been an
economic community. Coal and steel, atomic energy, agriculture,
the common market, the single currency – these have been the
building blocks of the European construction to date. Meanwhile,
the properly political elements of European integration remain
weak. What integrationists call 'political union' is little more than
the harmonisation of tax and fiscal policy, and perhaps the centralisation of foreign and defence decision-making by heads of
state and foreign ministers of the member states. 'Political union'
is not the explicit creation of a European government or of a
European state – even if this is what it will in fact become. On the
contrary, the true political nature of what is proposed is generally
disguised as increased co-operation or integration between
member states.

This dissimulation is partly a consequence of the bureaucratic
and unpolitical drift which afflicts all modern European politics at
both national and international level. It also is the result of the
original intention of the founding fathers of the European Union,
especially Jean Monnet, which was to bypass all potential political
obstacles to their plans for integration by creating institutions of
an apparently technical nature.

It is precisely for this reason that none of the institutions of the
European Community are democratic. They were never supposed
to be. Instead, they were supposed to make executive decision-
making easier, a goal which has traditionally been achieved by
conferring that decision-making to unaccountable and unelected
institutions. Indeed, Europe's hybrid constitutional nature (partly
intergovernmental, partly federal) causes all the institutions of
the European Union to favour executive and technical power over
legislative.

This is clearest in the supreme legislative organ, the Council of Ministers. The Council, which meets and votes in secret, is composed of ministers from the member states. This is about as thorough a confusion between the executive and the legislature as one can imagine: by allowing the governments of Europe's member states to transform themselves – as if with a wave of a constitutional wand – from members of executives into legislators, they can pass laws without having to submit to the bother or indignity of parliamentary questioning, let alone approval. No doubt this explains the great popularity of the European Community among the governments of the member states.

The Council is responsible to no parliament or electorate. Its members, the national ministers, are generally – but not necessarily – elected. But as a body, the Council is certainly neither elected nor accountable. Individually, individual ministers are theoretically accountable to their national parliaments and electorates; in practice, this amounts to nothing, because when votes are taken by majority, the link between national parliaments and ministers is irretrievably cut. A minister can claim that he was outvoted if a law is passed to which his national parliament was opposed. Because of the well-established principle that Community law overrides national law, there is nothing a national parliament can do in such cases.

Even in the rare cases where national parliaments take an interest in European legislation while it is in preparation – many parliaments, such as the French one, are not even consulted about European legislation while it is being drawn up – and even in the single case (Denmark) where the parliament actually gives ministers a defined negotiating mandate, the ultimate power of a national parliament to say yes or no to a measure is nil. The Council of Ministers is about as perfect an example of discretionary power as one can imagine: controlled by no one, it is accountable to no one.

Moreover, 80 per cent of the decisions taken by the Council are in fact prepared by their officials during negotiations prior to the actual meetings between the ministers. This accentuates the executive or *dirigiste* flavour of much European legislation. A convoluted and largely undisclosed process of bureaucratic dialogue between national and European bureaucracies is thus the principal source of European decisions, which emanate from the Council like the smoke from the conclave of cardinals electing a new Pope.

Procedures of this kind may be defensible for achieving technical and well-defined goals, such as the realisation of the single market, because the Council can be said to be exercising legislative authority by delegation from the national parliaments. They, the holders of democratic legitimacy, allow the Council to make laws in their place, on the basis that this is a better way to achieve such agreed goals than acting separately. However, such methods are obviously unacceptable as a constitutional model for general policy-making. They would certainly be completely anti-democratic if the power exercised by the Council came to be considered autochthonous – that is, not enjoyed by delegation from parliaments, but in its own right – or if the definition of the goals to be achieved were elastic. This will be the case with the Common Foreign and Security Policy, whose broad and varying aims are to be decided by majority vote.

Although the Council exercises supreme legislative power, the Commission is *de facto* the most powerful institution of the EU. It is composed of civil servants – that is, of unaccountable and unelected officials. Its role is to implement the policy guidelines laid down in the treaties, as agreed by governments. As the neutral guardian of the treaties, it enjoys constitutional independence from governments. Because the actual membership of the Council varies (different Ministers attend it according to the matter in hand: agriculture ministers for the Agriculture Council, Finance Ministers for the Economic and Financial Council, and so on), the Commission's power of influence is proportionally very great. Not only is it there permanently, but it also has a good deal of moral clout as the representative of the common interest. Its preponderance adds to the EU's well-known bureaucratic culture.

The last window on democracy will be closed if a monetary union is created, managed by an independent central bank. Then, all the levers of power will be in the hands of unaccountable and unelected bodies. The Bank, the Commission and the Council will share power between themselves, but none of the three will enjoy a democratic mandate, nor be accountable to any institution or electorate. Those who suggest that the European parliament can fill this gap, by one day becoming the parliament of the entire continent, are only displaying an embarrassing ignorance of what a parliament should be.

This means that the European monetary union will be unlike any other kind of political association. It will be a union of states which may retain their formal sovereignty, but all of whose essential political powers will be exercised by institutions over which their peoples have no control. The independent central bank will run monetary policy, the most important discretionary state power. The Council of Ministers (or the Stability Council, a body proposed by the Germans and since accepted by the Commission, which is supposed to unite the member states of the monetary union) will try to harmonise fiscal and budgetary policy in the name of that most unpolitical of things, monetary stability. There will be no 'European people' in whose name these powers are exercised. National governments will be technically responsible, but, when pressed on any policy, will invoke Europe as the reason why it is being undertaken.

Above all, it is the economist or unpolitical assumptions underlying the European construction which threaten democracy and the rule of law. It is widely assumed in Europe (and not just at a European level) that politics is simply the administration of the economy, and that it is sufficient to do this well, even in the absence of democracy. The European ideology, indeed, has not suddenly sprung into being. It is, on the contrary, the natural continuation of many trends which are alive and well in the member states of the European Union, where corporatism and *dirigisme* are the norm.

To holders of such views, statehood and the activity of politics appear messy and illogical. Far better, it seems, to organise the world rationally, to overcome division and squabbling, and to put in place politico-economic systems which encourage harmony rather than conflict. Many Europeans believe that such pan-Continental economic administration (what Jacques Delors and his supporters warmly call 'the economic government of Europe') can be pursued without thinking about – or in deliberate opposition to – the concepts of statehood and sovereignty.

But to ignore such concepts is to risk undertaking what are in fact political tasks in an unpolitical fashion. For example, European monetary union, if it occurs, will be completely different from the German monetary union between East and West Germany, where the former adopted the currency of the latter, and from which the European project draws some inspiration. That union was a political undertaking, honestly and publicly advanced as such, with a clear political aim: the complete political absorption, six months later, of East Germany into the Federal Republic. This implied the formal and real disappearance of the German Democratic Republic as a sovereign state, and the extension of the sovereignty of the Federal Republic to the territory it occupied.

No such clearly affirmed political plan is being advanced for European monetary union. By contrast, the intention is to occult what is in fact a process of political unification behind the smoke-screen of economic technicalities. There is no clearly proclaimed attempt to create a sovereign European state, even if this is what the likely effect of monetary union will be. Europe has, rather, a series of politicians who seem seldom to act with clearly stated political aims, and whose discourse resembles that of the accountant rather than that of the statesman. But to debase sovereignty is to debase statehood; and to debase statehood is to attack the very foundations of democracy and the rule of law themselves.

1. Sovereignty, legal personality, and the right to rule

> 'The idea of an inalienable sovereignty of the nation-state still carries weight, even though this sovereignty has long since become an empty shell'
>
> 'REFLECTIONS ON EUROPEAN POLICY', CDU/CSU
> PARLIAMENTARY GROUP, SEPTEMBER 1994

It is amusing that European ideologues have some difficulty locating the concept of national sovereignty in time, even though they seem to know that it is outdated. The Germans usually say 'nineteenth century', by which they presumably wish to evoke the century in which their own nation was unified, and which culminated in the rivalry and bloodshed of the First World War. Others say 'late eighteenth century', by which they presumably mean the French Revolution, which, among other things, proclaimed the sovereignty of the people.

Both dates are wrong: the concepts of sovereignty and nationhood are eternal. There are references to 'nations' as early as the Book of Genesis.[8] The power of the state is accepted as legitimate by both Christ and St Paul in the New Testament,[9] as well as by Church Fathers such as St Augustine.[10] The question of the absolute authority of the prince (especially the paradox that he was both the source of law and bound to God's law) animated centuries of medieval political thought.[11] Indeed, the modern formulation of the concept of state sovereignty dates from neither the nineteenth nor the eighteenth century: it is usually attributed to Jean Bodin's *Six Livres de la République* (1576), and to Thomas Hobbes' works *The Elements of Law* (1640), *De Cive* (1642) and *Leviathan* (1651).

The dates of the modern formulation of the theory are no coincidence. Although questions about government and sovereignty are as old as human civilisation itself, the suggestion that ultimate civil authority resides with the institutions of the nation-state is a modern, secular doctrine. It was formulated precisely to fill the gap left by the decisive decline of the idea that the source of political authority was God or the Church. This fact alone shows that the concept of sovereignty and that of democracy are profoundly linked.

Legal and political authority (which is sometimes referred to as 'power') are exercised in a state according to certain rules.[12] Even in a dictatorship, where power is exercised without reference to the rules of justice, there are rules which enable people to distinguish officers of the state from other citizens. A criminal thug who works for the secret police can be politically (if not morally) distinguished from a criminal thug who does not.

In most states, the fabric of rules which govern the exercise of legal and political authority is very complex. For any governmental action or legal ruling, there is a web of legal and constitutional relationships and rules which will determine whether this officer of the state, or that judge or court, has the right to take this decision or make that ruling. These justifications constitute the hierarchy of legal reasoning. We can ask, for instance, 'Why do European Community laws take precedence in British courts over national laws?' and the answer will be, 'Because the act of accession to the EC [the European Communities Act of 1972] implies acceptance of the EC's legal order, in which Community law takes precedence over national law.'

But at some point legal reasoning will stop and give way to a meta-legal fact. Such interwoven legal justifications, however complex, ultimately rest on a simple non-legal, political fact: the rule that courts should obey Parliament is, quite simply, the ultimate political fact on which the whole system of legislation hangs.[13] This is a statement about political authority. The body of rules which explains both the fabric of legal reasoning, and the ultimate political authority on which it rests, is called 'a constitution'.

As Noel Malcolm has so cogently shown, a constitution is the total body of rules governing the exercise of political authority in a legal order. The constitutions of some states (federated states, for instance) are subordinate to others. If the constitution of a state traces the ultimate source of political authority to somewhere outside itself, then that constitution is not independent and the state is not sovereign. If the people ruled accept that their state is subject to a higher political authority, then they recognise the higher authority as their sovereign. If, on the other hand, they do not accept it, then they will want to secede, which means declaring that they do not accept the higher authority. They will want to break the legal order in which they find themselves, so that in future the highest authority will lie within their own state. Then, their constitution will be autochthonous – that is, if the rules for the exercise of political authority will not include legal and political subjection to another power. Sovereignty, indeed, is constitutional independence.[14]

In other words, the overall validity of an independent constitution depends on politics, not law. Without political authority, a
structure of rules and legal order is a formal skeleton with no life in
it.[15] If the nature and source of that legal authority changes, such
as after a revolution, then the old legal order will be abandoned in
favour of a new one: legal authority has to be validated by the new
political authority. Political authority is simply the right to rule
which is recognised by the people who are subject to it, that is, the
citizens of the state. Political authority can be obtained by force, as
in a dictatorship, or by consent, as in a democracy: but unless it is
there, there will be no state, only anarchy. As such, just as political authority is the basis or necessary condition of sovereignty, so
sovereignty is itself the basis of civil law.

Sovereignty, therefore, belongs to all independent states. Its
quality is the same in all. It is false to claim, as many supporters of
the European ideology do, that federal states have a different kind
of sovereignty from unitary ones, or no sovereignty at all. The
sovereignty of a federal state like Germany is the same as that of a
unitary state like Britain. The rules for the exercise of political
authority may be different, but the constitutions of both kinds of
state are equally autochthonous. Sovereignty is absolute: either
you have it or you do not. As the great jurist H. L. A. Hart has
written:

> The theory [of sovereignty] does not merely state that there
> are *some* societies where a sovereign subject to no legal
> limits is to be found, but that everywhere the existence of
> law implies the existence of such a sovereign. On the other
> hand, the theory does not insist that there are no limits on
> the sovereign's power but only that there are no *legal* limits
> on it. So the sovereign may in fact defer, in exercising
> legislative power, to popular opinion either from fear of the
> consequences of flouting it, or because he thinks himself
> morally bound to respect it. Very many factors may
> influence him in this . . . and he may think and speak of
> these factors as 'limits' on his power. But they are not legal
> limits.[16]

This is why a constitution is essential to be able to answer the fundamental question of all politics, 'Who has the right to rule?' It answers that question by explaining by what rules political authority is exercised, and by whom. Without knowing where the buck stops, the question of the right to rule cannot be addressed. And without a distinction between power and authority, we cannot conceive of any of the most fundamental elements which make up human civilisation: the notions of contract, of crime, of legitimacy, of rights and duties. Expressions like 'legitimate government', 'usurper', 'coup d'état', 'government-in-exile' could not be explained.

Sovereignty, indeed, is a matter of authority, not power. The confusion between these two concepts lies at the very heart of the claim that nation-states, being weak, are no longer 'sovereign'. Even if it were true that nation-states could accomplish little on their own (a highly questionable claim) they would not necessarily not be sovereign. Their peoples and parliaments could still decide what to do in given situations, taking their weakness into account. To say that a state is not sovereign if it is weak – and, by extension, to imply that powerful states are more sovereign than weak ones – is to obscure the central function of law, which is to put the weak and the strong on an equal footing.

It is a primary principle of Western jurisprudence that legal rulings must explicitly state the source of their legitimacy – the precedents in common law, the statutes, the constitutional provisions. To abolish, whether explicitly or implicitly, all differences between authority and power – by saying that sovereignty is a meaningless or 'academic' concept, for instance – is to eradicate the distinction between lawful and illegal behaviour, and to reduce all human relations (and inter-state ones) to power relationships. As we shall see, people who do this do so because they think that government is purely a matter of using power scientifically to plan economic activity. Questions of right and authority do not enter into their equations. The idea, implicit in the European ideology, that notions of authority and right are irrelevant, thus risks tearing the heart out of legal systems.

This is why it is absurd to say that sovereignty is an anachronistic concept. Sovereignty never means 'total power', which is a nonsensical concept anyway. Neither of the great authors of the modern theory of state sovereignty, Jean Bodin or Thomas Hobbes, ever thought sovereignty meant total power. Bodin wrote of 'absolute' or 'sovereign' power ('*puissance*'), not of absolute force, and it is difficult to think of any serious political philosopher who would have made such a mistake. Instead, what they were describing was the source of ultimate political authority. Bodin was especially clear in stating that the sovereignty he attributed to the Republic established its independence from other states precisely because that sovereignty was itself based on the maintenance of a distinct system of domestic law.

Subsidiarity

These reflections should also make it clear that talk about 'centralisation' and 'decentralisation' is an irrelevant side-issue in the European debate. It is little more than an attempt to avoid the most important issue. The question is not at what level power is exercised, but *by what authority*. A state can be centralised and legitimate or decentralised and illegitimate: the level at which powers are to be exercised can be decided only when the overall constitution enjoys political authority.

In the European Union, the question of centralisation is usually discussed in terms of 'subsidiarity'. This principle, which is also enshrined in the German constitution, is supposed to ensure that a 'higher' level of government acts only when its action will be more 'effective' than a 'lower' level. There are many things wrong with this doctrine – quite apart from the fact that the obligation in Article C of the Treaty on European Union to respect in full the *acquis communautaire* (the accumulated body of policies which have been transferred to EU level) renders any true decentralisation impossible. Indeed, the German constitution has become increasingly centralised as a result of its subsidiarity clause.

The notion that government should be based on 'effectiveness' presupposes that the principal activity of the state is to do things. Obviously, governments must be able to act; but the liberal tradition also emphasises the role of government in concentrating mainly on maintaining intact the rule of law and the principles of justice, and adapting them to the daily shift and change of human circumstance, thus allowing people to do things for themselves. Subsidiarity, with its assumption of a unitarian, pyramidal hierarchy of executive functions, is based on a model which is at variance with that of a justice-based liberal legal order.

It is no coincidence if subsidiarity is a corporatist doctrine, elaborated by the Vatican in Rome in the heady days of Italian Fascism, and within two years of the Lateran accords which reconciled the Holy See and the fascist state. Indeed, the most charitable thing one can say about the Church's espousal of the doctrine in the Papal encyclical *Quadragesimo Anno* (1931), with all its corporatist implications, is that 'the Church was blind to the profound logic of the link between corporatism and fascism'.[17] But, given the benefit of hindsight which the Pope did not have in 1931, it is perhaps more difficult to make the same concession to modern Christian Democrats who still embrace the doctrine.

Moreover, 'centralisation' is not necessarily always bad. On the contrary, the centralisation of legislative authority and law is a prerequisite for democracy, to the extent that legislative decentralisation allows local potentates to establish political fiefdoms of their own. Just as the people traditionally looked to the king to mitigate the power of local nobles – and thus to overcome the constraints of feudalism – so democrats look to legal equality for all as the necessary condition for freedom. Decentralisation tends to be favoured in countries, like Germany, where the feudal model is still strong, for there politics is associated mainly with distributing state money – the exchange of allegiance for patronage – rather than with establishing the conditions for the free interaction of responsible citizens.

Sovereignty and the European Union

In the case of Europe, legal authority already resides at the European level in many areas. European Community law takes automatic precedence over national law, and member states are required to change their own laws if they are in conflict with those of Europe.

This absolute supremacy of European law over national law, and even over national constitutions, which was never laid down in any of the original treaties, was introduced by a series of highly questionable rulings of the European Court of Justice in Luxembourg in the 1960s and early 1970s. The Court adopted a 'dynamic' approach to EC law: it saw itself as an important 'motor' of European integration, charged with the task of pushing it forward. This is quite incompatible with the role of judges as it is understood in most legal systems, where they are supposed to apply the law rather than invent it. These claims to legal supremacy were challenged by the ruling of the German Constitutional Court in Karlsruhe in 1993, which said that ultimate political and legal authority continued to reside with the member states. It was no doubt in reply to this, and perhaps because of embarrassment that the primacy of EC law had never been ratified by treaty, that a reference to 'the jurisprudence of the ECJ' – and thus endorsement of the primacy of EC law – was surreptitiously introduced into an obscure protocol of the Amsterdam Treaty, signed in June 1997 between the EU heads of state and government. The effect of this protocol, if ratified, will be formally to abrogate the supreme legal authority of the member states, even though neither the electorates nor even the parliaments of those states are aware that they are thereby being asked to sign away their birthright. Although in all EC states – for the time being at least – it is recognised by explicit legal and constitutional reasoning that the EU's (or, more precisely, the European Community's) supreme legal authority derives only from the continuing will of the member states to remain members of the EC – in other words, from the ultimate political authority of the EU's constituent nations – this position, in which power is (formally at least) enjoyed by the EU only as a result of revocable delegation, will be severely undermined, and probably overturned completely, if monetary union is introduced, for by common consent the very purpose of monetary union is to bind together Europe's states in an *irrevocable* fashion.

If the daily exercise of power is transferred to the European Union, this does not of itself mean that the member states have ceased to be sovereign. The member states of the EU will only cease to be sovereign if and when they cease to have political authority as well as legal authority, that is, if their ultimate right to rule ceases to be recognised by their populations and their legal systems. It is conceivable that, on some policy difference or other, a conflict between the rights of the Union and a member state might raise just such a constitutional question. At that point, the outcome of the conflict would determine where ultimate political authority lay. Therefore, either the member states of the European Union will be sovereign or the European Union itself will be. 'Pooling' sovereignty is constitutional nonsense because sovereignty is absolute.

This is why it is wrong to assert that national sovereignty is already constrained by membership of other international organisations such as NATO. Pro-European commentators, mystified at the hang-ups of Euro-sceptics, often write such things as, 'Apart from powers ceded to European institutions, Britain shares sovereignty through membership of the United Nations, NATO and other international organisations. Britain is, after all, obliged to commit its armed forces immediately if any other NATO member is attacked, a far more demanding sharing of sovereignty than anything involved in the EU.'[18]

These arguments, which are unfortunately extremely common, display an ignorance of both constitutional issues and simple matters of fact. Firstly, as will be seen later, membership of treaty organisations in no way requires sovereignty to be 'shared' or diluted. Sovereignty is, on the contrary, the necessary prerequisite for the signing of treaties and for the undertaking of obligations. Secondly, the difference between most treaty organisations and the European Union is that the latter has a federal vocation. It is distinguished from all other international organisations by one fundamental difference: the quality of its law. Whereas under most treaty organisations, it is the states which are the subjects of the rights and duties which flow from them, European Community law applies directly to the *citizens* of the member states. Add to this the scope of EC policies, and the other trappings of proto-statehood such as a common parliament and a common passport, and the result is an embryonic federal union of states whose central provisions are intended to be 'irrevocable' (to quote Maastricht). This is constitutionally utterly different from a classical treaty organisation or alliance between sovereign states. Anyone who denies there is a difference between these two concepts is confused; and anyone who denies that the EU aspires to be the former is dishonest.

Thirdly, the comparison with NATO – a favourite with muddle-headed pro-Europeans – is simply wrong in fact. Unlike the WEU, which has always aspired to be a vehicle for political integration, NATO has always been explicitly based on the sovereignty of its member states. It has never had any pretensions to cover aspects of policy other than defence. The Washington Treaty thus does not and cannot override the sovereignty of its signatories. According to the crucial Article 5, 'each Party will assist that Party or Parties so attacked by taking forthwith . . . *such actions as it deems necessary*, including the use of armed force'.

Concretely, there is no question that NATO could or would prevent a state from carrying out a military operation on its own: the Gulf and Falkland Wars demonstrated this perfectly. By contrast, Europe aspires to have one integrated defence policy (as well as one integrated policy in all other areas too), and several articles and declarations of the Maastricht Treaty already restrict the ability of EU member states to take foreign policy or security action independently of the others. A pro-European commentator emphasises the difference: 'The Atlantic alliance is only a framework within which Member States agree on policies which concern their defence and security obligations under the Treaty of Washington. Meanwhile, the WEU, like the European Union, has the vocation to integrate its members politically.'[19]

Conflicts arise constantly within a state, and they are resolved under the law. But when a fundamental conflict arises about the source of law itself, it can be resolved only by politics or war. Therefore, to construct Europe on the basis that it is irrelevant to ask, 'By what authority are the peoples of Europe governed?' is to dismiss the most important question one can ever ask about a political system. This is not a very solid basis on which to build an entire trans-Continental and trans-national political structure.

Sovereignty and the outside world

These confusions are most evident when people say that states are no longer sovereign because they cannot resist international pressures. For instance, it is argued that France was forced to abandon her Socialist policies in 1983 as a result in the collapse of market confidence in her economy, and that therefore her state sovereignty has no meaning any more.[20] Alternatively, Britain and other European countries are said to have no 'monetary sovereignty', because their monetary policy is constrained by the decisions of the Bundesbank.[21] Or again, it is argued that sovereignty means 'a nation's practical capacity to maximise its influence in the world'[22] – a classic case of a definition cooked up to justify a foregone conclusion. Many say things such as: 'Technological advances in communication and transportation are eroding the boundaries between hitherto separate markets – boundaries which were a necessary condition for independent national economic policies,'[23] and that this is rendering the concept of national sovereignty otiose. Therefore, it is concluded that national political systems must adapt to the international economy, which is already an incontrovertible reality.[24] Because they are no longer very powerful on their own, states had better club together, and 'pool' their sovereignty in order to regain the 'sovereignty' they have lost.

All these arguments share the simple and hubristic false premise that the discretionary power of the government is equivalent to the sovereignty of the state. It is false to say that if a government is constrained to act in a certain way – such as under pressure from international capital flows – then the state is not sovereign. This is because the government and the state are two different things. Sovereignty, as we have seen, is a matter of authority: a constitution describes who is responsible for what. The concept of responsibility is obviously compatible with the fact of constraint:

indeed, it is a prerequisite for it. To equate the power of a state's executive (the government) with that of the state as a whole is to ignore the whole fabric of law which is supposed to ensure that executive power is exercised within certain limits.

States are persons in law. A person is a bearer of rights and duties. An individual's status as a person is not reduced if he or she is influenced by outside events. Persons take decisions, and interact with other persons, based on what has happened around them. The concept of personhood, and the structure of civil law, allows them to do so within a recognised framework. Like sovereignty, in other words, personhood *presupposes* lawful interaction with others. It in no way excludes it. It is as absurd to say that sovereignty means autarky or absolute power as it would be to say that only an individual with 'absolute power' were a person.

Persons are responsible for their actions, and they can thus be subject to rights and duties in law. If a person enters into a contractual obligation with another person, then he or she must accept the rights and duties which flow from that contract. A housewife might go to the market and buy a bag of tomatoes: she has the right to take the tomatoes home and eat them if she accepts her duty to pay for them.

Alternatively, if she tries to spend more money than she has, the bank may withdraw her chequebook, and the vendors may refuse to sell to her on credit. In such a case, the housewife's freedom to act would be reduced, but her personhood would not be. The constraints which burden her now are the result of the duties she assumed when she spent the money. If the bank feels there is no choice but to withdraw a chequebook from a spendthrift housewife, then this is its right in virtue of her decision to borrow more money than allowed. Far from being reduced, her personhood is therefore the very cause of her present predicament. She may plead attenuating circumstances – she has a family to feed – but can only do so within the general logic of personhood, that is, as a bearer of rights and duties. If personhood is not attenuated in such cases of extreme constraint, it is certainly not attenuated in daily commerce.

The relationship between states and the international money

markets is almost identical to that between a housewife and the market she visits. If a state goes into the money markets to borrow money, and later finds that its action is constrained by the way those markets (the states' creditors) judge the value of its debt in the light of the government's policies, then that is merely part of the deal. It no more limits the sovereignty of a state if the government feels constrained to change a policy by the judgement of the money markets, or for any other economic reason, than it affects the freedom and personhood of an individual to have to pay his debts. To say that the modern international economy restricts the liberty of states by being able adversely to judge their policies is like saying that personhood and individual liberty are eradicated by the growth in bank lending and the conditions attached to it. Just as consumer choice (and therefore liberty to buy) is increased in a free market, so the choice of states in general, and their freedom to act, is increased in a free market, not decreased. The French government may have been constrained to abandon its policies in 1983 because of the adverse judgement of the markets; but there are obviously many more examples of governments who have increased their ability to act by borrowing from the money markets more wisely.

Moreover, the market is not something 'out there'. It is, rather, a form of human interaction based on justice and the rule of law which should govern citizens of the state themselves, as well as those outside. The foreign exchange traders who go short on the franc are just as likely to be French as American or British, and if a sovereign state upholds the rule of law then it should accept this contractual censure of its executive actions, from whomever it comes. To say that the markets are wrong to sell francs is tantamount to saying that there can be no higher law than what the French government (the executive) decides. But this is obviously incompatible with any commitment to the rule of law either domestically or internationally. It is a pretty safe bet that governments which blame foreigners in this way would be happy to deny normal contractual rights to their own citizens too.

Ever since the seventeenth century, successive British political philosophers have understood that the role of the state is to uphold the rule of law, and thereby to ensure the free functioning of the market. The market, after all, is nothing but a regime in which free contracts are concluded by individuals within a legal regime which enforces them. It is a creation of law. Because some thinkers, especially Thomas Hobbes, realised the congruence of sovereignty and the market society, they understood that the state's power should be judicial rather than administrative, and that a free society requires a neutral arbiter in order to function. As Hobbes himself wrote, 'And therefore it belongeth to the commonwealth, that is to say, to the sovereign, to appoint in what manner all kinds of contract between subjects as buying, selling, exchanging, borrowing, lending, letting, and taking to hire, are to be made; and by what word and signs they shall be understood for valid.'[25] A sovereign, in other words, is needed to ensure conditions for the respect of contracts: far from being incompatible with the free market, it constitutes it.[26]

This law-based understanding of statehood contrasts with another model, more prevalent in Continental traditions, according to which the state's duty is not so much to uphold the validity of free decisions taken by its citizens (and foreigners), and to enforce the respect of contracts, but rather to direct the economy, much as a feudal lord directs the 'housekeeping' of his estates. According to this view, the state is a self-contained economic 'space'; and if the economy expands beyond the borders of the state, then state (or super-state) control needs to expand with it to master it. (This explains why it is a grave error of judgement to understand the EC as a free trade zone: while trade advantages may flow from membership of it, the EEC and its 'single market' were never intended to be a free trade zone between independent states, but rather an embryonic economic – and hence political – union.) Just as such a view is incompatible with the ensurance of market relations within the borders of the state, so it also presents the free market as a hostile, exterior force. This view is especially pronounced in France.[27]

The market, therefore, does not threaten sovereignty: nor do treaties. Statehood, like personhood, is a prerequisite for contractual and economic interaction under the law. If a state is obliged to follow a certain course because of its treaty arrangements, it cannot be said to be 'not sovereign'.[28] On the contrary, it is only when a state exists as a person in international law – that is, when it is sovereign – that it is free to engage in whatever agreements with the outside world it likes. As with any other agreement, this means that, in certain circumstances, it may be constrained to do this or that. Far from restricting sovereignty, the constraint which flows from a contractual arrangement is the very expression of it.

2. Sovereignty and the nature of law

> *'Justice is the bond of men in states, and the administration of justice, which is the determination of what is just, is the principle of order in political society'*
>
> ARISTOTLE[29]

Sovereignty is, therefore, a prerequisite for constitutionalism. The state enjoys inner and outer sovereign legal authority, which belongs to it absolutely – that is, which is not deduced from any other legal order – and over which it decides for itself. This definition says nothing about the amount or nature of the power sovereign states exercise: it merely helps explain the source of that power, and the conditions for its exercise. A sovereign state can be powerful or weak, rich or poor. The statement that European states can become more powerful by acting together may be true or false: it is doubtless true in many cases, but in the case of Yugoslavia it was manifestly false. But co-operation between states is different from political integration.

A constitution, in other words, is the guarantor of positive law. It does not limit sovereignty any more than a market does – although both may limit the discretionary power of the executive. A constitution merely stipulates (or rather, *is*) the rules for the exercise of executive power and legal authority. It is a great paradox, indeed, that those who equate sovereignty with unfettered executive power generally propose to abolish it, even though, being in fact the definition and even limitation of that power by a

legal order, sovereignty (constitutional independence) is the necessary (if not sufficient) condition for *preventing* the unfettered
exercise of executive power.

However, this paradox is no accident. The European ideology is
based precisely on a belief in the primacy of executive power –
which, as we have seen, has deep roots in the history of post-war
European integration – and on an ignorance of the nature and
importance of law. Or, to be more precise, the view of law implicit
in the European ideology is not a liberal one. This is because con-
stitutionality distinguishes the state from other structures of
command and obedience. The concept of a constitution, in the
most common use of the word, shows that the state is law-based. It
has permanence, as well as other qualities which distinguish it
from other kinds of order or association, while law is different
from a mere command. The view that the state has a role in directing the economy, or the equivalent European view that super-state
structures need to be created to keep up with the globalisation of
the economy – both of which by definition ascribe a *dirigiste* rather
than judicial role to the state – tends to overlook this.

There are theories of law and constitutions which hold that the
role of the state is to direct society by the means of its commands.
They are opposed by theories which argue that law is not the command of the state (nor indeed the command of anybody) but
something more subtle: it is a rule, or a code of behaviour, which
provides a meaningful framework for human action. According to
the latter view, such a code can be generated spontaneously: it can
undergo constant evolution, as a result of that permanent interaction between persons which is the very definition of human life.
As we shall see, each of these views interlocks with its own raft of
different views about the nature of the individual and the role of
the state: we shall also see that the European ideology tends to
support the first view, while traditional liberalism is based on the
latter.

The first view of the state understands laws to be commands.
The influential German positivist philosopher of law, Hans
Kelsen, was one of the principal proponents of this view. He said
that the law was a series of commands backed by threats, and

argued that all law could be interpreted as 'If you do x, then the state will do y.' He held law to be essentially coercive, and called the legal order an apparatus of constraint.[30] 'Law is a particular order or organisation of power,' he wrote.[31] At the basis of all legal hierarchies was a fundamental norm, the state. All individual norms could be deduced from that basic norm, and all legal norms thus had their basis in the constitution, the fundamental act of will which founded the state. The purpose of those norms was to bring about a desired social condition, and jurisdiction was essentially a form of administration. Indeed, Kelsen considered the difference between administration and jurisdiction to be only one of degree.

There are many difficulties with the analogy between a law and a command. Firstly, law is more permanent than a command, which dies with the occasion. The whole enduring character of the law and the constitution – formulated by medieval political thinkers with the well-known rubric 'the king never dies' – cannot be accommodated within the analogy. Secondly, the commander of a group does not give orders equally to the whole group, whereas laws, by contrast, are general and not addressed to anyone in particular.

To explain laws as commands backed by threats also crucially fails to provide any standard by which to distinguish a legal command from an illegal one. Law is 'obeyed' (if this is the right word) out of respect for legitimate authority, not out of simple fear of the consequences. Edmund Burke attacked the positivist notion that laws were merely commands backed by threats, and not an attempt to approximate to absolute notions of Right and Wrong, in a particularly splendid passage. 'On the scheme of this barbarous philosophy,' he argued, 'which is the offspring of cold hearts and muddy understandings . . . laws are to be supported only by their own terrors . . . In the groves of *their* academy, at the end of every vista, you see nothing but the gallows.'[32]

Kelsen's theories, which analyse the legal system of all states as being akin to a pyramid of instructions to the officers of the state to act in certain ways in response to certain situations, end up, like many similar 'scientific' theories, in emptying legal 'commands' of what most ordinary people would think was their definitive ethical-legal content. He holds, for instance, that there are no laws against murder, but only instructions to state officials (policemen, judges, prison keepers) to undertake certain actions (arrest, trial, prison) when a murder has been committed. The command of a policeman is lawful, the command of a bank-robber is lawless, and yet Kelsen uses the latter – the epitome of lawlessness – as an analogy for the former.

The view that law is a command also fails to take account of Natural Justice. The belief in Natural Justice or Natural Law has nourished centuries of traditional thinking about the role of the state, and it is a current of thinking which runs from Aristotle and Cicero through Aquinas to Edmund Burke and John Locke. Although varied, the Natural Law tradition holds that there is a system of law binding on men by virtue of their nature alone, and independently of all convention or positive law. Right and wrong are not expressions of preference or even of the state's say-so; they are rather objective values which exist independently of the state (although they may and even should be upheld by it).

The Austrian economist, philosopher and Nobel prize-winner, Friedrich von Hayek, attacked Kelsen, who excoriated the natural law tradition as unscientific humbug, and claimed that his pure theory of law was responsible for the definite eclipse of all traditions of limited government. He also attacked the statism of philosophers like Kelsen and economists like Knapp in the following terms: 'It was in Germany that the meta-legal principles which underlie the ideal of the rule of law were dismissed first.'[33] Law was confused with mere legality, and the *Rechtsstaat* was hollowed out into a merely formal concept. Illegal or even criminal acts were able to be pursued within the correct procedures of the state.

But just as St Augustine insisted that an unjust law was not a law, so it can be argued that legislative acts need to conform to certain criteria – abstractness, generality, conformity to justice – in order to qualify as laws. To think that a state can be said to observe the rule of law simply because orders (or legislative acts) are obeyed is false if those orders or legislative acts do not qualify as law. The notion of the rule of law therefore involves a definition of law itself.

Modern written constitutions are intended to make precisely this point clear. The 'rights' they enunciate are basically modern substitutes for the ancient concept of the Natural Law, according to which legislative acts, and government in general, was explicitly understood as being subordinate to Natural Right.

Like common law in England, Roman law was based overwhelmingly on jurisprudence, that is, the discovery of what the law is, rather than the invention of it. Common law – which drew largely on the Natural Law school of thought – does not, as is sometimes claimed, consist just of particular cases, but rather of general principles which are illustrated, realised and explained by those cases. Common law is not some valueless pragmatism, but rather a moral tradition which understands that the principles of justice do inhere in real, individual actions. They can therefore be found there, and they do not inhabit some elevated, abstract realm, separate from that of ordinary human behaviour. The classical Roman civil law, on which the great Code of Justinian was based, was almost entirely the product of law-finding by jurists, and only to a very small extent the product of legislation.

In common law, it is a well-established principle that if there is any conflict between the law (whether written or customary) and equity, it is equity which must prevail. To believe that law should conform to some higher standard of morality implies two things. It implies, firstly, that those standards are endangered if law is considered as having an instrumental function: civil law, according to the Natural Law school, has as its primary role the upholding of justice, not the discretionary regulation of society. Secondly, it implies that states should be extremely modest in the amount of legislation they pass: if civil law is an approximation to Natural Justice, then it can be assumed that this is a difficult task which takes time and effort. The Common Law and jurisprudence – the slow, painstaking and practical process by which cases and precedents are amassed in order gradually to suggest general principles – are the right way, from an epistemological point of view, to approach Right and Wrong.

An important conclusion to draw from this is that the much-used constitutional concept 'the sovereignty of Parliament' is misleading. We have already seen that sovereignty is a quality enjoyed by states, not institutions. It is false to say that the British Parliament has some kind of unfettered right to make or break any law: such absolutist behaviour would be contrary to the very legal traditions which the pre-eminence of Parliament over the executive is intended to safeguard.

Excess legislative zeal, therefore, is a danger to traditional liberties and to the rule of law itself. Tacitus, describing the legislative mania under the dictator Sulla, wrote: 'Never were there so many laws as when the state was the most corrupt.'[34] In contrast to such decadence, it was very difficult in the great ancient democracies to change the law: it could be done only through a complicated procedure involving a specially elected body. This in turn was based on the belief in the sacred and timeless origins of law. In the traditional understanding, indeed, law was conceived as being independent of human will, and therefore certainly not produced by it.

But the strongest argument against the view of law as a command is that it obscures the fundamental role of law as constitutive of a free society. One can, indeed, imagine a society run exclusively by the commands of the man at the top, but if this was that society's only 'law', then it would not be what we understand as 'the rule of law'. (It is no coincidence that Kelsen's 'Pure Theory of Law' was intended to apply to legitimate and illegitimate states alike: the theory was developed precisely to include all states and, as such, offers no means by which to distinguish a state of law from a dictatorship.) This is because the analogy between law and command completely fails to take account of any kind of contract law. It thus obscures one of the most important qualities of those parts of the law which do not enjoin any particular act whatever, but which instead give subjects of the law a legal framework within which to increase their powers of free action.

Although criminal law may display some analogies with commands backed by threats, contract law does not require people to act in certain ways. Laws governing contracts, wills, marriages, and so on, do not impose duties or obligations. Instead they provide people with facilities for realising their wishes, by conferring legal powers on them to create, by certain specified procedures, structures of rights and duties within the coercive framework of the law. In a sense, contract law makes individuals into private legislators: by their own free actions, they can create rights and duties.[35]

This power which the law confers on individuals to create their own legal relationships with other individuals is obviously one of the law's greatest contributions to social life. Indeed, it is constitutive of social life. If law did not exist, we would lack some of the most basic concepts of human life: marriage, death and wills, buying and selling, and so on.[36] Therefore, law does not only increase the domain of free action: it actually gives meaning to human life itself by defining and thus realising certain kinds of relationships. (It is significant that Kelsen regarded the difference between 'public' and 'private' law as largely spurious, since he claimed to detect the mere exercise of power in both cases.[37] His theory did not allow people to obey the law because they regard it as sensible or legitimate, but only out of a fear of the external constraint which disobedience would entail.)

To ignore this fundamental element of the law is to see the legal system, and by extension the entire constitutional order, as having a uniquely or mainly commanding or authoritarian function. It is to confine the operation of the law to what happens in a courtroom, or when a policeman gives an instruction, instead of understanding that law permeates the whole fabric of social, political, and thus human life. It also understands citizens not as responsible and free, but as mere recipients of instructions.

But citizens are not mere recipients of commands: they are free agents defined by the common acceptance of the public procedures by which the state is run. To ignore this is to ignore the fact that people act on the basis of their intelligent interpretation of the predicament in which they find themselves. Human actions and conduct are the ways in which people reveal their desires, choice, imagination, understanding and preferences. Likes and dislikes are not 'merely subjective', nor the mere products of determinist 'behaviour': they are an exhibition of intelligence capable of being investigated, explained and interpreted in intelligent terms. It is materialist to understand human behaviour in terms of psychological drives or genetic impulses, or even to assume that people necessarily all 'seek happiness' (as the Utilitarians claimed), for such theories obscure the intelligent nature of human action.

Another crucial element in the view that law is a system of commands is the idea that the commands have a purpose, and that the process of ruling involves determining the overall goals of society, and legislating in such a way as to achieve them. This in turn assumes that the legal system, and the other rule-based relationships which govern human interaction, can or should be directed by those in power. This view is implicit in much of the talk about 'the European construction', the 'European project', and so on.

Such a view has been questioned by many thinkers. Hayek, for instance, drew a famous distinction between '*taxis*' (an order which has been made) and the '*cosmos*' (an order which has grown up). *Taxis* is an association governed by orders which enjoin certain people to do certain things; *cosmos*, by contrast, is constituted of abstract, neutral rules which do not enjoin any action in particular, but which instead specify the terms which facilitate free interaction between individuals or groups. Hayek's paradigm for *cosmos* is the free market: a rule-based system of dispersed knowledge, which no one designed, and in which people can participate without knowing anything about the way the system functions.

Hayek used the distinction to attack what he called 'constructivism', to which he attributed most of the ills of the modern world, especially the rise of socialism and totalitarianism. In this, he greatly resembles Edmund Burke, whose great *Reflections on the Revolution in France* attacked as inhuman the idea that society could be invented and planned on the basis of abstract theory.

The mistake of constructivism is to think that order can exist only if it has been deliberately and consciously planned by someone, and that it can consist only of a structure of command or obedience. This is authoritarian. What Hayek called a 'spontaneous' or 'grown' (self-generated) order can evolve out of individual elements adapting themselves to circumstances which directly affect only some of them. Indeed, the order which grows up in this way is qualitatively different from a 'made' order: a spontaneous order does not have any single common purpose, precisely because it results from individuals interacting on the basis of their divergent needs, in circumstances which directly affect only some of them, and whose totality may not be known to anyone. Because of this, a spontaneous order generally extends to circumstances so complex that no mind can comprehend them all.

The free market, for instance, contains factors and elements of which most people are totally ignorant. If I order a coffee in a restaurant, the price I pay is the consequence of a huge web of nearly infinite economic relationships and variables: the price of coffee, the price of labour in the town, the manufacture of cups and saucers, the cost of land rent, the sugar market, the demand for sitting in bars and drinking coffee. All these factors combine to produce a price, and each of them is in turn affected by incalculable others: coffee and sugar prices by the weather; labour costs by wage policy, educational policy, immigration policy and demography, and so on. To describe all these relationships exhaustively might be actually impossible: it is certainly way beyond the ken of the man who orders the coffee. As a participant in the market, therefore, he is making use of a body of dispersed knowledge of which no one has mastery.

Among other things, this means that it is more difficult for any single person to gain control over an extended and more complex order than over a made order. Only in the most simple organisations is it conceivable that the details of all activities can be governed by a single mind. Although Hayek used the free market as a paradigm, he thought that law and civilisation were analogous to it. One of his central arguments against *dirigiste* state action in whatever domain, therefore, was that it was simply impossible to *know* what the outcome of a particular piece of interventionism would be: society was just too complex to be run by the government. It needs the subtlety of the law instead.

It is because society has not grown up as the result of deliberate design that its structures have attained a degree of complexity which far exceeds anything which could have been achieved by deliberate organisation. Therefore, the right way to reform society is to enforce and improve the rules conducive to its preservation. Because it is intellectually presumptuous – not to say megalomaniac – to believe that one man could devise a whole system of such rules, a ruler must act with prudence and modesty when he decides to change them.

Therefore, to maintain that we must deliberately plan modern society because it has become too complex – as many supporters of the European ideology, such as Jacques Delors, claim – is paradoxical and potentially destructive. If the myriad free interaction of intelligent individuals has generated rules, the imposition of new rules is always in danger of upsetting the spontaneous order and, thus, freedom and civilisation itself. Hayek writes, 'It was not through direction by rulers but through the development of customs on which expectations of the individuals could be based, that general rules of conduct came to be accepted.'[38]

So long as people act in accordance with rules, it is not necessary that they be consciously aware of them. Laws can be obeyed and can be said to exist even if they are not explicit. Most of us cannot give an accurate account of the grammar rules which govern our own language, even if we speak it correctly. Indeed, rules are often more general and abstract than anything that language can express. This is because such abstract rules are learned by imitating particular actions. By analogy, the individual acquires the capacity to act in other cases on the same principles without necessarily being able to state those principles. Something of the kind of knowledge described here is expressed by the French verb '*connaître*' (to know a person) as opposed to '*savoir*' (to know a fact). Moreover, in the kind of free society with which we are familiar, only some of the rules which people in fact observe, namely some of the rules of law, will be the product of human design. Many of the rules of morals and custom will have grown spontaneously.

The Cambridge philosopher Michael Oakeshott argued that when we recognise the authority of a language, a morality, or law, we subscribe to the intimations of virtue which those practices contain. We subscribe to the values within the language, and if we act with virtue or honour or integrity, it is not with respect to certain outcomes that these qualities can be recognised, but rather to the quality of the acts themselves. Like other languages, the language of morals is not a creation of grammarians, but of speakers. General principles and rules may be elicited from a practice, but they are not generated by prior thought. Practices of this kind do not specify certain acts; instead they intimate considerations to be subscribed in making choices. In other words, language, morality and common law presuppose intelligent free agents.

A practice of this kind is 'social' insofar as agents are connected with one another in terms of their understanding and enjoyment of specific practices. A practice is not only an art in terms of which an agent, having learned it, may reveal himself, it is also a procedure in which agents may be durably associated with one another while pursuing their own intelligently conceived purposes. The clearest example of this is a common language, but morality and common law unite people in their individual pursuits in a manner which is analogous to the speaking of a language.

As Oakeshott says: 'The conditions which specify practices may be said to be the "constitutions" of those numberless associations in which the conduct of agents declares its "social" character. Every such association is a *societas* of agents joined, not in seeking a common substantive satisfaction, but in virtue of their understanding and acknowledgement of the conditions, of the practice concerned and the relationship it entails.'[39] Later he goes on, '*Cives* [that is, the members of a civil association] are not neurophysiological organisms, genetic characters, psychological egos or components of a social process, but free agents whose responses to one another's actions and utterances is one of understanding; and civil association is not organic, evolutionary, teleological, functional or syndromic relationship, but an understood relationship of intelligent agents.'[40]

By contrast, certain types of association exist for the fulfilment of certain goals. One joins a political party or a commercial enterprise for purposes other than the membership itself. The nature of this kind of relationship, and of the rules which govern it, is quite different from those of civil association. For one thing, membership of an enterprise association is chosen, while membership of a civil association is not necessarily chosen. (Many practices, such as the speaking of a mother tongue, are not chosen at all.) Enterprise association is not only association in terms of a common purpose, it is association in terms of the management of the pursuit of that purpose, because membership of it assumes submission to the ongoing right of the association to decide to do this rather than that in response to a specific circumstance and with the common goal in mind. Enterprise association is thus a managerial engagement.

To be associated in terms of a practice (for example a language or a state) is precisely not to be associated in the reciprocal satisfaction of wants or in making or acknowledging 'managerial' decisions in pursuit of common purposes. Citizens are not partners or colleagues in an enterprise with a common purpose to pursue or a common interest to protect. As Oakeshott insisted, the conditions of civil association are moral considerations precisely because they are not instrumental to the satisfaction of substantive wants.

The following very common sentiment is thus inadmissible from a liberal point of view: 'In order for monetary union to be able to start with confidence in its stability, the Intergovernmental Conference must bring concrete and palpable progress for ordinary people. I am thinking for example of the effective fight against organised crime by a European police force, a single set of rules for asylum and immigration policy, and the capacity to speak with one voice in common foreign and defence policy.'[41] As the above arguments about the nature of civil association show, this kind of justification of the state's existence (or, in this case, of Europe's) in terms of the promotion of extraneous goals implies equating statehood with enterprise association. But in the liberal view, a constitution has authority if citizens' acceptance of that constitution is not a matter of satisfaction with the outcomes of executive actions taken by the government, but rather a matter of support for the public procedures by which general laws are made for the state, and particular cases adjudicated. This support persists even if the outcomes themselves are contested. We respect the will of parliament, or the ruling of a judge, even if we do not agree with it.

Here, at the very heart of civil association, therefore, it is important to be clear about the nature of legal decisions. The decisions of a court are judicial, not managerial. Its adjudication is concerned with the *meaning* of law in a given situation. The law must, in order to be law, be blind to the substantive outcome or consequence of this or that decision. It would be illegal for a judge to rule because he intended this or that outcome. Politics, like law, is predicated on conflict, for without conflict there would be no politics or law, only management. Similarly, legislation should be concerned with the desirable composition of a system of moral, not instrumental considerations. This is because law is to be understood not as instructions issued to the citizens of a state in pursuit of certain aims, but rather as a language in which citizens understand themselves and resolve their conflicts.[42] This means that it is wrong to understand the state of law as Kelsen did, that is, as a system of commands addressed to the citizens or to the officials of the state. Law is simply not a system of commands from a Chief to his Indians: it is rather a language of civil conduct.

Because civil association is intelligent, rule-based association, it should take note of pre-existing political realities. State structures should be adapted to the common historical and cultural experience of the people they govern, and will usually be determined by those factors; the regions or communities within that state will similarly reflect historical contingency; the law of the state will uphold the values in which people believe. Democracy is, therefore, inherently conservative.

It is difficult to see how the European construction is compatible with any of these considerations. Far from being a spontaneous, self-generated and piecemeal process of natural constitutional growth, its very name, 'the European construction', suggests a technocratic, artificial and deliberate construction – which, as Edmund Burke insisted, is in contradiction with law and traditional liberties. Far from going with the grain of popular will or even judicial evolution, it proposes to replace existing politico-legal systems with new-fangled invented ones: although it prides itself on its 'communitarian' image, it will sideline those political communities which already exist, the nation-states. The togetherness of a pre-existing European people does not exist, as the metaphor 'the European construction' precisely admits. And far from being compatible with an understanding that law is a neutral set of rules which permit order to emerge from the tangle of free interaction between people, it is a regulatory and *dirigiste* system which thinks of law as a 'directive', and of political life as akin to a common enterprise with goals to be pursued.

But this view of the state is widely held in many countries of the European Union, who often have a corporatist understanding of the state. There, the activities of government are identified almost entirely with spending money. Federal states are particularly prone to this understanding of statehood, because the bulk of their domestic politics is devoted to wrangling between the various layers of government over funds. This, in turn, is due to the proliferation of levels of government in federal states. Belgium, for example, has no fewer than seven legislative assemblies.

Similarly, because their country is divided up into *Länder*, Germans will often explain to you that their country is wonderfully decentralised. This, however, is untrue. The *Länder* have the same powers as local authorities in Britain, while the difference between the Scottish and English legal systems is greater than any difference within Germany. What Germany does have is a relatively high degree of administrative decentralisation (funds are raised by national taxation and then distributed downwards to the *Länder*, who spend money) together with fifteen high-profile regional governments who can block government legislation at national level in the Bundesrat.

However, the power to spend is not equivalent to regional political autonomy. Those who say that German federalism is a model for Europe are assuming that the desire for genuine national political independence – the right to makes one's own laws – can be quenched with mere transfers of money from someone else. They are assuming that the nature of government at regional level within a state is similar to that at state level itself. This is an unpolitical and clientilist understanding of statehood. If citizens subscribe to a

constitution, they are subscribing essentially to law-based procedures for deciding and adjudicating on general rules. If they accept
the validity of the state merely because it gives them money, then
this is not political association but feudal subjection.

3. Sovereignty, democracy and the common good

> 'A society whose members enter into opposition with one
> another tends towards dissolution'
>
> SAINT-SIMON

Human conduct thus presupposes two things: other people and
meaning. Society and language are thus two definitive elements of
human life. Without the notion of meaningful behaviour – that is,
behaviour which is intelligible in terms of the self-understanding
revealed by the people engaging in it – there would be no such
thing as human conduct, human freedom and human reason.
There needs to be a public dialogue for thought to be able to take
place. As Kant writes, 'Reason is not made to isolate itself but to
get into community with others.'[43]

Human reason develops by extracting or discovering universal
natures within the individual things which we encounter through
experience. But because this process is partial and continuous,
human intelligence and knowledge is a *chiaroscuro*. Areas of light
and clarity are encircled by zones of obscurity. Man acquires
knowledge by a slow, difficult, laborious and progressive process as
a result of long, patient and complex work. Indeed, he only ever
comes to have a partial knowledge of reality: he never even has
knowledge of the whole of any particular part of reality. Although
he may know the truth, the truths he knows are only partial, and
they need to be complemented by others. This partiality means
that human intelligence is also successive, that is, that our knowledge grows as one partial truth succeeds another.

Another way of expressing the same thought is to say that
human knowledge is discursive. Human intellectual knowledge is
expressed in speech. Like knowledge, speech is partial, successive

and progressive, and it derives from the interaction of intelligent beings engaged in common practices. This means that the common things in life are essential elements in the constitution of human reason. In other words, it is the experience of common-ness which gives meaning to human life. Without it, we would live in a state of idiocy, that is, on 'one's own' (*idion*). We need to live in a common world where the words we have in common possess an unquestioned meaningfulness. Social and political life – human life – could not exist without law and language. All our concepts of freedom, law and belonging together in democracy are communicated to citizens through the experience of statehood. Just as law presupposes a state, a people and a judge, so the common-ness of law, like that of any practice, is an integral part of man's nature as a political animal.

This explains why a common language is an important element of statehood and democracy. Without one, the commonality which is essential to judgement, evaluation and purpose in human life is impossible. It is indeed very difficult to exaggerate the importance of a common language as the constitutive element of politics and law. States and nations grow and persist as communities sharing a common tongue. Peoples arise out of languages, not languages out of peoples. A language is the means by which men make sense of the world and of themselves. Language is indispensable to commonality, intelligence, politics and freedom.

Whole swathes of the vocabulary of politics and law, indeed, reveal this deep link between speech acts and political acts. In French and German, the word for 'vote' is the same as the word for 'voice'; laws are passed by a *parlia*ment in which speeches are made and 'parleys' held; laws are 'promulgated', decisions are 'announced'; the government makes 'statements' to parliament; in a court, the parties 'plead'; investigative inquiries are 'hearings'; the domain in which rulings have validity is a juris*diction*; a judge speaks in the 'name' of the state he serves, and he passes a 'sentence'; the 'jury' is 'sworn in'; the witnesses 'swear' to tell the truth. Law and politics live in and through language – that is, in the public domain.

Meanwhile, Aristotle's definition of man as a political animal was intended not only to emphasise the difference between household life and the public realm of politics, but also to differentiate between the free citizen and the slave or barbarian who was *aneu logou* – deprived, of course, not of the faculty of speech, but of a way of life in which speech, and only speech, made sense, and where the central concern of all citizens was to talk with each other.[44] In the Middle Ages, the (public) splendour of majesty was contrasted with the darkness and obscurity of the private realm. Throughout the Middle Ages, indeed, and into the Renaissance, the public realm grew in importance as the *sine qua non* of the rule of law, and the idea that the king or feudal lord was the head of a household declined. Parliament, the arena of speech, became the realm in which political power had to be manifested for it to be legitimate. Politics is therefore part of what it is to be human, if 'politics' means the public association of individuals who understand themselves to be 'a people'. Without 'a people', there can be no rule by the people (democracy).

Ruling is therefore different from legislation or adjudication: it is 'policing' civil association.[45] The powers of policing do enable officials of the state to prohibit certain substantive actions, but this is in accordance with the procedures laid down in the law. This is because law postulates an apparatus of rule, since it cannot enforce or administer itself. There must therefore be the machinery of a state for law to exist. While ruling is a series of commands issued in pursuance of the law, law is not the rule-book of an enterprise. Even the etymology of 'rule' makes it clear that it is supposed to supply an invariable measure by which human behaviour can be judged (Father Copleston glosses Aquinas' view of law as 'a *measure or rule* of human acts, *a measure or rule* conceived by reason and promulgated with a view to the common good'[46]) – just as the etymology of prince indicates that he should be principled.

Law, therefore, presupposes citizens who respect the judge's authority to rule in case of conflict, and to say which interpretation of the law is the right one. Indeed, they are citizens precisely in virtue of their self-understanding as members of the *polis* who live under that authority. Law, in other words, presupposes a civil state, or rather is constitutive of it. As St Thomas Aquinas says in the *Treatise on Law*, 'Law is nothing else than the ordination of reason for the common good promulgated by the one who is in charge of the community.'[47] The pursuit of 'the common good' of which he speaks is not a substantive purpose like that pursued in Oakeshott's enterprise association. It is instead the self-definitive activity which flows from the acceptance that the 'good' in question is 'common' to the people who recognise themselves as citizens. The pursuit of the common good is the pursuit of those values which strengthen the community as a community. It is not the pursuit of a substantive goal extraneous to the fact of belonging to the community.

Law and policy are therefore public goods. What we understand as democracy cannot exist without a properly maintained public realm. Neither freedom under the law, nor one of its most important outcomes, the free market, can exist unless there are public spaces, guaranteed in law, where free interaction can occur, and public standards (language, the law) which make human action intelligible and free. Freedom, in other words, needs a public realm, and cannot be said to exist if it is confined only to private life. Anyone who has travelled to a Soviet country, where suspicion of strangers and the habits of extorting them run as deeply as can be imagined, and where common staircases in blocks of flats are filthy even if the apartments inside are spotless, will know what is meant by this destruction of the public realm.

Man would know nothing of inner freedom if he had not experienced a condition of being free as a worldly tangible reality. Law and political freedom must be real, not just formal, for them to have any worth. We first become aware of freedom in our intercourse with others, not in intercourse with ourselves. This is how we come to develop our minds and our self-awareness as persons. Without a guaranteed political realm, freedom would not be a demonstrable fact. Freedom is not something found in the obscurity of the heart, nor is it a mental state, as some Utilitarian philosophers seem to imply. Instead, politics and freedom coincide and interrelate to one another like two sides of the same coin.

That realm must be clearly described. For in order for law to be said to exist, there must a clearly defined area within which it is valid, and a clearly defined group of people to whom it applies. Good fences make good neighbours. In the ancient world, law 'was quite literally a wall, without which there might have been an agglomeration of houses, but not a city, a political community'.[48] The *polis* originally connoted something like 'ring-wall', just as *urbis* in Latin also expressed the notion of a circle and was derived from the same root as *orbis*. Indeed, 'town' and the German word *Zaun* (fence) are etymologically related, while the Greek word for law, *nomos*, is said to come from *nemein*, to distribute, to possess (what has been distributed) and to dwell. The combination of 'law' and 'hedge' in the word *nomos* enabled Heraclitus to pun, 'The people should fight for the law as for a wall.'[49] It is only in the Communist mind that a border is necessarily a closed barrier: for the classical understanding of law, it is precisely the definitive element of jurisdiction. In the Continental view, of course, a national border is as much economic as political. But, as we have seen, the British concept of sovereignty since Hobbes has included within it the idea that borders are commercially open.

Territorial clarity is thus a prerequisite for non-tribal organisation. All law requires jurisdiction, that is, a system for determining who is and who is not subject to its edicts. In a state containing various tribes, each governed by its own religious law, not only is political unity undermined: the idea is established in the minds of people that those who do not share their religious beliefs are in some important sense outside the law. Such an idea of jurisdiction is incompatible with the emergence of a state in which rights are offered regardless of confession. The safety, continuity and stability necessary to a rule of law are unobtainable until territory is secure. Only a territorial idea of jurisdiction will permit the final separation of law from confessional attachment.[50]

The national idea establishes a social loyalty suited to territorial jurisdiction: without territorial jurisdiction there is no possibility of a liberal state. It is for this reason that the history of the state of law and that of the national idea are inseparable. Nationality and jurisdiction, indeed, interpenetrate one another, and it is not absurd to envisage their relation in terms of that between body and soul.[51] Far from being a threat to the liberal order, the nation is the very prerequisite for it.

Constitutional independence, or national sovereign state-hood, is thus a prerequisite for democracy because it is only within a certain polity – that is, a group of people clearly consti-tuted by common rules and reference points – that democratic debate and democratic accountability can be assured. This is why it is dangerous to argue simply – as supporters of European integration do – that borders should be dismantled or made irrel-evant. Just as no one seems to be clearly saying that they want a European sovereignty, but rather that they want to dismantle the very notion of sovereignty, so European integrationists tend not to say they want to erect borders around the European Union (although this may very well be the consequence of what they propose) but rather that they are simply encouraging borders in general to disappear.

The claim that borders are barriers which must be dismantled is thus a denunciation of one of the essential instruments of law itself. The abolition of juridical borders implies the abolition of political nationhood, and this in turn implies the abolition of law and its replacement by bureaucracy or *dirigiste* legislative activity. Without politics – without the real existence of a clear, public realm – there can be no judgement, no morals and no law. It is precisely when the public realm of open law- and policy-making is blurred, in favour of decision-making behind closed doors, that the real danger in contemporary societies emerges: that of bureaucratic, technocratic and depoliticised structures, which encourage indifference, and which render citizens less discriminating, less capable of critical thinking, and less inclined to assume responsibility. This is the danger of abolishing national borders without explicitly creating new European ones (even though the latter would create a whole raft of new prob-lems), or of pretending that political life can or should exist without them.

4. The age of sophisters and calculators

'Economic power counts more than territorial power'
COLBERT[52]

It was in order to emphasise the role of the public realm in safe-guarding political freedom that the great liberal French philosopher, Benjamin Constant, drew a distinction between the freedom of the ancients and that of the moderns.[53] For the ancients, freedom was a public good – you were free if, as a citizen, you had the right to participate in politics – while what we now call private, individual freedom counted for little. By contrast, the modern world associates freedom with the freedom from state interference in the private life of the individual.

The ancients understood that the government of a republic can destroy freedom if it is based on the economist model of the household. (Housekeeping in Greek is *'economia'*.) They considered the private life of the family or the tribe to be the realm of necessity, while the public realm, in which all men were equal, was the realm of freedom. In the private domain, the commands issued by the chief or the master of the household were concerned with ensuring that the necessities of life (food, warmth) were obtained. The Roman tyrant Caligula was the first to be called *'dominus'*, master, a title which Augustus and even Tiberius would have regarded as an insult and a malediction.

The trends against which Constant was warning gained an important victory in the nineteenth century with the rise of a new doctrine which blurs the very distinction between public and private: the social. This concept encouraged the view that peoples and political communities should be treated like a family, whose everyday affairs have to be taken care of by that gigantic, nation-wide administration of housekeeping which we now call government.

The discipline which corresponds to this undertaking is no longer political philosophy or rhetoric, but rather the science of economics. 'Society' is conceived as being like one big household, and the essential distinction between the private and public realms is blurred by it. Phrases like 'the common European home' – regularly used as a slogan by Chancellor Kohl and others[54] – suggest that the correct model for politics is the domestic domain rather than the public realm.

The understanding of government as something based essentially on economics, rather than on policy and law, encouraged Marx and Engels to think that once the 'contradictions' of the 'capitalist' (that is, free) system had been resolved, the state would wither away, and that the government of men would be replaced by the administration of things.[55]

This was because members of this school of thought did not grasp the essentially intelligent nature of free human interaction under the law. Being the discipline which deals with the necessities of human life, economics assumes that men *behave* rather than *act* with respect to one another. It assumes that human behaviour can be explained in egocentric terms, or as the result of some physical or psychological drive. The Classical economists, and some tendencies in liberal thought, also share some of the blame for this, for they argue that man necessarily seeks his own happiness or well-being, and that it is possible to enjoy the liberal order without the conservative foundations – nationhood, law, tradition – which underlie it.

But, in fact, although all actions are ineluctably the agent's own, it is a travesty of humanity to argue that man's only motive is self-gratification. Such a theory removes all notions of freedom and intelligence from the equation. By the same token, the idea that society is statistically pretty uniform, and that the national economy can be directed towards one end which is its interest, is incompatible with a truly free and liberal legal order.

This is because the application of the law of large numbers and long periods to politics and history signifies nothing less than the wilful obliteration of their very subject matter, which is the exceptional. Politics, being an integral part of human freedom, involves taking free decisions which, being genuinely free, cannot be theorised in advance: the sovereign, in Carl Schmitt's famous definition, is the one who takes the decision in exceptional circumstances.[56] It is a hopeless enterprise to search for meaning in politics, or significance in history, when everything which is not everyday behaviour or automatic trends has been ruled out as immaterial.

The myth of the necessarily egocentric agent is thus a denial of agency. To think that society has one interest, perhaps discernible by economic science, is to adopt a universalist and materialist view of human nature. It is a view of man which fails to take account of the fact that, though men are identical in their nature, they are all different in fact, each influenced by his upbringing, time, beliefs, country and all the other qualities which make a man a particular person. In other words, to say that all men's – or all nations' – interests are alike (as the foreign policy spokesman of the ruling Christian Democrats in Germany has affirmed, in defence of European integration[57]) is to ignore the possibility that people will perceive their interests differently. It is thus to ignore the possibility of intelligent disagreement.

This is why some liberal economists (especially those of the Austrian school, whose philosophy is infused with the understanding of human nature outlined in this chapter) have themselves explicitly attacked modern economists' obsession with numbers, and their tendency to believe that 'good numbers would inevitably make for good policy'.[58] Indeed, it was precisely against the Micawberish and even megalomaniac tendency latent in much econometrics that Hayek pleaded that the paradoxical task of economists was to show how little economics could show. Economism, as a branch of scientism, falls easily prey to the hubristic belief that it can know and plan the whole of society.

The economist vision of the state is especially pronounced on the Continent. Inspired by a unitarian and corporatist model of society, many Continentals believe that social cohesion can exist only if everyone agrees all the time, and if the state engages in significant redistribution of income. In their different ways, the political cultures of France, Germany, Belgium, the Netherlands – among others – are based on this erroneous 'unitarian' visions of politics: Germany boasts of her 'consensual' approach to politics, in which everyone agrees with everyone else, and in which differences of opinion are cushioned and muted by generous government hand-outs; while French political discourse usually assumes that the interests of the 'whole' are morally superior to those of the individual, and that the French nation is somehow a common project.

In contrast to Continental European constitutional theories or practices which assume or aspire to political harmony, the British and American systems realise that conflict is the stuff of life. In the liberal tradition, true solidarity exists when two people who are in conflict or competition with one another nonetheless accept the authority of the same rules by which to solve the dispute. Rather than trying to iron out conflict, Anglo-Saxon countries have learned to develop constitutional systems which allow it to flourish. The British parliamentary system gives absolute priority to the principle of disagreement by ensuring that there is always an opposition.

The American tradition is similar: in the Federalist Papers, Publius explains that the spirit of faction is inevitable and must be channelled correctly, not suppressed: 'Liberty is to faction what air is to fire, an aliment without which it instantly expires. But it could not be less folly to abolish liberty, which is essential to political life, because it nourishes faction, than it would be to wish the annihilation of air, which is essential to animal life, because it imparts to fire its destructive agency.'[59] Conflict, in other words, leads to the common good. Where there is no conflict, there is no politics, only management. Politics lives off enmity, the opposition between parties and interests and ideologies, the antagonism between different opinions, values and goals.

The liberal tradition also understands that the practice of civil association is infinite, unpredictable and conflict-ridden. Its terms are not imposed on citizens as already shaped and articulate engagements, but are rather that which is generated by the miscellaneous and unforeseeable intelligent choices and transactions which people make in their daily lives. Indeed, civil association is predicated on dispute and difference of opinion, even on how the terms of law relate to contingent circumstances. Civil association therefore postulates an authoritative adjudicative procedure for resolving uncertainties and disputes. Citizens are related to each other in political association as suitors to a judicial court, not as

partners in a common undertaking.[60] For those who hold a unitarian or harmonist view of politics – for whom this last
affirmation will be shocking – by contrast, multiplicity implies
disorder.

Some strands of modern liberalism, as much as bureaucratism
and socialism, must share some of the blame for the drift towards
economism and away from politics. The view has been encouraged
that freedom is primarily a private matter. But politics is the art of
decision-making. A political act is a public act, that is, the decision taken bears the personal hallmark of the man taking it.
Politics is prudential: the choices made in deciding policy and law
need to be accommodated to the contingent conditions of time
and place in which they are taken. By contrast, bureaucratic government does not take place in public – its essence is not
parliamentary – but in the corridor or behind closed doors.
Bureaucratic management is neither personal nor authoritative:
the decisions taken are anonymous and pretend at objectivity (sci-
entificity). Technocracy is precisely that which seeks to influence
political decisions without taking responsibility for them.

Ever since the beginning of the modern age, the administration
of the ever-increasing sphere of social and economic life has over-
shadowed the political realm. But where the necessities of life are
at stake – in economics – all action is by definition under the
sway of necessity. If politics were only the preservation of life,
then courage would be considered a foolish and vicious contempt
for life and its interests. On the contrary, it is the prerequisite for
all political action.

The dominance of economics, the growth of modern state
bureaucracies, the increased power of technocrats, the general pres-
tige of science – all these contribute to the view that the things
which matter in human society are susceptible of pure, certain, scientific knowledge. Politics, by contrast, is regarded as being little
more than 'party politics', and as an almost secondary activity to
that of economic management. This can lead to decisions being
taken for exclusively economic reasons which ignore the constitutional, legal and political implications of what they propose, as is
the case with European Monetary Union. By debasing politics as a

separate, genuine and potentially worthy activity, therefore, modern scientism tends to ignore and dismiss as chimeras the knowable bases of politics, and thus of free societies.

Politics is not a science. It is impossible to construct a model or a mechanism for taking political decisions, as the Maastricht Treaty loves to do. To confide political power in the hands of the bureaucrat, or a bureaucratically-minded politician, is to divert it from its proper place. The bureaucrat hates the humorous, the eccentric and the creative: but true politics should be all of these, and more. All apparatuses lead to an abandonment of responsibility and a neutralisation of decision-taking: politics is the enemy of the apparatus.

Because politics is real (not ideal, like a scientific theory or a political -ism), the relation between means and ends is always critical, not scientific. Politics is the art of deciding when to take what measure which may have been suggested by advisers in order to achieve a certain end. This implies that it is necessary for a political act that the actor possess intuition of the measure which seems the most opportune, as well as a sense of responsibility for the cause being defended. The errors or successes of such an action will be revealed only during the course of the action itself, for politics is precisely actions taken in certain circumstances. No end can ever be pursued in politics without surprises and unexpected occurrences, for politics is human life. These unexpected circumstances may require a change of tack, a new strategy, an abandonment of the aim. Politics, being part of human life, is a continuous, risky and unpredictable process. Thus it is dangerously unpolitical to want to put an end to all conflict, or to believe that a state (let alone a continent) can be ruled by a supposedly neutral and technocratic institution like a central bank.

5. The strange alliance between liberals and socialists

These reflections help us to understand the following paradox: how can it be that the project of European integration, which was undertaken in the name of the market, became a project for political harmonisation and unification with pronounced illiberal elements? To put the problem another way: how was it that Margaret Thatcher, whose opposition to political union was as strong as it was instinctive, was unable to provide a convincing alternative vision to the one proposed by her nemesis, Jacques Delors?

The answer to these riddles lies in confusion about the role of the state. Margaret Thatcher had spent nearly ten years 'rolling back the frontiers of the state' when the project to integrate Europe politically got under way. Having built her reputation as an anti-statist, her determination to maintain national borders and national state control seemed self-contradictory. Similarly, European integrationists tended to argue that their abolition of national borders was an act of liberalisation, not of increased central control.

These paradoxes can be resolved only by saying that the point about Thatcherite and Reaganite 'liberalisation' was not so much to *reduce the quantity* of state action (although it was partly that) but rather to *change its quality*. Conservative liberalism sees the state having a principally judicial rather than executive function. As we have seen, the maintenance of a (primarily judicial) state is, in fact, the prerequisite for political and economic liberties. Therefore, defenders of a lightly regulated economy, with a maximum degree of political freedom are – paradoxically – also supporters of a strong state in the areas which matter, especially in upholding the rule of law and a framework for genuine democratic debate. By contrast, the project of European integration has used the *language* of liberalisation to advance something very different: the simple replacement of national controls by supranational ones.

The conundrum also produces an equal and opposite paradox. It is that technocratic liberals, who ignore the importance of conservative things like the state and the nation, can quickly slip into socialistic positions. There has, indeed, been an alliance in Europe between technocratic liberals and socialists, of which Sir Leon Brittan and Jacques Delors (who both agree on the need for the single currency) are a good example.

Such technocratic liberalism is therefore not the opposite of socialism. Unlike conservatives, technocratic liberals think you can have the cherry of the liberal order without the cake of nationhood, law and politics which must underlie it. Caring little for these conservative values, which are the inexplicable results of history and accident, they can therefore become the supporters of grandiose socialistic projects to replace old orders with new ones, such as that of European unification. And, just like econometrics, with which it shares a materialist view of man, such technocratic liberalism quickly slips into a plannificatory *dirigisme*.

The modern European project is not the first time in history when anti-conservative liberals (or libertarians) have become transmogrified into organisational or even proto-totalitarian socialists hostile to the liberal order. In the nineteenth century, Henri Comte de Saint-Simon began life as a liberal, close to industrial circles, and a follower of the great French liberal economist, Jean-Baptiste Say. He and his colleague, Auguste Comte, ended up as influential theoreticians of proto-totalitarian plannificatory socialism.

As with many modern economists and libertarians, Saint-Simon's fatally scientific approach to politics came from his love of economics. He was convinced that human life was messy and irrational, and that it should be scientifically planned. In one of his first publications, in 1803, he proposed that a subscription should be opened before the tomb of Newton to finance a 'Council of Newton'. Mathematicians, physicists, chemists and other scholars would be elected to this council by the whole of mankind, and together they would rule the planet. The supreme Council of Newton would divide the world into local Councils of Newton, which would organise worship and scientific instruction throughout the whole world: Saint-Simon was convinced that science, not morals or law, should rule the world.

In 1814 Saint-Simon published 'On the Reorganisation of European Society, or On the Necessity of Grouping Together the Peoples of Europe into One Body Politic, While Conserving the National Independence of Each'. In this early plan for European federal union, Saint-Simon expressed his conviction that Europe was 'disorganised', and that it was necessary to overcome this disorganisation by uniting the continent politically. To do this, political homogeneity was necessary: all Europe's nations had to have the same political institutions. Because he was still in his liberal stage, Saint-Simon looked to England for his model, and wanted Europe to emulate the British parliamentary system: each country was to have its own parliament, but they would 'recognise the supremacy of a general parliament placed above all national governments, and invested with the power to judge their differences'.[61]

Together with the historian Augustin Thierry, who became his assistant, Saint-Simon developed what became known as 'positivist politics'. Such politics were intended to be scientific, purged of the abstract metaphysics of morality. Thierry, who had co-authored the 'Reorganisation', later became the new leader of a schools of historians which developed a history of the masses that was profoundly to influence Marx. Meanwhile, Auguste Comte writing in the positivist review, Le Censeur, also published similar ideas, such as 'On the European Situation, On the Causes of Its Wars, and On the Means by Which to Put an End to Them'. In this, he suggested for the European government the same tasks as Saint-Simon had: public works, communications and infrastructure, and the colonisation of uncivilised parts of the world.

Thierry, Saint-Simon and Comte believed that the forces of industry had to be given a greater role in the planning of the economy. In their reviews, L'Industrie and Le Censeur, they developed the idea that politics in general should be subsumed into economic planning. In Le Censeur européen, they attacked the theory of the balance of power in Europe, which they saw as nothing but the rivalry between militaristic nations. Against this, they opposed the idea of the identity of all nations' commercial interests. Augustin Thierry wrote that the definition of liberalism was 'a regime founded on industry, "commercial government", as the English say'.[62] They saw Europe developing from a feudal age into a modern industrial age where all interests were the same. In a spirit very close to that of his liberal colleagues at the time, Saint-Simon wrote, 'The sole purpose towards which all our thoughts and all our efforts ought to be directed [is] the organisation of society most favourable to industry in the widest sense of the word.'[63]

By concentrating on economics, Saint-Simon and Thierry wanted to devote political organisation entirely to the satisfaction of the necessities of life. Within the framework of his analysis of history as developing towards industrialisation, Saint-Simon advocated the integration of industry into the state. He wrote that politics is the 'science of production',[64] and – like those who talk of 'UK PLC' today – considered a nation as 'nothing but a large industrial company'.[65] There can surely be fewer bleaker statements of the unpolitical mentality than these.

Influenced partly by the authoritarian traditionalism of Joseph de Maistre, but rejecting the theological foundations of De Maistre's thought, Comte and Saint-Simon increasingly wanted to replace the Church and theology with a clergy of scientists, in order to perfect industrial society. Comte in 'The Organiser' and Saint-Simon in 'Industrial System' (1820) and 'Catechism for Industrialists' (1822) called for the formation of corporations of industrialists to strengthen the scientific nature of government.

Saint-Simon began to see more clearly than most socialists that the organisation of society for a common purpose was incompatible with individual freedom, and that it required the existence of a power which 'can choose the direction to which the national forces are to be applied'.[66] He became more and more disenchanted with 'the vague and metaphysical idea of liberty' which was 'contrary to the development of civilisation and to the organisation of a well-ordered system'.[67] The parliamentary system was bad and unscientific because it allowed different ends to compete. He even once suggested that people who did not comply with the state's commands were idiots who should be treated 'like quadrupeds'.

Comte, meanwhile, came to the view that there was no such things as liberty of conscience, for differences of view would soon by ironed out by social physics.[68] He called on artists to 'exercise on the common masses sufficient action to determine them to follow irrevocably in the direction indicated and to assist their natural leaders in that great co-operation'.[69]

The new society, wrote Saint-Simon, would not be governed: it would be administered. In a completely industrialised society, there would be no more governments, only administrators. He thought that the principal activity of politics was balancing the budget, and that meant that the essence of politics was administration. Saint-Simon thought that man, who was destined to live in society, had hitherto lived in governmental society: henceforth he would live in an *administered* or *industrial* society.[70] He attacked 'the judicial order' as 'very damaging', and affirmed 'the superiority of the principles of political economy over those of civil law'.[71]

Saint-Simon also called for industry in general to be controlled by the corporation of all industrial corporations, the banks, for banks linked credit and thus the whole industrial economy. Banks were 'the general agents of industry'.[72] Thus, as in feudal society, there would be a hierarchy of functions, with bankers at the top.

After his death in 1825, Saint-Simonians continued their master's thought, publishing an *Exposition* of it in 1829–30. Perhaps the most intriguing development from the point of view of this book, is that the authors of the *Exposition* foresaw a world in which all industrial activity was organised, foreseen, and perfected by one 'social institution', the banking system, crowned by 'a unitary, directing bank' which was to serve as the planning body:

> The social institution of the future will direct all industries in the interest of the whole society and specially of the peaceful workers. We call this institution provisionally the general system of banks . . .
>
> The system will comprise in the first instance a central bank which constitutes the government in the material sphere; this bank will become the depository of all wealth, of the whole productive fund, of all the instruments of production, in short of everything that today makes up the whole mass of private property.[73]

As Hayek comments, this may be the first occurrence of the term 'central bank'. It was not to be the last.

An *assignat*, the paper currency of Revolutionary France, at the top of which stand the following warnings: 'THE LAW PUNISHES THE COUNTERFEITER BY DEATH' and 'THE NATION REWARDS THE DENUNCIATOR'. Edmund Burke wrote that the *assignat* was 'depreciated paper which is stamped with the indelible character of sacrilege'.

V

MONEY MATTERS

'This is why all goods must have a price set on them; for then there will always be exchange and, if so, association of man with man'
ARISTOTLE[1]

It is typical of the unpolitical mentality which inspires the European ideology that the plan to create political union in Europe centres around a currency and a central bank. There is no European Garibaldi or Bismarck openly proclaiming the intention to constitute a new state. There is only a technocratic plan to introduce an unavowed political union by the back door, by creating a European Central Bank, and by replacing the national currencies with a new centrally managed European one. Europe is faced, in other words, with a proposal to set up the apparatus of state power (or super-state power) without proposing to channel the exercise of that power through the authoritative structures of a politically legitimate constitution. Nowhere, indeed, is the confusion between power and authority greater than in monetary questions.

Technocrats have long been fascinated by the power of banks precisely because they epitomise unpolitical power, as Saint-Simon's story shows. Jacques Attali and Jacques Delors are also instances of this: the former, the biographer of Warburg, wanted his career in the corridors of power to be crowned with the presidency of the 'European bank'. The latter, meanwhile, began his career as an official in the Bank of France, and finished it with the single currency project.

The arguments in favour of monetary union are thus seldom explicitly political. Supporters of it usually tend to hide the political significance of what they propose behind a fog of technocratic jargon about currency management, transaction costs, and the requirements of the single market. This only serves to obscure political and constitutional issues of the first importance.

Moreover, this decisive change in the economic and political structure of Europe – not to mention in the lifestyle of its citizens – is being undertaken in the name of internationalism, but in the notable absence of any serious reflection about what is best for the international monetary system as a whole. Instead of looking at alternative monetary regimes and weighing up their relative merits, the architects of EMU have decided merely to reproduce at supranational level the same monetary regime which exists in all the world's states. In particular, little attention has been devoted to the compatibility between the world's present monetary system and the values of the market, to which everyone professes attachment.

Money, the market and society

> 'Sound money . . . was devised as an instrument for the protection of civil liberties against despotic inroads on the part of governments. Ideologically it belongs in the same class with political constitutions and bills of rights'
>
> LUDWIG VON MISES[2]

In the twentieth century, the world lost its way in monetary matters and is now astray in a gloomy wood. It has forgotten the true function of money, and its importance as a constitutive element of a free society, because it is victim of the delusion that money is principally an instrument of state power, or an expression of the strength of the economy. It lives in preoccupying ignorance of how even relatively recent monetary regimes worked.

The truth is that money is a commodity selected by the market as a common means of exchange. Any non-Communist society involves the exchange of goods and services, and money grows from the desire all men have to exchange goods and services in a peaceful and mutual fashion. It is the term in which the commensurability of human action is expressed. It serves as a means of expressing in the same language the rights that buyer and seller enjoy over different things.

Money is civilised because it represents a higher stage than barter, the most primitive form of exchange. People who want what other people have may not have what the latter want, and therefore a single commodity usually emerges which everyone will accept in payment for a good or a service, knowing that they can in turn exchange the commodity for another good or a service they desire. If it gains currency, this commodity becomes money, and, like any other commodity, its value is determined by supply and demand.

At different times and places, different commodities have served the function of money. In the most primitive economies, oxen, shells, or bushels of wheat served the purpose. One anthropologist at the beginning of this century discovered huge immovable round stones being used as money on the Micronesian island of Yap.[3] In more modern times – for instance in Communist countries where the official currency was debased, or in other conditions of monetary disorder – goods like cigarettes have emerged as the true currency: in Ceauşescu's Romania, for instance, all important payments (bribes for schoolteachers, doctors' fees) were made with packets of Kent.

But one kind of commodity has prevailed more frequently and for longer than any other: the precious metals, gold and silver. Various explanations have been given for their popularity, from the mystical to the practical: these metals are, for instance, malleable and durable enough to be made into coins which last. Also, apart from their inherent attractiveness, the quantity of these precious metals which is mined each year is a small fraction of the total amount in circulation. This is especially true of gold, whose value is not subject to huge swings as a result.[4]

The original understanding of money as a commodity is visible in the names of currencies. As Adam Smith shows, the English 'pound' under Edward I was a pound, Tower weight, of silver. The French *livre* contained in the time of Charlemagne, a pound, Troyes weight, of silver. A 'shilling' was also originally a denomination of weight.[5] A 'mark' was about 0.234 grams – it was made the basic imperial unit of weight in Germany at Esslingen in 1524[6] – while a 'shekel' is originally a Jewish weight (about half an ounce), the word 'shekel' coming from the Hebrew for 'to weigh'.

A commodity having been selected as money, it becomes the standard unit of all riches. Regardless of which commodity is picked, the commodity which serves as a means of exchange has (or should have) value in its own right, independently of its function as money. As we shall see, the twentieth century has fatally lost sight of this important truth, and consequently, it has no light by which to be guided through the dark and treacherous thicket of monetary affairs.

In particular, it has been forgotten that money is not – and should not be – the creation of the state. The state may well, however, uphold its soundness by ensuring the respect of contracts. It will do this as part of its overall policing of the rule of law. Under such circumstances, money is not 'political', in the sense of being the subject of daily partisan dispute; but it is eminently political, in the sense that it is a vitally important element in the constitution of a state. Like a constitution, indeed, money defines the terms of (constitutes) citizens' interaction with one another.

The view that money is the creation of the state is, unfortunately, very old – even if the opposite view has an even older and nobler pedigree. From the earliest times, the head of the king or emperor was imprinted on coins, and this gave the impression that money was an emanation of his power. In truth, however, a state emblem on a coin no more gives the state the right to tamper with the value of money than the state emblem in a courtroom gives the king or the prince the right to interfere in the judicial process. As Edmund Burke wrote, who had a rare and brilliant understanding of the constitutional role of money, 'We entertain a high opinion of the legislative authority; but we have never dreamt that parliaments had any right whatever to violate property, to overrule prescription, or to force a currency of their own fiction in the place of that which is real, and recognised by the law of nations.'[7]

Despotic princes habitually did debase the currency for their personal gain. In many cases, this debasement should be understood not only as the consequence of greed, but also as having a more profoundly political aim. For instance, the French king Philip the Fair (1285–1314) was notorious for plundering his country to finance his perpetual dynastic wars, which he did by taxing (and eventually destroying) the trade fairs of Champagne – which had been a hub of local and international commerce during the High Middle Ages – and by repeated confiscatory levies on groups or organisations with money.[8] As a result of it, he is now credited with being the first French king who used depreciation of the currency as a means of raising revenue. Dante has consequently handed his name down to posterity with a mark of infamy for '. . . the woe he worked / With his adulterate money on the Seine'.[9]

But his destruction in 1308 of the wealthy Order of the Templars, whose spiritual control over currency and foreign exchange gave it a crucial role in the growth of international finance,[10] was not simply a matter of grabbing its funds for the royal treasury. It was part of his overall attack on spiritual authority – it was he who seized the Pope in Rome and transferred the Papacy to Avignon – which at that time represented a check on the otherwise despotic power of a rapacious king. (From the time of ancient Babylon, indeed, power over money had been vested in the spiritual domain. Temples had had important banking functions, providing credits and raising taxes, which explains why there were money-changers at the temple in Jerusalem for Christ to chase out.) As we shall see, because it was part of an overall project to increase state power, Philip the Fair's attack on the Templars is therefore a historical precedent for the nationalisation of central banks by governments in the twentieth century.

Modern dictators have similarly cemented their oppression of their own people with stringent restrictions on the way money is used. One of the most vicious Communist dictatorships of all, Pol Pot's – famous mainly for exterminating one third of the

Cambodian population – perfected the Communist system by actually outlawing money altogether.[11]

For these reasons, therefore, those committed to the rule of law have always sought to channel state power into the framework of justice in the monetary domain as much as in the political. They argue that it is a very significant part of human freedom under the law to be able to own and exchange property without being robbed either by the state or by another individual. It is only when the law protects the right of individuals to hold and exchange goods and services that people are truly free. The maintenance of the rule of the law thus requires the state to have the power of coercion over malefactors: property law defines when and where the police should intervene. This is why free economic activity itself is an outgrowth from the general juridical structure which imposes social peace, and why the principle of sound money is a central element of classical liberalism. If human action is intrinsically linked to the desire to exchange goods and services in a spirit of mutuality and sociability, and according to the law, then it is clear that sound money lies at the very heart of all civilised human society.

Conversely, if the state uses a discretionary power (not a law) to restrict economic activity, or to change the terms of contracts which have been concluded, then it does not ensure the protection of property rights, and thus its citizens cannot be said to be free. As John Locke realised,

> The reason why it [the definition of the currency in terms of precious metal] should not be changed is this: because the public authority is guarantee for the performance of all legal contracts. But men are absolved from the performance of legal contracts, if the quantity of silver under settled and legal denominations be altered . . . the landlord here and the creditor there are each defrauded of twenty per cent of what they contracted for and is their due . . .[12]

Therefore, the two essential institutions which ensure human freedom are the judicial system and the mechanism of free prices.

The mechanism of price is that which co-ordinates the activities of men in a regime where real rights are ensured. The mechanism allows a collective order to emerge from the chaos of individual wills, and allows each individual to exercise his rights in proportion to the extent to which he enjoys them. In this sense, the fair operation of the price mechanism is a true plebiscite (not a majoritarian representative system) in which each individual, however humble he may be, can make his voice heard. By contrast, the function of money, which is to express rights and duties, is destroyed in a planned economy because demand has no influence on supply: the latter is not governed by the needs of consumers and producers, as expressed through the price mechanism, but rather by central diktat.

In modern times, it has been the Austrian school of economics (especially Friedrich von Hayek and Ludwig von Mises) which has done the most to emancipate economics from the state theory of money. Like the theory of legal positivism which underpins it (legal positivists hold that there are no independent moral or judicial values, and that justice is what the state says it is), this theory reached its apogee in the late nineteenth-century Germany, culminating in Georg Friedrich Knapp's *The State Theory of Money*. But although it may have been nurtured in Germany, it is now a very widely held view. In 1953, for instance, the US Chamber of Commerce declared abruptly, 'Money is what the government says it is.'[13]

Apart from its obvious authoritarianism, the state theory of money tends to ignore the fundamental function of money, which is to act as a means of exchange between individuals. It tends to regard it only from a macro-economic point of view. At best, it regards the currency as an expression of the total value of the economy's production; at worst, as an instrument with which the state can control it. In general, this monetary nominalism – the view is nominalist because it believes that money has no essence in itself, but derives its value only from the imprimatur of the state – corresponds to the view that there is no natural justice in the world, and that the role of the state, in the absence of independent standards or values, is to issue commands to society. By contrast, the view that money is a commodity which has a value, independently of its role as money, corresponds directly to the view that there are judicial and moral values which are independent of the will of the state, and which the state has a duty to uphold. The state has a duty to ensure the soundness of the currency, just as it has a duty to ensure the respect of the rule of law.

Thus, from the earliest times, it was considered an infraction against natural law for the prince to put copper into gold coins. As bank notes increasingly replaced coins from the middle of the seventeenth century onwards, classical liberals sought to ensure that the 'content' of fiduciary money was not subject to discretionary meddling by the government. Thus was the principle established that the holder of a bank note had the right to redeem his bank note for a contractually predetermined weight of gold on demand. Indeed, bank notes would never have come into existence had such a right not been guaranteed. Bank notes in the modern period were originally receipts for gold deposited with goldsmiths. As those receipts gained currency – that is, as people came to believe in the good name of the goldsmith – they began to circulate as money.[14] Ever since metallic convertibility was abandoned on the eve of the First World War, this simple mechanism has been abolished.

As modern banking flourished, the guarantee to redeem bank notes for gold coin on demand was not understood as a technical mechanism chosen for prudential reasons as an effective way of managing the currency. It was instead a principle which defined the relationship between the issuer and the user of currency. A contractual relationship between them was established, and thus the simple principle which governs the free market – the principle of the respect of contracts – prevailed in the monetary domain as well. By contrast, the dissociation of currencies from a definitive and unchangeable gold parity made the value of money a plaything of politics.

Although not primarily a prudential choice, many technical advantages flowed from respecting the principle of contracts in the monetary domain. If a user of money felt that the issuing bank could not be trusted, he could return the bank note, which had failed to fulfil its service as a sound indicator of value, and get his gold back. To convert bank notes back into gold in this way is to reduce the amount of fiduciary money in circulation. In other words, the amount of money in circulation was based on the confidence and needs of the market. There was thus an automatic and decentralised regulation of the money supply, and thus of the economy itself. The balance of power between the producer and user of money thus also created a powerful weapon of deterrence against bad producers. Similarly, the amount of credit in the economy – the largest single element in defining what modern economists call 'the money supply' – depended on the needs of the market, and not on the decisions of the state.

To ensure the metallic convertibility of a currency was not to 'fix' or 'peg' the currency to gold. It was instead to use gold – or rather convertible substitutes for it – as the currency. It meant allowing the value of the currency to be determined by the same law which determines the value of any other commodity, that of supply and demand. When metallic convertibility is suspended, by contrast, a paper currency ceases to be a receipt for a commodity, and becomes an expression of nothing but itself.

Paper currencies are 'forced' or 'fiat' currencies. A 'fiat' currency is a medium of exchange which is neither a commodity, nor a consumer or producer good, nor a title to any such commodity. It is an irredeemable paper currency. In contrast, 'commodity money' refers to a medium of exchange which is either a commercial commodity or a title thereto.[15] The French, indeed, have a good term for fiat currencies. *Cours forcé* or 'forced tender' are the words given to them, because by dispensing the issuing bank of its contractual obligation to reimburse its bank notes in cash, the state *forces* the bearers of bank notes to keep their notes, or to convert them into goods, generally at inflated prices. The decree of *fiat* or *forced currency status* is the equivalent of nationalisation in other sectors of economy, and it is obviously a necessary condition for the unilateral increase by the state of the money supply, and thus for the inflation which is characteristic of all contemporary monetary regimes. In turn, the decree of legal tender is a prerequisite for the decree of forced tender: legal tender is the obligation on creditors to accept the notes of a certain bank (the central bank) as payment from debtors.

The growth of central banking

That bank notes were originally issued by individual goldsmiths underlines the fact that there is nothing inevitable about central banks. The institution of the central bank only arose after the government intervened. In England, for instance, the Bank of England was created in 1694 to provide a war loan of £1,500,000 to the Crown, in exchange for the privilege to enjoy an important monopoly, that of joint-stock formation with more than six partners in England and Wales.[16] In consequence, throughout the eighteenth and nineteenth centuries, other English banks only had limited access to capital funds. By the time that particular privilege was removed, the Bank of England dominated the capital market in London, and new privileges replaced it.

For instance, when the Pitt government ran into debt in order to finance the war with France, the metallic convertibility of Bank of England notes was suspended in 1797 by an Act of Parliament. This amounted to a legalisation of the bankruptcy of the bank. The suspension of convertibility may have been very profitable for the Bank of England, but it created a precedent which led the public in future always to expect the government to come to the aid of the central bank in difficult circumstances.

But the most important power granted to the central bank was that of note issue. Although not originally an exclusive power – private banks continued to issue their own throughout the eighteenth and nineteenth centuries – the Bank of England's size and privileged relationship to the state meant that it quickly established a monopoly of note issue in London. In 1833, Parliament bestowed legal tender status on the Bank's notes ('legal tender' denotes a currency which creditors are obliged to accept in payment) and in 1844, the Bank Charter Act restricted the power of other banks to issue rival notes.

The 1833 Act encouraged country banks to pay out Bank of England notes at times of rush when their own notes were presented for redemption, and so the ultimate demand for gold fell on the Bank of England. Therefore it was natural that the country banks should keep the greater part of their reserves in the form of balances at the Bank of England. In this way the Bank of England became the holder not only of the gold reserve of the whole country, but of the banking (cash) reserve.[17] This established the Bank of England as a regulating institution holding a special position of duty in the currency and credit system of the country, and thus it came to acquire the characteristics of a central bank.

The 1844 Act ensured the ultimate monopoly of the note issue in the hands of the Bank of England. The Act certainly had much to recommend it: the heart and soul of the 'currency' principle which inspired it was a rigid tie of Bank of England note issue to a 100 per cent gold reserve. (The Currency School held that policy should be governed by rules; by contrast, the Banking School thought that the authorities should be allowed discretion.) But unfortunately, as might have been expected, the link to gold was suspended very soon afterwards (in 1847), and so the only thing which remained was the central bank monopoly, on which all countries have modelled their monetary constitutions ever since. Indeed, the 1847, 1857 and 1866 crises – which supporters of free banking blamed on the centralised control of the money supply – showed that the government was always prepared to abrogate the Bank Act whenever it felt the need. This naturally undermined all credibility in the clause in the Act limiting the fiduciary issue of the bank. As Vera Smith notes,

> The relations between the Bank and the Government were, in fact, too long established for either the Bank or the Government to envisage anything other than full Government support to the Bank in times of stress. It had always been a privileged and protected institution, and it was in the interests not only of the Bank but also of the Government that it should remain so.

The Bank's directors were extremely loath to recognise the
delicacy of the Bank's position in a system which, as the result
of a long series of Governmental manipulations, had made it
the controlling element in the country's credit structure.[18]

In other words, it was only by an incremental process of increasing government control that central banks came to play the role
they all play today, that is, of discretionary monetary management, and the regulation and support of the banking system. The
'lender of last resort' function completes the state's control over
the credit system, for it gives the central bank the responsibility of
accommodating demand for high-powered money in times of
crisis, thus preventing panic-induced contractions of the money
stock.

That central banking is neither historically nor theoretically
inevitable is amply demonstrated by the monetary regime known
as free banking. Under this regime, the state does not enjoy a
monopoly in the issue of fiduciary money (bank notes). In 1717,
for instance, the privilege of issuing bank notes, which had been
confided to the Bank of Scotland, was abolished. Until the monetary regime set up in England in 1844 was extended to Scotland
in 1845, Scotland survived without a central bank, and the country was not under the control of the Bank of England.[19] The law
stipulated what a pound was in terms of gold, but on that basis different banks were able to issue bank notes, just as modern banks
all issue cheques. (A bank note is, indeed, nothing but a cheque
made out to the bearer for a round amount.) A historical reminder
of this is the fact that, to this day, Scottish clearing banks still
enjoy the right to issue bank notes – even if that right has as little
real significance as the 'promise to pay the bearer' still written on
English bank notes, because Scottish banks can issue only as many
bank notes as the Bank of England allows them to. The essence of
the free banking system, competition between the banks, has
obviously been abolished.

The free banking system allowed a proliferation of financial
institutions and a development of financial services; durable
growth and balanced financing of that growth; a near-absence of

banking collapses; and an escape from the business cycle at a time when other regions which had a centralised banking system suffered from depression caused by a credit crisis. (The snowball effect of inflationary credit is a common characteristic of monetary systems which give one institute a monopoly right to issue currency.[20])

Free banking arrangements have, however, been the exception. The rule has been a monetary regime ensuring metallic convertibility, but in which the currency and the central bank enjoy a privileged status. Even under regimes of metallic convertibility, central banks have usually enjoyed the monopoly right to issue the currency. This monopoly, granted by the state, is, however, substantially moderated by the contractual relations which govern the relationship between the issuer (producer) and the user (consumer) of money. Its abrogation, however, amounts to nothing other than the dispensation by the state of the central bank's duty to honour its cheques (bank notes).

The Classical Gold Standard

'And because silver and gold have their value from the matter itself; they have this first privilege, that the value of them cannot be altered by the power of one, nor of a few commonwealths; as being a common measure of the commodities of all places. But base money, may easily be enhanced, or abased . . . But that coin, which is not considerable for the matter, but for the stamp of the place, being unable to endure the change of air, hath its effect at home only; where it is also subject to the change of laws, and thereby to have the value diminished, to the prejudice many times of those that have it'

THOMAS HOBBES[21]

The regime of metallic convertibility (with or without a central bank) is usually referred to as 'The Gold Standard' for shorthand. The classical Gold Standard was the monetary regime to which most of the civilised world adhered from 1880 to 1914. Although the experiences of this time are very interesting and illustrative, the important point is not so much this relatively short-lived period of international monetary harmony, but rather the millennial principle of commodity money.

For this reason, it is misleading to think that the definitive element of the Gold Standard was fixed exchange rates between currencies. This egregious error was committed by those, like the former British Chancellor of the Exchequer, Nigel Lawson, who compared the European Exchange Rate Mechanism to the Gold Standard.[22] Fixed exchange rates between currencies were only a consequence of the fact that the world's currencies were, until 1914, merely different national expressions of the same commodity, gold. Gold was, in truth, the world's single currency. In other words, it was only because the regime of convertibility protected rights *domestically* (by enforcing a contractual arrangement between the issuer and the users of money) that it created exchange rate stability *internationally*. Rights were protected domestically because money was not created by the state.

In other words, as its fascist and Nazi opponents realised only too clearly, the Classical Gold Standard was fundamentally the outcome of a liberal world view. It was indissociable from a belief in the rule of law and free trade, of which the nineteenth century represents the most glorious flourishing. It was founded on an integrated set of norms which were embedded in the prevailing classical liberal consensus of the latter nineteenth and early twentieth centuries, and based on institutions which themselves expressed beliefs about the proper organisation of economic life.

Contrary to the belief of many modern politicians and economists, the Classical Gold Standard as an international monetary regime did not last because of co-operation between central banks, but rather because of its absence. Central banks co-operated bilaterally to arrange liquidity transfers in times of need, but their main preoccupation was with the domestic soundness of their currencies, not with its external value. If the latter was stable, it was because they were successful in pursuing the former. Both the origin and the stability of the Gold Standard were in fact outcomes of a more diffuse and decentralised process than the conventional thinking on the Gold Standard suggests. As one historian explains, 'Co-operation fails to explain the origin and stability of the regime. In fact, it was a failure to co-operate that led to the emergence of the regime in the 1870s . . . Moreover, monetary relations under the Gold Standard were highly consistent with prevailing national interests, and the regime showed a harmonious and self-enforcing nature.'[23]

Nor was the Classical Gold Standard successful because of the power of the British Empire. (The pound sterling was the world's main international currency in the nineteenth century, and many historians have attributed its success to British hegemonic influence over the world's financial system.) The same historian remarks, 'Time and time again, Britain had the opportunity to bring about a regime which was in its interest, and time and time again it failed to do so.'[24]

It is therefore strange that modern economists denounce the Gold Standard as an excessively rigid system. Perhaps some people find the obligation to pay debts unnaturally constricting, but all that the regime of metallic convertibility ensures is that there is no free lunch, not even for central banks. On the contrary, far from being inflexible, the Gold Standard, like any other market regime, is far more flexible than the statist control of the money supply under which we suffer today. Precisely what that regime did was to allow the market, not the state, to regulate the amount of credit in the economy, and therefore the money supply. Letters of credit, or any other market-generated means of payment, expanded or contracted in number according to the needs of commerce: a stock of precious metal easily served as the basis for a circulation of other means of payment which greatly exceeded it. The only essential point was that, however complex the network of credit, everyone respected their promises.

Indeed, given what we know about the growth of finance and trade in the nineteenth century, the charge of inflexibility is historical nonsense. There was a huge growth in credit instruments: public bank notes, private bank notes, cheques, transfer orders, certificates of deposit, commercial bills, financial bills, drafts, storage certificates, stock market securities, T-bonds, mortgages, warehouse receipts and clearing-house loan certificates: these represented over 90 per cent of the growth in the collective money supply of the eleven leading economies of the time.[25] It was precisely the growth of these credit instruments (always subject to the ultimate demands of convertibility) which kept national gold stocks from varying more than they might have under the exclusive use of gold in national and international transactions.

Indeed, the international system of credit functioned under the Gold Standard precisely because of the public and private confidence in international convertibility. This is why the international Gold Standard coincided with an explosion in foreign investment, and why the world enjoyed highly abundant capital flows compared with periods before and since. Liquidity was plentiful (with foreign exchange increasingly supplementing gold), elastic (because of limited capital controls) and geographically dispersed.[26] This monetary regime, based primarily on domestic and private interest, contrasts with the growth in 'international cooperation' after the Second World War. This is why our historian concludes that 'the most pervasive element in the workings of the gold standard was the liberal [that is, decentralised] nature of the regime'.[27] He argues,

> Among the group of nations that eventually gravitated to gold standards in the latter third of the nineteenth century (i.e. the gold club), abnormal capital movements (i.e. hot money flows) were uncommon, competitive manipulation of exchange rates was rare, international trade showed record growth rates, balance-of-payments problems were few, capital mobility was high (as was mobility of factors and people), few nations that ever adopted gold standards ever suspended convertibility (and of those that did, most returned), exchange rates stayed within their respective gold points (i.e. were extremely stable), there were few policy conflicts between nations, speculation was stabilizing (i.e. investment behaviour tended to bring currencies back to equilibrium after being displaced), adjustment was quick, liquidity was abundant, public

and private confidence in the international monetary system remained high, nations experienced long-term price stability (predictability) at low levels of inflation, long-term trends in industrial production and income growth were favourable, and unemployment remained fairly low . . . The pre-war gold standard . . . supported both micro- and macro-economic efficiency, accommodated domestic diversities (i.e. protected domestic autonomy), contributed to harmony beyond monetary relations, achieved a fairly desirable distribution of gains and burdens among gold-club nations, controlled inflation, facilitated trade and investment, maintained employment and income growth, minimized misalignments, maintained confidence, provided liquidity, and facilitated adjustment.[28]

Crucially, the Gold Standard also ensured a near perfect stability in prices. For example, Britain had a constant definition of the pound sterling in gold terms for 220 years from 1711 to 1931, during which time prices rose by a mere 29 per cent. By contrast, prices in a typical European country, France, have risen by a factor of 2,558 (in terms of gold) in less than eighty years.[29] Indeed, it is an indication of the degradation of the modern world that 'price stability' can mean annual inflation rates of several per cent a year, even when 'price stability' is laid down as a constitutional or legal obligation, as in Germany. The supposedly stable D-Mark, indeed, has in fact depreciated in value by some 200 per cent in a single generation. Such constant inflation (albeit at supposedly low annual rates) is a phenomenon which is now taken for granted, but which did not exist systematically before 1914.

Even in periods when new gold was discovered, inflation was very low by modern standards. During the sixteenth century, for instance, when the amount of gold tripled because of Spain's exploitation of South America, prices tripled.[30] A comparison with the figure for twentieth-century France just quoted shows this to be a minute level of inflation in modern terms. This gives the lie to the very common (yet absurd) claim that the Gold Standard handed influence over the gold price to gold-producing countries.

This system was abandoned in 1914. European states, faced

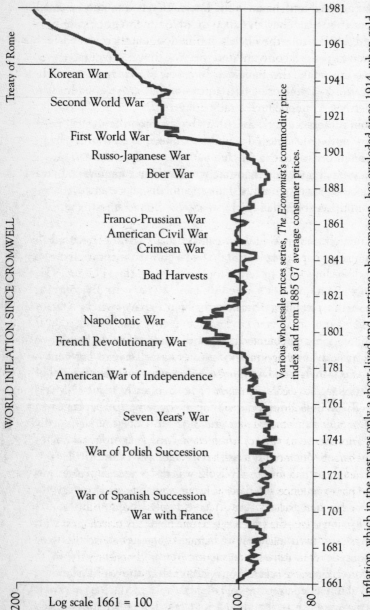

WORLD INFLATION SINCE CROMWELL

Treaty of Rome

Korean War

Second World War

First World War
Russo-Japanese War
Boer War

Franco-Prussian War
American Civil War
Crimean War

Bad Harvests

Napoleonic War
French Revolutionary War

American War of Independence

Seven Years' War

War of Polish Succession

War of Spanish Succession
War with France

Various wholesale prices series, *The Economist*'s commodity price index and from 1885 G7 average consumer prices.

Inflation, which in the past was only a short-lived and wartime phenomenon, has exploded since 1914, when gold convertibility was abandoned.

1981
1961
1941
1921
1901
1881
1861
1841
1821
1801
1781
1761
1741
1721
1701
1681
1661

200

Log scale 1661 = 100

100

80

with the need to fight the First World War, had to arrange quick access to funds. They therefore absolved their central banks of the duty to honour their debts. In the words of the Act by which France suspended convertibility in 1914, 'Until it is decided otherwise by a law, the Bank of France . . . is released from the obligation to reimburse its bank notes in cash.'[31] At the time, the measure was intended to be only provisional.

It is therefore erroneous to say that the Gold Standard 'broke down'. It did not 'break down': the whole grim apparatus of state intervention was needed to destroy it. Very often, these included measures which were even more obviously authoritarian than the basic suspension of convertibility itself: when convertibility was suspended in the United States in 1933, for instance, Americans were forbidden by law from holding gold. Contracts which had been concluded in gold convertible dollars were retrospectively declared null and void.

The Gold Exchange Standard

> 'We therefore consider it necessary that the system of international exchanges be re-established, as was the case before the world's great misfortunes, on an indisputable monetary base which bears the mark of no country in particular. What base? In truth, there can in this regard be no other criterion or standard than gold. Eh! oui. Gold, which does not change its nature, which can be cast indifferently into bars, ingots or coins, which has no nationality, which is held eternally and universally as the inalterable fiduciary value par excellence . . . Obviously one cannot dream of telling other states what to do in their internal affairs. But the supreme law, the golden rule as one might say, which must be reinstated and honoured in international economic relations, is the obligation to balance, from one monetary zone to another, the balance of payments resulting from exchange with real transfers of precious metal'
>
> CHARLES DE GAULLE, 1965[32]

What did 'break down', however, was the monetary system introduced after the First World War. This system bore only a
tangential relationship to the Classical Gold Standard, and,
indeed, it destroyed one of the Gold Standard's most important
central features. The new system was known as the Gold Exchange
Standard, and was created at Genoa in 1922.

Resolution 9 of the International Conference at Genoa dismantled one of the central provisions of the Classical Gold
Standard. Previously, central banks had been allowed to issue
currency only against gold, or against credits in national currency
like bills of exchange or government bonds. Genoa recommended
reducing the role of gold and using foreign currency reserves
instead. Thus it allowed central banks in 'peripheral' countries
(for example in continental Europe) to count in their monetary
reserves dollars and pounds sterling, the so-called 'key currencies' which remained a direct link to gold. They could use these
holdings in key currencies to issue their national currency.

The great French economist, Jacques Rueff, known mainly for
his lucid and impassioned writings in favour of the Classical Gold
Standard, and whose influence reached its apogee under one of the
most ardent champions of national sovereignty, General de
Gaulle, was a bitter and impenitent critic of this Gold Exchange
Standard. He first attacked it in 1926, when he predicted that it
would lead to a boom and bust. The credit bubble in the latter half
of the 1920s, the Wall Street Crash of 1929, and the ensuing
Great Depression, only proved him all too correct.

As Rueff showed, the Gold Exchange Standard dismantled
one of the most important elements of the Classical Gold
Standard because it dispensed the 'key' countries from the normal
disciplines of the market. Under the Classical Gold Standard, if
a country was a net importer of goods and a net exporter of capital, the capital outflows would reduce the quantity of money
(gold) in the economy and cause the interest rate to rise. Because
it became more expensive to borrow money in that currency,
imports would cost more, tend to fall, and the system would
balance itself out.

Under the Gold Exchange Standard, by contrast, net capital

outflows did not result in a contraction of credit in the key countries. Dollars or pounds paid for goods went abroad, but were
immediately repatriated by their holders on the money markets in
London and New York. Thus repatriated, they could serve as the
basis for new credit. Payments of money from, say, America to
France (in exchange for French exports to America) increased
the amount of money in circulation in France (because the Bank
of France could use the dollars to issue francs) but did not
correspondingly diminish the amount of money in circulation in
America.[33]

This meant that the countries with the 'key' currencies (Britain
and America before the Second World War, only America after it)
received the extraordinary privilege of being able to buy things
from abroad without their internal money supply ever diminishing.
Their balance of payments could thus remain permanently in
deficit, because everything happened as if the deficit did not exist.
Rueff aptly called this 'the deficit without tears'.[34] It was thus
inevitable that the United States ran a permanent balance of payments deficit – as it continues to do – because the system cut the
link between the total volume of purchasing power of a country
and the state of the country's current account on its balance of
payments.

We still live with this system today, because the dollar enjoys
status as a world reserve currency. As a consequence of its pre-emi-
nent position, large sectors of world trade are subject to the
important swings in its value, while central banks are obliged to
take measures to support it, for fear of seeing their reserves evaporate. As the US Treasury Secretary John Connally once remarked
smugly to the rest of the world, 'The dollar is our currency, but it's
your problem.'[35]

Because the Gold Exchange Standard provided no brake on
the deficit country, therefore, it could continue creating credit
indefinitely until the whole house of cards came crashing down, as
it did in 1929. The crash of 1929, based on an artificial credit
boom in 1927–28, made the depression into a great depression:
during 1927–28, money had flowed from the USA and the United
Kingdom to the Continent in great quantities, but the monetary

reserves of those countries remained unchanged. The Gold Exchange Standard thus accumulated indefinite amounts of new credit made on the basis of a mass of gold which did not exist. Indeed, because of this endless duplication of credit, all countries with convertible currencies suffered from permanent inflation. This exposed all countries to the dangers of recession which the collapse of the double pyramid of credit caused by the Gold Exchange Standard inevitably brought about.

In other words, what collapsed in the 1930s (and again in 1971–73) was not the Gold Standard, but a grotesque caricature of it. But the Gold Exchange Standard was defended precisely because of the characteristics which Rueff spent so much of his life attacking: governments, like most people, like to think that there *is* a free lunch, and they were delighted with a system which increased their discretionary room for manoeuvre.

Bretton Woods

This is presumably why the world repeated exactly the same error after the Second World War as it had committed after the First. What Genoa had done for the pound and the dollar, Bretton Woods did for the dollar alone – and with the same results.

The entire system was centralised around the dollar. The structure of the system was thus that of a wheel with spokes: the dollar was at the centre of the system, and the other currencies orbited around it. Foreign central banks held dollars in their reserves (as they do to this day) and the dollar price of gold was fixed at $35 per ounce.

As the holdings by foreign central banks of potentially convertible dollars increased, the United States realised that it could not honour its debts. On 15 August 1971, in defiance of its treaty obligations, the United States unilaterally revoked its obligation to sell gold to other central banks at $35 an ounce. The last link to a commodity had been cut, and the oil price in debased dollars obviously rose immediately.[36] The era of inflation and economic decline had begun.

Because the Gold Exchange Standard within Bretton Woods absolved the United States of the duty to settle its foreign debts, Rueff never ceased to hold it responsible for the persistent American dual deficits in its balance of payments and in its budget – problems which are still obstinately with us to this very day. It is amusing, indeed, given the latest attempt (in 1995) to balance the US budget deficit, to be reminded that in 1963, 1965 and 1968, successive American leaders were even then confidently predicting the imminent balancing of the budget deficit. Rueff insisted that the budget and balance of payments deficits would never be solved until this aspect of the monetary regime was corrected, and that those who wanted to balance the budget first before correcting the monetary regime were simply putting the cart before the horse. The Republican congressman, Jack Kemp, and the candidate for the Republican presidential nomination, Steve Forbes, both concurred with this view in 1996.

Indeed, it was precisely because it failed to prevent the accumulation of debt that both the monetary regime established at Genoa in 1922, and that established at Bretton Woods, New Hampshire, in 1944 (coming into force in 1947) were doomed to ineluctable failure. The United States cut the link between the dollar and gold because it knew that it could not afford to pay its debts in gold. The significance of this step cannot be overestimated. Even President Nixon himself called it 'the most important event in the financial history of the world'[37] – although he obviously approved of it.

Yet it is extraordinary that the decision by a government unilaterally to revoke its duty to pay its debts should not be more reviled to this day. After all, this was hardly the first time that a government had tried to get itself out of excessive debts by debasing the currency or refusing to honour its commitments. This is especially strange, since it set in motion a train of events with whose consequences we are still living today. Not the least of these is the inevitable decision by the world's oil-producing cartel to increase the price of oil in depreciated dollars.

While Bretton Woods restricted neither inflation nor the accumulation of government debt, it had at least ensured exchange rate stability between the participating currencies. But in the era of generalised fiat currencies which dawned after its collapse, all countries in the world now operate monetary systems which are pyramidal in structure, national in content and statist in essence.[38] The exchange rate stability of Bretton Woods thus remained impossible to re-establish: as the sorry history of the European Exchange Rate Mechanism shows, state-controlled currencies can, *in virtue of their fiat status*, never achieve either internal or external stability.

The concept of world monetary disorder

> 'Cecily, you will read your Political Economy in my absence. The chapter on the Fall of the Rupee you may omit. It is somewhat too sensational for a young girl. Even these metallic problems have their melodramatic side'
>
> MISS PRISM IN *THE IMPORTANCE OF BEING EARNEST* BY
> OSCAR WILDE, ACT II

Because fiat (paper) currencies are the creation of the state, they are incompatible with a market order. The widely held belief that the fluctuating exchange rates which have existed between currencies since 1973 are the expression of a market order is, therefore, false. Far from being evidence of a market order, floating exchange rates are the proof of its very absence.

To be sure, there is a market in currencies: we see evidence of it nearly every night on TV screens, when the 'business reports' show a dealing room to give the impression of interesting, up-to-the-minute news. In fact, however, the high technology and the elaborate financial instruments in the foreign exchange and money markets are no more the expression of a high degree of market development than the increased sophistication of burglar alarms is evidence of a greater degree of public security. For the products being traded in such massive quantities twenty-four hours a day around the globe are, as we have seen, state-controlled. This control is exercised through the twin legislative instruments of

legal tender and forced (or fiat) currency status, that is, the obligation on creditors to accept the currency as payment, and the
refusal by central banks to reimburse their bank notes in cash.

There is, then, no free market in currencies in the modern
world. There is, instead, a distorted market in state currencies.
The fact that the prices of currencies vary does not mean that this
market is free: prices fluctuate on the world cereal markets, too,
but no one would pretend that they are free. Both the world currency markets and the world's cereal markets are perverted by
subsidy and dumping: in both cases, the product (money, cereal)
is either monopolistically produced by the state (this is the case
with paper money) or heavily subsidised by it (as is the case with
cereals).

Indeed, it is because the supply of the world's currencies is based
on that most insubstantial thing of all, the policies – and even the
nods and winks – of each government, that fluctuations occur in
the value of currencies which are not based on changes in the
real economy. States cannot dictate currency movements
absolutely. But because they determine the supply of their currencies, and because the management of the money supply is therefore
so eminently political, the currency markets devote their main
efforts to trying to second-guess the meaning of what politicians
and central bankers say. Many of these fluctuations are patently
absurd: the dollar once rose on the markets because President
Clinton hired a good lawyer to defend himself from charges of
sexual harassment.[39]

Similarly, a state can certainly pursue a long-term policy of
having an undervalued currency (the dollar is a case in point),
while state influence can often have absolutely spectacular results
in the short term: in September 1995, for instance, the German
Finance Minister, Theo Waigel, was able to send the Italian lira
crashing through the floor with a mere leaked remark about the
size of Italy's budget deficit.

Indeed, if states did not maintain the two legislative instruments of legal tender and fiat status in place, state-controlled
paper currencies would probably disappear. Who, after all, would
prefer a valueless piece of paper to one which guaranteed the

bearer of it a right of ownership of a commodity? Their existence is maintained *only* by the legislative apparatus which created them in the first place.

A simple thought experiment can help us to see this. (It also helps to rebut the common charge that supporters of the gold standard are somehow opposed to the forces of the market.) If there were a truly free market in currencies, banks and individuals would be allowed to issue currency. It is obvious that an individual or a bank who issued a paper ticket which was a title to nothing, would find little use for it. It would, indeed, be utterly worthless. By contrast, a title to a commodity would have value. If private banks and private individuals were able to issue their own currencies, then it is likely that state-controlled paper currencies would rapidly be driven out of the marketplace by better, convertible ones.

Moreover, it is precisely under such conditions that truly sound currencies would emerge: providing that they were subject to the common law against fraud, banks or individuals who issued notes convertible into precious metals, and whose name was good, would, in all likelihood, capture an important part of the bank-notes market. To put it another way, state-controlled paper currencies can only exist where there is a monopoly of note production, and where free entry to the note-production business is restricted.

This model also enables us to see the shortcomings of proposals to allow the competition – in Europe, say – between national paper currencies. Such competition might improve matters, but it would not substantially alter the nefarious role played by modern states in the economy. It would be better to allow competition in the issuing of currency, providing that the state stipulated convertibility. It would thus ensure respect for the law by clamping down on rogue or unreliable issuers of bank notes.

Therefore, no amount of international 'markets' can compensate for the basic unfairness of having government-controlled currencies. Large banks and international financiers may be able to play the currency game to their advantage, but this is at the expense of the fair, free market relations which would otherwise be enjoyed by ordinary citizens. It is no coincidence if the man in the street regards the wild activities of young men in red braces to be as alien as those of international bureaucrats. As Edmund Burke realised, state currencies – which inevitably become the substance of speculation – are corrosive of the real economy:

> But where the law, which in most circumstances forbids, and in none countenances, gaming, is itself debauched, so as to reverse its nature and policy, and expressly to force the subject to this destructive table, by bringing the spirit and symbols of gaming into the minutest matters, and engaging everybody in it, and in every thing, a more dreadful epidemic distemper of that kind is spread than has yet appeared in the world. With you a man can neither earn nor buy his dinner, without a speculation. What he receives in the morning will not have the same value at night. What he is compelled to take as pay for an old debt, will not be received as the same when he comes to pay a debt contracted by himself; nor will it be the same when by prompt payment he would avoid contracting any debt at all. Industry must wither away. Oeconomy must be driven from your country. Careful provision will have no existence . . . The truly melancholy part of the policy of systematically making a nation of gamesters is this, that tho' all are forced to play, few can understand the game; and fewer still are in a condition to avail themselves of the knowledge.[40]

There is, therefore, an important difference between the unfairness of the currency markets and those of other markets perverted by the interference of governments in their goods. Money is not just any commodity: it is the very means of exchange itself. It is, as Burke said, the 'nerve centre of everything'.[41] A market functions freely only if prices are not subject to state influence or control. If the value of a contract freely concluded between two parties is subject to discretionary change by the state, then the market cannot be said to be free. Therefore neither the currency markets – nor indeed any market in any good or service, whether national or international – can be said to be truly free in a world of fiat currencies.

Consequently, although currency fluctuation may not decrease the volume of international trade, it perverts it. Currency fluctuations can wipe out at a stroke increases in productivity which have been painstakingly obtained over an entire year. As such, those opponents of the ERM who advocate floating exchange rates because they allow a country to 'adjust' (that is, devalue) if the economy is uncompetitive, are simply protectionist. Taking discretionary state action (for example by keeping the currency undervalued) is incompatible with free and fair trade.

Fluctuating rates disturb international commerce because they impose an extra cost on business. It should be obvious to anyone that while the dollar can lose 5 per cent in a few days, and certainly 10 per cent in a few months, most businesses break their backs to increase profits by a few percentage points in one year. It is not sufficient to say, as many supporters of floating rates do, that companies can hedge against risk. First, such hedging represents a cost. Second, even hedging cannot change the fact that the long-term devaluation of a currency over time represents an unfair advantage to the uncompetitive companies in the devaluing country. If an exporting company bills in dollars, its revenue will drop over time if the dollar falls, without that company having changed the terms of its contracts with its clients. By intervening in this way in contracts concluded between two parties, the monetary policy of a country inevitably perverts free trade.

The reason why floating exchange rates are not a market order is precisely that the producers of money are not obliged to respect the law of contract. Floating rates – which are the direct consequence of the nationalisation of the production of money – resemble a centrally directed war economy more closely than a market one.

'Doomed to all the horrors of a paper circulation'[42]

'A paper circulation not founded on any real money deposited or engaged for . . . and this currency by force substituted in the place of the coin of the kingdom, becoming

thereby the substance of its revenue, as well as the medium
of all commercial and civil intercourse, must put the whole
of what power, authority, and influence is left, in any form
whatsoever it may assume, into the hands of the managers
and conductors of this circulation'

EDMUND BURKE[43]

It should not be forgotten that the Bank of England's private business continued to be of critical importance until the end of the nineteenth century, and not without significance even in the inter-war years. The Bank was not formally incorporated into the machinery of state economic management until 1946.[44] Full metallic inconvertibility dates only from 1971. In other words, the discretionary central control by the state of the credit system, the money supply and thus of the whole economy, which we now take for granted, is in fact a very recent historical occurrence.

But the constitutional implications of fiat currencies are as grave as the economic ones. Even though the state has always increased its control over monetary policy by means of the institution of central banking and the imposition of fiat currencies (indeed, even before then, states imposed centralisation of minting, yet there is no reason why there should be a single state mint), the suspension of convertibility represents a qualitative increase of state control, not just a quantitative one. For in a regime of forced currencies, the state's control becomes discretionary and not legislative.

When the state nationalises the currency through the suspension of convertibility, the executive muscles in and abrogates the rule of law in monetary matters. A currency is forced on to the population, whose value lies entirely in the hands of the managers of it. That value therefore becomes dependent on trade-offs between other political considerations, not on the forces of the market.

Moreover, the state's power to decide the money supply is exercised with little or no input from the parliament. In countries with 'independent' central banks, interest rates are fixed with absolutely no consultation of Parliament whatever. In countries where interest rates are fixed by the government (that is, where the central bank is under the control of the Minister of Finance), there is at least some parliamentary accountability, because the minister has to account for his decisions after the event to parliament.

Both systems stand in stark contrast to a regime of metallic convertibility, where monetary policy is subject to the law. David Ricardo, the great theoretician of international trade and champion of the Gold Standard, argued for the return to gold after its abandonment during the Napoleonic Wars precisely because he thought that, without gold convertibility, the Bank of England was usurping the rights of Parliament and the law.[45]

Furthermore, monetary policy has become the single most important instrument the government wields to influence the state of economy. As one authoritative source rather coyly admits, fiscal policy has not proven in practice to be as flexible a macro-economic tool as monetary policy. The former is more unwieldy and slower in its operation, the latter much easier for the government to act directly.[46] He fails to add that it has the advantage – in the eyes of governments – of being discretionary.

But the constitutional implications of this are very grave. A liberal state is one in which the government is express and conscious. Individuals should look after their personal interests and after those of their dependants, and the state must fulfil its role as a moral person, charged with achieving collective and social ends, and with upholding and defining the rules which permit and encourage social interaction (the rule of law).

In a liberal regime, the state should perform this and other functions only by using those resources which it has been explicitly given. This means money raised from tax or borrowing. Tax rates can be high or low, borrowing can be high or low, but these resources must be known if the regime is to be considered liberal. A transparent budget obliges the government not to undertake actions of which the public disapproves.

If instead the government effectively raises money covertly by inflation – even at the supposedly low rate of 2 per cent a year – then it is raising money without the express consent of

Parliament. Whereas liberal government is express, the raising of revenue by inflation is occult. Inflation is now taken for granted, but it should be rejected as firmly as if the government were able to take a variable amount of, say, between £2 and £5 annually out of every £100 in people's bank accounts, without the consent of Parliament. Parliamentary control of government finances works only if the government is not in a position to provide for unauthorised expenditure by increasing the circulating amount of fiat money. Inflation, after all, is a tax. As Ludwig von Mises has written,

> The excellence of the Gold Standard is to be seen in the fact that it renders the determination of the monetary unit's purchasing power independent of the policies of the government and political parties. Furthermore, it prevents rulers from eluding the financial and budgetary prerogatives of the representative assemblies. Parliamentary control of finances works only if the government is not in a position to provide for unauthorized expenditures by increasing the circulating amount of fiat money. Viewed in this light, the Gold Standard appears as an indispensable implement of the body of constitutional guarantees that make the system of representative government function.[47]

If government spending is not limited to taxation and borrowing, the government will be released from the fundamental law of civilisations with real rights: it will be able to take without giving, and to obtain without asking. Raising money through inflation dissipates government responsibility, and the resulting attribution of false rights damages the judicial mechanism. Regimes with false rights are in a state of social disorder. As soon as one passes from a contractual system to a discretionary system – in whatever domain – one passes from the order of a free society to the disorder of a statist society. Viewed in this light, the gold standard can be seen to be an indispensable element in the body of constitutional guarantees which make the system of representative government function.

Authoritarian government is government which acts without using tax to pay for its actions. The cost merely falls on society instead. Authoritarian government takes the form of a command. It implies the subjection of individual wills to governmental decisions, by the institution of sanctions which render undesirable all acts other than those which the government commands to be accomplished. In a liberal regime, government accountability is concentrated largely in control over tax. But Parliament's control over government finances is severely attenuated when convertibility is suspended.

Central bank independence – a trap

The concept of central bank independence is thus a dangerous political trap. Supporters of Maastricht argue that central banks, especially the European Central Bank, ought to be free from government control. But the comparison with the Gold Standard shows that whether the bank is independent or not, the money supply is manipulated centrally by the discretionary power of the state, and not by the market.

Central bank independence does not depoliticise currency management. It merely places what is inevitably a political activity in the hands of people who are not democratically accountable. Currency management is inevitably political in a regime of metallic inconvertibility, because the value of the currency depends exclusively on what the markets think that the monetary authorities are going to do. It is therefore imperative for the central bank to cultivate an 'image' or a reputation for stable currency management. But the cultivation of such an image is an eminently political activity, because to convince others that you are likely to behave in a certain way you need to act in public – that is, politically.

Monetary policy cannot produce price stability unless the overall economic management of the monetary union is sound. The famously 'independent' Bundesbank, like any other central bank, is an integral part of the whole fabric of written and unwritten political practices which enjoin the pursuit of monetary stability in

Germany. One example of this is the 1967 'Act to Promote Economic Stability and Growth' which requires the Bundesbank's co-ordination with the central, regional and local authorities, trade unions and enterprise associations. Indeed, the federal structure of the Bundesbank itself, of which the Germans are so proud, is precisely supposed to root the bank's decisions in what is happening in the real economy. The Bundesbank recognises that its own success is indissociable from the tissue of financial, social and economic relations which govern the workings of the German state. If the Bundesbank did not act politically, by communicating and negotiating with government and other associations, then it would be unable to contribute to the overall stability for which post-war Germany is reputed.

Being at the very heart of Germany's overall political and economic order, therefore, the (relative) success of the Bundesbank cannot be understood in purely technical terms. People often refer to Germany's inflationary history and the present 'culture of stability' as reasons why the D-Mark is strong. But arguments which invoke history and culture prove precisely that in general, political authority derives from established practice, not from legislative fiat nor technical arrangements. Indeed, all power is ultimately political.

Instead of central bank independence, what is needed is for rulers to be forced to spend only what, by virtue of duly promulgated laws, they have collected as taxes. Parliamentary control of government spending, indeed, makes sense only if the back door to inflation is closed. This means that, in a truly parliamentary regime, it should be the law which stipulates the framework for monetary policy and the market which regulates it. In short, Parliament in Britain should force the Bank of England to honour its promise to pay the bearer, on demand, the sum indicated on its cheques (bank notes). The re-introduction of the Gold Standard would represent an increase of law-based parliamentary control and a decrease in the discretionary power of the executive. By contrast, making central banks independent reduces the amount of parliamentary (and therefore law-based) control and increases the discretionary power of state authorities.

This is no doubt why the German Bundesbank is so hostile to gold. Helmut Schlesinger, the former President of the Bundesbank, said once that he was hostile to gold because it would 'put us in the hands of the Russians and the South Africans'.[48] This comment combines ignorance about the functioning of the gold market with a rather distasteful assumption that foreigners will control us if we allow our markets to open. In a similar vein, the present President of the Bundesbank, Hans Tietmeyer, patronisingly told a meeting of Swiss businessmen in April 1996 that 'the constitutional link between the Swiss franc and gold seems to me to be of no practical importance. It is just a relic from the long-distant era of the gold standard.'[49] He failed to mention the uncomfortable fact that the allegedly perfect D-Mark has depreciated by one third of its value against the Swiss franc since 1972, or that it has also lost 75 per cent of its value against gold since the Bundesbank was created in 1957.

A corrupt understanding of the role of money

> 'To destroy the bourgeois system, it is sufficient to corrupt
> its currency'
>
> LENIN[50]

Perhaps the gravest consequence of the state control of the money supply is the way it has perverted our understanding of the role money plays in society. Previously understood as a means of exchange and measure of value by which to conduct commerce and trade without interference by the government, inconvertible money has instead come to be understood as an instrument by which the state can regulate the economy. Few so-called free marketeers seem to see this problem. In Britain, for instance, the man supposed to be at the cutting edge of free-market thinking, John Redwood, was able to write approvingly that 'the interest rate is the most important lever the government currently operates to influence the state of the economy'.[51] Indeed it is, but one would have thought that a man who believed in free markets would hold that the government cannot and should not have such a lever. There is little difference, indeed, between Redwood's thought and Stalin's recommendation of the control of the economy via the rouble.[52]

But this is exactly how modern economies function. The monetary operations of governments and central banks are deliberately aimed at influencing the performance of the nation's economy. They do this by raising or lowering interest rates – the price the central bank charges for lending money to other banks – in order to influence the amount of credit in the economy. Unlike the regime of convertibility – in which credit, and therefore the money supply, are allowed to expand or contract according to the needs of the market, and where prudent credit is encouraged because of the basic soundness of the currency – with forced currencies the state arrogates to itself the role of deciding how much money there should be in the economy.

This represents economic *dirigisme* of a kind which would be rejected as incredible if it were proposed for any other sector of the economy. Modern governments look at the economy and try to decide how much credit it needs, but if they tried to do the same for steel or motor cars, they would rightly be considered dangerously megalomaniac. It is just as impossible to know how much credit there should be as it is impossible to know how may cars, or how much steel, there should be.

This extraordinary degree of central control over the economy is, surprisingly, not even contested by most economists who claim to favour the free market. Monetarists, for instance, hold that the quantity of money has a major influence on economic activity and the price level, and that monetary policy should target the rate of growth of the money supply. Thus, although it is supposed to be a free market system, monetarism in effect advocates the rationing of credit by the state: if it is deemed that there is too much money in circulation, the state tries to turn down the credit tap by raising interest rates, and vice-versa. The state thus tries to operate comprehensive economic *dirigisme* using the bluntest of instruments, the money supply. As such, the right-wing doctrine of monetarism, which asserts that the state must restrict the money supply in order to control inflation, is little but a kind of perestroika of what is essentially a Soviet-style system.

One can even question the almost universal commitment to 'price stability', which is at the heart of all monetarism and, obviously, at the heart of the project to create a single currency in Europe. Measuring inflation is arbitrary. Why pick this basket of goods rather than that one? Similarly, the pretence that the state can or should maintain the stability of all prices has something slightly totalitarian about it. Money might rise in value as well as fall. The Austrian school of economics bases its analysis of money as a means of exchange on the instability inherent in human life and action. Money emerges as a relatively stable reference point with which to deal with this instability. But, as common sense tells us, there is no reason why prices should be stable: they can go up or down. Certainly inflation is a bad thing, but it is always the result of state action.

State control of the money supply also means that policy is always directed to the past and not to the future: currency management is based on data about what has happened in the economy in the past – the prices of an arbitrarily fixed basket of goods, factory costs, labour costs, and so on. By contrast, a state policy of maintaining gold convertibility requires the guardians of the currency to ensure that users of money maintain confidence in the currency for the future. It is no coincidence if the suspension of convertibility has been accompanied by the massive accumulation of debt, which simply means that we are mortgaging our children's future for the sake of living beyond our means now.

By interfering at the very heart of contracts, the suspension of metallic convertibility has corroded the notions of duty and personal responsibility. It has encouraged the view that people can enjoy infinite rights without the corresponding duties, and – in politics as much as in economics – the sentiment that one can permanently be owed things by other people ('society') without ever owing them or society anything in return. The endless demands for 'rights' (many of which are little but demands for state hand-outs), uncomplemented by the recognition of duties, are nothing but the demand to live at other people's expense. Because the 'promise to pay the bearer', which is still hollowly proclaimed on British bank notes, is never respected, we live in a world where the cornerstone of the free market, the principle of the respect of contracts, is ignored by the very institution which is supposed to uphold it.

The European Monetary System

As has been seen, the failure of the European Monetary System was inevitable. Metallically inconvertible currencies can *only* fluctuate in value against one another, because they are unwieldy, state-controlled products. Their value is not based on the value of any commodity, but merely on the policies pursued by the government and the central bank. Attempts to fix or even co-ordinate the value of such currencies against one another are thus always futile.

Any comparison between the gold standard and the EMS is, therefore, deeply flawed. Because paper currencies are state instruments for regulating the economy, to base the exchange rate of one currency on another currency is, *a fortiori*, to base the economic and monetary policy of one country on that of another country. Therefore, as Bernard Connolly has shown, rather than de-politicising currency management, the ERM politicised it to the most extreme degree.[53] Moreover, the Gold Standard produced centuries of inflation-free growth, while the ERM produced a decade of huge currency crises and high unemployment. The Gold Standard was a self-regulating system in which national and private interests created a natural balance and harmony on the one hand; the ERM was a cartel of states trying hypocritically to pretend that their interests were the same, and stifling growth in their economies by doing so.

For various reasons, the D-Mark achieved a dominant position within the EMS (even though it was not supposed to function in this way) and so participating countries had to agree to copy German monetary (and therefore economic) policy if they wished to maintain exchange rate parity with the Mark.

Countries supported their own membership of the EMS because they thought that copying the anti-inflationary policies of the German central bank would help them bring down their own inflation. However, the system generally required them to maintain interest rates higher than those in Germany: precisely because their currencies had inflationary reputations, the market regarded their currencies as more risky than the D-Mark, especially in the long term.

In order to make their currencies more attractive on the markets, countries needed to keep their interest rates higher than the D-Mark in order to keep parity with it. This had a long-term depressing effect on their economies, and entrenched Germany's strength relative to them. Germany, therefore, profited doubly. Firstly, as an exporting country, it benefited from an undervalued currency, for which undervaluation the countries with overvalued currencies paid. Secondly, it benefited from low short- and long-term interest rates, while those of its competitors were generally higher. (The Netherlands and Austria were an exception to this trend.)

This was the reason for the repeated crises which afflicted the EMS throughout its existence. In 1981, 1983, 1986, 1992 and 1993, European currencies were forced to devalue against the D-Mark. The last two of these crises were especially dramatic, the first leading to the ejection of the pound and the lira from the Exchange Rate Mechanism, the second leading to the effective dissolution of the ERM itself. (The permitted fluctuation bands were enlarged from +/– 2.25 per cent to a huge and meaningless +/– 15 per cent.) In each case, the markets took the view that the deflationary pressures on the non-German economies were too great to withstand continued high interest rates, and they speculated that the currencies would devalue and cut rates.

Not only was the EMS subject to speculation, it also actively encouraged it. By announcing the rate they were prepared to defend, national monetary authorities gave the markets an easy target. If the markets guessed correctly that a devaluation was impending, the winnings were immense because the devaluations occurred only after a crisis. During such a crisis, central banks intervened massively on the market to buy their currency at the overvalued prices. The more currency traders sold to the central bank at an overvalued price, the more likely a devaluation became (because the reserves of the bank started to run low) and the bigger were the winnings. As Europe has discovered after the bands were extended to +/– 15 per cent, these pressures disappear once currencies are effectively no longer defended.

On the other hand, those opponents of the ERM who argued that fluctuating rates are compatible with the single market were historically disingenuous. Not only did this view fail to accept that fluctuating rates are the expression of nationalised currencies, it also failed to acknowledge that the exchange rates between the European currencies were fixed when the Treaty of Rome was signed, in virtue of Bretton Woods. Stable exchange rates were an integral component of the single market when it was conceived.

Sovereignty

Many Europeans think that state sovereignty is threatened by the world's foreign exchange and money markets. They argue that it is no longer realistic, in an interdependent international economy, to maintain independent monetary policies. They argue that monetary union is necessary so that states can be stronger collectively than they are individually, and thus better able to affirm themselves against the markets.

Almost everything is wrong with this argument. Firstly it is wrong to say that states can no longer pursue independent monetary policies. There are plenty of countries which pursue independent monetary policies, and even those states who belong to fixed-rate currency arrangements like the EMS are limiting their room for manoeuvre of their own free (sovereign) accord.

Secondly, to say that a state is 'less sovereign' or 'weak' because it cannot 'stand up to the market' is to assume that the market is something 'out there'. In fact, of course, a state of law is defined precisely by the extent to which law and market relations prevail within its territory. A *fortiori*, the influence of market forces, whether national or international, on its government's policies, is merely a natural consequence of the game whose rules a state of law should obey. Metallic convertibility ensures that the government provides the framework which upholds free contracts concluded between individuals, by specifying and guaranteeing – in law – the national currency in terms of a certain quantity of gold.

The phrase 'monetary sovereignty' is meaningless. Sovereignty is not something which pertains to a particular area of government policy: it is the defining characteristic of a constitutionally independent state. To talk of 'sovereignty' over this or that question is therefore intrinsically wrong, because sovereignty has only a tangential relationship to power. To say that a state is sovereign is to say that it is responsible for the laws passed on its territory, and that its constitution does not require it to defer to a higher authority.

The reason for the misunderstanding is precisely that the modern exercise of state power in the monetary domain *does* have more to do with the sheer wielding of power than with the upholding of law. In regimes of metallic inconvertibility, the state wields brute executive power with a view to manipulating the economy, and thereby the value of independently concluded contracts. This means, among other things, that one state's monetary policy can affect another's: national economies are subject to great pressure from the monetary policies of the dominant regional power.

By contrast, in a regime of convertibility – that is, if the currencies used are commodities – then the monetary policy of each state does not affect that of the other. The strength and credibility of one currency in terms of gold does not affect the strength or credibility of gold itself. A monetary regime of metallic convertibility, in other words, increases practical national autonomy. It was precisely because Charles de Gaulle – that great champion of national independence – realised that the Classical Gold Standard was the *sine qua non* for national sovereignty that he called for its restitution in 1965.

Indeed, it is testimony to the hypocrisy of our times that an age which presents itself as one of openness, globalisation and internationalism maintains nationalised monetary policies of the kind usually only found in wartime. Meanwhile, the period which is usually decried as being that of absolute national autarky, the nineteenth century, had, in effect, a supranational monetary regime with all the limitations on discretionary executive power which that implied.

Defining the currency in terms of a certain weight of gold is a sovereign act which is used to define what the national currency is, comparable to the promulgation of a new element of contract law. It enables citizens and residents of a country to formulate their prices in an official monetary unit whose soundness the government is committed to protect. It is only on this basis that a sound credit system can be founded.

It is therefore imprecise to speak of the national sovereign right to issue currency. What is referred to here as a sovereign right is in fact nothing other than the sovereign's duty to ensure the soundness of the currencies circulating in the state. If coins have always had the heads of kings and emperors on them, this does not signify their right to play fast and loose with the currency. It is rather a sign that the coin in question is issued under, and guaranteed by, their authority.

The suspension of convertibility therefore represents an abuse of national sovereignty, for the government of the day thereby absolves itself of the duty to uphold, and to abide by, the law. But when the national sovereignty of a state is usurped, the usurper is not recognised as legitimate. Marshal Pétain's government in Vichy was not recognised as legitimate by De Gaulle, because it installed itself in power after the defeat, and governed only with the consent of the occupying forces: taking orders from the Germans, it could not be regarded as either legitimate or sovereign. Similarly, the civil war in England was fought over the issue of whether the king should hold all the sovereign powers himself, or whether he should exercise them through Parliament. The victories of Cromwell, and especially of William of Orange over James II, established the doctrine which is known as the 'sovereignty of Parliament'. Any power not exercised through Parliament is regarded as illegitimately exercised. It is curious that, although monetary policy in a regime of metallic inconvertibility gives the government massive discretionary power over the entire credit system and the entire economy – a power which it exercises with minimal or no reference to Parliament – this point is not more widely understood.

The constitutional implications of European Monetary Union

> 'We want the political unification of Europe. If there is no monetary union, then there cannot be Political Union, and vice-versa'
>
> CHANCELLOR KOHL[54]

> 'The single currency is a strongly federalising element. The opponents of a federal Europe are right about that. It is my conviction that the euro will lead to a European economic government'
>
> KAREL VAN MIERT, EUROPEAN COMMISSIONER
> FOR COMPETITION[55]

Because the imposition of forced currencies represents a grave constitutional imbalance in favour of the executive, and to the detriment of the legislature, it is clear that the creation of a single European currency has very great constitutional implications as well. To create a monetary union in Europe is to transfer a very important executive power from the nation-state to Europe. The transfer would be so great that the member states of Europe would cease to be self-governing entities. They would no longer have the right to govern themselves by taking decisions about the economy independently. Although a single currency might not formally create a new state, therefore, it would create one in fact.

To centralise European monetary policy in the hands of an independent European central bank, but in the absence of a properly constituted state, will be to wield monetary power with no parliamentary control whatever. It is not even clear that this power will be exercised with any formal consent: after all, it is the declared intention of Chancellor Kohl to use the single currency to make European union 'irreversible'. This suggests that member states are not expected to be able to revoke their consent to the monetary union. As the President of the Bundesbank has said, 'The path to monetary union is a path of no return.'[56]

Not only is this discretionary power being confided to an unaccountable institution, it is not even circumscribed by law. The Central Bank's overriding commitment will be to 'price stability', but the meaning of this is not defined anywhere in the treaty. The Bundesbank Law also requires the Bundesbank to pursue this aim, but being similarly undefined, German inflation has very often been above 5 per cent and never 0 per cent. In other words, the (German) model on which the European Central Bank is based differs crucially from that employed by the Bank of New Zealand, where the Central Bank operates like a contractor for the government, committed to getting inflation within a specified target. If it fails, then the governor of the bank suffers a cut in salary and can lose his job. The European central bankers, by contrast, are provided with high salaries and guaranteed pensions, and they cannot be sacked.

Sometimes the political decisions which are taken by independent central bankers are legitimate. It is, for instance, legitimate that a central banker charged with maintaining price stability decides to pursue monetary rigour rather than short-term growth. But sometimes – as usually happens with power exercised in a discretionary fashion – the power of central bankers is not exercised legitimately. The Bundesbank, for instance, has flexed its muscles on several occasions to ensure that its own power is not compromised either by the Bonn government or by foreign governments. It has also acted in co-operation with the Bonn government, most notably to pursue Chancellor Kohl's foreign policy aims of creating a political union between Germany, France and the Benelux countries. This is why the former German Chancellor, Helmut Schmidt, has claimed that the Bundesbank wields greater influence in world politics than the German foreign minister.

All of this should emphasise that, whatever its statute, the very existence of a central bank is evidence of state control over the financial system. As the Bundesbank itself never fails to make clear, indeed, monetary stability cannot be ensured within a monetary union without a coherent fiscal framework. In other words, political union is necessary if monetary union is to work: monetary policy cannot be practised *in vacuo*. It has been shown persuasively that nineteenth-century monetary unions often broke down because of the unstable finances of the participating states.[57] What was true then is truer now, because discretionary monetary policy plays an even more integral role in overall economic management than it did under the Gold Standard at that time.

Consequently, any institutional arrangements – such as the 'Stability Council' proposed in 1995 by the German Finance Minister, Theo Waigel, or, for that matter, like the Maastricht Treaty itself – which would enable the European Council to tell a state to cut its deficit, would represent a huge transfer of political power to the central organs of Europe. It is not a matter of obeying the impersonal rules of good housekeeping, such as those upheld by the market forces of the Gold Standard, but rather of allowing European institutions to govern Europe's member states. When the German Finance Minister opined in September 1995 that Belgium ought to privatise more rapidly in order to qualify for EMU, this was a clear illustration of the degree of mutual interference which economic and monetary union will introduce.

To transfer the bulk of one's economic decisions to Europe on this basis is dangerous for democracy. Power will be shared between three constitutionally unaccountable institutions: the Central Bank, the Council of Ministers, and the Commission. Instead of doing this, the challenge for Europe ought to be to force its governments to spend only what they have collected in tax by virtue of duly promulgated laws.

A modest proposal

> *'This volume collects and repeats all the exploded fallacies on the subject of the standard of value and currency. Its authors bewail the darkness of the age which adheres to a standard*

which was adopted in the reign of Queen Elizabeth, and which they consider wholly unsuitable as a measure of value now, considering the extent of our commerce, and the increase of pecuniary transactions in number and amount. They might with equal justice complain, that since travelling has been increased by the completion of railways, the foot measure is adhered to'

SIR ROBERT PEEL, SPEECH IN THE HOUSE OF COMMONS, 6 MAY 1844, ATTACKING A REPORT BY THE OPPONENTS OF HIS BANK CHARTER ACTS[58]

It is typical of the European ideology to hijack good arguments and divert them towards bad causes. It is a good thing, for instance, to want to depoliticise money management; but a central bank and a single currency, which are intended to be the crow-bars by which to force the political integration of Europe, will only politicise it to the most extreme degree. It is a good thing to have price stability, but the D-Mark has not enjoyed it and nor will the Euro. It is a good thing to have a common reference point for trade, but the European single currency will not only divide the single market between those countries which are in the monetary union and those outside it, it will also tend to separate Europe from the rest of the world. All of the arguments which link the need to trade with the need for a single currency are, therefore, curiously self-contradictory: their logical conclusion is a world currency, not a European one.

Instead of dealing with the degradation in the world monetary system, European Monetary Union will only entrench the status quo of discretionary fiat currencies. It will neither improve Europe's monetary regime, nor respond to the destructive financial and economic consequences of international monetary decline. It will not put an end to the privilege of the dollar, nor will it bring issuing banks back under normal contract law by abrogating their privilege of being exonerated from paying their debts and of creating fiduciary money out of nothing.[59]

There are two solutions which could re-establish a liberal international monetary order. The first would be to create a European currency, in parallel to the national European currencies, defined by a weight of gold. Not only would such a currency be genuinely objective and politically neutral, unlike the proposed European single currency, it would also be stronger than the D-Mark. Such a parallel currency would introduce itself progressively, according to the wishes of people and the needs of the market. Bank notes and deposits could be issued in gold convertible ecus by the European central bank, national central banks and commercial banks. It is to be hoped that the emergence of a gold currency in Europe would encourage the United States to reinstate the gold convertibility of the dollar, as the Republican candidate Steve Forbes had promised to do anyway. Bob Dole's running mate, Jack Kemp, also supports the gold standard.

Alternatively, the fiat status of all national European currencies could simply be abolished. This would automatically bring national monetary systems back under the law of the market and the law of contract. This solution, unlike the previous one, would not produce a visible single European currency. It would therefore have the advantage of placing supervision of the monetary order under Parliament, instead of delegating the discretionary exercise of monetary policy to the government or the central bank.

Such a solution would also be compatible with the declared aim of Europe to create a single market. A free market is defined by competition between producers and the free choice of consumers. The replacement of different national currencies within the single market by one new common currency cannot be said to increase competition: on the contrary, it decreases it. Monetary integration coherent with the spirit of the single market would have allowed Europe's citizens a greater, not a smaller choice of currencies. Legal tender could have been extended to all Europe's currencies, and consumers might thereby have chosen which currencies to use.

The way to achieve this second solution in Britain would be for the Royal Mint to create a gold sovereign, and for bank notes to be issued in pounds, convertible into these coins. The Bank of England could be privatised, reduced to its purely supervisory functions as the watchdog of the City of London, or brought under proper parliamentary control with a committee specially created for the purpose.

Only then would market principles – that is, the rule of law – be introduced into the final domain which remains impervious to it. Thus would the goals of Richard Cobden, the radical nineteenth-century free trader, be realised:

> I hold all idea of regulating the currency to be an absurdity. The very terms of regulating the currency and managing the currency I look upon to be an absurdity; the currency should regulate itself; it must be regulated by the trade and commerce of the world; I would neither allow the Bank of England nor any private banks to have what is called the management of the currency . . . I should never contemplate any remedial measure, which is left to the discretion of individuals to regulate the amount of currency by any principle or standard whatever.[60]

Who's falling into whose lap? Yevgeni Primakov and Javier Solana
shake hands at the NATO summit in Berlin, June 1996.

VI

THE THIRD ROME

'We won the Cold War together'

YEVGENI PRIMAKOV[1]

It is seldom realised that the plan to integrate the states of Western Europe around a single currency, grandiose though it is, is only part of an even larger plan. 'European integration' is not an exclusively Western European affair. Indeed, the very purpose of suggesting the institutional restructuring of Western Europe around a hard core, according to the plan's German authors, is to permit the creation of a common (Western) European foreign and security policy, which will in turn be based on a 'lasting partnership with Russia'.[2] The German government has repeatedly stressed that it is 'the advocate of pan-European, not just West European, thinking'.[3]

By arguing, as they often do, that the need for such integration is 'more important than ever'[4] now that the Cold War is over, supporters of pan-European integration are saying that the international system has become more unstable because the world is no longer divided into two blocs. This view is widely held, and is nourished by the dangerous fiction that nationalism and 'ancient hatreds' (such as in Yugoslavia) have erupted following the end of the 'discipline' of Communism. Just as with their faulty diagnosis of 'the nineteenth century', so the underlying assumption is that, if free, people will kill each other.

The principal manner in which it is proposed to create this pan-European structure is by strengthening the provisions for majority voting on foreign policy within the EU, and by creating a 'European Defence Identity' within NATO. This will involve making the hitherto moribund Western European Union (WEU) into the defence arm of the European Union. The idea is then to construct a pan-European security architecture with Russia. In other words, the institutional reforms which are being undertaken in Western Europe, especially the institutionalisation of the hard core through monetary union, are the necessary prerequisite for the larger vision of one single politico-military system for the whole European continent. As the former German president, Richard von Weizsäcker, said: 'A common foreign policy can be created only via the single currency. Getting used to a single currency is the only possible means of achieving a single foreign policy.' The hard core in the West is to be the Western 'pillar' of a pan-European security structure, of which the Eastern 'pillar' will presumably be Russia and her associated states. It is no coincidence if this larger goal is being advocated with the same language of European integration as the smaller, Western European one.

Similarly, the view that the entire Eurasian continent can be governed by one single politico-military structure is inspired by the same unitarian and administrative vision we have encountered elsewhere. It is inspired by a deep reluctance to draw lines in the sand, or to have meaningful borders of any kind. It is inspired, above all, by the Utopian wish that politics can be spared the need ever to make the choice between friend and enemy.

Big ideas on the Moscow–Bonn hotline

> 'When the Russian and the German get together, they are invincible'
>
> GERMAN PROVERB[5]

Germany, which has placed herself at the centre of the process of Western European integration (principally by her leading position within the process of monetary union), is set to place herself at the centre of the process of pan-European integration as well. She has always boasted of her pan-European agenda: she is the primary advocate of the eastward enlargement of the European Union and NATO, and she is also the primary advocate of the lasting partnership with Russia. Meanwhile, the French attachment to the idea of a 'European' defence identity (as opposed to an Atlantic one) is very long-standing.

It is also in Germany that thinking on matters European – whether monetary or geopolitical – is the most coherent and therefore the most forceful. This explains why Germany's policies tend to carry the day against those of more intellectually muddled neighbours. As was seen in Chapter III, the geopolitical arguments of the original CDU document which proposed the 'hard core', 'Reflections on European Policy', were very limpid. The paper argued that, with the end of the Cold War, Germany was exposed to potential instability on her eastern flank: she proposed to deal with this threat by drawing the Eastern European states into the German/Franco-German orbit, while at the same time constructing a lasting partnership with Russia in order not to offend the Eastern superpower.

Even before the publication of that document, and certainly ever since, German and French politicians alike have frequently stressed the need to build European security on the basis of an alliance with Russia. Chancellor Kohl has said on many occasions that he wants to develop 'a pan-European security system' by enlarging NATO to the East and developing a privileged partnership with Russia.[6] The German Foreign Minister, Klaus Kinkel, has confirmed this on many occasions. The foreign policy spokesman of the CDU/CSU parliamentary group, Karl Lamers, indicated in March 1996 that he could not foresee any circumstances in which this policy would change, and did not feel that the Chechen war gave any reason to change it. His argument was that Russia just *was* a European country, and that therefore it should be part of an integrated European security structure. He made it clear that the very purpose of creating a European defence system was to reduce the American component in NATO. Russia was not afraid of NATO as such, he said, she was afraid of

America, and a European defence was thus a way of diluting the American component and thereby reassuring the Russians.[7]

These ideas have since gained wide acceptance among European federalists, and they are the official policy of many European states and institutions. For instance, the Belgian Prime Minister, Jean-Luc Dehaene, speaking in his capacity as Chairman of the WEU, declared in June 1996 that 'Russia must have its place in the European security structure. It must not be an isolated and frustrated nation, but a partner in a democratic Europe.'[8] It is also official European policy to integrate the WEU into the EU.[9] Similarly, President Chirac indicated in October 1995 that he was determined to show French understanding for Russian opposition to NATO enlargement.[10] His Prime Minister, Alain Juppé, suggested 'a vast partnership' with Russia, which was detailed when President Yeltsin visited Paris on 20 October 1995. Juppé indicated that such a partnership could include a charter or treaty between the Atlantic alliance and Russia.[11]

Pan-European collective security is, indeed, an old French dream as well as a German one. They understand the anti-American implications of it well enough, after all: ever since De Gaulle, France has always been ready to cosy up to Russians if they can thereby escape the American yoke. François Mitterrand famously called for 'a permanent structure for the whole of Europe'.[12] Edouard Balladur continued a similar version of the same idea with his European Stability Pact, which he kicked off in Paris in May 1994 and which was signed a year later.[13] Finally, the French felt able to re-integrate themselves fully into NATO's military command when, in June 1996, NATO agreed to allow a European defence identity 'under the political and strategic direction of the WEU'[14] within its structures, and with the intention of thereby creating – in Jacques Chirac's words – 'a European security organisation in which Russia has her full place'.[15]

Chancellor Kohl's belief in the possibility of a 'lasting relationship with Russia' dates, no doubt, from 1989, when the former Soviet president, Mikhail Gorbachev, decided to allow German reunification to go ahead. Since then, Kohl's political friends have frequently evoked the heady days when the unification deal was signed in 1990, and the picture of Genscher, Kohl, Gorbachev and Shevardnadze informally sitting around a wooden table in the Caucasus during a break in the negotiations is now a symbol of Russo-German bonhomie during those momentous days.

However, the Germans' faith in the continuing possibility of building an axis with Moscow after the formal dissolution of the Soviet Union, and after Mikhail Gorbachev's fall from power, also reflects a deep convergence of geopolitical requirements, as well as shared views about political philosophy and the role of the state. This was confirmed in May 1994 when Boris Yeltsin visited Bonn, an occasion when the harmony between the Russian and German views of Europe could hardly have been greater. Yeltsin was at pains to emphasise that the relationship between Germany and Russia (the two largest countries in Europe, as he pointed out) was crucial to the future political construction of Europe. 'Never forget, we are a European country,' he declared. Delighted, Chancellor Kohl replied to his Russian interlocutor that 'lasting security can be achieved only if individual countries are not excluded: the security of Europe cannot be guaranteed without, but only in close co-operation with Russia'.[16] Boris Yeltsin and Helmut Kohl agreed to install a telephone hotline linking their two offices.

But it was on the common vision of a politically united European continent that the Russian and German views converged most during Yeltsin's 1994 visit. As has been seen in Chapter III, German political culture is deeply infused with the desire for, and belief in, generalised harmony. The whole of Ostpolitik, indeed, was predicated on the Genscherite argument that the reunification of Germany could come only with détente and 'overcoming the division of Europe' by drawing closer to the Soviets and Eastern Europeans.

Much of this resulted in simple appeasement and even outright support for the Communist dictatorships: the moneys paid in the name of rapprochement by the Federal Republic of Germany to the German Democratic Republic, for instance, represented a signifi-cant financial crutch to the otherwise moribund and murderous East German regime.[17] So generous in diplomatic and financial terms was the policy of *détente*, indeed, that the veteran Soviet dissident, Vladimir Bukovsky, confesses to having believed that it had been orchestrated on the Kremlin's initiative. He writes of his surprise when he learned that, even if Russia milked it for all it was worth and probably manipulated some of its leading lights, the policy had, in fact, been invented by the German Social Democrats.[18]

But this German need for harmonisation became so strong that one German commentator has described the hallmark of West German foreign policy as being 'an insatiable striving after international harmony on all sides'.[19] Boris Yeltsin was therefore speaking the very language his hosts wanted to hear – and which the two sides had been exchanging for decades anyway – when he declared to his German hosts,

> A new unified Europe cannot be an exclusive club of the
> chosen. No more than security questions can be the privilege
> of the chosen. A united political, economic and spiritual
> architecture for our continent must not isolate countries or
> groups of countries, or separate them according to the crite-
> rion of friend or enemy, but it must integrate them into a
> unified organism. It is unworthy to divide Europe into zones
> of greater and lesser security. The politico-military institutions
> of our continent, born in the conditions of confrontation and
> the Cold War, are to be overcome . . . In our view, the path to
> this is via the development of the CSCE as an effective
> regional organisation. Under its roof, the co-ordinated efforts
> of the NATO Co-operation Council, the Western European
> Union and the Commonwealth of Independent States can
> find new content.[20]

The speech could have been written by Hans-Dietrich Genscher; but in drawing this beatific tableau of a united Europe, Yeltsin was saying nothing new. Moscow had long dreamed of the day when NATO would disappear, or be neutralised by a pan-European collective security system in which Russia would play a major role. Indeed, the first Russian proposal for a European security conference or treaty was made by Soviet Foreign Minister Vyacheslav Molotov, who had served under Stalin, at Berlin in 1954. At the same time, Stalin's would-be successor, Lavrenty Beria, who lost the battle to take over the Communist Party to Nikita Khrushchev, proposed to reach an understanding with the West on the reunification of Germany, for which he wanted $10 billion.[21] Again, in 1966, the Bucharest declaration of the Warsaw Pact called for the dissolution of both blocs, and their replacement by a system of collective security. In May 1968, when General de Gaulle was on a state visit to Romania, the dictator Nicolae Ceauşescu exploited his undeserved reputation in the West as a dissident in the Soviet camp – undeserved because Brezhnev put him up to it – to propose a structure of pan-European defence to the French president. When President Nixon went to Romania in 1969, the same idea was floated again.

Although the creation of such a security structure did not occur in 1969, these initiatives did bear some fruit, because they led in August 1975 to the first Conference on Security and Co-operation in Europe (CSCE), held in Helsinki. This was a triumph for Soviet diplomacy: Moscow's aim in signing the Helsinki accords was to get the West to recognise Soviet hegemony in Eastern Europe. The West responded by agreeing to do so, on condition that the Soviet Union recognise human rights. Thus was *détente* between East and West to be encouraged. In reality, of course, Western governments ignored the Soviet Union's continuing human rights abuses, and pursued the policy of *détente* anyway, arguing that there was no alternative to it. This policy took the international pressure off the Soviet Union, allowed it to re-arm and achieve military supremacy over the West by the end of the 1970s, and culminated in the Soviet invasion of Afghanistan in 1979.

What the Soviet Union valued in the Helsinki process was that it gave it an institutionalised say in European affairs, within a structure in which the American role was diluted. Soviet hostility to NATO, indeed, was above all hostility to the dominant American role in Western Europe. NATO's very existence was a challenge to Russia's pretensions to be the rightful European super-power.

Where other European institutions were concerned, the Soviets also quickly realised that what was 'European' was, by definition, not American. When the EEC was created in 1957, the Soviets attacked it as a consolidation of the Western bloc they so resented. But they opposed this 'false Europe' to a 'true' pan-European grouping, evoking the possibility of all-European integration as an ideal. Privately, they discussed whether the EEC might one day evolve into an anti-American bloc and, as such, be in their interests. By 1962, this idea had developed, especially as the Gaullist rejection of British membership encouraged the belief that the EEC would be independent from the USA. Time and again since then, the Soviets have stated that all-European integration is the right answer and that partial, EEC-style integration is a mistake.[22] It was in this vein that Leonid Brezhnev declared on a visit to Bonn in 1981, 'Whatever may divide us, we still inhabit a common European home.'[23] As one Russian pro-European commentator has written, 'Even in the Brezhnev era of "soft totalitarianism" the USSR showed interest in setting up an all-European system of security and co-operation.'[24]

Just three years later, the future General Secretary, Mikhail Gorbachev, was to exploit Brezhnev's slogan with far greater success. He referred to the 'Common European Home' in a speech to the House of Commons in 1984,[25] and later made it his hallmark. Inasmuch as the slogan meant anything, it indicated a Europe no longer divided between two power blocs, which in turn implied the reunification of Germany and the restructuring of the world away from its bipolar division. Above all, it meant that European countries – that is, Russia and not America – should determine the security and policies of the continent. In keeping with this aim, the Soviet Union declared 1987 to be 'the year of Europe', and gave new emphasis to the old theme of the need for wide-ranging European co-operation.[26]

Gorbachev's widely sold but seldom read personal manifesto, *Perestroika: New Thinking for Our Country and for the World*, devoted a whole chapter to attacks on NATO, and to Soviet desire to replace it with all-European co-operation instead. As part of his overall attack on American defence policy, Gorbachev tried to present American culture as foreign and dangerous to Europe: 'A serious threat is hovering over European culture, too. The threat emanates from an onslaught of "mass culture" from across the Atlantic . . . Indeed, one can only wonder that a deep, profoundly intelligent and inherently humane European culture is retreating to the background before the primitive revelry of violence and pornography and the flood of cheap feelings and low thoughts.'[27]

As Gorbachev was still explaining in 1995, his concept of the Common European Home was by no means in contradiction with those European institutions which already existed. On the contrary, he expected them to fit into his pan-European structure like parts of a Russian doll.[28] Thus would Russia 'integrate herself fully' into the continent. Like previous Soviet leaders, therefore, Gorbachev trained his sights on the CSCE as the framework with which to build a pan-European structure. On a visit to Paris in 1989, he declared himself in favour of 'a Europe from the Atlantic to the Urals' – the old phrase which De Gaulle had made famous, and which is geopolitical nonsense, because the Ural mountains cut Russia in two, and represent no political border whatever. If anything they are the mountain range which links Europe and Asia within one country, Russia.

However, Gorbachev's vague but compelling rhetoric about a united Europe, and the wind of change which swept the Eastern bloc in 1989, caused the CSCE to be suddenly reactivated in 1990. The meeting of the heads of state held in Paris in November 1990 concluded with the signature of a 'Charter for a New Europe' which spoke of the signatories' firm will to create a Europe 'from Vancouver to Vladivostock'. The CSCE also received institutions, as Gorbachev had proposed, and in 1994 became the OSCE (Organisation for Security and Co-operation in Europe) on a German/EU proposal. This reflected 'the intention of Russia to emphasise the OSCE as a regional organisation'.[29] Moreover, Russia succeeded in inserting into the Budapest summit's communiqué a commitment 'to launch in the CSCE a broad and comprehensive discussion on all aspects, as appropriate, aimed at devising a concept of security for the twenty-first century'.[30] In other words, the member states are committed to examining ways of subordinating NATO to the OSCE. Russia was getting close to realising her old aims: as Eduard Shevardnadze wrote in 1992, 'Perestroika has substantially determined the movement towards a new united Europe.'[31]

Indeed, a significant step towards the common European security structure of which Russia has dreamed for so long was taken when NATO and Russia signed a 'Founding Act on Mutual Relations, Co-operation and Security' on 27 May 1997. This document, which legitimised Russian 'peace-keeping' missions around the world, created a 'Joint Council' for policy-making between NATO and Russia. Although a proviso was inserted that the Joint Council could not be allowed to infringe the sovereignty, or to influence the policy-making, of NATO, Russia, or any of NATO's member states, the rest of the agreement reflected the desire for a very broad co-operation in security matters between East and West indeed. The policy areas listed for potential co-operation under the aegis of the Joint Council make up an entire page: in fact, it is clear that they are intended to cover the whole gamut of security and political issues. Elements listed include such catch-all concepts as 'issues of common interest related to security and stability in the Euro-Atlantic area'; 'conflict prevention'; 'peace-keeping operations'; 'regional air-traffic safety'; 'exchanges on nuclear weapons issues'; 'co-operative projects in defence-related economic, environmental and scientific fields'; and 'combatting terrorism and drug trafficking'.

The Chechen war: how the West was won

While Mikhail Gorbachev was Soviet president, and especially after the fall of the Berlin Wall, the Western reaction to Soviet proposals to create a Common European Home was extremely warm. NATO declared peace on the Warsaw Pact in 1990, and East–West relations have since then been predicated on the assumption that Russia is becoming more liberal and more democratic.

This policy, like much modern bureaucratic policy-making, remains on the same track, even though the assumptions which originally guided it are no longer obviously valid. This is the case with two central policy areas: the increasingly authoritarian rule of President Yeltsin, and Russia's attitude to the former Soviet Republics and the former member states of the Warsaw Pact.

As the Chechen war has shown, it is difficult to call Russia a liberal, democratic state. The initial bombardment of the Chechen capital, Grozny, in December and January 1994–95, was ferocious. Tens of thousands of civilians were killed in a matter of weeks by indiscriminate aerial bombing. After a year of fighting – by March 1996 – the estimated death toll was 40,000,[32] and there were millions of refugees in the region. This was proportionally the same as had been killed in the Bosnian conflict in four years. Ceasefires and withdrawals were regularly announced by the Kremlin, but the fighting continued throughout the first half of 1996, and included the assassination by the Russians of the rebel leader, Djokhar Dudaev.

However ferocious the bombing, and however high the civilian death toll, the West always insisted that the Chechen war was an internal Russian matter, and that it therefore did not concern them. In March 1995, the EU Foreign Affairs Commissioner, Hans van den Broek, travelled to Moscow to protest that Russia was blocking some EU imports, but he studiously refrained from any criticism of Russia's war against its own citizens in the Caucasus. When asked about it, he said that it was an internal matter and that the Chechen demands were unreasonable.[33] This compromising attitude contrasted with that of the president of the parliamentary council of the normally emollient Council of Europe, after President Yeltsin instructed Russian delegates to resist all interference in Russia's internal affairs: 'Human rights are never an internal affair. Chechnya is not an internal Russian affair because Chechnya never subscribed to the treaty which created the Russian federation.'[34]

But Hans van den Broek's attitude recalled that of Chancellor Kohl, who visited Moscow in February 1995. He emphasised the need for Western 'understanding' of Russian hostility to NATO enlargement, and preferred not to condemn the Chechen war. Similarly, when the French foreign minister, Hervé de Charette, travelled to Moscow on 23 January 1995, he declared that Russia was still on the path to reform, and that the Chechen war was 'a regrettable hitch'. *Le Monde* described as 'almost obscene' Charette's description of Yevgeni Primakov, the new foreign minister and former head of Russian's foreign intelligence services as 'a friend'[35] – especially as on the same day, Sergei Kovalov, the Russian human rights campaigner, had resigned as an adviser to Yeltsin, saying that the Russian leader had 'definitively abandoned democratic reforms'. (One wonders why Mr Kovalov did not realise this in October 1993, when Boris Yeltsin ordered the bombing of the Russian parliament, and when, in order to put down a parliamentary rebellion, three days of urban warfare left hundreds dead and wounded.)

Therefore, when the war broke out, international reaction was as mild as possible. The procedure for Russian admission to the Council of Europe was suspended – but Russia was admitted a year later anyway. The partnership and trade accord with the EU was frozen, and the EU demanded that there be a 'political' solution to the conflict – but the trade accord was signed seven months later, in July 1995, once the fighting had temporarily disappeared from jaded Western television screens. (This agreement was announced, incidentally, just after the Serb attacks on the UN safe haven of Srebrenica in July 1995, a coincidence which must have sent a clear message to both the Serbs and the Russians that aggression pays.) The UN's Human Rights Committee criticised Russia, and the OSCE sent a mission to Russia to 'promote respect for human rights' – but that mission was denied access to all the important areas.

It was obvious, in fact, that the West was not going to let a few rebellious Chechens get in the way of constructing a pan-European political and military condominium in which Russia would have her full place. Its reaction to the massively bloody campaign in the Caucasus was therefore not only to turn a blind eye: it was also to give formal approval to Russia's actions there. Indeed, the very fact that military operations in Chechnya did not begin until just after Boris Yeltsin had attended the summit meeting of the Organisation for Security and Co-operation in

Europe, in Budapest in December 1994, suggests that the Russian president had secured tacit approval from his interlocutors in Budapest for the operation.

Not surprisingly, Russia just ignored what little international pressure there was. Between the adoption of the agreement to send the OSCE mission on 11 April 1995 and the anticipated despatch of the team on 23 April, particularly vicious fighting occurred.[36] Fighting continued uninterrupted between the time of the freezing of the EU trade agreement and its final signature.[37] When hostages were taken in a village in Daghestan in February 1995, hundreds of civilians were killed in the Russian response, which was to blow the entire village to kingdom come – in full and flagrant view of the world's television cameras. On 26 March 1996, the Organisation for Security and Co-operation in Europe published a report which attacked the human rights situation in Chechnya. It concluded that the Russian army's behaviour was deliberately intended to terrorise the civilian population. It cited numerous atrocities, including the shooting by a helicopter of a civilian lorry. The helicopter landed, the survivors were captured and put into it, it took off – and then they were thrown out in mid flight.[38] Unperturbed by this, the International Monetary Fund made its biggest loan ever, $10 billion, in order to support 'reforms' in Russia – on the very same day.

Moreover, as Russian troops were bombing the Chechen villages of Bamut and Orechovo in March 1996, and as an estimated 600 civilians were killed in a day or two in the bombing of Samashki,[39] flooding neighbouring Ingushetia with 50,000 or more refugees, a consortium of German banks lent Russia DM 4 billion. To emphasise the political nature of this loan, it was announced by a German government spokesman.[40] Although the local OSCE representative said there was no chance of peace in the short term, later the same month a further four big German banks (Commerzbank, Deutsche Bank, Dresdner Bank and Westdeutsche Landesbank Girozentrale) lent a further DM 1 billion to the region of Cheliabinsk. Russia was also admitted as an observer to the 'Paris Club' of world creditors in March.[41] Meanwhile, France lent Russia 2 billion francs 'to support the process of economic transition'.[42] Finally, in May, the World Bank lent Russia $200 million to support 'Russian social services' in Novosibirsk, Rostov and other regions.[43]

By the end of April 1996, Western creditors had signed the biggest and most generous debt-relief package ever, agreeing to re-schedule $40 billion of Russian debt over twenty-five years.[44] So spectacular was this support that some commentators warned that the West was rather putting itself in hock to a massive debtor which could not, or would not, pay. The debt, which had been greatly inflated from 1985 onwards, was held overwhelmingly (75 per cent) by Western Europe, with Germany holding by far the largest part. By February 1996, indeed, Germany admitted offi-cially to having supported Russia to the tune of $75 billion in credits and financial aid.[45] Much of it, such as the DM 89.9 mil-lion given to Russia for 'projects set up by Germans living in Russia' has been given to 'help the unification of Europe', in the words of the Russian nationalities minister.[46] Germany was also a major contributor to the new IMF loan package, and Kohl's influence was decisive in bringing the loan about. But even though the Soviet Union had unilaterally ceased payment of the capital on its debt in December 1991, Russia continued to enjoy a comfortable trade surplus, while capital outflows from Russia into tax havens in the West were estimated to have reached between $70 billion and $100 billion by 1991: money was presumably being placed there to escape creditors. There was a whiff of blackmail in the air.[47]

Indeed, the West's candidate having announced during the pres-idential election campaign that he would withdraw Russian troops from Chechnya, the re-elected President Yeltsin swiftly ordered a new military offensive there on 10 July. The village of Mekhety, where the new rebel leader was believed to be, was liquidated.[48] Three hundred and seventy people were bombed to death and 170 wounded in a single week.[49] By August – despite the appointment of a man supposed to be opposed to the violence perpetrated against the Chechens, General Alexander Lebed, as Chairman of Boris Yeltsin's 'Security Council' – Moscow was threatening the Chechens with a war 'using all means'.[50] Meanwhile, President

Yeltsin appointed as his new defence minister the man who had organised the bloody suppression of a pro-democratic demonstration in the Georgian capital, Tbilisi, on 9 April 1989, when over twenty people were killed.

A European Commission official gave vent to the prevailing EU attitude to such objections when he commented, 'Yes, but the Chechens are a load of bastards.' This seemed to make the bombing of civilians acceptable, much as similar views about the Yugoslavs had encouraged the West to turn a blind eye to atrocities committed during the Balkan war. But it is difficult to imagine the EU, the OSCE or the Council of Europe reacting with similar indulgence if, on the basis that 'the Irish are a load of bastards', the British decided to carpet-bomb Londonderry. Indeed, it is difficult to imagine anything but deserved outrage even if, as British Conservative MP Alan Clark suggested in October 1997, the British government attempted to resolve the IRA insurgency by shooting dead 600 Republicans.

Russian hostility to NATO enlargement

During this time a second aspect of Russian policy seemed to destroy the premises of East–West *rapprochement*, without Western policy changing concomitantly. It was the definitive and unambiguous abandonment of the so-called 'Sinatra doctrine'. The Sinatra doctrine, the successor to the 'Brezhnev doctrine', according to which Moscow would maintain a tight rein over Warsaw Pact states by using the Red Army if necessary, was announced in October 1989 on American television by the Soviet Foreign Ministry spokesman, Gennadi Gerasimov. He said: 'We now have a Frank Sinatra doctrine. He had a song, "I had it my way [sic]." So every country decides, on its own, which way to take.'[51]

By 1994, however, this policy had been abandoned. Russian hostility to NATO, and her preference for a pan-European collective security structure, was expressed with increasing stridency. Indeed, it rapidly became the central plank of Moscow's foreign policy. In May 1994, General Gratchev, the then Russian defence minister, called for Russia to be given the right to partake in NATO decision-making mechanisms (to have a veto over NATO, in other words), and for NATO to be subject to the OSCE.[52] A Russian document leaked (presumably deliberately) in the autumn of 1995 even threatened invasion of the Baltic states should Poland join NATO,[53] while Communist officials in Belarus, who work in close co-operation with the Russian Communist Party, declared in November 1995 that Russia would invade the Baltic states if they joined the Atlantic alliance.[54] In December 1995, the then Russian foreign minister, Andrei Kozyrev, said, 'The NATO bloc must transform itself into something new, and Russia must certainly participate in that something new.'[55] Russia also continued to pursue her old aim of creating a European Security Council – an arbiter over European security questions, perhaps within the OSCE – knowing that she would be able to exert decisive influence over any such body by having a permanent seat on it.

Andrei Kozyrev's replacement, Yevgeni Primakov, reaffirmed Russia's goal of getting rid of NATO. In February 1996 he called for a pan-European security charter which would 'define the fields of intervention of each organisation' within it – that is, subjugate NATO to the OSCE.[56] The new structure would, he said, include NATO, the EU, the WEU and the Pact of Tashkent, to which former Soviet Republics belong. Instead of enlarging NATO to Eastern Europe, the Russian proposed that 'mutual guarantees' be made by NATO and the Pact of Tashkent to the states of Eastern Europe.[57] The Russian defence minister continued to press for a 16 + 1 arrangement for European security (integrating Russia into NATO's decisions), saying, 'NATO would be transformed not by broadening its zones of responsibility but by transforming it into an instrument of pan-European collective security.'[58]

At the same time, Russia undertook rearmament programmes and other actions which seemed incompatible with the spirit of co-operation which was inspiring Western policy. She repeatedly lied about the true state of her biological weapons, and failed to dispose of her 40,000 tonnes of chemical weapons.[59] She also publicly flouted the Conventional Forces in Europe treaty. She did not respect the treaty's deadline of 1 January 1996 for the destruction of thousands of tanks and other military equipment beyond the Urals,[60] and announced several times that she would ignore the treaty's central provisions limiting the number of troops Russia may amass on another country's border. In November 1995, General Gratchev said, 'Russia is not prepared to observe the CFE treaty.'[61] Similarly, Belarus, which is now Russia's Western border following the integration of the two countries into the Union of Sovereign Republics, has also been happily disregarding the Conventional Forces in Europe treaty:[62] it has refused to destroy the weaponry on its border with Poland – citing economic problems and hostility to NATO expansion as an excuse – and Russian soldiers now guard the Belarus–Poland border. By June 1996, Russian intransigence had succeeded: she obtained a further three years (until the end of May 1999) to fulfil her commitments under the treaty.[63]

As the EU Intergovernmental Conference began in Turin at the end of March 1996, Russian declarations against NATO enlargement increased in vigour. NATO kow-towing, however, only became more pronounced. On the very eve of the IGC, the Secretary-General, Javier Solana – a former anti-NATO, pro-Soviet Spanish socialist politician, appointed in January 1996 on Germany's suggestion – declared that it was essential for the West to reassure Russia 'that NATO has changed'[64] – as if it were Russia, not the West, which needed reassurance. A changed NATO was, of course, what Russia had always wanted. Solana also pointed out that the creation of a common European foreign and security policy would facilitate the creation of 'a European defence council', something which sounded very much like the realisation of the old Russian goal of creating a European security council.[65]

Despite these significant changes in Russian policy, the Western approach to Russia remained the same. Russian threats were met with accommodation. When Moscow accused NATO of genocide against the Bosnian Serbs when the alliance started its long-overdue air strikes in September 1995, the German foreign minister, Klaus Kinkel, rang Andrei Kozyrev, his Russian counterpart, 'to calm Russian fears of being isolated'. Kinkel argued that it was important to show Russia with deeds that she should be brought into the European decision-making process. The German government explained that it wanted the aim of overarching pan-European security co-operation to be preserved. Kinkel declared: 'Russia remains an important partner . . . We say "yes" to Russia taking her place at the European table: we want that.'[66]

Again, at the WEU summit in Birmingham in May 1996, Germany called for 'a security partnership between Russia and NATO', as well as for 'a political and economic partnership' between Moscow and the European Union.[67] No one seemed to care that, that very week, Russia had decorated Radovan Karadjic, the Bosnian Serb leader accused of genocide by the International Tribunal in The Hague, with the Prize of Saint Andrew, one of the highest Russian distinctions, for 'his qualities as a statesman'.[68]

The Council of Europe

German policy towards Russia did extend to actions as well as words. It was German pressure that was decisive in the decision to admit Russia to the Council of Europe in February 1996. Despite the atrocities being committed in Chechnya, the German government and the CDU set in motion the process for Russia's admission to the body in September 1995. The German Foreign Ministry claimed that restarting the admission process would give a blessing to Russia's attempt to find a peaceful solution in Chechnya. This reflected an old German conviction that 'integration' is a universal panacea, and a useful substitute for robust policy towards a foreign country. For some reason, however, the same logic did not apply to Croatia, whose application for membership was turned down on much lesser charges than those against Russia in June 1996.

Chancellor Kohl himself addressed the assembly of the Council of Europe on 28 September 1995. He reaffirmed that the aims of German policy were EMU and political union, the eastward expansion of NATO and the development of an 'unambiguous and lasting partnership with Russia and the Ukraine'. He wanted to 'draw Russia further and further into the fashioning of Europe's future'. He said, 'We want to develop a pan-European security system by enlarging NATO to the East and developing a privileged partnership with the Ukraine and Russia.'[69]

It was argued that Russian admission to the Council of Europe would enable pressure to be exerted to make Russia improve its human rights record. But as the French daily, *Le Monde*, commented on the day of the vote, 'Fascinated by the potentates of the Kremlin, and obsessed with an erroneous conception of stability, the West is repeating the same error it committed with Mikhail Gorbachev and his predecessors. It is supporting the Russian president as if he were the rampart against the arrival of Communists and nationalists, when in fact he is their very harbinger.'[70] For his part, the president of the pan-European union, Otto von Habsburg, called it 'a day of shame' for the Council of Europe, saying that the Russian delegation was led by one of the 'highest bloodstained functionaries of the KGB, Foreign Minister Primakov'.[71]

When the Russians were admitted, their reaction was as jubilant as it was contemptuous. A spokesman for the Russian Ministry of the Interior, whose troops were carrying out most of the terror killing in Chechnya, snarled, 'Give us some subsidies. Then we might think about some reforms.'[72] President Yeltsin said that the vote showed Western understanding for his policy in Chechnya, a policy he described thus: 'You have to kill mad dogs.'[73] Another senior official said that Russia would not abolish the death penalty, even though this was a condition of membership to the body. (Eighty-six people were executed by firing squad in Russia in 1995, and the number of appeals for clemency which Yeltsin rejected increased. In February alone, he rejected thirty.[74]) The official also said that the conditions in Russian prisons would not change, where people die of cold and hunger – and occasionally of cannibalism.[75] Yeltsin also immediately instructed the Russian delegates to the Council of Europe to 'block all initiatives for exerting pressure on Russia or for interfering in our internal affairs', by which he principally meant Chechnya.[76] Indeed, when the Council of Europe held a plenary summit of all its forty members in October

1997, i.e. after well over a year of Russian membership, Human Rights Watch issued a report showing that the human rights situation had actually worsened in Russia since it joined the organisation. Such an unimportant detail was, however, not allowed to disturb the general bonhomie, and the speeches of heads of state like Yeltsin and Shevardnadze were politely listened to by their peers. Indeed, as if to underline that the West will continue to appease Russia whatever happens, the Council of Europe's summit coincided with the announcement by the 'London Club' of world debtors that a further $33 billion of Russian debt was to be rescheduled.[77]

The idea that Russia could somehow be controlled by being admitted to the Council of Europe is vitiated by the same simple paradox which affects the similar argument about controlling Germany through monetary union: why does the state in question want admission to the body which is supposed to control it? The answer in Russia's case is that, as her long-standing support for pan-European structures shows, she has a deliberate policy of entering European institutions in order to influence them, and thereby to increase her general influence over the affairs of the Continent.

This policy of entryism has been explicitly stated on several occasions. When Russia was admitted to the Council of Europe, the head of the Duma's delegation to it, Vladimir Lukin, a 'liberal' politician, made this clear. He welcomed the vote, saying that now Russia would have 'to work hard in order to become a member of *all European institutions*'.[78] In saying this, he was only repeating the very words used by President Yeltsin during the state visit to Germany in May 1994, who also spoke of Russian membership 'of all European organisations'.[79] Russian entry into NATO, the World Bank, the IMF, the Council of Europe and even the European Union itself, were discussed – and welcomed by his German hosts. As a *quid pro quo* for German friendship, Yeltsin announced that he would support a permanent seat for Germany on the UN Security Council. On that occasion, indeed, Russia made it very clear that its goal was to place European security in the hands of an overarching security structure, the OSCE, and to make NATO subordinate to it.

The West is actively encouraging this policy. The Russian ambassador to NATO, Vitaly Churkin, is already inside NATO's councils, and the Russians have established a permanent representation at NATO's military headquarters in Mons, Belgium, as part of the 'Partnership for Peace' initiative. Russia has even asked for the three-star general stationed at SHAPE in Mons to become a permanent observer at NATO, and for the Russian presence to be increased in other NATO bodies. NATO has agreed with this in principle. Volker Rühe, the German defence minister, has welcomed the idea, saying it showed the Russians were ready for dialogue.[80]

But the process of Western appeasement came to a head at the NATO summit in Berlin in June 1996, when NATO agreed to allow a 'European pillar' to be constituted within the Alliance. Henceforth, operations will be able to be conducted in NATO's name, and using NATO's structures, but without the participation of the United States. Such operations would be conducted 'under the political and strategic direction of the WEU',[81] the very institution which European federalists wants to make into the defence wing of the European Union, and which has always had a vocation to act as a vehicle for the political integration of Europe.

Two events underlined the fact that this change represents a crucial dilution of the American element in NATO. The first was that France immediately announced that she was able to re-take her place in this new NATO. Having spent thirty years as a semi-detached member of the Alliance, after De Gaulle withdrew France from NATO's integrated structures in order to escape perceived American hegemony over the Continent, Jacques Chirac announced in June 1996 that France was now ready to take her full place in a changed NATO. He called for 'a renewed Atlantic alliance, and a European security organisation in which Russia has her full place'.[82]

The second, even more dramatic illustration of the implications of this change came in the sudden volte-face towards NATO operated by Moscow. Yevgeni Primakov, who attended the Berlin summit, and was treated, according to one German newspaper, 'like a star',[83] promptly inflected his country's opposition to NATO enlargement. He said that Russia no longer minded if other countries joined, providing that NATO troops were not stationed on their soil. It was, in other words, just as Karl Lamers has said: Russia did not mind NATO as such; what she minded was the American component. Once Europeanised, and detached from the USA, NATO, in Russia's view, would be neutralised. Moscow's long-standing aim had been achieved.

European ideology and the myth of 'nationalism'

On one level, this astonishing Western support for Russia can be read simply as an attempt to keep Boris Yeltsin in power and to influence Russia from outside. The approach can certainly be criticised: IMF officials noted with dismay from April 1996 onwards that all the rules attached to their loan were being broken during the election campaign, as both the Russian president and his prime minister constantly announced populist new spending packages at successive electoral meetings. As a Russian government official remarked, 'The IMF has made it clear that it will give the money in any case. The fund is completely ignored by the government.'[84] In addition, it can be argued that excessive political and financial investment in one candidate (Yeltsin) is putting all one's eggs in one basket-case.

But there is a deeper reason for the West's compliant reaction to the Russian demands. It is that the integration of Russia into Europe's political and military structures corresponds precisely to the same model which France and Germany have in mind for Western Europe: a Europe 'without borders'. This is inspired by the same unitarian and unpolitical view of government and statehood which has been analysed in previous chapters.

This mentality, which wants to sweep all conflict away under the rug of apparent consensus, eschews any notion of division in Europe and any notion of 'friend' and 'enemy' in politics. President Yeltsin himself explicitly said in Bonn in 1994 that 'a united political, economic and spiritual architecture for our continent must not isolate countries or groups of countries, *or separate them according to the criterion of friend or enemy*, but it must integrate them into a unified organism'.[85]

And yet the distinction between 'friend' and 'enemy' is precisely that which defines the activity of politics.[86] The distinction between friend and enemy is the difference between association or dissociation: political life – the activity of politics – is the domain in which the possibility of making the distinction obtains. Politics exists only where there is conflict, and it lives off the opposition between different parties, interests and goals. It also presupposes a distinction between citizen and foreigner, which is itself the *sine qua non* for peaceful or conflict-ridden interaction with other states, and for the clear delineation of juridical space.

This definition of politics does not rule out peace between peoples or states, or even neutrality. Far from peace being the absence of an enemy, or the absence of antagonism or conflict, peace is the absence of war. Moreover, one can only make peace with an enemy. It would be contrary to the essence of politics to want to suppress one's enemies, or to dissipate the distinction between friend and enemy into obscurity. In foreign policy as in domestic policy, peace denotes a certain equilibrium between opposing parties. If peace is not the absence of conflict, the difference between peace and war is simply that, in peace, a state or a person does not seek to destroy the enemy, but rather recognises him as a legitimate equal despite all his differences. Accordingly, any so-called proclamation of peace which implies the suppression or the negation of the enemy is in reality a camouflaged declaration of war. This is the danger of Yeltsin's remark. To put it bluntly, if the price of peace with Russia after the Cold War is the disappearance of the states of Western Europe in any meaningful sense, then that price is too high.[87]

However, Western leaders are generally in hock to an ideology which believes that such distinctions should no longer be made. Especially in Europe (and above all in Germany) they believe that the solution to all foreign policy questions is integration. It is as if their intention is to blur the difference between domestic and foreign affairs, and to transform both from politics into economic management. It is because of their unitarian, administrative understanding of politics that Western politicians, like their Russian counterparts, attribute stability to the *grands ensembles* (such as the European Union or the Soviet Union) and regard nations as irrational, destabilising and irritating.

This prejudice has given rise to a deep-rooted myth, which perverts much Western policy-making: the myth of nationalism. World leaders, egged on by numerous commentators, seem convinced that conflicts in Europe are liable to erupt – or have erupted – because there is no overarching structure to contain them. 'Ethnic conflict' is usually blamed. A typical comment is that of the Secretary-General of the OSCE, Dr Wilhelm Höynck: 'Most of the existing or potential conflicts in the OSCE have a strong ethnic root.'[88]

The myth was propagated strongly as the Soviet empire began to collapse. Empires have never liked nations, after all. Mikhail Gorbachev argued in 1990 for a 'European Conflict Prevention Centre' to be created – even though no conflicts had erupted by then – as if the loosening of the iron grip of Communism over Eastern Europe were a cause for worry rather than optimism. In the summer of 1995, the former Soviet president was still peddling the same line. 'Today, Europe is a zone which is particularly exposed to the risk of war,' he wrote. This, he argues, is because of the destabilising effect of nations, and the lack of a supranational framework to contain them: 'Local tensions and quarrels between nations can henceforth degenerate into open conflicts.'[89]

Since Gorbachev fell from power, Yeltsin has continued to sing the same song. Just as, for fifty years, the Soviet Union had based its bogus legitimacy on being 'anti-fascist', so the Russian president told the German government in 1994 that 'nationalism' has caused the wars in the CIS.[90] Russia, which had fought the war from 1941–45, 'knows what nationalism means', Yeltsin said. Similarly, the former Russian foreign minister, Andrei Kozyrev, made attacks against 'aggressive nationalism' his hallmark, and he lost no opportunity to say that 'political extremism, based on xenophobia and aggressive nationalism' were gaining ground.[91] In particular he used to accuse the Baltic States of 'nationalism', 'particularism', and 'mistreatment' of the sizeable Russian minorities there.[92] He seemed not to care that the Russians were all staying there, rather than leaving these allegedly repressive countries. Similarly, when the new Russian foreign minister, Yevgeni Primakov, went to the Council of Europe in April 1996, he emphasised to the body Russia had just joined that he considered the Russian national minorities in the Baltic States to be in danger from 'nationalists' there.

Many Western commentators and institutions have picked up the same theme. Self-appointed opinion-formers have warned of 'the new tribalism of today'.[93] The American commentator Patrick Moynihan wrote a book called *Pandaemonium: Ethnicity in International Politics*.[94] Robert Kaplan wrote *Balkan Ghosts*; Misha Glenny, *The Rebirth of History*, and so on. In a similar vein, the Council of Europe, as part of its overall goal of 'cultural cohesion', launched a European Youth Campaign against Racism, Xeno-phobia, Anti-Semitism and Intolerance. This took such forms as 'Trains of Tolerance' shuttling across the continent to promote the slogan: 'All different, all equal.' In Hungary, this resulted in a series of video clips shown at metro stops featuring a black person, a Native American, homosexuals, a yuppie, a prostitute and a Hungarian peasant travelling together harmoniously in the same compartment.[95]

Western leaders have also been in the forefront of this vision. It became a universally accepted truth that the war in Yugoslavia was 'ethnic', and the result of ineradicable ancient historical legacies. Gerald Ford, the former American president, spoke of the Yugoslav conflict as 'the stubborn ethnic conflict which was already ancient when I was born'.[96] Richard Holbrooke, President Clinton's peace envoy, said, 'The people of Central and Eastern Europe now have a real opportunity to create a lasting peace. But to do so, they must be prepared for one final act of liberation, this time from the unresolved legacies of their own tragic, violent and angry past.'[97] Jacques Poos, the foreign minister of Luxembourg, sounded like a mini-Metternich in 1992 when he declared that the idea of national self-determination was 'dangerous as the basis for international order . . . It would release an explosive develop-ment.'[98] When he was French foreign minister Roland Dumas declared, 'The right of peoples to self-determination cannot be

allowed to be the cause of instability, and France will not support
anything which seems in danger of causing such instability.'[99] On
another occasion, he added, 'It is not the role of the EC to promote the independence of peoples.'[100]

Perhaps the greatest Western exponent of this view was the
former French president, François Mitterrand. He was well known
for his disdain for the bothersome multiplicity of small nations,
and for his faith in great geopolitical groupings. He was also a
great believer in the principle of stability imposed from above. In
December 1985, he received the Polish dictator Wojciech
Jaruzelski in Paris – a decision which shocked even his political
friends – because he believed Jaruzelski's presentation of himself as
the thin blue line which had held Poland back from the brink of
anarchy and Soviet invasion. (KGB archives released in August
1993 have since shown that, on the contrary, Jaruzelski had *asked*
for a Soviet intervention in 1981, which the Kremlin had turned
down.[101])

Mitterrand also organised a notorious conference in Paris in
March 1992, whose title, 'Tribalism or Europe', suggested that
anyone opposed to European integration was 'tribalist'.[102] He used
that conference to express his conviction then that the war in
Yugoslavia was just one example of the kind of conflict which
would erupt all over the Continent if not contained by a pan-
European structure: 'The example of Yugoslavia will precede
others, but it has the advantage of giving us a testing ground for
what must be done and what must not be done . . . It is a classic
example, taken on a limited area of a small region of Europe, but
one which is formidably representative.'[103] In fact, of course, he
was wrong – the Yugoslav conflict is the only one to have broken
out in Eastern Europe – but this did not cause him to abandon his
belief that free nationhood was a cause of instability.

In 1991, indeed, Mikhail Gorbachev and François Mitterrand
had agreed that the Soviet president's favourite slogan, 'a common
European home', corresponded exactly to what Mitterrand understood by 'a European confederation'. At a meeting in Latche,
Mitterrand's small country house in Burgundy, on 30 October
1991, Gorbachev said, 'There will be two points of support [to this

European structure]. The European Community in the West, and the Union of Sovereign States, which will replace the USSR in the East. The co-operation between them will be founded on the principles laid out in the Charter of Paris.' Mitterrand reassured his guest that France would never do anything to encourage the break-up of the Soviet Union, and that the future Europe had to be made with Russia.[104]

He was true to his word. Repeatedly during 1989, Mitterrand stressed the need to contain what optimists called 'the springtime of nations' within manageable structures. When the Berlin Wall came down, Mitterrand himself declared, 'This happy event shows how liberty is progressing in Europe. It is likely that this great popular movement will be contagious and that it will continue elsewhere and go further'[105] – his use of the word 'contagious' showing how deeply he really welcomed what was happening. Again, when the Soviet *putsch* occurred, Mitterrand instinctively sided with the *putsch*-ists, because he had been convinced that a strong hand was needed to hold the Soviet Union together. He held that Gorbachev's liberalisation programme would inevitably lead to the break-up of the Soviet Union, an outcome he found undesirable, and which he thought he had cleverly predicted.

But perhaps the most limpid example of a leading Western politician swallowing the myth of nationalism was when the then British Prime Minister, John Major, told the House of Commons that 'the biggest single element behind what has happened in Bosnia is the collapse of the Soviet Union and of the discipline that that exerted over the ancient hatreds in the old Yugoslavia. Once that discipline had disappeared, those ancient hatreds reappeared, and we began to see the consequences when the fighting occurred. There were subsidiary elements, but this was by far the greatest.'[106]

It is difficult to know where to begin with this statement. Yugoslavia ceased to be under Soviet 'discipline' in 1948; the Yugoslav peoples have been to war with each other on their own account less than the French and Germans; Communism was not a 'discipline' which controlled these hatreds: it was itself a regime based on hatred, which was quite happy to use rabid nationalism to its advantage when it wanted – from Stalin's use of nationalism after the German invasion in 1941, to the vile nationalism of Communist dictators Slobodan Milosevic in Serbia, Todor Zhivkov in Bulgaria or Nicolae Ceauşescu of Romania. Finally, these regimes were – in virtue of the very collapse to which Major refers – not stable at all.

People who subscribe to such views tend to attribute historical determinism to events in the distant past, while ignoring the very recent history of the countries they analyse. They will prefer, for instance, to cite anecdotes about medieval atrocities (which are probably no worse than those committed in Western Europe at that time) rather than to ask who is in power now, and what their functions were two or three years previously. Alternatively, they will prefer to dig up colourful figures from the fascist or authoritarian inter-war history of these countries (which are also no worse than those of Western European countries) and, with a kind of stage shudder, present them or their inheritors as a 'danger' to the democratic development there. At the same time, they will take at face value the declarations by the Communist former leaders of these countries: that they have miraculously abandoned their life-long beliefs and become converts to the free market and the liberal order instead.

This is especially worrying because of the general failure in Eastern Europe to throw judicial light on the Communist period. The acquittal of Todor Zhivkov, the Bulgarian dictator, in early 1996 (he had only been on trial for corruption anyway), means that there is now no former Communist ruler from any country of the old Eastern bloc behind bars. Both big and small fish have been allowed to swim away. In Poland, the murderer of Father Popieluszko was set free in 1994 for good behaviour. In Romania, the last officials imprisoned for involvement in the massacres of December 1989 were released in 1993. No one who ordered or carried out the imposition of martial law in Poland in 1981, or the squashing of the Hungarian uprising of 1956, has been held accountable. Indeed, Hungary now boasts a prime minister who makes no secret of having served in the vigilante squads that helped the Russians mop up after the 1956 uprising.[107]

The myth of nationalism therefore obscures the role of specific people with the conveniently vague veil of all-determining historical forces. Neither does it explain why some regions 'explode' while others do not: why Bosnia and not Macedonia? Why did the Russians in Tiraspol, Transdniestria, protest against Moldavian independence, and 'call in' the 14th Russian army, when Russians are more numerous elsewhere in Moldavia? Why do 'ethnic conflicts' spring up and suddenly die down again? What has happened to the 'Gagauz' minority in Moldavia or the Russians in the Crimea?

Above all, the very fact that the greatest danger is supposed to come from 'nationalism' implies that the enemy is no longer 'external' (as the Soviet Union was) but rather 'internal'. Once this has been established as an accepted truth, the answer – provided largely under Russian impetus – is supposed to be the creation of a pan-European security structure, including Russia, whose 'common strategy' will be against 'nationalist extremisms', to use Andrei Kozyrev's words.[108] Such ideas can only augment the power of states and institutions with a supranational agenda.

Russian imperialism and the ideology of European integration

Russia is obviously such a state, for Russian politicians from all parts of the political spectrum want to re-establish Moscow's traditional imperialist hegemony. The desire of the Russian government to reconstitute the Soviet Union, albeit not in an explicitly Communist form, was made official on 14 September 1995, when Boris Yeltsin signed a decree entitled 'The Strategic Plan of Russia Concerning Its Relations With the Member States of the CIS'.[109] It repudiated the idea of a Western-oriented identity for Russia after the collapse of the Soviet Union, and rejected the military, economic and political independence of the states of the former Soviet Union. It also declared the aim of re-creating a smaller version of the Warsaw Pact to counter what it perceived to be the threat from NATO expansion.

'Our policy is intended,' the document said, 'above all to make the CIS into an integrated grouping, capable of playing a primary role in the international community.' The 'grand objectives' of Russia were 'to contribute to the emergence of politically and economically stable states whose policy is friendly to Russia; to make Russia into the motive force of a new system of political and economic relations within the former Soviet space; and to accelerate the process of integration within the CIS.'[110]

The document spoke of 'the progressive enlargement of a customs union to states linked to Russia by a very integrated economy, and by a strategic and political partnership'.[111] It declared the 'border security' of the CIS states to be 'the affair of all'.[112] It stated the intention 'to resolve the border questions, and to give a juridical contractual basis to the presence of Russian border guards in the states of the CIS' as well as 'to study the possibility of creating unified regional border guard commands with the objective of having a unified system of border control'. The net effect of all this, and of the call for stronger military ties between Russia and the CIS states, would be to legalise Russian control of the armed forces of the former Soviet states, reuniting them in what would amount to a new Soviet army. Russia would also seek to form a united front with the former Soviet Republics to deal collectively with international institutions such as the United Nations and the European Union: foreign-policy dealing with the outside world would be possible only with Moscow's approval.[113]

That Russia should have this goal is hardly surprising. Russia and the Soviet Union did not exactly achieve a revolution in 1991 when the Soviet Union was dissolved: it would be more accurate to say that she experienced a collapse, which left many of her old power structures sullen and demoralised, but intact.[114] Indeed, the break-up of the Soviet Union owed more to the internal power-struggles within the Kremlin than to any genuine desire on the part of Moscow to undertake decolonisation. As the French Sovietologist, Françoise Thom, has shown, it was a manifestation of the extreme degeneracy of the Soviet system in the later Gorbachev years that the only way of getting rid of a political enemy was to suppress the post he occupied: Gorbachev would suppress the Secretariat of the Central Committee to get rid of Ligachev, or the Council of Ministers to get rid of Ryjkov.[115] As such, the dislocation of the Soviet Union itself was merely the raising of this principle to the highest power: creating the Commonwealth of Independent States was a way of getting rid of Gorbachev, the Soviet president, by a kind of internal constitutional coup.

Indeed, the very fact that the creation of the Commonwealth of Independent States on 8 December 1991 pre-dated and triggered the dissolution of the Soviet Union shows that the chief political protagonists of the Soviet Union's dislocation did not intend to divide the Soviet Union up into genuinely independent states, but rather to rearrange the institutional furniture in the Soviet space. Since then, Russia has made no pretence of abandoning her imperial ambitions: the Voice of Russia World Service (the former Radio Moscow) devotes regular news broadcasts to 'Commonwealth update'. It is rather as if, the policy of British decolonisation having been announced in the 1950s, the BBC had continued to broadcast 'Commonwealth updates' with the intention of showing how the British empire was growing back together again.

But Russia gets away with it because she exploits Western intellectual confusion and uses the ideology and language of European integration to justify the reconstitution of the old Soviet empire. On 2 April 1996, Russia and Belarus signed a treaty of union which created the Union of Sovereign Republics. The fact that the Russian abbreviation for this, SSR, is only one letter short of the Russian for USSR (SSSR), was not lost on Belarus' citizens, many of whom demonstrated in the streets in protest. By the stroke of a pen, the military and political borders of Russia were suddenly extended westwards by several hundred miles, and once again reached those of Poland.

The protagonists of this new union (which was founded within the Commonwealth of Independent States, and intended to be a kind of 'hard core' to speed up the latter's integration) made explicit comparisons between what they were doing and the process of Western European integration. The First Deputy Minister of Foreign Affairs of Belarus specifically said that the new treaty was modelled on the Maastricht Treaty, while Boris Yeltsin's press secretary also made a direct comparison between the new entity and the European Union.[116] The Belarussian minister pointed out that integration would be enhanced between the two states by the creation of inter-state legal bodies, and the introduction of a single currency.

This was not the only occasion when a comparison had been drawn between the reintegration of the Soviet Republics and the integration between the states of Western Europe. The week before Belarus and Russia signed their treaty, and on the same day as the summit meeting in Turin on 29 March 1996, when the EU heads of state and government met to set in motion the Intergovernmental Conference to revise the Maastricht Treaty, the heads of state of four former Soviet republics – Russia, Belarus, Kazakhstan and Kyrgyzstan – met in Moscow to sign a separate treaty on economic integration. The symmetry seemed deliberate. At any rate, if the intended comparison escaped anyone, President Boris Yeltsin of Russia made it clear: 'Within a single day,' he said at the ceremony, and with no apparent irony, 'four countries have arrived at a level of integration which the countries of the European Union have taken years to achieve.'[117] Mr Yeltsin's remark confirmed a long-standing trend: that European ideology had become a significant weapon in Russian geopolitical strategy: these four republics alone represent 92 per cent of the territory of the former Soviet Union and 88 per cent of its population.

Indeed, in the months leading up to the signature of these two treaties, Russian politics had been replete with references to 'integration'. The Russian foreign minister and former spy chief, Yevgeni Primakov, had outlined his two aims as foreign minister when he was appointed: to prevent the enlargement of NATO, and to deepen relations with the 'near abroad'. He suggested that this latter might take the form of economic integration on the Western model.[118] Similarly, in January 1996, the Communist leader Gennadi Zyuganov had made the same analogy: he said that he supported the integration of the former Soviet states 'on the model of the European Union'.[119] The 'Strategic Plan' document published in September 1995 was also noteworthy for presenting the Russian plan to guard the borders of the former Soviet Republics in Euro-speak like 'abolishing border controls' (between Russia and the republics), and in the name of 'the Community' (of 'Independent' States).[120]

Indeed, the European Community had even been held up as a model for the Soviet Union at a plenum of the Central Committee of the Communist Party of the Soviet Union in December 1990 – and not by the most liberal speakers.[121] It is not difficult to see that one of the main premises of European integration – that the community of states takes precedence over the narrow interests of individual ones – can also serve Russia's natural imperialism.

At any rate, the treaty signed between the four republics set up a 'single market' for 'goods, services, capital and persons'. Defence and foreign policy between the signatory states was similarly to be 'harmonised' and placed under a common 'mechanism' – a euphemism for the Red Army's continuing rearmament. There were to be supranational organs, including a rotating presidency and a 'Committee for Integration'. Meanwhile, the Russian–Belarussian union created a 'Supreme Council' (or 'Soviet' in Russian) as well as an executive committee.[122]

Throughout 1997, efforts continued to consolidate the structures of the old Soviet Union. On 5 September 1997, Russia proposed to a CIS meeting in Bishkek, Kyrgyzstan, that 'a single border protection space' be created. The commander of Russia's Federal Border Service (the reincarnation of the old KGB border troops) suggested that his troops protect the external borders of all CIS states. And on 29 August Armenia and Russia agreed to 'protect jointly' Armenia's borders with non-CIS countries. (Armenia's longest non-CIS border is with NATO member Turkey: this is an interesting way of implementing Russia's stated desire that NATO should not approach Russia's borders.) As one commentator observed, among the general disarray of Russian policy, 'if there is an operative foreign policy in Russia today, it is the political, military and economic integration of the CIS states.'[123]

It was, of course, never clear just to what extent the original 'integration' had ever disappeared. In some countries – notably Belarus and Tadjikistan – Russian troops had continued to guard the frontiers after the formal dissolution of the Soviet Union. Indeed, the Red Army prosecuted a long and bloody war in Tadjikistan throughout the early 1990s. Similarly, the administrators of the old Soviet Union were seldom disbanded: old bureaucratic Soviet structures remained in place even when the constituent republics became nominally independent. Finally – most importantly, but very difficult to assess – the KGB in the successor states maintained strong links and maybe even an integrated pan-Soviet structure.

At the same time, much remained to be formally re-consolidated. As early as 1994 Yevgeni Primakov had put the West on guard that Moscow's redomination of the former Soviet empire was – to use a Euro-word – inevitable. 'It is *hopeless* to resist the centripetal tendencies within the Commonwealth of Independent States,' he said, 'and *counterproductive* at the same time.'[124] Even before that, in 1990, supporters of the old Soviet Union had attacked the demands for more autonomy by the Soviet republics as being incompatible with the global trend towards 'internationalisation'.[125] One is reminded of Karl Lamers' statement that it would be irrational to resist the magnetic force the hard core will exert on peripheral nations. Indeed, just as the Franco-German 'hard core' is supposed to encourage the rest of Western Europe to follow suit and integrate around it, so the Russian Prime Minister, Victor Chernomyrdin, insisted that the Russian–Belarussian union would also play the role of motor, driving the overall reunification of the other Soviet republics. 'We want others to join it,' he said. No doubt he does.

The treaties reflected Russia's long-standing preference for economic mechanisms, rather than political ones, to encourage 'integration'. In October 1994, the member states of the Commonwealth of Independent States created an executive organ for economic union. The necessity of a free trade, customs and payments union was evoked.[126] Meanwhile, the 'Strategic Plan' decree published in September 1995 devotes one of its two most substantial sections to 'Economic Co-operation' (the other is devoted to 'National Security') in which the formation of a payments union, common rules for the organisation of the market, and fixed exchange rates between currencies with a view to introducing the rouble as the reference currency for the whole CIS 'in the near future' are all mentioned as part of the plan.[127]

Indeed, in 1992, Arkadi Volski, the former head of the military–industrial complex and president of the Union of Russian Industrialists, organised a 'Congress of the International Council of Industrialists and Entrepreneurs'. All the republics of the former Soviet Union, all the countries of the former Eastern bloc (that is, all the members of COMECON, the old Soviet 'common market') plus China, were represented. The meetings were held in Russian. Since then eight meetings have been held, at the seventh of which, in Bucharest in 1994, the then Romanian President Ion Iliescu advocated the re-orientation of his country to the East and called for 'the re-establishment of economic relations, the restructuring of commercial and financial links within this economic zone'. For his part, Volski – who is a friend of Yevgeni Primakov, and probably an agent of the security services himself – spoke of a 'return' and of the 're-establishment' of the 'traditional links' between the countries concerned. Interestingly, he suggested that the clearing bank for this new economic union be situated in . . . Brussels.[128] In 1995, he united all the former Soviet republics at a conference entitled 'Towards Integration Based on Understanding Between Peoples', and he obtained the accord of four republics – Russia, Ukraine, Belarus and Kazakhstan – for further integration.

This is because 'economic integration' suits the post-Soviet world rather well. It allows Russia to rebuild old power-structures without being obliged to answer for them before the court of international law. It opens considerable avenues for the clandestine exercise of power over and above the constitutional clarity of creating one new state with clear lines of responsibility. Similarly, one of the central doctrines of Communist theory was that the state would 'wither away' and with it, the central institution of the state, law. The 'contradictions' generated by 'capitalism' would be replaced by a world without conflict. In 'full communism' society was supposed to exist and flourish without a controlling state. At that point, the 'government of people' gives way to the 'administration of things'. The institutions which permitted that free individual action – money and the law – which the Communist mind finds anarchic, unplanned and selfish, would be abolished. To put the same point less philosophically, a world in which the rigour and clarity of the law is replaced with bureaucracy and discretionary administrative fiat – that is, one of the kind which European integration has, in many respects, already introduced – would hardly be unsuited to the mentality of subterfuge and corruption which reigns in former Soviet republics.

Therefore, just as the European ideology claims that the harmonisation of everything from monetary to defence policy will leave the EU member states' sovereignty intact, so, on the occasion of the signature of the Russian–Belarussian union, Boris Yeltsin's office worked hard to correct the impression which had been given by Alexander Lukashenko – the authoritarian Belarussian president, and a declared enthusiast for the old Soviet Union – that a new state was being created. On the contrary, insisted the Russian presidential spokesman, the EU model showed that a new single emblem and anthem for the two countries did not mean that Belarus and Russia were no longer independent states.[129] In reality, of course, everything will be controlled from Moscow.

This in turn explains why 'integration' is welcomed by all sections of Russian political opinion. One of the reasons why President Yeltsin pressed ahead with his treaties of integration and union was precisely that he wanted to pre-empt the pressures towards the reconstitution of the Soviet Union from his various political opponents. In April 1996 *Newsweek* published details of a document prepared by Mr Yeltsin's advisers which advocated the reconstitution of the Soviet Union by the year 2005.[130] This may well have been a classic piece of Soviet-style '*desinformatsiya*' to give the impression domestically that the reconstruction of the empire was on track, but the leader of the Russian Communist Party, Gennadi Zyuganov, declared that it was 'very gratifying'[131] to see Mr Yeltsin sign the treaty of integration in April 1996 between the four republics, because only two weeks previously his own party had successfully voted in favour of abrogating the decree which had put an end to the Soviet Union in 1991. (The Belarussian president, Alexander Lukashenko, had spoken of his treaty of union with Russia as 'a correction of the historic error of 1991'.[132]) As Mr Zyuganov reminded everyone, the Communist Party also aimed to 'accelerate integration between former Soviet Republics'.[133] Similarly, Vladimir Zhirinovsky said that the union of Russia and Belarus was 'the implementation of the programme of the Liberal Democratic Party . . . We support that, this is necessary, this is good.'[134] And those like Eduard Shevardnadze or Gregory Yavlinski, who opposed the vote in the Duma on 15 March, did so not because they are opposed to the goal of integration, but, on the contrary, because they said that the vote would discredit it.

If the EU project can clothe grandiose Franco-German designs in respectability, then similar structures in Boris Yeltsin's Russia are no less likely to afford cover for hidden channels of control. After all, the idea that integrated states can retain their independent status on the international stage is little but a modern variant of Stalin's insistence that the Soviet republics of Byelorussia and Ukraine have seats at the United Nations. If the same principle were extended to other CIS states, as Russia clearly hopes it will be, then the international system would contain states which, although theoretically independent, would in reality be dependent on Moscow.

This is why even Gennadi Zyuganov also insisted that the integration which he proposed between the Soviet states would leave their sovereignty intact. Using exactly the same arguments as those used in Western Europe – defending the imposition of centralised control in the name of lifting controls between 'member states' – Zyuganov said that there was no question of infringing the sovereignty, independence, culture, traditions or way of life of

other countries: it was just a matter of allowing 'children' to travel
freely from Kiev to Moscow again.[135]

The ideology of European integration also serves other Russian
aims. Just as the documents of the Council of Europe, the OSCE
and the European Union are full of references to the need to avoid
'new divisions in Europe', so when the Russians want to express
their opposition to NATO, they habitually use precisely this
phrase, thus exploiting the European ideology's hostility to the
concept of borders for their own hegemonic purposes. Russia can
thus attack NATO expansion as divisive and un-European. Boris
Yeltsin even stated his own version of the 'Monroe doctrine'
('America for the Americans') on 8 September 1995, in a furious
response to the United States' presence in Bosnia. He called for
the South Slav crisis to be resolved by 'Europe' and 'without trans-
Atlantic dictates'. He added, of course, that NATO as a defence
organisation should be dismantled and that a new military force
under shifting command be set up which would be highly mobile
and capable of 'resolving conflicts' in Europe.[136]

Yeltsin returned to this, a favourite theme, in October 1997 at
the Council of Europe's plenary summit meeting. Calling for 'a
greater Europe without dividing lines', he used pronounced anti-
American rhetoric when he said that Europe could do very well
without the help of 'any uncles'.[137] Indeed, during the state visit of
Russia by the French president the previous week, the old Russian
determination to get the Americans out of Europe had been on full
display again. As Le Monde's defence correspondent wrote, 'One
would have thought we were back in the old days of the Cold
War, when the Kremlin never stopped suggesting an organisation
for the European continent in which there would be no counterweight to its own power.'[138] Chirac, who was awarded Russia's
highest state honour, called for Russia and the EU to establish a
'privileged partnership' with one another, a suggestion which only
nourished the eager talk in Moscow of 'a Paris–Bonn–Moscow
axis'. (In a separate development, the French also agreed to re-
schedule $3 billion of Russian debt in a meeting at the IMF
summit in Hong Kong.[139])

In this vein, the Russian delegation to the OSCE, in its report

'Regarding the Work on a Model of Universal and Comprehensive Security for Europe in the Twenty-first Century', declared its desire to 'create a common space of security, stability, and co-operation, free from dividing lines'.[140] Similarly, General Gratchev, the former Russian defence minister, who had declared in 1994 that it was 'unacceptable' that NATO decisions be taken without Russian consent, was still expressing the same thought two years later, when in March 1996 – as part of a general statement of Russian hostility to NATO enlargement – he denounced 'blocs' (by which he meant NATO) and said that instead 'European security should involve all European countries', that is, Russia and not America.[141]

Similarly, the former Soviet President, Mikhail Gorbachev, writing in 1995, said that 'an organisation which groups together only a part of the states of Europe is not in a position to play the role of policeman for the whole continent'.[142] Warming to an old Soviet theme, he called for the insertion of NATO's activities into the OCSE framework, and for a Security Council to be created for Europe within the latter organisation. 'This structure should act in the name of all Europeans and not in the name of a part of them.'[143] Another example of the same thing was the 'Declaration on the fiftieth anniversary of the termination of the Second World War', inserted into the 1994 Budapest summit document on Russian initiative. The OSCE states said that they were 'ready to make full use of CSCE potential in preventing new rifts and divisions in the CSCE region'.

Furthermore, when President Yeltsin engineered the public *rapprochement* with China in April 1996, Beijing's support for Moscow's opposition to NATO expansion was also expressed in this language: China declared that it, too, regarded 'blocs' as unsuitable for ensuring security.[144] Mr Yeltsin travelled to Beijing with the presidents of Kazakhstan, Kyrgyzstan and Tadjikistan, and agreements were signed between the four states and China. The Kazakh authorities suppressed separatist movements within their own country (peoples who felt closer to the Chinese than to the Kazakhs), announcing that separatism was 'the political AIDS of the twentieth century'.[145]

It is unfortunate that these concepts and phraseology have made their way into the lexicon of Western European political discourse, most notably in the British prime minister's address to the Western European Union on 23 February 1996: 'Creating a Europe whole and free . . . means extending to the East the stability and prosperity that we have for so long taken for granted in Western Europe, whilst guarding against the appearance of new divisions.'[146]

In other words, the very idea of having dividing lines in Europe is considered bad. But, as we saw in Chapter IV, it is only in the Communist mind that a border is a closed barrier. In the traditional and liberal views, a border is the line which delineates a political entity, and the abolition of a border must therefore imply the abolition of the political entity it describes. But the same idea also enables Russia publicly to oppose the extension of NATO to her borders, while in fact herself covertly extending those borders eastwards.

But the most intriguing comment about the union between the four republics came from President Nazarbayev of Kazakhstan. He declared that the treaty would be 'a springboard to *Eurasian* union'.[147] 'Eurasianism' has a specific meaning for Russians: it indicates a viscerally anti-liberal movement, born in the 1920s, based on hatred of Western civilisation and a conviction of Russia's unique mission in the world. It is a current of thought which unites Russian Communists, nationalists and moderates.

Eurasianism has returned to popularity in recent years in Russia as something of an *ersatz* for the apparent collapse of Communist ideology. Indeed, the recent *rapprochement* between Russia and China, Russia and Iran, and Russia and the former Soviet Central Asian states, is best understood in terms of a growing tendency towards Eurasianism within President Yeltsin's entourage. It has been brought about largely by the appointment of Yevgeni Primakov as Russian foreign minister – a man whose speciality is Iran and the Middle East – even if Gorbachev himself spoke of 'Eurasia', and organised a conference in Moscow in 1993, attended by Hans-Dietrich Genscher, which concluded that there was a need to 'defend Eurasian civilisation'.

But the origins of Eurasianism lie in a school of geopolitics initiated in 1921 by the publication of a book, *Exodus to the East*, written by N. Troubetskoy, P. Souvtchinsky, G. Florovsky and P. Savitsky. The school attempted to solve the inherent schizophrenia of Russia's geopolitical identity by saying that Russians were neither Europeans nor Asians, but Eurasians, a mixture of the sedentary peoples of the forest and of the nomadic peoples of the steppes.

Eurasianism is clearly an anti-Western ideology, and, as such, its theoreticians do not support the unification of 'Europe' in the sense in which most European federalists understand the term. They were indeed glad that Bolshevism had terminated Russia's Western orientation and made their country Europe's enemy. On the other hand, Eurasianism has two other things which certainly are in common with (Western) European federalism. The first is a geopolitical mentality of the kind examined in an earlier chapter; the second is the view that Western Europe, Russia, and the former Soviet states should somehow form a common 'space'. Eurasians believe that the division between Europe and Asia is artificial, and that the two continents are in reality one. Russia, indeed, is the country which unites them. In other words, they believe, like West European federalists, that political entities are or should be determined by geography. The Eurasians' rejection of 'Europe' as a model does not mean that they think that Russia should play no role in Europe: on the contrary, they think that a Eurasian Russia should expand and conquer Europe.

Just as in 1917, when the Tsarist empire was reconstructed by the Bolsheviks who conquered Russia first (many of the future Soviet republics enjoyed brief periods of independence in the aftermath of the civil war, before the Bolsheviks re-conquered them), so modern Eurasians see the new Russian republic as the springboard to pan-Soviet and perhaps pan-Eurasian union. 'Eurasianism,' writes one theoretician, 'is the new niche which will save the Soviet Union.'[148]

Eurasians are supporters of the kind of 'great space/*Großraum*' thinking which we encountered with the Nazi geopoliticians. Like the Nazis, they are convinced that there is an irreducible opposition between maritime and terrestrial powers, which is incarnated in the

enmity between the 'thalassocratic' powers – Britain and America –
and the Continent, whose 'heartland' (to use the original geopolitical term coined by the geopolitician Halford J. Mackinder) is
dominated by Eurasian Russia. 'Only the strategic interests of Russia
are strictly identical to those of the continent,' writes one modern
Eurasian. 'Only continental integration centered around Russia can
ensure real sovereignty for all the peoples of Eurasia . . . the peripheral territories are indispensable for Russia if she wants to become a
truly sovereign continental geopolitical force.'[149]

This mentality is obviously by definition hostile to any 'division'
of that unitary mass which is the Eurasian continent. Like the
Germans, the Russians find fragmentation of that land-mass a
threat: they feel that it is playing the game of the Atlantic powers.
The American dominance of the Western part of that continent
enfeebles the Eastern part, and therefore there should be a new
'Eurasiatic' strategic bloc which would include 'the Franco-German
bloc, which is avid to liberate itself from the Atlanticist tutelage',
and 'an Asian bloc constituted of China, India and the Muslim
world'.[150] In Europe, it is above all the Berlin–Moscow axis which
has to be constituted, while encouraging Germany to reconstruct
Mitteleuropa, because 'Germany has always been the enemy of
Anglo-Saxon colonial conquests, and has always tried to create a
purely terrestrial, continental and autarkic civilisation'. In Asia, the
sworn enemies of the Atlantic powers, the Islamic fundamentalists,
have to be supported, and secular Turkey has to be eliminated, for
it is the Atlantic powers' principal pawn in the region.

Geopolitical thinking of this kind is not by any means relegated
to a few obscure journals. The Communist leader, Gennadi
Zyuganov, praised Ivan the Terrible for his geopolitical insights:
'The tsar understood clearly the geopolitical needs of his empire.
He saw that Russia's state and national interests demanded that
Russia control maritime regions.' As for Peter the Great, he 'did
not so want to open a window to the West [by founding St
Petersburg] but rather to ensure the security of Russia and guaran-
tee it against a possible invasion from the sea'.[151]

The Russian Eurasians particularly look to Islamic fundamentalists as allies. They admire their hatred of liberalism, of the free

market, and of America. It is no surprise, therefore, if Vladimir Zhirinovsky is a lucid advocate of Eurasian union. When the treaty between the four republics was signed in March 1996, he said, 'There is a need to act more rapidly. Next comes Eastern Ukraine, Kazakhstan, Kirghizia [Kyrgyzstan], Tadjikistan – once again the road to India.'[152] Earlier, in 1994, he had explained that the process of re-creating the empire needed to begin with the expansion of Russia towards warm waters in the south and the west. Only then would her edification on the continent be complete. 'Annexations and conquests are not necessary for this. All that is needed is a strategic anti-Atlantic alliance with the continental European and Asiatic powers.'[153]

In other words, any analysis of developments in the former Soviet Union which fails to take this overriding geopolitical and strategic agenda into account is likely to be deficient. And yet – just as in Western analysis of, and political reaction to, the Yugoslav war – it is just this analysis which has been lacking. Just as the phrase 'Serbia's war aims' was absent from Western pronouncements on Yugoslavia, so Russia's aims in the hot-spots of the former Soviet Union are systematically obscured by the veil which the myth of nationalism throws over them.

A fig-leaf for Russian expansionism

The process of maintaining or re-establishing control from Moscow over the former Soviet republics did not begin with the publication of the strategy document in 1995, however. It began in 1991. Or, to be more precise, it was never abandoned: Gorbachev's attachment to the myth of nationalism was itself intended to show that 'integration' and supranational structures (under the influence of Moscow, of course) were the answer to it. Indeed, it was in order to give credibility to this vision that both Yeltsin and Gorbachev have manipulated 'minorities' in regions of strategic importance in order to counter any genuine drives for independence on the territory of the former Soviet Union.

Perhaps the most flagrant example of this exploitation of

national minorities was in the Transdniestrian region of Moldova. This slither of land had been created by Stalin before the Second World War and given the name 'Soviet Republic of Moldavia' even though it had not been part of pre-1914 Romania. This same name was then given to the formerly Romanian province of Bessarabia, when it was incorporated into the Soviet Union after the Second World War.

When the Soviet Republic of Moldavia (which corresponded approximately to the old Romanian province of Bessarabia, disputed with Russia since the Napoleonic wars) declared its independence from the Soviet Union after the August 1991 *putsch*, its Russian minority in Transdniestria in turn declared independence from Moldavia. Fighting broke out in 1992, and the Russian 14th army moved in to 'protect' the Russians. The Russian army's right to move into the region went largely uncontested internationally, even though Transdniestria was either in Moldavia or in Ukraine – both of which were supposed to be independent countries – but by no stretch of the imagination in Russia.

In fact, of course, the reason why Russian troops went in was to protect Russia's strategic interests in the region. Tiraspol is a strategically very important Russian military base. It was described by the general commanding the 14th army, Alexander Lebed, as 'the gateway to the Balkans', and is indeed a nodal point for energy supplies to Moldavia. The fact that there are more Russians in the rest of the Moldovan republic than in Transdniestria, where Russians are actually spread more thinly than elsewhere in the republic, gave the lie to the instant analyses by Western commentators that this was a reaction to the 'nationalism' of the Moldavian authorities.

In other words, what Moldova in fact provides is not an example of the dangers of nationalism, but rather a text-book case of how minorities can be manipulated for classical great power politics. Just like the Gagauz, a Turkic Christian people who protested to Gorbachev in favour of a language they had not spoken for two centuries when the first rumblings of Moldovan independence occurred in 1989–90, the Transdniestrian crisis soon brought the secessionist Moldovan government to heel. All dreams of reuniting with Romania were squashed, former Communists were soon installed back in place, Moldova joined the CIS, and suddenly the ethnic problems miraculously disappeared. However, the Russian 14th army remained.[154] Indeed, when the Moscow-friendly Petru Lucinschi came to power in Moldova, Moscow even quietly dropped their erstwhile stooges in Tiraspol.

Similar artificial flare-ups of tensions and hostility can be observed elsewhere in the former Soviet Union. If these disputes had been true grass-roots nationalist problems, then there would be a progressive hardening of attitudes on both sides. In fact, in every case, the opposite has happened. Old Communists have returned to power following the 'disturbances', playing the card of moderation and *rapprochement* with Moscow. In Ukraine for instance, a Russian independence movement surfaced in the Crimea when Ukraine had a moderately independence-minded government, and when the carve-up of the Black Sea fleet was still in dispute. Although the Ukrainian question has not yet stabilised, it was striking how things went quiet again in the Crimea once the pro-Moscow Leonid Kuchma was elected in Kiev.

But the region in which Russian exploitation of national minorities has been the most vicious is the Caucasus. This is a region of great traditional strategic interest to Russia. Imperial Russia traditionally tried to crush the Northern Caucasus peoples, because they blocked easy Russian access to the rich Caucasus lands. Several peoples, such as the Oubikhs, were simply eradicated and replaced by Russian colonists.[155] Throughout the nineteenth century, heavy-handed and often spectacularly cruel Russian action in Chechnya met with very stubborn resistance. The Chechen and Daghestani peoples rose against the Soviet Union in 1920–21: they were put down then and, even more cruelly, in 1937. In 1944, nearly all Chechens were deported. Their record of ferocious independence even led Alexander Solzhenitsyn to write glowingly about them in *The Gulag Archipelago*.

In the twentieth century, new but similar strategic interests applied. The Caucasus is not only the cusp on which Christian

Russia meets the Muslim world, it is also a region where there are massive oil reserves still waiting to be tapped in the Caspian Sea. The significance of these oil reserves is twofold. Firstly, oil is obviously a source of income for the state and for the new 'private' owners of oil companies. (Azeri oil is managed by the President's son.) Secondly, Russia (and, formerly, the Soviet Union) has a long track record of using energy as leverage to advance Kremlin priorities in the old territory of the USSR. Ever since the Siberian pipeline project in 1989, when Moscow sought to foster Western European dependence on Soviet natural gas, the Baltic states, Ukraine, Kazakhstan, Georgia and Azerbaidjan have all been victims of the Russian use of energy to dominate her neighbours.

The case of the Baltic states in this regard was especially flagrant. Energy supplies were simply cut off to Vytautas Landsbergis' fiercely independent Lithuania, and only switched on again when the former Communist Party First Secretary, Algirdas Brazauskas, was returned to power. Similarly, in neighbouring Latvia in 1993, pro-Moscow politicians campaigned on a three-word slogan describing what they offered, one of which was 'warmth'.

Throughout the former Soviet Union, indeed, leading politicians often run energy companies, like the Russian Prime Minister, Victor Chernomyrdin, who heads the massive Russian gas conglomerate. The net effect of all this is that there is not one single country on the territory of the former Soviet Union where the Popular Fronts which mushroomed in the late 1980s to oppose Russian hegemony are still in power. In some countries, such as Belarus, Georgia, Azerbaidjan, and others, their leaders have even been arrested or forced into exile.

Because of the need to control the new oil which is to be exploited in Azerbaidjan, Russia has been playing power-politics in the Caucasus with considerable skill.[156] Ever since the 'collapse' of the Soviet Union, Russia has successfully and brutally made sure that its own men are in charge in the Caucasus republics. Russia is, in particular, keen that Baku's oil should pass through Russia itself, and this means through Chechnya. (Chechnya is also the only part of the former Soviet Union where kerosene is mined.) An alternative route, which may be built in time, runs through Georgia to the Black Sea.

Therefore it is no coincidence if Georgia, Azerbaidjan and Chechnya have been the scenes of massive unrest. In Georgia and Azerbaidjan, presidents were freely elected who had long records of anti-Communism and who, unlike so many recent converts to 'the free market', were genuinely interested in national independence for their countries. Both of them, Zviad Gamsakhurdia and Abulfaz Elcibey, were soon overthrown in military coups, and replaced by senior Communist party stooges: the former Soviet foreign minister, Eduard Shevardnadze (known as 'the butcher of Tbilisi' in his home country for his brutal reign as Party First Secretary in Georgia in the 1970s), and the former member of Leonid Brezhnev's Politburo, Geidar Aliev, in Baku. Both Aliev and Shevardnadze then proceeded to have themselves fraudulently 'elected'. In 1992, Shevardnadze was the only candidate – just like in the good old days of Soviet elections – while the election which brought Aliev to power was openly rigged.[157]

'Divide and rule' has always provided a useful rule of thumb for Russia in the region, and Moscow skilfully exploited the national-minorities question throughout the Caucasus to further these aims. In Georgia, Russia gave military support to poorly armed peoples – the Ossetians and the Abkhaz – in order to foster 'ethnic conflict'. In Azerbaidjan, Russia supported both sides in the war with Armenia over Nagorno-Karabakh. These conflicts duly brought in a number of prominent figures from the Gorbachev–Yeltsin political establishment, including, most recently, the Russian foreign minister, Yevgeni Primakov, to 'manage' them.

One-worldism: an old socialist and Russian dream

All this explains why Russia is so interested in pan-European institutions and in the process of pan-European integration generally. Such institutions tend to have an international and bureaucratic flavour which is not ungermane to Communist or neo-Communist

aspirations for control over the European continent. They are, by
definition, hostile to genuinely free nationhood, and their interests
can therefore coincide with those of imperial powers like Russia.

Moreover, being based on the belief that stability comes from
on high, and not from the free interplay between individuals or
nations, such institutions are often one-worldist. They incarnate
the view that politics and human behaviour can be scientifically
planned, and that such planning is preferable to what too many
people are happy to regard as irrational and incomprehensible
local conflicts.

One-worldist ideology, of the kind to which international
institutions are naturally disposed, has a lot in common with
Communism. They share the same grandiose pretensions to uni-
versality. As former Soviet foreign minister Eduard Shevardnadze
once said, 'The rational organisation of human existence at the
global level is an absolute necessity.' He wrote that, 'For the first
time, we are beginning to be aware of the necessity of regulating
numerous aspects of human existence at the global level.'[158]
Similarly, Mikhail Gorbachev argued in his Fulton speech on 7
May 1992 that 'the world is becoming conscious of the fact that
it is indispensable to create forms of global administration in
which all members of the international community would take
part'.[159]

Like most socialist thought, such thinking is infused with the
Utopian belief in a 'new order' governed by an elite of administrators and planners, and with the conviction that the past must be
definitively abandoned if the future is to work. Gorbachev was still
writing in 1995 that 'traditional methods' of guaranteeing security
were no longer any use. He claimed that what is needed is 'the creation of a global system of common security'.[160] Indeed, the
frequent use of words like 'architecture' or 'system' in such con-
texts presupposes the existence of an architect or planner who
will structure the new world. Indeed, like all socialist thought,
such 'new thinking' is predicated on a radical rejection of humanity as it is now, and indeed of liberty – for liberty, which is not
susceptible to planning, can only produce the unpredictable. The
fact that such plans for pan-European government are invariably

accompanied by affirmations of the need for supranational social policy only underlies their inherently socialist nature.

Indeed, the whole Gorbachevite and one-worldist ideology of 'common human values', like that of 'the common European home', presupposes the dissolution of political life into uniform world-wide administration. Such 'common values' are always opposed by their partisans to the 'conflict' and 'division' which they say they regret in the world. But, in fact, conflict is an inherent consequence of human liberty, and a natural facet of human behaviour. To wish to abolish it because people are 'all the same' is to display an administrative, unpolitical, and hence unnatural view of human nature. It was in this vein that Eduard Shevardnadze wrote in 1992: 'The old idea of a united Europe is being given a chance. The European countries now proceed from the assumption that they have a common destiny, common problems and common interests . . . It is Europe that faces the noble task of showing the rest of the world that the further progress of our civilisation is possible only on the basis of universal human values.'[161] Or, as his boss Mikhail Gorbachev wrote: 'It is precisely this notion of co-operation and of mutual support which is at the origin – at the heart – of the concept of the "Common Home".'[162]

It is not surprising, therefore, if the ideology of one-worldism is so popular on the international Left. The Soviet dissident Andrei Sakharov, for instance, who described his own views as 'profoundly socialist', spent years writing about the possibility and desirability of 'convergence' between the socialist and capitalist 'systems', rather than about the triumph of free capitalism over dictatorial Communism.[163] Sakharov openly advocated the 'scientific method of directing policy' and specifically attacked 'the division of mankind' as the source of all woes and of mankind's potential future destruction. He favoured massive international taxation to effect financial transfers from rich countries to poor, and wrote of 'the monstrous relations in human and international affairs brought forth by the egotistical principle of capital when it is not under pressure from socialist and progressive forces'.[164]

The link between this straightforward socialism and grandiose – even megalomaniac – constructivism is amply illustrated by a

magnificent flight of political science fiction in which Sakharov
indulges. Writing that he is 'not one of those who consider the
multiparty system to be an essential stage in the development of
the socialist system, or, even less, a panacea for all ills', Sakharov
warned that unless the Communist Party adopted the 'scientific
democratic method', the multiparty system would come about and
socialism would collapse. As part of the process of 'convergence',
he foresaw an 'expanded role for the intelligentsia' (to plan all this,
one assumes) and a process of world industrialisation in which
'gigantic fertilizer factories using atomic power will be built, the
resources of the sea will be used to a vastly greater extent . . . and
gigantic factories will produce synthetic amino acids and synthe-
sise proteins, fats, and carbohydrates'. By the final stage of
'convergence' (1980–2000), there would be 'world government
and the smoothing of national contradictions'. For good measure,
he added that 'during this period, the expansion of space explo-
ration will require thousands of people to work and live
continuously on other planets and on the moon, on artificial satel-
lites, and on asteroids whose orbits will have been changed by
nuclear explosions'.[165]

Stripped of their science fiction, the constitutional arguments
have not changed much since Sakharov wrote these words in
1968. The head of the Moscow 'Institute for Europe', Yuri Borko,
explained the origins and ideals of the 'convergence' theory
Sakharov outlined. 'The theory of convergence was the first
attempt to escape the rigid dichotomy of "capitalism versus socialism" . . . Actually, the theory of convergence precipitated the
"discovery" of what later became universally recognised – the
global interdependence of all peoples, nations and social systems.'
As he rightly points out, Helsinki was 'the first international document to manifest the approach of convergence: not to change
"social systems" but to recognise the territorial and sociopolitical
status quo'.[166]

These ideas now form the staple diet of much of the international Left's great and good. For instance, a report written by 'The
Commission on Global Convergence' – the name says it all – entitled 'Our Global Neighbourhood' concludes: 'In an increasingly

interdependent world, old notions of territoriality, independence, and non-intervention lose some of their meaning. National boundaries are increasingly permeable – and, in some important respects, less relevant.'[167] The conclusion, predictably enough, is that there is a need for World Government. 'The time is now ripe – indeed overdue – to build a global forum that can provide leadership in economic, social, and environmental fields.' The establishment of an Economic Security Council is proposed, whose goals would include providing 'long-term strategic policy framework' for the planet. One of the instruments for this, it is proposed, would be an enhanced role for the IMF in 'having oversight of the international monetary system . . . to ensure that domestic economic policies in major economic countries are not mutually inconsistent or damaging to the rest of the international community'. Its 'capacity to support nominal exchange rates in the interest of exchange rate stability' would be improved.[168] It will come as no surprise to Europeans to learn that Jacques Delors, among many other luminaries, sits on this Commission.

Indeed, Mikhail Gorbachev himself was still actively pushing the idea of a world government in 1996. His 'Gorbachev Foundation' in California organised a 'State of the World Forum' in San Francisco in February 1996 with topics for discussion like 'Ecology: the New Science of the Sacred' and 'The Global Crisis of Value and the Search for Meaning'. The president of the Gorbachev Foundation, Jim Garrison, called for the establishment of an 'earth charter'. As he told the San Francisco Weekly his real goal was making a blueprint for 'the next phase of human development . . . Over the next twenty to thirty years, we are going to end up with world government. It's inevitable.'[169]

Collective security, Russia, and the OSCE

The one-worldist ideology is also predicated on the assumption that borders are barriers which should be brought down, or at least to be 'spiritualised' away into political irrelevance. It sees no difference between internal and external policy, and certainly no rational reason for drawing the distinction, because we all live in one interdependent world. In fact, of course, a border is a line which delineates a jurisdiction and the difference between 'internal' and 'external' is therefore, or should be, the very cornerstone of statehood and the rule of law.

Above all, the view that security – like the rest of government – must be collective is a doctrine which differs radically from that on which classical defence alliances like NATO are based. They are directed outwards towards external enemies, and they provide for common action in case of attack from an external aggressor. It is therefore incompatible with the understanding of NATO as a defence alliance for Chancellor Kohl to insist that 'NATO expansion is not directed against anyone'.[170] A defence alliance is, *by definition*, directed 'against' someone, because it is intended to defend its member against a state, a group of states or all states in general which do not belong to the alliance. Defence alliances are predicated on the difference – and certainly on the divergence of interests – between different states, and they never pretend that they can settle political disputes within a member state, or that they should be vehicles for general political integration.

By contrast, any organisation which did this would not be a defence alliance, but instead a kind of supranational government. Indeed, those who, like Mikhail Gorbachev, believe that 'security is not just a military problem. It is instead mainly a political problem,' hold that security can therefore be ensured only by common, supranational government.[171] The same mentality allows 'security' to justify the need for government in all areas of policy: the Commission on Global Convergence proposes world government in the form of an Economic *Security* Council.

It is precisely because it is central to the philosophy of the Organisation for Security and Co-operation in Europe (the re-named Conference on Security and Co-operation in Europe which grew out of the Helsinki Conference in 1975) that 'security' is not a matter of militarily defending states from external attack, but rather a matter of governing them all together, that Russia has long regarded it as a useful vehicle for asserting her leading role in Europe by replacing NATO with a pan-European security structure, and thereby of entrenching and augmenting her influence over the European continent. It is therefore significant that the OSCE has enjoyed something of a renaissance in recent years.

Since 1994, the OSCE has committed its member states to collective security, as the Russians have always wanted. The concluding document of the Budapest summit said, 'The participating states will base their mutual security relations upon a co-operative approach. They emphasise in this regard the key role of the CSCE ... The participating States will co-operate in ensuring *that all such security arrangements are in harmony with CSCE principles and commitments under this Code*.'[172]

As one of the foremost advocates of European collective security, the supposedly moderate former Russian foreign minister, Andrei Kozyrev, has insisted, 'The CSCE has become the irreplaceable instrument of the construction of the new Europe.'[173] According to him, it is part of 'the pan-European process'.[174] In geopolitical phrases which, as we shall see, are heavy with significance, he has called for 'a union of states which is at once transatlantic and Eurasiatic'.[175] Evoking the usual mantra about 'aggressive nationalism' being the main danger, Kozyrev calls for the OSCE to be transformed into 'a genuinely effective pan-European organisation' in order to combat it.[176] He goes on: 'The security of the new democratic Europe can only be common and global ... The unity of democratic Europe implies the indivisibility of the security of European peoples.'[177]

All this means that, far from being a defence alliance like NATO, the OCSE aspires to be a pan-European government. In the words of the Chairman of the OCSE, the Hungarian foreign minister, László Kovács: 'Comprehensive security means more than mere military security.'[178] As he made clear at the 1994 summit in Budapest, the OSCE deals not only with the relations between states, but also with the relationship between the state and the citizen. Thus the philosophy of the OSCE blurs the very distinction between internal and external affairs.

Indeed, its documents use much of the same vocabulary as the European Union: they speak of 'a secure and stable CSCE *community*, whole and free'; of 'the *integration* of states in resolving security

problems'; or of 'our goal of a community of nations with no divisions, old or new'. Its declarations are replete with the kind of
anti-national one-worldism which we have analysed above, and it
shares the EU's animosity to borders, considering them to be only
factors for division and causes of potential conflict, and they typically speak of 'a Europe without walls, without ideological barriers
and without political animosities'.[179]

The very wide definition given to security, and the mythology
of complete harmony which underlies it, encourages the OSCE to
argue that any 'conflict' should either be dissipated or 'managed'.
Indeed, precisely because the OSCE adheres to the bureaucratic
dogmas of 'crisis management' and 'conflict prevention', it devotes
great effort to developing new 'instruments' and 'mechanisms' for
dealing with these conflicts. In the words of the 1994 Budapest
summit conclusions: 'The participating states shall commit themselves to co-operate . . . to counter tensions that may lead to
conflict . . . [they] stress the importance both of early identification of potential conflicts and of their joint efforts in the field of
conflict prevention.'[180]

Such phrases are incapable of precise legal definition, and they
thus give potential blank cheques to the international community
to intervene – or not to intervene – wherever it likes. This pretence is formally recognised in a whole series of rights enunciated
in the OSCE's documents, including rights for workers, women,
disabled persons and national minorities. All these elements fall
under the label 'The Human Dimension'.

The role of the OSCE in protecting the rights of national
minorities is especially important in giving the OSCE its character of embryonic pan-European government. This is because there
are so many minorities, especially across Central Europe and in the
former Soviet Union. As we have seen, the existence of significant
Russian minorities in the former Soviet republics has also given
Russia excellent legal justification for its neo-imperialist concept
of the 'near abroad'. Indeed, it was Russia which has introduced
'aggressive nationalism' as a key OSCE concept,[181] and Russia
which has succeeded in getting the term inserted into various
OSCE norm-creating documents. As a consequence, the OSCE

appointed a High Commissioner on National Minorities in 1995 in order to ensure the 'prevention of the spread of ethnic conflict and nationalism',[182] and the CSCE's and OSCE's documents are full of 'declarations on aggressive nationalism, racism, chauvinism, xenophobia and nationalism'.[183]

Indeed, the OSCE's powers to deal with national minorities were significantly augmented in 1991 when the so-called 'Moscow document' introduced a series of new commitments, including an important provision on the rights of minorities. That document made reference to a previous report by the OSCE on national minorities, thereby bringing the substance of that report into the body of OSCE 'law'. The report had found that 'issues concerning national minorities . . . are matters of legitimate international concern, and consequently do not constitute exclusively an internal affair of the respective state'.[184]

The OSCE's pretence that it can pacify the whole gamut of political antagonisms from women's and workers' rights to national minorities – itself a rather mistaken aim – risks making it more like a transcontinental military police force than a defence alliance. Moreover, states which are deemed to have minorities might be required by the OSCE to do anything from providing education in minority languages to establishing local autonomy. This is why one legal expert has concluded that the CSCE is 'the source of an overarching European constitutional order to which all national and political institutions in Europe must conform'.[185] This will give Russia the right to pressurise her former colonies to 'respect' the national rights of the Russians who still live there.

On the other hand, the OSCE philosophy of national minorities is also crucially intended to prevent minorities within a state from ever achieving genuine political independence. By reducing nationhood to a matter of 'identity' – language teaching in schools and local autonomy, as if this is what is meant when a people decides it is a people – the OSCE seems determined to make sure that minorities remain minorities. It is, of course, the definition of a secessionist demand by a people who are not happy remaining a minority: by protecting the 'rights' of minorities, the OSCE therefore seems designed to prevent them from ever really rocking the boat. As one pro-OSCE commentator has written: 'International organisations should refrain from making further concessions to secessionist drives: their primary goal should remain the protection and promotion of the rights of minority groups within existing states.'[186] Or as the Director of the OSCE office for Democratic Institutions and Human Rights states: 'Attempts made by certain minorities seeking secession from the State in which they reside to claim that they are a people and that they are entitled to self-determination are not well founded . . . Self-determination does not mean complete independence.'[187]

This presentation of the position may have the merit of honesty. It would be practically impossible to guarantee a right to political independence in law: independence from a state cannot be demanded in the name of a legal 'right' within the state's political and legal system, since the desire is precisely to leave that system. But it hides a deeper agenda. On the one hand, the liberal state can be undermined from the outside in the name of its internal minorities; on the other hand, minorities in illiberal countries (like Russia) are themselves denied what they truly want, namely genuine political independence.

A concrete example of how these two facets of the question can combine to favour Russian interests was when, on 12 January 1995, the OSCE's Permanent Council gave clear support to the principle of the territorial integrity of Russia with respect to the Chechen question. Of all the compliant international reactions to the start of the Chechen war in late 1994, indeed, that of the OSCE was the most pro-Russian.

The OSCE's compliance was probably due, at least in part, to the inclusion within its normative documents of a politico-military Code of Conduct, which was incorporated into the decisions of the Budapest summit as Chapter 4. The Russians being good chess-players, they knew how to use this when the time came, for its twenty-fifth paragraph enshrines the principle of territorial integrity thus: 'The participating states will not tolerate or support forces that are not accountable to or controlled by their constitutionally established authorities.'[188] The Russians were then able to use this Code as a means by which to legitimise the Chechen campaign.

Indeed, the OSCE can already decide to send peace-keeping missions to the territory of one of its member states without needing the approval of the United Nations' Security Council. Because of the UN's commitment to the peaceful resolution of disputes (Chapter VIII of the UN Charter), coercive measures require the approval of the Security Council. But the Western European Union – the organ which European federalists want to integrate into the EU in order to give it an army and a defence policy – can undertake coercive measures without Security Council approval, if the OSCE asks it to intervene in a state whose government is trying to recover sovereignty over the whole of its territory from secessionist forces.[189]

Moreover, Western policy-makers had already explicitly condoned the principle of Russian 'peace-keeping' in the 'near abroad'. In December 1993, the then British Foreign Secretary, Douglas Hurd, co-authored an article in the *Financial Times* with Kozyrev, which specified the conditions under which Russia might be allowed to conduct 'peace-keeping' operations in former Soviet republics. Since that article, the OSCE has sanctioned the despatch of Russian 'peace-keeping' troops to Azerbaidjan; the Russian 14th army was illegally in Moldova *at the time the article was written*; and Russia has also signed military and other integration accords with Belarus (which means that Russian troops are now once again on the Polish border) and Georgia.[190]

So when the war broke out, the OSCE pointed to the Code of Conduct and criticised Russian 'excesses' – an OSCE mission which visited Moscow and Chechnya from 23–29 January 1995 concluded merely that there had been a 'disproportionate' amount of bombing – but as a body the OSCE reaffirmed its unqualified support for the territorial integrity of Russia, that is, its opposition to Chechen claims for independence.[191] It is hardly surprising that Russia called the OSCE's attitude 'constructive': one wonders what level of bombing the OSCE would have found 'proportionate'. Indeed, *Izvestiya* concluded that the OSCE 'sympathised with Russia'.[192] This is in spite of the fact that Russia's behaviour was clearly in conflict with the Geneva Convention of 1949, and with its second additional protocol of 1977. As one commentator

phlegmatically puts it: 'The question is whether . . . Russia will be
able to use the OSCE to flout the principle of the self-determination of peoples with utter impunity, and by using the methods of
another age.'[193]

The other main Russian interest in the OSCE is that it will
inevitably neutralise Western Europe. International bodies of this
kind have a natural tendency to be sclerotic, because they gravitate towards the lowest common denominator. For instance, the
Budapest summit communiqué in 1994, which was supposed to
survey the state of European security, made no mention of the
Bosnian war because of Russian opposition.

Andrei Kozyrev himself has unwittingly explained why it is
that such pan-European structures will neutralise Western Europe.
He compared the OSCE to a 'net' in which states would be 'intertwined' with each other.[194] That the institution is already
institutionally and culturally likely to do just that is clear whenever one reads any of its literature. Read, for example, what the
Secretary-General of the OSCE writes about Chechnya:

> Chechnya has demonstrated the efficiency of another
> OSCE instrument of early action: executive initiative of the
> Chairman-in-Office. The Budapest summit has considerably
> strengthened this means. In a number of well-considered steps
> and based on solid support from OSCE states, the Hungarian
> Chairmanship clearly addressed the violation of OSCE com-
> mitments and secured the co-operation of the leadership of
> the Russian Federation. Consensus was then reached in the
> Permanent Council to establish a continuous OSCE presence
> in this conflict area. On this basis, the OSCE Assistance
> Group in Chechnya has been deployed since April this year
> [1995]. Acting through the head of the Assistance Group,
> Hungarian Foreign Minister, László Kovács, has used the
> Group's potential to make essential contributions towards a
> peaceful settlement of the conflict. Working virtually under
> the roof of the Assistance Group, the parties have agreed to
> the cessation of hostilities and are ready to work for a lasting
> peaceful solution. For the first time, a permanent and peaceful

solution has been addressed clearly and in detail. Many problems remain, however, and the OSCE will be engaged in
post-conflict confidence-building, including monitoring
elections in Chechnya.[195]

One wonders how a Chechen refugee mother, her family
bombed to death, her house reduced to rubble, would react if told
that the initiative of the Chairman-in-Office represented an effi-
cient OSCE instrument. Lost in the fog of bureaucratic waffle and
prevented from action by the stagnancy of committees and mechanisms, any Western response to any Russian pressure or mis-
behaviour will inevitably be one of inertia.

Just as with the Council of Europe, an increased role for the
OSCE will result in an institutional imbalance. In the Council of
Europe, Russia will have the largest parliamentary delegation
(being the largest country) and she will in due course appoint a
judge to the European Court of Human Rights in Strasbourg. This
means that her parliamentary delegates and judges will partake in
determining the policies of the Council of Europe and the rulings
of the Court. As many member states – including Britain – know,
this can result in political rulings made against them: Britain was
criticised by the Court of Human Rights for the shooting of three
IRA terrorists in Gibraltar and ordered to pay compensation to the
families of the dead. Also, in September 1996, the Court questioned the right of a step-parent to discipline a violent child, even
though the man in question had been acquitted of using excessive
force by due process in a British court. But Russia herself has publicly announced her intention not to abide by the Council of
Europe's rules, and to block any attempts by Council delegates to
interfere in Russia's internal affairs.

The role of the OSCE will be similar. Contrary to popular
belief, international institutions often augment the influence of
powerful countries rather than weaken it. The European Union,
indeed, provides a telling example of how France and Germany
have been able to increase their hold over European affairs
through it. Within the OSCE – just as within the Helsinki process
ever since it began – Russia will demand a say in the internal

affairs of other states (in the name of national minorities, for instance) while at the same time refusing to abide by any of the restrictions the OSCE might try to place on her. Like Germany, Russia has every interest in dissolving other people's statehood, while continuing to preserve and exercise her own influence by occult means instead.

VII

A CONTINENT IN DECLINE

In a joint statement published in 1995, a group of French and German parliamentarians insisted that 'the realisation of Economic and Monetary Union serves fundamental political and strategic goals', of which the main one was 'the creation of a new economic and social world order'.[1]

We have heard calls for a new world order before. But in fact there is little genuinely novel about the project of European monetary union, except inasmuch as it represents a departure from the way that the states of the EC have hitherto interacted. In terms of its underlying motives, the project is striking mainly for its intellectual timidity. Faced with declining competitiveness, low growth, mass unemployment, and sclerotic and often corrupt political structures, European countries are undertaking to reproduce their present systems at supranational level rather than to reform them at home. Similarly, instead of asking how the world's monetary system as a whole might be reformed to render the globalisation of the economy fairer and freer, they prefer to pursue an exclusively intra-European project whose effect will be to close the continent in on itself.

This is because the desire to cushion European states from world competition by creating a European 'bloc' is becoming an increasingly important motive for European integration. While

France's hostility to the world market is legendary, the view is also becoming more explicit in Germany that monetary union is needed to shield the country from the twin dangers of declining competitiveness and an overvalued currency. 'If EMU failed,' says one supporter, 'the D-Mark would suffer an over-valuation which would cause very grave difficulties for our exports and which would bring about, within a few years, new massive transfers of jobs abroad. In the middle term, our competitiveness would suffer. We would be probably be faced with a more tense social situation.'[2]

German business is increasingly seeing that it needs a devaluation, by transforming the D-Mark into the Euro, if Germany is to maintain the level of her European exports. Faced with very high levels of German investment flowing outside Germany – and even outside continental Europe – German policy-makers know that it is only by locking the rest of Europe into the same currency area that the needs of Germany's export industry can be met. This kind of bloc thinking, however, will inevitably lead to a more or less closed continental economic space.

European businesses know that they are suffocating from social over-regulation in the name of a social security system which is falling apart. German businesses now have to obey 1,000-page books of personnel regulations in dealing with their workers, and a company needs written permission from the regional government whenever it wants to ask people to work overtime on Sundays. And yet the political systems of European states are unable to grasp the nettle of reform in anything other than a bureaucratic and book-keeping way. The crash course in financial prudence being undertaken to fulfil the Maastricht criteria by 1998 is like any diet: without a fundamental change in mentality, these countries will only fall back on bad old habits when it is over. The only alternative European governments see, therefore, is to create a single economic space in which everyone is burdened with the same weaknesses, and to hope that Europe can somehow hobble along for a while by defending itself against outside pressure.

This inability of states to tackle reform is political. Europeans often regard their social systems as an essential element in their political life: the Germans fear that their post-war consensus will break down if state hand-outs dry up, while the French president has described his country's bankrupt social security system as 'the foundation-stone of the Republican pact'. This means that their political systems are systemically unitarian, and unable to manage (let alone encourage) the kind of lively conflict within the law which is at the heart of the liberal order. On the contrary, they prefer to dissipate all conflict away into false bonhomie and social 'consensus'.

Such unitarianism is also reflected in these countries' neo-corporatist economic structures. In France, state and industry interpenetrate each other to a very great degree: high-flying civil servants from ENA or *Polytéchnique* flit between government and industrial management as if there were no difference between the two activities. In Germany, industry is largely controlled by the banking sector, which in turn is under the overall control of the central bank, itself a crucial part of the consensual framework linking government and 'social partners'. The powerful men who sit on the boards of the big German banks invariably hold a stack of directorships in German big business, and the banks themselves have very significant holdings in Germany's big companies.

This neo-corporatism is the essence of the 'Rhenish capitalism' which appeals so much to the Left after the failure of the Soviet and Social Democratic models. It is for this reason that, from the Bundesbank downwards, German policy-makers express such contempt for the 'casino capitalism' which exists in the more liberal, Anglo-Saxon systems of capital ownership: a free market, after all, cramps their style. Because European tax levels are dramatically higher than those of Asia and the United States; because European states consume huge portions of GDP (in France, 55 per cent); because European wage levels are grossly distorted above their true value by social costs, German labour being now the most expensive in the world; and because of a massive development of the dependency culture (only 28 per cent of the Belgian population works), liberal tendencies within these states are structurally hostage to the system and its vested interests.

To unite Europe politically around a single currency, with all the control over monetary, financial and industrial policy which the adoption of the German model implies, is therefore not only to make that which should be most politically neutral – money – into a highly politicised crow-bar by which to force the pace of history of an entire continent, it is also to transfer a system which is failing in individual countries to the European level, in the absence of parliamentary control or the institutions necessary for democratic debate. Such intellectual laziness and lack of imagination can only be a symptom of Europe's general cultural decline. It is small wonder that Europe's share of world trade has declined by 25 per cent in a decade. This decline will not be arrested, only aggravated, by building castles in the air.

And what a castle! In 1990, Jacques Delors – the man charged with realising the project of (Western) European integration, declared himself 'frightened' by the prospect of the Soviet republics introducing their own currency, as if the end of Communist dictatorship and the springtime of nations were a cause for worry.[3] In 1991, on the day after the Moscow *putsch* – of which he wrote in *Le Figaro* the following day that it might have 'positive consequences' – he told the European Parliament that 'we cannot unite the states of Western Europe and at the same time encourage the breakaway of Soviet republics'[4] – as if the process of Western European integration were substantially the same as that of Russian imperialism. Again in 1994, he expressed great surprise to a senior Russian official when the Soviet rouble-based clearing system was abandoned. He exclaimed: 'But how can you have abandoned something like that, when we drew inspiration from your system by introducing the ECU?! Our ECU is a European adaptation of what you did in COMECON.'[5] Convergence between capitalism and Communism – rather than the victory of one over the other – was not, it seems, only a Soviet idea after all.

Those opposed to European integration are often accused of being negative, and of not providing positive alternatives to the

European plan which is being proposed. This charge is partly a
trap: its formulation begs the very question: 'Should there be a
plan at all?' According to the political philosophy expounded in
this book, there should not be one – at least not a 'plan' in the
sense in which the question is posed.

Certainly there may be this or that project which the states of
Europe can achieve together; but there may also be projects which
other constellations of states can achieve too. These self-evident
truths are irrelevant to the fundamental question of European
integration, one of whose greatest intellectual faults is to confuse
co-operation between states with their political integration, and to
defend the latter in the name of the former.

But life cannot be planned in the way the question suggests. It
is escapist to think that the kind of problems outlined above can
be resolved by confused institutional tinkering in a Europe which
leaves the fundamental questions unaddressed. It is a far greater
challenge to re-establish clearly the principles upon which free
political life is based, and to entrench them in institutional
arrangements. Indeed, Eurosceptics should take heart from Psalm
118, Verse 22 – 'The stone which the builders refused is become
the head stone of the corner' – for their task must be to retrieve
the eternal principles of a just society, which are being so brutally
cast aside by the pro-Europeans.

Those principles are: accountable government (democracy),
the rule of law, and sound money. To institutionalise them, the
national parliaments across Europe would have to be reformed
before any European construction proceeds. Necessary reforms
would include abolishing proportional representation – which, in
the name of greater representation, actually divorces parliaments
from the people – and dissolving the excessively close link
between political parties and the state which exists in many continental countries, notably Germany. Both these are currently
suffocating democracy in Europe, and making a mockery of the
continent's national parliaments. Released from the hard constraints of true accountability – the simple link between the man
in the street and his member of parliament, which is broken by
continental party list systems – parliaments rapidly become

grotesque political circuses which represent no one except the interests of a self-serving and cynical political elite.

Parliamentarian government is the antithesis of bureaucratic government, and the latter encourages the erosion of the rule of law. In France, fiscal measures are frequently sabotaged by lobby groups *after* they have been passed by parliament: a powerful ministry can simply bury them, and they languish unapplied. When regulatory power is confided in the hands of bureaucrats, power slips out of the public domain, and democracy suffers.

The law of sound money needs to be re-established in the way suggested in Chapter V. The rule of law, by which is meant the intelligent association outlined in Chapter IV, is the only way Europeans can interact more freely with one another. It is dishonest for European federalists to have peddled the idea of a single market – which could have united the peoples of Europe by means of free and spontaneous interaction – when what was in fact being hatched was not a free market at all. On the agenda instead is a self-contained and centrally directed economic space which is intended to serve as the basis for a political union. The one cannot be defended in the name of the other, any more than integration can be defended in the name of co-operation. The one is a noble cause, the other is not.

The case of Belgium, with which this book began, illustrates the dangers of forgetting these lessons. If Belgium had remained liberal, as it was for much of its history, then its multinationalism would have mattered little. Flemings and Walloons would have regarded themselves principally as citizens of a state of law, and not as semi-tribal members of 'communities'. But when the state's finances and debts become as bloated as they are in Belgium (which has the highest per capita debt in the industrialised world), the state can only act as a factor for division, not unity. Political life can only descend into a grubby fight over who gets which government funds, and who escapes the burden of the debt. If Europe follows the Belgian model and combines multinationalism with illiberalism – by trying to create a fake European identity with empty promises of prosperity, hand-outs or other political 'projects' – then it will suffer the same fate.

That fate involves the inflation of political institutions. Belgium has six parliaments, all with overlapping and confusing powers. Like any inflation, this one has debased the value of the individual elements, and all these parliaments are basically irrelevant – a fact which was illustrated by the spectacular decision in July 1996 effectively to close down the federal parliament and rule the country by decree.

This development was, however, inevitable. As the European Union itself proposes to do, it is only natural to want to replace parliamentary institutions with ones which are sealed off from parliamentary or electoral control (like the Commission, the Central Bank and the Council of Ministers) if those parliamentary institutions have made themselves irrelevant or absurd, as they have already done across the continent. The European Union would be delighted to have the European Parliament squabbling with national parliaments for powers: it is a perfect recipe for over-riding the lot of them, and introducing authoritarian rule by unaccountable institutions. It is no coincidence that parliamentary rule was suspended across Europe in the 1930s, for parliaments had made themselves irrelevant and absurd then as well. Anyone who cannot see the dangers of losing sight of these fundamental principles seems dangerously blind.

The 'plan', therefore, should be to stick to the principles of the free society. This is difficult. But human life is unstable and uncertain. Only the law, democracy and sound money can allow that natural uncertainty to become intelligible and even stimulating. By contrast, any attempt to remove uncertainty by artificial political means is self-defeating and contrary to human nature. After all, the only escape from uncertainty lies in the graveyard.

NOTES

Chapter I: The Withering State (pages 1 to 8)

1. Speech at the Catholic University of Louvain, Belgium, 5 February 1996.
2. Karl Lamers, foreign policy spokesman of the German CDU/CSU parliamentary group, speech to the Institut Français des Relations Internationales, Paris, 7 November 1994.

Chapter II: Fascists and Federalists (pages 11 to 80)

1. 'Das Europa der Zukunft' ('The Europe of the Future'): speech to Czech intellectual workers and journalists, 11 September 1940, reprinted in Walter Lipgens (ed.), *Documents on the History of European Integration* (De Gruyter, Berlin and New York, 1985), p. 73.
2. Speech at the Catholic University of Louvain, Belgium, 5 February 1996.
3. Speech by Professor Dr Helmut Hesse to the Stadtsparkasse Osnabrück, 31 October 1995, reprinted in *Auszüge aus Presseartikeln*, Deutsche Bundesbank, No. 75, 7 November 1995, p. 7.

4. 'Movimento Federalista Europeo', *Political Theses and General Directives*, 27–28 August 1943, reprinted in Lipgens, op. cit., pp. 514–16.

5. *Europa. Handbuch der politischen, wirtschaftlichen und kulturellen Entwicklung des neuen Europa. Herausgegeben vom Deutschen Institut für Außenpolitische Forschung, mit einem Geleitwort von Joachim von Ribbentrop* (Helingsche Verlagsanstalt, Leipzig, 1943), pp. 239ff.

6. Speech to the Nazi Party rally in Nuremberg, 13 September 1937.

7. 'Europas Schicksalskampf im Osten. Ausstellung zum Reichsparteitag 1938 unter Schirmherrschaft des Stellvertreters des Führers, Reichsministers Rudolf Hess'.

8. Alfred Rosenberg, 'Krisis und Neugeburt Europas' in *Nationalsozialistische Monatshefte*, No. 33, December 1932.

9. Pierre Drieu La Rochelle, *Socialisme fasciste* (Gallimard, Paris, 1934), pp. 10, 114.

10. *Europa*, op. cit., p. 239.

11. Professor Dr Antonio de Luna, 'Europa – von Spanien gesehen' in *Europa*, pp. 61, 62.

12. Virginio Gayda, 'Italien und die europäischen Nationalitäten' in *Europäische Revue*, July/August 1943, p. 227.

13. Karl Heinz Pfeffer, 'European Consciousness' in *Zeitschrift für Politik*, Vol. 34, No. 10–12, October/December 1944, pp. 377–85; reprinted in Lipgens, op. cit., p. 171.

14. Werner Daitz, *Wiedergeburt Europas durch Europäischen Sozialismus, Europa-Charta* (Zentralforschungsinstitut für Nationale Wirtschaftsordung und Großraumwirtschaft, De Amsterdamsche Keurkamer, Amsterdam, 1944), p. 135.

15. Op. cit., p. 136.

16. Daitz, *Der Weg zur Volkswirtschaft, Großraumwirtschaft und Großraumpolitik* (Zentralforschungsinstitut für nationale Wirtschaftsordnung und Großraumwirtschaft, Dresden, 1943), Part III, pp. 11–29; reprinted in Lipgens, op. cit., p. 113.

17. Friedrich Stieve, *Deutsche Tat für Europa: Von Armin bis Hitler* (Rütter & Loening Verlag, Potsdam, 1944), p. 286.

18. Karl Olivecrona, *England oder Deutschland* (Lübeck, 1941), pp. 11, 25.

19. Arthur Seyss-Inquart, meeting of the *Auslandsorganisation* of the Nazi Party, 26 July 1940; reprinted in Lipgens, op. cit., p. 72.

20. Walther Funk, 'Das wirtschaftliche Gesicht des neuen Europa' in *Europäische Wirtschaftsgemeinschaft* (Verein Berliner Kaufleute und Industrieller & Wirtschafts-Hochschule Berlin, Berlin, 1942), p. 41.

21. Francis Delaisi, *La Révolution européenne* (Editions de la Toison d'Or, Brussels, 1942), p. 7.

22. Karl Megerle, the official in charge of information matters on Ribbentrop's staff, in 'European Themes', a memorandum written probably in the autumn of 1941, reprinted in Lipgens, op. cit., p. 95.

23. Vidkun Quisling, 'Norway and the Germanic Task in Europe', 25 September 1942, reprinted in Lipgens, op. cit., p. 105.

24. Cecile von Renthe-Fink, 'Note on the Establishment of a European Confederation', August 1943, reprinted in Lipgens, op. cit., p. 138, and 'Draft Memorandum on the Establishment of a European Confederation', Autumn 1943, reprinted in Lipgens, op. cit., p. 150.

25. Megerle, 'Positive Themes for Press and Propaganda', 27 September 1941, reprinted in Lipgens, op. cit., p. 86.

26. Quoted in *Europa*, op. cit., p. 2.

27. See Joseph Goebbels, *Tagebücher aus den Jahren 1942–1943* (L. P. Loechner, Zurich, 1948), pp. 323ff (8 May 1943).

28. See Paul Otto Gustav Schmidt's record of a conversation between Hitler and Count Ciano at Hitler's headquarters on 25 October 1941, reprinted in Lipgens, op. cit., p. 89.

29. Ibid.

30. Op. cit., p. 52.

31. 'Dal principo di nazionalità all'imperialismo: Origini, vita e superamento delle nazionalità' (Turin, 1942).

32. L. Gangemi, *Europa Nuova* (Ed. Italiane, Rome, 1941), pp. 48–9.

33. 'The Problem of Reconstruction' in *Critica Fascista*, 24 July 1943, unpublished, reprinted in an anthology edited by R. de Felice, *Autobiografia del fascismo 1919–1945* (Minerva Italica, Bergamo, 1978), pp. 553–66.

34. P. J. Morgan, 'The Italian Fascist New Order in Europe' in M. L. Smith & Peter M. R. Stirk (eds.), *Making the New Europe: European Unity and the Second World War* (Pinter, London, 1990), p. 27.

35. Alberto de Stefani, 'The Reorganisation and Pacification of Europe' in *Rivista italiana di scienze economiche*, October 1941, reprinted in Lipgens, op. cit., pp. 188–9.

36. *Civiltà Fascista*, December 1942.

37. Reprinted in Lipgens, op. cit., p. 190.

38. Op. cit., p. 193.

39. Camillo Pellizi, letters to Ugoberto Alfassio-Grimaldi, 12 August and 4 September 1943, reprinted in Lipgens, op. cit., p. 195.

40. Published by Washburn & Sons, London, 1958.

41. Mosley, op. cit., p. 19.

42. Op. cit., p. 30.

43. Op. cit., p. 39.

44. Op. cit., p. 40.

45. Lipgens, op. cit., pp. 190, 192–3.

46. Megerle, 'Positive Themes for Press and Propaganda' in Lipgens, op. cit., p. 88, and 'European Themes' in Lipgens, op. cit. p. 95.

47. Anton Adriaan Mussert, 'The Dutch State in the New Europe', August 1942, published by the Dutch National Socialist Publishing House, Utrecht, and reprinted in Lipgens, op. cit., p. 98.

48. Goebbels, 'Das Europa der Zukunft', reprinted in Lipgens, op. cit., p. 73.

49. Op. cit., p. 75.

50. Op. cit., p. 73.

51. Ibid.

52. Reich Chancellery memorandum, 'Organisation of the German Economy', 9 July 1940, reprinted in Lipgens, op. cit., p. 57.

53. Quisling, 'Norway and the Germanic Task in Europe', reprinted in Lipgens, op. cit., p. 105.

54. Professor Dr Heinrich Hunke, 'Die Grundfrage: Europa – ein geographischer Begriff oder eine politische Tatsache' in *Europäische Wirtschaftsgemeinschaft*, op. cit., p. 214.

55. Lipgens, op. cit., p. 57ff.

56. Op. cit., p. 58.

57. Memorandum of 1 June 1940 to the Foreign Minister by Ritter, reprinted in Lipgens, op. cit., p. 61.

58. Daitz, *Der Weg zur Volkswirtschaft, Großraumwirtschaft und Großraumpolitik*, reprinted in Lipgens, op. cit., p. 111.

59. Speech to the Reichstag, 7 March 1936.

60. Hunke, Berlin, 1940; see also John Brech, 'Europa findet sich: Konturen einer Festlandwirtschaft' in *Das Reich*, 26 May 1940; Brech, 'Europa ohne Übersee' in *Das Reich*, 16 June 1940.

61. Colin Ross, 'L'Avènement d'une Europe nouvelle dans le cadre d'un nouvel ordre mondial', Les Conférences du Groupe 'Collaboration', Paris, October 1941, p.47.

62. Daitz, 'Der Weg zur völkischen Wirtschaft' in *Deutschland und die europäische Großraumwirtschaft* (Felix Meiner Verlag, Leipzig, 1939), pp. 7–12.

63. Op. cit., p. 52.

64. Daitz, *Wiedergeburt Europas durch Europäischen Sozialismus, Europa-Charta*, op. cit., p.34.

65. Alfred Oesterheld, *Wirtschaftsraum Europas* (Gerhard Stalling Verlagsbuchhandlung, Oldenburg and Berlin, 1942), p.14.

66. Op. cit., p.9.

67. See my article 'The Thousand Year Reich' in the *Spectator*, 21 June 1991.

68. Hunke, 'Einführung' to *Europäische Wirtschaftsgemeinschaft*, op. cit., pp. 7–16.

69. Op. cit., p. 23.

70. Hunke, 'Die Grundfrage: Europa – ein geographischer Begriff oder eine politische Tatsache' in *Europäische Wirtschaftsgemeinschaft*, op. cit; see also Dr Horst Jecht, 'Die Entwicklung zur europäischen Wirtschaftsgemeinschaft' in the same work.

71. Dr Anton Reithinger, 'Europäische Industriewirtschaft' in *Europäische Wirtschaftsgemeinschaft*, op. cit., p. 102.

72. Funk, 'Das Wirtschaftliche Gesicht des neuen Europa' in *Europäische Wirtschaftsgemeinschaft*, op. cit., p. 25.

73. Ibid.

74. Op. cit., p. 41.

75. Op. cit., p. 26.
76. Ibid., emphases in original.
77. Op. cit., p. 29.
78. Hunke, op. cit., p. 11.
79. Joachim von Ribbentrop, speech on the prolongation of the anti-Comintern pact, 26 November 1941, reprinted in Lipgens, op. cit., pp. 90ff.
80. Ribbentrop, 'European Confederation', 21 March 1943, reprinted in Lipgens, op. cit., pp. 122–3.
81. Hans Frohwein, 'Basic Elements of a Plan for the New Europe', 7 June 1943, reprinted in Lipgens, op. cit., p. 137.
82. Von Renthe-Fink, 'Note on the Establishment of a European Confederation', reprinted in Lipgens, op. cit., p. 138.
83. Ibid.
84. Ibid.
85. Daitz, 'Lebensraum und Gerechte Weltordnung, Grundlagen einer Anti-Atlantikcharta' in *Ausgewählte Aufsätze von Werner Daitz* (De Amsterdamsche Keurkamer, Amsterdam, 1943), p. 218.
86. Goebbels, 'Das Europa der Zukunft', reprinted in Lipgens, op. cit., p. 75.
87. Ibid.
88. Dr Philipp Beisiegel, 'Der Arbeitseinsatz in Europa' in *Europäische Wirtschaftsgemeinschaft*, op. cit., p. 128.
89. Megerle, 'Positive Themes for Press and Propaganda', reprinted in Lipgens, op. cit., p. 87.
90. Op. cit., p. 95.
91. Seyss-Inquart, 'Vier Jahre in den Niederlanden,' quoted by Lipgens, op. cit., p. 117, note 1.
92. *Signal*, No. 1, 1942; quoted by M. L. Smith in 'The Anti-Bolshevik Crusade and Europe' in *Making the New Europe: European Unity and the Second World War*, op. cit., p. 61.
93. Mussert, 'The Dutch State in the New Europe', reprinted in Lipgens, op. cit., p. 99.
94. Reithinger, 'Europäische Industriewirtschaft' in *Europäische Wirtschaftsgemeinschaft*, op. cit., p. 106.
95. Goebbels, 'Das Europa der Zukunft', reprinted in Lipgens, op. cit., p. 75.

96. Quisling, 'Norway and the Germanic Task in Europe', reprinted in Lipgens, op. cit., p. 105.

97. Von Renthe-Fink, 'Draft Memorandum on the Establishment of a European Confederation', reprinted in Lipgens, op. cit., p. 152.

98. Op. cit., pp. 152–3.

99. Op. cit., p. 155.

100. See also Gustav Königs, 'Europäische Verkehrsfragen' in Europäische Wirtschaftsgemeinschaft, op. cit., p. 141.

101. Frohwein, 'Basic Elements of a Plan for the New Europe', reprinted in Lipgens, op. cit., p.136.

102. Note for the Reich Foreign Minister, probably September 1939, prepared by Cecile von Renthe-Fink and reprinted in Lipgens, op. cit., p. 55.

103. Beisiegel, 'Der Arbeitseinsatz in Europa' in Europäische Wirtschaftsgemeinschaft, op. cit., p. 123.

104. Op. cit., p. 161.

105. Lipgens, op. cit., p. 161.

106. See also Herbert Backe, 'The Future of European Agriculture', 29 June 1944, reprinted in Lipgens, op. cit., p. 166.

107. Von Renthe-Fink, 'Draft Memorandum on the Establishment of a European Confederation', reprinted in Lipgens, op. cit., p. 158.

108. Op. cit., p. 159.

109. Op. cit., p. 158.

110. Op. cit., p. 159.

111. Europa, op. cit., p. 52.

112. Ibid.

113. Königs, 'Die Zukunft gehört der Motorisierung' (The Future Belongs to Motor Transport), from 'Europäische Verkehrsfragen' in Europäische Wirtschaftsgemeinschaft, op. cit., p. 156.

114. Funk, 'Die wirtschaftliche Neuordnung Europas', speech to the domestic and foreign press, 25 July 1940 (M. Müller & Sohn, Berlin, 1940), p. 5.

115. Jecht, 'Die Entwicklung zur europäischen Wirtschaftsgemeinschaft' in Europäische Wirtschaftsgemeinschaft, op. cit., p. 62.

116. Funk, 'Das wirtschaftliche Gesicht des neuen Europa' in Europäische Wirtschaftsgemeinschaft, op. cit., p. 35.

117. Ibid.
118. Morgan, 'The Italian Fascist New Order in Europe' in *Making the New Europe: European Unity and the Second World War*, op. cit., pp. 32–3.
119. Daitz, 'Die wirtschaftliche Neuordnung Europas', op. cit., p. 10.
120. Assessor Joachim Radler, 'Europäische Wirtschaft im Querschnitt' (Subtitle: 'Kann man heute schon von einer europäischen Wirtschaftsgemeinschaft sprechen?') in *Europa*, op. cit., p. 131.
121. Funk, op. cit., p. 38.
122. Op. cit., pp. 38–9.
123. Funk, 'Der wirtschaftliche Aufbau Europas' in *Europa*, op. cit., p. 90.
124. Dr Bernhard Benning, 'Europäische Währungsfragen' in *Europäische Wirtschaftsgemeinschaft*, op. cit., p. 162.
125. Georg Friedrich Knapp, *Die Staatliche Theorie des Geldes*, translated as *The State Theory of Money* by H. M. Lucas and J. Bonar (London, 1924).
126. Op. cit., p. 175.
127. Ferdinand Fried, 'Les Problèmes sociaux dans l'Europe nouvelle', Préambule de Henri Clerc, Les Conférences du Groupe 'Collaboration', Paris, August 1941, p. 41.
128. Jean Maillot, 'La Révolution technique et ses conséquences', Préambule de Jacques Duboin, Les Conférences du Groupe 'Collaboration', Paris, April 1941, pp. 5–6.
129. 'La moneta-lavoro e la scomparso dell'oro', August 1940, in De Stefani, *Sopravvivenze e programmi nell'ordine economico* (Ed. Italiane, Rome, 1942), pp. 271–3, 302–6.
130. Daitz, 'Der Weg zur völkischen Wirtschaft', op. cit., p. 139.
131. Mosley, op. cit., p. 45.
132. Von Renthe-Fink, 'Draft Memorandum on the Establishment of a European Confederation', reprinted in Lipgens, op. cit., p. 158.
133. Megerle, 'Positive Themes for Press and Propaganda', reprinted in Lipgens, op. cit., pp. 87–8.
134. Delaisi, *La Révolution européenne*, op. cit., p. 147.
135. Op. cit., p. 184; on Nazi theories about price stability, see also unsigned article in *Europäische Revue*, May 1942, p. 283.

136. Op. cit., p. 161.

137. Op. cit., p. 119.

138. Ibid.

139. Op. cit., p. 281.

140. Op. cit., p. 170.

141. Op. cit., pp. 150, 179.

142. Op. cit., p. 182.

143. Op. cit., p. 196.

144. Op. cit., p. 195.

145. Op. cit., p. 167.

146. G. Bottai, *Contributi dell'Italia fascista al 'Nuovo Ordine'* (INCF, Rome, 1941), pp. 8–9.

147. Dino Cofrancesco, 'Ideas of the Fascist Government and Party on Europe' in Lipgens, op. cit., p. 182.

148. 'Discorso pre lo stato corporativo' in Eduardo and Duilio Susmel (eds.), *Opera omnia*, XXVI: *Dal Patto a Quattro all'inaugurazione della Provincia di Littoria* (La Fenice, Florence, 1958), p. 91.

149. H. W. Neulen, *Eurofaschismus und der zweite Weltkrieg. Europas verratene Söhne* (Munich, 1980).

150. 'L'economia alla base della nuova civiltà europea', November 1941, in R. Riccardi, *La collaborazione economica europea* (Ed. Italiane, Rome, 1943), p. 125.

151. V. Gayda, *Profili delle nuova Europa. L'economia di domani* (Il Giornale d'Italia, Rome, 1941), p. 36.

152. Gangemi, *Europa Nuova* (Ed. Italiane, Rome, 1941), Chapter 4; M. Gianturco, *Lineamenti della nuova Europa* (Fratelli Bocca, Milan, 1941), Chapter 8.

153. Resistance pro-Europeans wanted this, according to Lipgens, op. cit., p. 17.

154. Morgan, 'The Italian Fascist New Order in Europe' in *Making the New Europe: European Unity and the Second World War*, op. cit., p. 30.

155. See 'The Dark Years' by Robert Tombs, *Times Literary Supplement*, 28 January 1994.

156. See *La Propagande sous Vichy 1940–1944. Ouvrage publié sous la direction de Laurent Gerverau et Denis Peschanski* (Collection des Publications de la Bibliothèque de Documentation

Internationale Contemporaine, Paris, 1990), p. 98, Picture
No. 3.

157. Op. cit., p. 91.

158. See Jean Madire, *La Brigade frankreich. La tragique aventure des SS français* (Fayard, Paris, 1973), illustrations.

159. Ibid.

160. See the documentary film by Claude Chabrol, *L'oeil de Vichy*, which is a collage of Vichyite newsreels and propaganda films.

161. I am grateful to Eugen Weber, Professor of Modern European History at the University of California, Los Angeles, for correcting the impression I gave in the first edition of the book that there was no difference between the two groups.

162. Robert O. Paxton, *Vichy France: Old Guard and New Order 1940–1944* (Columbia University Press, New York, 1972), p. 67.

163. Quoted by Jean Thouvenin, *Avec Pétain* (Paris, 1940); and Paxton, op. cit., p. 77.

164. Jacques de Lesdain, 'Notre Rôle européen', Les Conférences du Groupe 'Collaboration', Paris, June 1941, pp. 28–9.

165. Jean Weiland, 'Pourqoui nous croyons en la collaboration', Les Conférences du Groupe 'Collaboration', Paris, December 1940, p. 24.

166. Paul Otto Gustav Schmidt, representing the bureau of the Reich Foreign Minister, recorded the conversation between Von Ribbentrop and Darlan on 11 May 1941, reprinted in Lipgens, op. cit., pp. 81ff.

167. Ibid.

168. Admiral Darlan to Hitler on 14 May 1941, quoted in Paxton, op. cit., p. 118.

169. Op. cit., p. 119.

170. Published by Bernard Grasset, Paris, 1937.

171. Otto Abetz, *Histoire d'une politique franco-allemande 1930–1950. Mémoires d'un ambassadeur* (Librairie Stock, Paris, 1953), p. 61.

172. Marc Ferro, 'Histoire parallèle', television programme, Arte, broadcast 11 May 1996.

173. Rita Thalmann, 'Du cercle de Sohlberg au Comité France–Allemagne: Une evolution ambigue de la co-operation franco-

allemande' in Hans Manfred Bock *et al.* (eds.), *Entre Locarno et Vichy: les relations culturelles franco-allemandes dans les années 1930* (CNRS Editions, Paris, 1993), p. 68.

174. Abetz, op. cit., p. 31.

175. Thalmann, op. cit., p. 75.

176. 'Le Couple France–Allemagne' (unsigned) in *Cahiers franco-allemands / Deutsch-Französische Monatshefte*, No. 5, 1938, pp. 361–3.

177. These are all taken from 1940 issues.

178. These are all taken from 1938 issues.

179. Editorial in the January 1942 issue.

180. Editorial in the March/April 1942 issue.

181. Editorial in the March/April 1941 issue.

182. See, for example, the September 1938 issue.

183. 'Das Jahr Europas' in *Cahiers franco-allemands / Deutsch-Französische Monatshefte*, November/December 1940, pp. 313–16.

184. Document 'Politische Arbeit in Frankreich', 30 July 1940, quoted by Thalmann, op. cit., p. 84.

185. Friedrich Grimm, 'Faisons la paix franco-allemande' in Hans-Georg Gadamer *et al.* (eds), *Regards sur l'histoire* (Sorlot, Paris, 1941), pp. 239, 240.

186. 'Friedrich Grimm – patriote allemand, européen convaincu' by Fritz Taubert in *Entre Locarno et Vichy*, op. cit., p. 107.

187. Bertram M. Gordon, *Collaborationism in France during the Second World War* (Cornell University Press, Ithaca and London, 1980), pp. 230ff.

188. Robert Herzstein, *When Nazi Dreams Come True* (Abacus, London, 1982), p. 122.

189. Introduction by René Pichard du Page to Weiland, op. cit., p. 7.

190. Rheinbaben is quoted by Jean Montigny in the Introduction to 'Vers une Europe nouvelle' by Baron Werner von Rheinbaben, Les Conférences du Groupe 'Collaboration', Paris, April 1941, p. 7.

191. Op. cit., p. 9.

192. Op. cit., p. 10.

193. Op. cit., p. 11.

194. Ibid.
195. Op. cit., p. 22.
196. Op. cit., p. 38.
197. Du Page, Introduction to Ross, op. cit., p. 6.
198. Ross, op. cit., p. 50, emphases and capital letters in the original.
199. De Lesdain, op. cit., p. 6.
200. Op. cit., p. 21.
201. Op. cit., p. 22.
202. Op. cit., p. 23.
203. Marcel Braibant, 'L'Europe, espace vital de l'agriculture française', Les Conférences du Groupe 'Collaboration', Paris, September 1941, p. 7.
204. Op. cit., p. 18.
205. Dominique Rossignol, *Histoire de la propagande en France de 1940 à 1944: l'Utopie Pétain* (Presses Universitaires de France, Paris, 1991), p. 181.
206. Op. cit., p. 29.
207. Described by *L'Illustration*, 12 July 1941; quoted by Rossignol, op. cit., p. 182.
208. Gordon, op. cit., pp. 231, 239.
209. Herzstein, op. cit., p. 122.
210. Kurt Vowinkel, '. . . ein zweiter Napoleon?' in *Zeitschrift für Geopolitik*, 1941–42, pp. 371–6.
211. Thalmann, op. cit., p. 74.
212. Interview in *Paris-Midi*, 28 February 1936; see Zeev Sternhell, *Ni Droite, Ni Gauche. L'Idéologie fasciste en France* (Editions Complexe, Brussels, 1987), p. 18.
213. Paxton, op. cit., p. 161.
214. Schweizer's speeches, 'Les Jeunes de l'Europe nouvelle et la révolution nationale' and 'Vers l'Union de la jeunesse française' at the JEN Regional Congress in Vichy on 9 January 1944 are reprinted in Schweizer, *La Jeunesse française est une jeunesse européenne* (Jeunesse de l'Europe Nouvelle, Paris, 1944), pp. 20 and 32 respectively.
215. Gordon, op. cit., p. 237.
216. Quoted by Jean-Louis Loubet del Bayle, *Les Non-conformistes des années trente* (Seuil, Paris, 1969), pp. 317–27.

217. Denis de Rougemont, *Penser avec les mains* (Gallimard, Paris, 1972), p. 232.

218. De Rougemont, *Politique de la personne* (Je Sers, Paris, 1934), p. 8.

219. De Rougemont, *Journal des deux mondes* (Gallimard, Paris, 1947), p. 46.

220. *Mission ou démission de la Suisse* (La Baconnière, Neuchatel, 1940), p. 183.

221. De Rougemont, *Journal d'une époque. 1926–1946* (Gallimard, Paris, 1968), p. 371.

222. *Ordre Nouveau*, No. 5, November 1933, p. 13.

223. Op. cit., p. 8.

224. Ferdinand Kinsky and Franz Knipping (eds.), *Le Fédéralisme personnaliste aux sources de l'Europe de demain. Hommage à Alexandre Marc* (Nomos Verlagsgesellschaft, Baden-Baden, 1996), p. 2.

225. Alexandre Marc and René Dupuis, *Jeune Europe* (Plon, Paris, 1933), pp. 125–6.

226. Henri de Man, 'Jenseits des Nationalismus' in *Europäische Revue*, January 1943, p. 5.

227. Letter from Jacques Maritain to Emmanuel Mounier, 2 November 1932, quoted in John Hellman, *Emmanuel Mounier and the New Catholic Left 1930–1950* (University of Toronto Press, Toronto, 1981), p. 6.

228. Op. cit., p. 58.

229. Ibid.

230. Op. cit., p. 59.

231. Op. cit., p. 63.

232. Emmanuel Mounier, 'Was ist der Personalismus?' in *Cahiers franco-allemands / Deutsch-Französische Monatshefte*, 1936.

233. Hellman, op. cit., p. 73.

234. Op. cit., p. 72.

235. 'Esprit au Congrès franco-italien sur la corporation', *Esprit*, No. 33, June 1935, pp. 474–80; see Sternhell, op. cit., p. 308.

236. Hellman, op. cit., p. 133.

237. Op. cit., p. 115.

238. *Esprit*, No. 51, December 1936; see Hellman, op. cit., p. 134.

239. 'Révolution communautaire' in *Esprit*, No. 28, January 1935; see Hellman, op. cit., p. 83.

240. Sternhell, op. cit., p. 326.

241. Op. cit., p. 161.

242. *Sohlbergkreis*, No. 7, April 1935; *Esprit*, No. 41, February 1936; *Jeune Europe*, No. 3, 1936; see Hellman, op. cit., p. 115.

243. *Esprit*, No. 46, July 1936; *Jeune Europe*, No. 3, 1936, p. 3.

244. Hellman, op. cit., p. 107.

245. Martin Conway, *Collaboration in Belgium: Léon Degrelle and the Rexist Movement* (Yale University Press, New Haven and London, 1993), passim.

246. Raymond de Becker, *Le Livre des vivants et des morts* (Brussels, 1942), pp. 203, 207, 209; Hellman, op. cit., p. 122.

247. Hellman, op. cit., pp. 124–5.

248. T. J. Knight, 'Belgium Leaves the War, 1940' in the *Journal of Modern History*, XLI, 1, March 1969.

249. Published by the Nouvelle Société d'Editions, Brussels, 1942.

250. Hellman, op. cit., pp. 125–6.

251. Robert Aron, *Histoire de Vichy 1940–1944* (Fayard, Paris, 1954), pp. 196–217.

252. Philippe Pétain, 'L'Education nationale' in *Revue des deux mondes*, 15 August 1940.

253. Hellman, op. cit., p. 169.

254. François Perroux, *L'Indépendance de l'économie nationale et l'interdépendance des nations* (Aubier-Montaigne, Paris, 1969).

255. Tony Judt, *Past Imperfect: French Intellectuals 1944–1956* (University of California Press, 1992), passim; *Esprit*, June 1946, pp. 970–85; Laurent Monterini, 'Mounier, Maritain et la Revue Esprit' in *L'Ordre français*, May 1975, pp. 30–45.

256. Marc Fumaroli, *L'Etat culturel. Essai sur une religion moderne* (De Fallois, Paris, 1991), pp. 91–113.

257. Philippe Burrin, *La Dérive fasciste. Doriot, Déat, Bergery (1933–1945)* (Seuil, Paris, 1986), pp. 88–90, 340–1, 466 and notes 58–62; see also Zeev Sternhell, op. cit.

258. Jean-Marie Domenach's reply to John Hellman is on p. 138 of *Le Personnalisme d'Emmanuel Mounier, hier et demain* (Seuil, Paris, 1985).

259. See Michel Bergès, *Vichy contre Mounier. Les non-conformistes face aux années 40* (Economica, Paris, 1997).

260. Hellman, op. cit., p. 182.

261. John Hellman, *The Knight Monks of Vichy France: Uriage 1940–1945* (McGill-Queen's University Press, Montreal, 1993), p. 38.

262. Hellman, op. cit., p. 40.

263. Hellman, op. cit., pp. 41–2.

264. Op. cit., p. 57.

265. Bernard Comte, *Une Utopie combattante. L'école des Cadres d'Uriage 1940–1942* (Fayard, Paris, 1991), p. 184.

266. On the continuities between the Coal and Steel Community and the German management of north-east France, Belgium and Luxembourg during the war, under Albert Speer and Jean Bichelonne, Vichy's industry minister, see 'From Albert Speer to Jacques Delors' by John Keegan in *The Question of Europe*, ed. Peter Gowan and Perry Anderson (Verso, London, 1997).

267. Raymond Poidevin, *Robert Schuman, homme d'état* (Paris, Imprimerie Nationale, 1985), pp. 120–4.

268. The event is recounted in Sir Edward Spears, *Two Men Who Saved France* (Stein & Day, New York, 1966), pp. 134–5.

269. Henry Beyer, *Robert Schuman. L'Europe par la réconciliation franco-allemande* (Lausanne, 1986), pp. 16–23; see also Michel-Pierre Chélini, 'Robert Schuman et l'idée européenne (1886–1963)' in *France-Forum*, October–December 1996, pp. 21ff.

270. Michael Salewski, 'Ideas of the National Socialist Government and Party' in Lipgens, op. cit., p. 52, note 92, and p. 53.

271. Ibid.

272. Emmanuel N. Roussakis, *Friedrich List, the Zollverein, and the Uniting of Europe* (College of Europe, Bruges, 1968).

273. Frank Ebeling, *Geopolitik. Karl Haushofer und seine Raumwissenschaft 1919–1945* (Akademie Verlag, Berlin, 1994).

274. Op. cit., pp. 18, 24.

275. Op. cit., pp. 23–4.

Chapter III: Holding the Centre (pages 83 to 156)

1. Immanuel Kant, 'Zum Ewigen Frieden', second section, first clause, paragraph 2.

2. Horst Fuhrmann, 'Wer hat die deutschen zu Richtern über die Völker bestellt? Die deutschen als Ärgernis im Mittelalter' in *Matinee im Bayerischen Landtag*, published by Bayerischer Landtag, Munich, July 1994, pp. 12ff.

3. Ernst Kantorowicz, *The King's Two Bodies: A Study in Medieval Political Theology* (Princeton University Press, Princeton, 1957), p. 94.

4. Title of Book IV, Chapter II of *Policraticus*, for example as edited and translated by Cary J. Nederman (CUP, Cambridge, 1990), p. 30.

5. Kantorowicz, op. cit., p. 20.

6. Richard Marienstras, *Le Proche et le Lointain; sur Shakespeare, le drame élisabéthain et l'idéologie anglaise au XVIe et XVIIe siècles* (Minuit, Paris, 1981), Chapter 5.

7. Address, 31 May 1960.

8. President Herzog of Germany, in a speech given in Berlin on 8 May 1995.

9. Both quotes from *Frankfurter Allgemeine Zeitung*, 16 October 1995.

10. Report published by the Economic Advisory Council in the German Federal Economics Ministry in 1995, quoted by Professor Dr Otmar Issing, Member of the Directorate of the German Bundesbank, in a speech in Frankfurt on 4 November 1995, reprinted in *Auszüge aus Presseartikeln*, Deutsche Bundesbank, 7 November 1995, No. 75, p. 5.

11. Karl Lamers, Speech to TRUST in London, 17 November 1994.

12. 'Deutschland, Großbritannien und die Zukunft der Europäischen Union': speech by Wolfgang Schäuble to the British Chamber of Commerce in Cologne, 8 March 1993.

13. 'Rückkehr in die Zukunft': speech by the Federal President in Berlin, 8 May 1995.

14. François Duchêne, *Jean Monnet: The First Statesman of Interdependence* (W. W. Norton & Co., New York, 1994), p. 364.

15. Speech at the Catholic University of Louvain, Belgium, 5 February 1996.
16. By Ludwig Dehio (Krefeld, Sherpe, 1948).
17. Otto Gierke, *Political Theories of the Modern Age*, translated and with an Introduction by F. W. Maitland (first published by CUP, Cambridge, 1900, reprinted by Beacon Paperbacks, Boston, 1958), p. 95.
18. Michael Sheehan, *The Balance of Power: History and Theory* (Routledge & Kegan Paul, London, 1996).
19. Jacques Bainville, *Histoire de deux peuples* (Fayard, Paris, 1933), p. 22.
20. Bainville, *Les Conséquences politiques de la paix* (first published 1919, reprinted by Editions de l'Arsenal, Paris, 1995), p. 70.
21. Henry Kissinger, *Diplomacy* (Simon & Schuster, New York, 1994), p. 66.
22. Quoted in Jörg Wollenberg, *Les Trois Richelieu. Servir Dieu, le Roi et la Raison*, translated into French by Edouard Husson (François-Xavier de Guibert, Paris, 1995), p. 145. The book's original German title is *Richelieu. Kircheninteresse und Staatsräson* (Bielefeld, 1976).
23. De Stael, 'De l'Allemagne', 1810.
24. Kissinger, op. cit., p. 21.
25. Emmerich de Vattel, quoted from 1758 by F. H. Hinsley in *Power and the Pursuit of Peace* (CUP, Cambridge, 1963), p. 166; see also Kissinger, op. cit., p. 68.
26. *Hansard*, 1 March 1848, Col. 122.
27. *Politische Testamente der Hohenzollern* (Richard Dietrich, Munich, 1981), pp. 61, 68.
28. Op. cit., p. 96.
29. Op. cit., p. 97.
30. Op. cit., p. 199.
31. Letter to Pourtalès, 30 July 1912, quoted by Gregor Schöllgen in *Die Macht in der Mitte Europas: Stationen deutscher Außenpolitik von Friedrich dem Großen bis zur Gegenwart* (C. H. Bech, Munich, 1992), p. 21.
32. A. J. P. Taylor, *The Course of German History* (Hamish Hamilton, London, 1945), p. 18.

33. William Shakespeare, *Richard II*, Act 2, Scene 1, lines 43ff.

34. See James Buchan, *Frozen Desire: An Enquiry into the Meaning of Money* (Picador, London, 1997), Chapter 5.

35. Friedrich List, *Schriften / Reden / Briefe*, edited by Friedrich List Gesellschaft, 10 vols., Berlin, Reimar Hobbing, 1927–36, Vol. VI, p. 425.

36. List, *Works*, op. cit., Vol. VI, p. 210; an English translation, from which this quotation is taken, is *The National System of Political Economy*, translated by Sampson S. Lloyd (Lomgans, Green & Co., London, 1885), p. 175; italics in the original.

37. See Harold James, *A German Identity: 1770 to the Present Day* (Phoenix, London, 1994), p. 59.

38. List, *Works*, op. cit., Volume VI, p. 417; see also *The National System of Political Economy*, op. cit., pp. 423–4.

39. List, *Schriften / Reden / Briefe*, op. cit., Vol. I, p. 493.

40. List, *Das Nationale System der Politischen Ökonomie* (A. Sommer, Basle, 1959), p. 176.

41. List, *Schriften / Reden / Briefe*, op. cit., Vol. VII, p. 553; emphases added.

42. Murray Forsyth, *Unions of States: The Theory and Practice of Confederation* (New York, 1981), pp. 173–4.

43. Emmanuel N. Roussakis, *Friedrich List, the Zollverein and the Uniting of Europe* (College of Europe, Bruges, 1968).

44. Roman Szporluk, *Communism and Nationalism: Karl Marx versus Friedrich List* (OUP, Oxford, 1988), pp. 145–6.

45. Ralf Dahrendorf, *Society and Democracy in Germany* (Doubleday, New York, 1969), pp. 54–5.

46. A. J. P. Taylor, op. cit., p. 63.

47. Henri Richelot, *L'Association douanière allemande* (Capelle, Paris, 1845), p. 170.

48. A. de Klinkowstroem, *Mémoires, documents et écrits divers laissés par le prince de Metternich chancelier de cour et d'état* (Plon, Paris, 1880–84), Vol. V, No. 1135, pp. 517–36.

49. Heinrich Triepel, *Unitarismus und Föderalismus im Deutschen Reich* (Tübingen, 1906).

50. Triepel, *Die Hegemonie: ein Buch von führenden Staaten* (W. Kohlhammer Verlag, Stuttgart and Berlin, 1938), p. 289.

51. Triepel, *Die Hegemonie*, op. cit., p. 557.

52. Quoted by K. E. Jeismann, *Das Problem des Präventivkrieges im europäischen Staatensystem mit besonderem Blick auf die Bismarckzeit* (Freiburg and Munich, 1957), p. 86.

53. Quoted by John C. G. Röhl in *The Kaiser and His Court: Wilhelm II and the Government of Germany* (CUP, Cambridge, 1994), p. 173.

54. Ibid.

55. Kaiser Wilhelm II to Poultney Bigelow, 15 August 1929; see Röhl, op. cit., p. 210.

56. Kaiser Wilhelm II to Alwina Gräfin von der Goltz, 28 July 1940 and 7 August 1940; see Röhl, op. cit., p. 211.

57. Kaiser Wilhelm II to Margarethe Landgräfin von Hessen, 3 November 1940; see Röhl, ibid.

58. Kissinger, op. cit., p. 137.

59. Op. cit., pp. 169–71.

60. Volker Berghahn, *Quest for Economic Empire: European Strategies of German Big Business in the 20th Century* (Berghahn Books, Providence, USA, and Oxford, England, 1996), p. 10.

61. Georges-Henri Soutou, *L'Or et le Sang: les buts économiques de la première guerre mondiale* (Fayard, Paris, 1989), p. 25.

62. Op. cit., pp. 26–7; the quotations are from a letter of Rathenau's dated 7 September 1914.

63. Op. cit., p. 27.

64. Op. cit., p. 48.

65. Kissinger, op. cit., p. 83.

66. Lucas Delattre, *Le Monde*, 1 January 1996.

67. Bainville, *Les Conséquences politiques de la paix*, op. cit., p. 34.

68. Op. cit., p. 41.

69. Walter Lipgens (ed.), *Documents on the History of European Integration* (De Gruyter, Berlin and New York, 1985), Vol. 1, p. 5.

70. On the history of the SPD and its attitude to Europe, see 'Posteuropäisch national' by Eckhard Fuhr in *Frankfurter Allgemeine Zeitung*, 3 November 1995, and '"Das Deutsche Reich muß als staatliches Ganzes erhalten bleiben" Kurt Schuhmacher und die nationale Frage' by Dr Heinrich August Winkler in *Frankfurter Allgemeine Zeitung*, 31 October 1995.

71.   W. H. Roobol, 'The Prospects for the German Domination of Europe in the Era of the World Wars' in M. L. Smith and Peter M. R. Stirk (eds.), *Making the New Europe: European Unity and the Second World War* (Pinter, London, 1990), p. 20.

72.   Kissinger, op. cit., p. 283.

73.   Karl Haushofer, *Wehrwille als Volksziel. Wehrkunde, Wehrgeographie im Rahmen der Wehrwissenschaften* (Stuttgart, 1934), p. 20.

74.   Frank Ebeling, *Geopolitik. Karl Haushofer und seine Raumwissenschaft 1919–1945* (Akademie Verlag, Berlin, 1994), p. 89.

75.   Halford J. Mackinder, *The Scope and Methods and The Geographical Pivot of History* (first published in 1887, reprinted by E. W. Gilbert, London, 1951), pp. 38ff.

76.   Erich Obst, 'England' in *Die Großmächte vor und nach dem Weltkriege* (Karl Haushofer und Rudolf Kjellén, Leipzig and Berlin, 1930), pp. 70–109.

77.   Hermann Jahrreiß, *Deutschland und das Reich* (Cologne, 1939), p.55.

78.   Obst, 'Berichterstattung aus Europa und Afrika' in *Zeitschrift für Geopolitik*, 1925, p. 440.

79.   Karl C. von Lösch, 'Der Kampf für das Recht im Osten' in *Zeitschrift für Geopolitik*, 1941/1942, pp. 481–96.

80.   Hans K. E. L. Keller, 'Einheit und Vielfalt im rechtlichen Weltbild' in *Zeitschrift für Geopolitik*, 1937, pp. 246–8.

81.   Karl-Richard Ganzer, 'Das Reich als europäische Ordnungsmacht' in *Reich und Reichsfeinde. Schriften des Reichsinstituts für Geschichte des neuen Deutschland* (Band 2, Hamburg, 1942), pp. 7–80.

82.   Ebeling, op. cit., p. 129.

83.   Op. cit., p. 97.

84.   Arnold Weingärtner, 'Jenseits des Nationalismus' in *Nation und Staat* (Werner Hasselblatt, Vienna, 1942/1943), pp. 258–60.

85.   Otto Muck, 'Der Großeuropäische Wolhfahrtstraum' in *Zeitschrift für Geopolitik*, 1943, pp. 16–21.

86.   Hans Kaiser, 'Wenn der Sieg kommt. England und die USA gegen Europa' in *Das neue Europa. Kampfschrift gegen das*

englisch-amerikanische Welt- und Geschichtsbild (Pressedienst, Walter Körber, Stuttgart, 1942), No. 24, p. 8.

87. Wolfgang Höpker, 'Die Ablösung Zwischeneuropas' in *Zeitschrift für Geopolitik*, 1940/1941, p. 189.

88. Ebeling, op. cit., p. 182.

89. See 'Was der "eigentliche Fall" Carl Schmitt sein soll': letter from Professor Dr Ernst-Joachim Mestmäcker, *Frankfurter Allgemeine Zeitung*, 29 January 1996, writing in response to 'Freischwimmer von rechts' by Rüdiger Altmann, *Frankfurter Allgemeine Zeitung*, 18 January 1996.

90. Karl Megerle, 'Positive Themes for Press and Propaganda', reprinted in Lipgens, op. cit., p. 86.

91. Ibid.

92. Cecile von Renthe-Fink, 'Draft Memorandum on the Establishment of a European Confederation', reprinted in Lipgens, op. cit., pp. 155–6.

93. Joseph Goebbels, 'Die Vision eines neuen Europa' in *Das Reich*, 6 December 1942.

94. Joachim von Ribbentrop, speech on the prolongation of the anti-Comintern pact, *Monatshefte für Auswärtige Politik*, 1941, pp. 1053ff., also reprinted in Lipgens, op. cit., pp. 90ff.

95. Friedrich Grimm, 'Allemagne et France: hier, aujourd'hui et demain', Les Conférences du Groupe 'Collaboration', Paris, January 1941, p. 9.

96. *Das Neue Europa*, No. 1, 15 October 1941, p. 4.

97. Op. cit., No. 2, 1 November 1941, p. 6.

98. Op. cit., No. 5, 1 March 1942, p. 3.

99. Op. cit., No. 3, 1 February 1942, p. 5.

100. Dr Wolff Heinrichsdorff, op. cit., No. 9, 1 May 1942, p. 2.

101. Dr Reinhald Hoops, op. cit., No. 9, 1 May 1942, p. 6.

102. Liviu Rebreanu (a Romanian), op. cit., No. 8, 15 April 1942, p. 5.

103. Dr Hans Hohenstein, op. cit., No. 13, 1 July 1942, p.1.

104. Walter Freund, op. cit., No. 13, 1 July 1942, p. 5.

105. Dr K. W. Rath, op. cit., No. 14, 15 July 1942, p. 1.

106. Dr Hans Baatz, op. cit., No. 15, 1 August 1942, p. 3.

107. Dr Hans Kaiser, op. cit., No. 15, 1 August 1942, p. 5.

108. Kaiser, op. cit., No. 2, 1 November 1941, pp. 6–8.

109.   Dr Ruth Gänsecke, op. cit., No. 16, 15 August 1942.

110.   Dr Walter Flemmig, op. cit., No. 19, 1 October 1942, p.4.

111.   Staatssekretär Dr Paul Bang, op. cit., No. 22, 15 November 1942, p. 5.

112.   Op. cit., No. 23, 1 December 1942, p. 8.

113.   Freund, op. cit., No. 4, 1 December 1941, p. 6.

114.   Op. cit., No. 1, 15 October 1941.

115.   Op. cit., No. 2, 1 November 1942, p. 4.

116.   Op. cit., No. 4, 1 December 1941, p. 7.

117.   Op. cit., No. 3, 15 November 1941, pp. 4ff.

118.   Friedrich Stieve, *Deutschlands europäische Sendung im Laufe der Jahrhunderte* (Aschendorffsche Verlagsbuchhandlung, Münster, 1942), p. 23.

119.   Stieve, *Deutsche Tat für Europa: Von Armin bis Hitler* (Rütten & Loening Verlag, Potsdam, 1944), p. 334.

120.   Ibid.

121.   Op. cit., p. 315.

122.   Op. cit., pp. 335–6.

123.   Op. cit., p. 337.

124.   Werner Frauendienst, 'The Internal Reorganisation of the Reich as a Contribution to European Order' in *Jahrbuch der Weltpolitik*, 1942, pp. 112–39; reprinted in Lipgens, op. cit., p. 114.

125.   Dr Hans Pflug, 'Deutschland – das Herz Europas' in *Europa* (Helingsche Verlagsanstalt, Leipzig, 1943), pp. 134ff.

126.   Walther Darré, *Blut und Boden* (Munich, 1940), p. 519.

127.   Adolf Rein, *Europa und das Reich* (Essener Verlagsanstalt, Essen, 1943), p. 8.

128.   Ebeling, op. cit., p. 233.

129.   Daitz, 'Das Reich als europäischer Ordnungsgedanke' in *Nationale Wirtschaftsordnung und Großraumwirtschaft*, 1941, No. 5/6.

130.   Paul Schmidt, 'Die Achse als Grundlage des neuen Europa' in W. Haas, *Europa will leben: die nationalen Erneuerungsbewegungen in Wort und Bild* (Berlin, 1936), pp. 13ff.

131.   Cecile von Renthe-Fink, 'Note on the Establishment of a European Confederation', reprinted in Lipgens, op. cit., p. 138.

132. R. Höhn, *Reich, Großraum, Großmacht* (Wittich, Darmstadt, 1942), p. 104.

133. Victor Farias, *Heidegger et le Nazisme* (Editions Verdier, Paris, 1987). See also Elzbieta Ettinger, *Hannah Arendt: Martin Heidegger* (Yale University Press, New Haven and London, 1995), p. 10. I am indebted to Dr John London for having drawn my attention to an error on this point in the first edition of *The Tainted Source*.

134. Martin Heidegger, *Einführung in die Metaphysik* (first published 1953, reprinted by Max Niemeyer Verlag, Tübingen, 1987), p. 28.

135. See Werner Weidenfeld, *Der deutsche Weg* (Siedler Verlag, Berlin, 1990).

136. Timothy Garton Ash, *In Europe's Name: Germany and the Divided Continent* (Jonathan Cape, London, 1993), p. 41.

137. Op. cit., p. 79.

138. Op. cit., p. 24.

139. Op. cit., p. 97.

140. Horst Köhler, interview in *Le Monde*, 6 February 1996.

141. Speech at the Catholic University of Louvain, Belgium, 2 February 1996.

142. 'Das verhängnisvolle Irrtum eines Entweder-Oder: eine Vision für Europa' in *Frankfurter Allgemeine Zeitung*, 17 July 1989.

143. Bainville, *Bismarck* (first published 1932, reprinted by Editions Godefroy de Bouillon, Paris, 1995), p. 12.

144. *Le Monde*, 6 February 1996.

145. Interview with *Süddeutsche Zeitung*, 28 December 1995.

146. See for example *Agence France Presse*, 1 October 1992.

147. Interview with *Die Woche*, 3 May 1996.

148. Lecture at the Institute for Capital Markets Research in the Johann Wolfgang Goethe University, Frankfurt, 25 April 1996; reprinted in *Auszüge aus Presseartikeln*, Deutsche Bundesbank, No. 27, 30 April 1996, p. 1.

149. Bernard Connolly, *The Rotten Heart of Europe: The Dirty War for Europe's Money* (Faber & Faber, London, 1996), pp. 253–5.

150. Address to the 9th European Finance Convention in Madrid, 29 November 1995, reprinted in *Auszüge aus Presseartikeln*, Deutsche Bundesbank, No. 82, 8 December 1995, p. 11.

151. 'Überlegungen zur europäischen Politik' by CDU/CSU-Fraktion des Deutschen Bundestags, 1 September 1994, p. 3 (Bonn, unpublished).

152. Op. cit., p. 6.

153. Op. cit., p. 8.

154. *Le Monde*, 14 March 1996.

155. Karl Lamers, 'Where Does Europe Go from Here?' in the *European*, 18–24 November 1995.

156. Speech to IFRI, Paris, 7 November 1994.

157. Schäuble, speech to the British Chamber of Commerce, Cologne, 8 May 1995.

158. Quoted by the Bundesbank's Chief Economist, Professor Dr Otmar Issing, in a speech in Frankfurt on 4 November 1995, reprinted in *Auszüge aus Presseartikeln*, Deutsche Bundesbank, No. 75, 7 November 1995, p. 5.

159. Triepel, *Die Hegemonie*, op. cit., p. 557.

160. Issing, speech to the Autumn Plenum of the Academia Scientarium et Artium Europea in Frankfurt, 4 November 1995; reprinted in *Auszüge aus Presseartikeln*, Deutsche Bundesbank, No. 75, 7 November 1995, p. 5.

161. Triepel, *Die Hegemonie*, op. cit., pp. 135–6.

162. Goethe, *Faust*, Erster Teil, 'Am Brunnen'.

163. Professor Dr Martin Seidel, *Deutsche Verfassung und Europa*, 30. Bitburger Gespräche, 13 January 1995, Westfälische Wilhelms-Universität, Münster, reprinted in *Auszüge aus Presseartikeln*, Deutsche Bundesbank, 1 March 1995, p. 8.

164. Lamers, 'Where Does Europe Go from Here?', op. cit.

165. James, op. cit., Chapter 4.

166. Murray Rothbard, *Economic Thought Before Adam Smith* (Edward Elgar, London, 1995), p. 36.

167. '*Ein gemeinsamer Währungsraum*' mentioned by Edgar Meister in a speech to the Friedrich Ebert Stiftung, Trier, 24 October 1995, reprinted in *Auszüge aus Presseartikeln*, Deutsche Bundesbank, No. 73, 27 October 1995, p. 6; see also speech by Reimut Jochimsen, Munich, 10 October 1995, reprinted in op. cit., p. 9. For '*europäischer Wirtschaftsraum*' see Issing, speech in Frankfurt, 4 November 1995, reprinted in op. cit., No. 75, 7 November 1995, p. 5; and for '*Deutschland ist . . . in die Mitte*

des gesamteuropäischen Wirtschaftsraumes gerückt' see speech by Helmut Hesse, Osnabrück, 31 October 1995, reprinted in op. cit., p. 8. At his speech at the Catholic University of Louvain, Belgium, Chancellor Kohl also spoke of the world's *'Wirtschaftsräume'*.

168.   Fritz Stern, 'A New Beginning in Germany' in the *Washington Post*, 29 July 1990.

169.   Louis Dumont, *The German Ideology: From France to Germany and Back* (University of Chicago Press, Chicago, 1994), p. 52.

170.   Thomas Mann, *Reflections of a Nonpolitical Man*, translated by W. D. Morris (New York, 1983), p. 246.

171.   Jean-Pierre Chevènement, *France–Allemagne. Parlons franc* (Plon, Paris, 1996), p. 152.

Chapter IV: The European Ideology (pages 159 to 211)

1.   Helmut Hesse, speech to the Stadtsparkasse Osnabrück, 31 October 1995, reprinted in *Auszüge aus Presseartikeln*, Deutsche Bundesbank, No. 75, 7 November 1995, p. 7.

2.   For example Kenichi Ohmae, 'New World Order: the Rise of the Region-State' in the *Wall Street Journal Europe*, 17 August 1994.

3.   See, for instance, Karl Lamers in debate with Jean-Pierre Chevènement, in the magazine *Géopolitique*, Spring 1996, p. 73; or Lamers again, 'Beyond the Nation-State – a German Vision of Europe' in *The Times*, 27 April 1996.

4.   *Die Welt*, 15 June 1996.

5.   *Géopolitique*, Paris, Spring 1996.

6.   Quoted by Niall Ferguson in 'The Kaiser's European Union' in *Virtual History: Alternatives and Counterfactuals*, ed. Niall Ferguson (Picador, London, 1997), p. 229. Ferguson's source is D. E. Kaiser, 'Germany and the Origins of the First World War' in the *Journal of Modern History*, LV (1983), pp. 442–74.

7.   Jean-Luc Mathieu, *L'Union européenne* (Presses Universitaires de France, Collection 'Que sais-je?', Paris, 1994).

8.   For example, Genesis 22 : 18.

9.   For example, Matthew 22 : 21; Romans 13 : 6–7.

10. St Augustine, *City of God*, translated by Henry Bettenson (Penguin, Harmondsworth, 1984), passim.

11. Ernst Kantorowicz, *The King's Two Bodies: A Study in Medieval Political Theology* (Princeton University Press, Princeton, 1957).

12. In what follows, I am indebted to Noel Malcolm's *Sense on Sovereignty* (Centre for Policy Studies, London, 1991), probably the most lucid modern statement on this subject. It is surely rare to find a short paper to which one can profitably turn again and again, as I have on numerous occasions in the years since it was published.

13. H. W. R. Wade, 'The Basis of Legal Sovereignty' in *Cambridge Law Journal*, 1955, p. 189. See also Malcolm, op. cit., p. 18.

14. Malcolm, op. cit., p. 20.

15. Ibid.

16. H. L. A. Hart, *The Concept of Law* (Clarendon Press, Oxford, second edition 1994), p. 67.

17. Alain Cotta, *Le Corporatisme* (Presses Universitaires de France, Collection 'Que sais-je?', Paris, 1984), p. 67.

18. Peter Riddell, *The Times*, 11 June 1996.

19. Patrice van Ackere, *L'Union de l'Europe occidentale* (Presses Universitaires de France, Collection 'Que sais-je?', Paris, 1995), p. 59.

20. See Andrew Marr, 'The Real Enemy is the Money Market' in the *Spectator*, 9 September 1995.

21. Sir Leon Brittan, 'The Discarded Image' in the *Spectator*, 15 December 1990.

22. Sir Geoffrey Howe, 'Sovereignty and Interdependence: Britain's Place in the World' in *International Affairs*, Vol. 66, 1990, pp. 675–95.

23. David Held, 'The Decline of the Nation-State' in Stuart Hill and Martin Jacques (eds.), *New Times: The Changing Face of Politics in the 1990s* (Lawrence & Wishart, in association with *Marxism Today*, London, 1989), p. 193.

24. See Lamers in *Géopolitique*, op. cit., p. 68.

25. Thomas Hobbes, *Leviathan* (first published 1651, edited and abridged by John Plamenatz and reprinted by Fount Paperbacks, London, 1983), p. 234.

26. See also C. B. Macpherson, *The Political Theory of Possessive Individualism: Hobbes to Locke* (OUP, Oxford, 1962), II, 5, iii ('Congruence of Sovereignty and Market Society'), pp. 95ff.

27. See, for example, 'La grande révolte française contre l'Europe libérale' in *Le Monde diplomatique*, January 1996.

28. For example Held, op. cit., p. 191.

29. Aristotle, *Politics*, translated by Benjamin Jowett, with introduction, analysis and index by H. W. C. Davis (Clarendon Press, Oxford, impression of 1926, first edition 1905), Book I, 1253a.

30. Hans Kelsen, *Reine Rechtslehre: Einleitung in die rechtswissenschaftliche Problematik* (F. Deuticke, Leipzig, 1934), p. 32.

31. Op. cit., p. 70.

32. Edmund Burke, *Reflections on the Revolution in France* (first published 1790, edited by Conor Cruise O'Brien and reprinted by Penguin, Harmondsworth, 1986), pp. 171–2.

33. Friedrich von Hayek, *The Constitution of Liberty* (Routledge & Kegan Paul, London, 1960), p. 237.

34. Tacitus, *Annals*, III, 27.

35. Hart, op. cit., pp. 27–8.

36. Op. cit., p. 28.

37. Kelsen, op. cit., p. 111.

38. Hayek, *Law, Legislation and Liberty* (Routledge & Kegan Paul, London, 1982), Vol. I, p. 82.

39. Michael Oakeshott, *On Human Conduct* (OUP, Oxford, 1975), p. 87.

40. Op. cit., p. 112.

41. Horst Köhler, *Stuttgarter Zeitung*, 12 December 1995; reprinted in *Auszüge aus Pressartikeln*, Deutsche Bundesbank, No. 84, 14 December 1995, p. 6.

42. Oakeshott, op. cit., pp. 132–41.

43. 'Reflexionen zur Anthropologie' No. 897, *Gesammelte Schriften* (Prussian Academy edition, 15: 392); quoted in 'Lectures on Kant's Political Philosophy' by Hannah Arendt, edited by Ronald Beiner (University of Chicago Press, Chicago, 1982), p. 40.

44. Hannah Arendt, *The Human Condition* (University of Chicago Press, Chicago, 1958), pp. 26–7.

45. Oakeshott, op. cit., p. 143.
46. F. C. Copleston, *Aquinas* (Penguin, Harmondsworth, 1955), p. 211; emphases added.
47. St Thomas Aquinas, *Treatise on Law*, Qu. 90, IV.
48. Arendt, *The Human Condition*, op. cit., pp. 63–4.
49. Ibid.
50. See Roger Scruton, 'In Defence of the Nation' in *The Philosopher on Dover Beach* (Carcanet, London, 1990), pp. 321ff.
51. Ibid.
52. Quoted by Ines Murat, *Colbert* (Fayard, Paris, 1980), pp. 199–207.
53. Benjamin Constant, *De l'Esprit de conquête et de l'usurpation* (first published 1814, reprinted by Flammarion, Paris, 1986).
54. For example *Die Welt*, 5 June 1996.
55. *Anti-Dühring* (*Herrn Eugen Dührings Unwälzung der Wissenschaft*), third edition, 1894, p. 302.
56. Carl Schmitt, *Politische Theologie. Vier Kapitel zur Lehre von der Souveränität* (first published 1922, reprinted by Duncker & Humblot, Berlin, 1991), p.11.
57. Lamers, speech to TRUST in London, 17 November 1994.
58. Rothbard, op. cit., p. 303.
59. *The Federalist, or the New Constitution*: papers by Alexander Hamilton, James Madison and John Jay (The Heritage Press, New York, 1945), p. 56.
60. Oakeshott, op. cit., p. 131.
61. *Oeuvres de Saint-Simon 1868–1875*, Vol. I, p. 197; quoted by Elie Halévy in *L'Ère des tyrannies. Études sur le socialisme et la guerre* (Gallimard, Paris, 1938), p. 32.
62. *Le Censeur européen*: Vol. I, p. 93, 'Du système de l'équilibre européen'; Vol. II, p. 67, 'Considérations sur l'état présent de l'Europe, sur les dangers de cet état, et sur les moyens d'en sortir'; see Halévy, op. cit., p. 35.
63. *Oeuvres de Saint-Simon*, Vol. XVIII, p. 165.
64. *L'Industrie*, prospectus, April 1817; *Oeuvres de Saint-Simon*, Vol. II, pp. 12–13; see Halévy, op. cit., p. 38.
65. *L'Industrie*, Vol. I, second part, by Augustin Thierry; *Oeuvres de Saint-Simon*, Vol. II, pp. 68–9.

66. 'Des Bourbons et des Stuarts' (1825) in *Oeuvres Choisies de C.-H. de Saint-Simon* (Brussels, 1859), Vol. 2, p. 447; quoted by Hayek, *The Counter-Revolution of Science: Studies on the Abuse of Reason* (Liberty Press, Indianapolis, 1979), p. 249.

67. 'Système industriel' in *Oeuvres Choisies*, Vols. 21 and 22; quoted by Hayek in *The Counter-Revolution of Science*, op. cit., p. 249.

68. Quoted by Hayek, op. cit., p. 254.

69. Op. cit., p. 245.

70. 'Cathéchisme des industriels' in *Oeuvres Choisies*, Vol. 8, p. 87. See Halévy, op. cit., pp. 46–7. Hayek writes that the formula was originally Auguste Comte's, and that it was later taken over by the Saint-Simonians, in whose publications it occurs once in the form, 'Il s'agit pour lui non seulement *d'administrer* les choses, mais de gouverner les hommes, oeuvre difficile, oeuvre saint' (*Globe*, 4 April 1831). Engel's use of the expressions runs in the original: 'An die Stelle der Regierung ueber Personen tritt die Verwaltung von Sachen. Der Staat wird nicht "abgsechafft", *er stribt ab.*' See Hayek, op. cit., p. 251 n. 58.

71. 'L'Industrie' in *Oeuvres Choisies*, Vol. 3, pp. 124–5; see Halévy, op. cit., p. 48.

72. 'Système industriel' in *Oeuvres Choisies*, Vol. 5, p. 47; see Halévy, op. cit., p. 46.

73. *Doctrine de Saint-Simon. Exposition*, Première Année, 1829 (Paris, 1830); Deuxième Année, 1829–30 (Paris, 1932), edited by C. Bouglé and E. Halévy ('Collection des economistes et réformateurs français', M. Rivière, Paris, 1924), pp. 272–3; see Hayek, op. cit., pp. 279–80.

Chapter V: Money Matters (pages 213 to 259)

1. Aristotle, *Nicomachean Ethics*, translated by David Ross (OUP, Oxford, 1986), Book V, Section 5, p. 120.

2. Ludwig von Mises, *The Theory of Money and Credit* (Liberty Press, Indianapolis, 1980), p. 454.

3. Milton Friedman, *Money Mischief: Episodes in Monetary History* (Harcourt Brace & Co., San Diego, New York and London, 1994), pp. 3–5, quotes William Henry Furness III's book, *The Island of Stone Money* (J. B. Lippincott & Co., Philadelphia and London, 1910).

4. An excellent account of monetary history, and especially of the pre-eminence of gold over silver, can be found in *The Evolution of Modern Money* by William Warrand Carlile (Burt Franklin, New York, 1901, reprinted 1967). See also the extremely informative and highly readable *The History of Money* by Jack Weatherford (Crown, New York, 1997).

5. Adam Smith, *An Inquiry into the Causes and Nature of the Wealth of Nations* (OUP, Oxford, 1976, reprinted by Liberty Press, Indianapolis, 1981), Chapter IV, 'On the Origin and Use of Money'.

6. Wolfgang Stützel, *Über unsere Währungsverfassung* (Walter Eucken Institut Vorträge und Aufsätze No. 56, J. C. B. Mohr [Paul Siebeck], Tübingen, 1975), p. 10.

7. Edmund Burke, *Reflections on the Revolution in France* (first published 1790, edited by Conor Cruise O'Brien and reprinted by Penguin, Harmondsworth, 1986), p. 261.

8. Murray Rothbard, *Economic Thought Before Adam Smith* (Edward Elgar, London, 1995), pp. 67ff.

9. Dante, *Paradise*, Canto XIX, line 117.

10. René Guénon, *Le Règne de la quantité et les signes du temps* (Gallimard, Paris, 1945, reprinted 1972), p. 110; Achille Dauphin-Meunier, *La Banque à travers les ages* (Banque, Paris, 1937), Chapter 3.

11. Rothbard, *Classical Economics* (Edward Elgar, London, 1995), p. 333.

12. John Locke, *Further Considerations Concerning Raising the Value of Money* (1695); quoted by Rothbard, *Economic Thought Before Adam Smith*, op. cit., p. 322.

13. *The Mystery of Money* (Economic Research Department, Chamber of Commerce of the United States, Washington, 1953), p.1.

14. Vera Smith, *The Rationale of Central Banking and the Free Banking Alternative* (first published by P. S. King & Son,

London, 1936, reprinted by Liberty Press, Indianapolis, 1990), p. 11.

15. Hans-Hermann Hoppe, 'How is Fiat Money Possible? Or, The Devolution of Money and Credit' in *The Review of Austrian Economics*, Vol. 7, No. 2, 1994, pp. 49–74.

16. Bank of England Act 1694 (5 & 6 Will & Mar c 20) in *Halsbury's Statutes* (Butterworth's, London, fourth edition reissued 1987), Vol. 4, p. 435.

17. Vera Smith, op. cit., p. 19.

18. Op. cit., pp. 22–3.

19. See Philippe Nataf, 'An inquiry into the free banking movement in nineteenth-century France, with particular emphasis on Charles Coquelin's writings' (William Lyons University, San Diego, 1987); see also Lawrence White, *Free Banking in Britain: Theory, Experience and Debate, 1800–1845* (Institute of Economic Affairs, London, second edition 1995).

20. See 'Les crises commerciales' by Charles Coquelin in his *Dictionnaire de l'économie politique* (Hachette, Paris, 1854).

21. Hobbes, *Leviathan*, op. cit., Chapter XXIV, 'Of the Nutrition and Procreation of a Commonwealth', p. 235.

22. Nigel Lawson, *The View from No. 11: Memoirs of a Tory Radical* (Bantam, London, 1992, reprinted by Corgi, London, 1993), p. 67.

23. Giulio Gallarotti, *The Anatomy of an International Monetary Regime: The Classical Gold Standard 1880–1914* (OUP, Oxford, 1995), p. 13.

24. Op. cit, pp. 7–8.

25. Gallarotti, op. cit., quoting Robert Triffin, 'The Evolution of the International Monetary System: Historical Reappraisal and Future Perspectives' in *Princeton Studies in International Finance* (Princeton University Press, Princeton, 1964), No. 12.

26. Gallarotti, op. cit., pp. 31–4.

27. Op. cit., p. 54.

28. Op. cit., pp. 18–19.

29. See Bernard Cherlonneix, 'Les Degrés de la convertibilité monétaire' (unpublished paper), p. 4.

30. Rothbard, *Economic Thought Before Adam Smith*, op. cit., Vol. I, p. 99.

31. 'Loi portant augmentation de la faculté d'émission des banques de France et de l'Algérie, établissant à titre provisoire le cours forcé de leurs billets et approuvant des conventions passées avec ces établissements', 5 August 1914.

32. Press conference, 4 February 1965, in Discours et messages (Plon, Paris, 1970), Vol. 4.

33. Jacques Rueff, Le Péché monétaire de l'Occident (Plon, Paris, 1971), pp. 16–18; also L'Age de l'inflation (Payot, Paris, 1963), pp. 11–12; and La Réforme du système monétaire international (Editions France-Empire, Paris, 1967), p. 16.

34. Rueff, Le Péché monétaire de l'Occident, op. cit., p. 24.

35. Quoted by Armand van Dormael, La Guerre des monnaies (Editions Racine, Brussels, 1995), p. 110.

36. The link between the two events is well explained by Robert L. Bartley in The Seven Fat Years and How to Do it Again (The Free Press, New York, 1992), Chapter 2.

37. Quoted by Rueff, La Réforme du système monétaire international, op. cit., p. 10.

38. Cf. Pascal Salin, L'Union monétaire européenne, au profit de qui? (Economica, Paris, 1980), p. 35.

39. Thomas L. Friedman, 'It's a Mad, Mad, Mad World Money Market' in the New York Times, 8 May 1994.

40. Burke, op. cit., pp. 310–11.

41. Burke, Discours sur la monnaie de papier (no publisher, Paris, 1790).

42. This was the reaction of the distinguished playwright and Whig MP, Richard Sheridan (1751–1816) to the government's decision to 'force' the Bank of England to suspend specie payments in 1797. Quoted by Rothbard in Classical Economics, op. cit., p. 161.

43. Burke, Reflections on the Revolution in France, op. cit., p. 307.

44. See The New Palgrave Dictionary of Money and Finance (Macmillan, London, 1992), Vol. I, p. 164.

45. Marcello de Ceco, 'The Gold Standard' in The New Palgrave Dictionary of Money and Finance, op. cit.

46. David E. Lindsey and Henry C. Wallich, 'Monetary Policy' in The New Palgrave Dictionary of Money and Finance, op. cit.

47. Ludwig von Mises, *The Theory of Money and Credit* (Liberty Press, Indianapolis, 1980), pp. 456–7.
48. Private conversation, February 1996.
49. Speech to the General Assembly of the Union of Swiss Businesses in Germany, Zurich, 12 April 1996, reprinted in *Auszüge aus Presseartikeln*, Deutsche Bundesbank, No. 25, 15 April 1996.
50. Quoted by Schumpeter in *Capitalisme, socialisme et démocratie* (Payot, Paris, 1951), p. 351.
51. 'A Superstate Set Up by Stealth' in *The Times*, 21 August 1995.
52. Quoted by Rueff in *Le Péché monétaire de l'Occident*, op. cit., p. 47.
53. Bernard Connolly, *The Rotten Heart of Europe: The Dirty War for Europe's Money* (Faber & Faber, London, 1995).
54. Speech to the Council of Europe, 28 September 1995, reported in *Frankfurter Allgemeine Zeitung*, 29 September 1995.
55. Interview in *Elsevier* magazine, Netherlands, 30 August 1997.
56. Lecture to the German Academy of Sciences, 13 June 1996, reprinted in *Auszüge aus Presseartikeln*, Deutsche Bundesbank, No. 38, 17 June 1996.
57. Theresia Theurl, 'Sprengsatz war immer das Budget: Die Vorläufer der Europäischen Währungsunion scheiterten an der Etatfinanzierung souveräner Staaten. Die Geldbünde des 19. Jahrhunderts' in *Frankfurter Allgemeine Zeitung*, 12 August 1995.
58. *Hansard*, 3/LXXIV/722–49.
59. See Charles le Lien, 'Overcoming the Sisyphian Project of European Monetary Union' in the *European Journal*, May 1996, p. 19.
60. Richard Cobden, quoted, without reference, by Rothbard in *Classical Economics*, op. cit., p. 246.

Chapter VI: The Third Rome (pages 261 to 320)

1. *Le Monde*, 15 January 1996.
2. CDU/CSU parliamentary group, 'Reflections on European Policy', September 1994.

3. *Frankfurter Allgemeine Zeitung*, 21 May 1994.

4. Issing, op. cit.

5. Quoted by Johann Georg Reißmüller in 'Lieber Gelmut, schön war's bei Ihnen', *Frankfurter Allgemeine Zeitung*, 17 May 1994.

6. For example in his speech to the Council of Europe on 28 September 1995, quoted by *Le Monde*, 30 September 1995.

7. Private conversation with the author, 20 March 1996.

8. *Frankfurter Allgemeine Zeitung*, 7 June 1996.

9. *Frankfurter Allgemeine Zeitung*, 9 October 1995.

10. *Le Monde*, 20 October 1995.

11. Ibid.

12. *Le Monde*, 3 March 1992.

13. *Le Figaro*, 26 May 1994.

14. *Le Monde*, 5 June 1996.

15. *Le Monde*, 9–10 June 1996.

16. *Frankfurter Allgemeine Zeitung*, 13 May 1994.

17. Jerzy Lisiecki, 'Financial and Material Transfers Between East and West Germany' in *Soviet Studies*, Vol. 42, No. 3, July 1990, pp. 513–34.

18. Vladimir Bukovsky, *Jugement à Moscou. Un dissident dans les archives du Kremlin* (Robert Laffont, Paris, 1995), p. 307.

19. Hans-Peter Schwarz, *Die gezähmten Deutschen. Von der Machbessessenheit zur Machtvergessenheit* (Deutsche Verlags-Anstalt, Stuttgart, 1985), p. 35; quoted in Timothy Garton Ash, *In Europe's Name: Germany and the Divided Continent* (Jonathan Cape, London, 1993), p. 40.

20. *Le Monde*, 13 May 1994.

21. Bukovsky, op. cit., p. 115.

22. Iver Neumann, *Russia and the Idea of Europe* (Routledge & Kegan Paul, London, 1996), pp. 135–6, 139–40.

23. *Pravda*, 24–25 November 1981.

24. Yuri Borko, head of the Institute for Europe, Moscow, in Vladimir Baranovsky and Hans-Joachim Spanger (eds.), *In from the Cold: Germany, Russia and the Future of Europe*, with a foreword by Eduard Shevardnadze (Westview Press, Boulder, Colorado, 1992), p. 40.

25. *Pravda*, 19 December 1984.

26. Neumann, op. cit., p. 161.

27.   Mikhail Gorbachev, *Perestroika: New Thinking for Our Country and the World* (HarperCollins, London, 1987), p. 208.

28.   Gorbachev, 'Plaidoyer pour une "Maison Commune"' in *Politique Internationale*, No. 68, Summer 1995, p. 111.

29.   John Borawski, 'The Budapest Summit Meeting' in *Helsinki Monitor*, Vol. 6, No. 1, p. 11.

30.   Heather Hulburt, 'Russia, the OSCE and European Security Architecture' in *Helsinki Monitor*, Vol. 6, No. 2, p. 5.

31.   Baranovsky and Spanger, op. cit., p. ix.

32.   *Le Monde*, 16 March 1996.

33.   *Europe Today*, BBC World Service, 18 March 1996.

34.   *Le Monde*, 14 March 1996.

35.   *Le Monde*, 25 January 1996.

36.   Hulburt, op. cit., p.15.

37.   *Le Monde*, 19 October 1995.

38.   *Neue Zürcher Zeitung*, 27 March 1996.

39.   *Le Monde*, 22 March 1996.

40.   *Le Monde*, 8 March 1996.

41.   *Le Monde*, 16 March 1996.

42.   *Le Monde*, 8 March 1996.

43.   *Le Monde*, 3 May 1996.

44.   *Wall Street Journal Europe*, 30 April 1996.

45.   *Wall Street Journal Europe*, 23–24 February 1996.

46.   *Frankfurter Allgemeine Zeitung*, 17 November 1995.

47.   Pierre Verluise, *Le Nouvel Emprunt russe* (Odilon Média, Paris, 1995); see also my review of the book, 'Is Russia Blackmailing the West?' in the *Wall Street Journal Europe*, 26–27 April 1996.

48.   *Neue Zürcher Zeitung*, 11 July 1996.

49.   *Le Monde*, 12 July 1996.

50.   *Frankfurter Allgemeine Zeitung*, 30 July 1996.

51.   *Guardian*, 26 October 1989.

52.   *Frankfurter Allgemeine Zeitung*, 26 May 1994.

53.   Robert Seely, 'The Truth About Russia's Foreign Policy' in the *Wall Street Journal Europe*, 25 October 1995.

54.   Private conversation between Anatolij Lashkevitsch, Secretary of the Central Committee of the Communist Party of Belarus, and the author, Minsk, October 1995.

55.   *Le Monde*, 29 December 1995.

56. *Le Monde*, 15 February 1996.
57. *Le Monde*, 15 February 1996.
58. Quoted by Baroness Park of Monmouth in a speech to the House of Lords on the security services, 13 March 1996. The speech was reprinted in the *Guardian*, 19 March 1996 and in the *European Journal*, April 1996.
59. Ibid.
60. *Le Monde*, 3 January 1995.
61. *Frankfurter Allgemeine Zeitung*, 16 November 1995.
62. Michael Mihalka, 'Restructuring European Security' in *Transition*, Vol. 1, No. 11, 30 June 1995, pp. 3–4.
63. *Neue Zürcher Zeitung*, 3 June 1996.
64. *Le Figaro*, 28 March 1996.
65. Ibid.
66. *Frankfurter Allgemeine Zeitung*, 14 September 1995.
67. *Le Monde*, 9 May 1996.
68. *Le Monde*, 2 May 1996.
69. Speaking to the Council of Europe on 28 September, see *Le Monde*, 30 September 1995.
70. *Le Monde*, 27 January 1996.
71. *Frankfurter Allgemeine Zeitung*, 29 February 1996.
72. *Le Monde*, 30 January 1996.
73. Ibid.
74. *Le Monde*, 16 March 1996.
75. *Le Monde*, 30 January 1996.
76. *Le Monde*, 14 March 1996.
77. *Le Monde*, 8 October 1997.
78. *Frankfurter Allgemeine Zeitung*, 27 January 1996; emphasis added.
79. *Le Monde*, 13 May 1994; *Frankfurter Allgemeine Zeitung*, 13 May 1994.
80. *Die Welt*, 15–16 June 1996.
81. *Le Monde*, 5 June 1996.
82. *Le Monde*, 9–10 June 1996.
83. *Die Welt*, 5 June 1996.
84. *Wall Street Journal Europe*, 18 April 1996.
85. *Le Monde*, 13 May 1994; emphases added.
86. According to the conservative German jurist, Carl Schmitt.

See *Der Begriff des Politischen* (first published 1932, third edition 1963, reprinted by Duncker & Humblot, Berlin, 1991).

87. I expounded these arguments in 'The Philosophy of Europe', *The National Interest*, Spring 1995, pp. 58ff.

88. 'What can the OSCE do to manage crises in Europe?': speech by the Secretary-General of the OSCE, Dr Wilhelm Höynck, Pielavesi, 3 September 1995, reprinted in *OSCE 1995: The Year in Print* (OSCE, Vienna, 1996).

89. Gorbachev, 'Plaidoyer pour une "Maison Commune"', op. cit., pp. 105–12.

90. *Frankfurter Allgemeine Zeitung*, 13 May 1994.

91. Andrei Kozyrev, 'OSCE: L'Avenir du vieux continent' in *Politique Internationale*, No. 68, Summer 1995, p. 97.

92. *Frankfurter Allgemeine Zeitung*, 1 April 1996.

93. For example Helmut Freudenschuß, 'Five Antidotes to Nationalism: an Austrian Perpective', in Armand Cleese and Adam Daniel Rotfeld (eds.), *Sources and Areas of Future Possible Crises in Europe* (Luxembourg Institute for European and International Studies, Luxembourg, 1995), p. 63.

94. Published by OUP, Oxford, 1993.

95. I am grateful to Johnathan Sunley's 'Post-Communism: An Inflantile Disorder' in *The National Interest*, No. 44, Summer 1996, for this anecdote.

96. President Gerald Ford's remarks in Helsinki, Finland, 1 August 1995; reprinted in *OSCE 1995: The Year in Print*, op. cit.

97. Address by Richard C. Holbrooke, Assistant Secretary of State for European and Canadian Affairs, to the spring session of the North Atlantic Assembly, Budapest, May 1995; quoted in Sunley, op. cit.

98. Quoted by Mark Almond in *Europe's Backyard War* (Heinemann, London, 1994), p. 32.

99. Quoted by Alain Généstar in *Les Péchés du prince* (Grasset, Paris, 1992), p. 116.

100. Interview on *The World at One*, BBC Radio 4, 5 July 1991; quoted by Almond in *Europe's Backyard War*, op. cit., p. 237.

101. Bukovsky, op. cit., pp. 448–50.

102. *Le Monde*, 3 March 1992.

103. Speech at the Palais Chaillot to the conference, 'Les Tribus ou

l'Europe', 29 February 1993, reported in *Le Monde*, 3 March 1992.

104.   Andrei Gratchev, 'L'Histoire vraie de la fin de l'URSS' (Editions du Rocher, Paris, 1992).

105.   Quoted by Généstar, op. cit., p. 110.

106.   Hansard, 23 June 1993, Col. 324; the person who has done the most to publicise this remark, and its appalling implications, is Noel Malcolm. See, for instance, his *Bosnia: A Short History* (Macmillan, London, 1994), p. *xx*.

107.   Sunley, op. cit.

108.   'L'espoir d'une "stratégie commune"' in *Le Figaro*, 14–15 November 1992.

109.   The decree was published in French translation by the Documentation Française (the official French state publisher) in *Problèmes politiques et sociaux*, No. 760, 1996, and by the quarterly review *Commentaire*, No. 73, Spring 1996, pp. 207ff.

110.   Op. cit., I, 4.

111.   Op. cit., II, 7.

112.   Op. cit., III, 13.

113.   Seely, op. cit.

114.   James Sherr, 'After the Cold War: The Search for a New Security System': speech to the Institute of International Relations, Kiev University, 4 May 1995, within the seminar series 'Defence in a Democracy'.

115.   Françoise Thom, *Les Fins du communisme* (Criterion, Paris, 1994), pp. 109–10.

116.   Reports on Belarussian radio, Minsk, 1700 GMT on 21 March 1996, and Moscow NTV, 1600 GMT on 23 March 1996, respectively. See BBC *Summary of World Broadcasts*, 25 March 1996 (SU/2569 B/14).

117.   *Le Monde*, 31 March–1 April 1996.

118.   *Frankfurter Allgemeine Zeitung*, 29 January 1996.

119.   *Frankfurter Allgemeine Zeitung*, 27 January 1996.

120.   See Seely, op. cit., and *Le Monde*, 9 November 1995.

121.   *Pravda*, 13 December 1990; see also 'The European Community as Seen from Moscow: Rival, Partner, Model?' by Vladimir Baranovsky of the Institute of the World Economy and International Relations, Moscow, in Neil Malcolm (ed.),

Russia and Europe: An End to Confrontation? (Pinter, London 1994), p. 74.

122. *Frankfurter Allgemeine Zeitung*, 3 April 1996.

123. See 'Russia's Un-Neighbourly Relations' by Therese Raphael in the *Wall Street Journal Europe*, 11 September 1997.

124. *Wall Street Journal Europe*, 22 January 1996.

125. *Literaturnaya Gazeta*, 30 January 1991.

126. *Frankfurter Allgemeine Zeitung*, 22 October 1994.

127. See 'Le Plan stratégique russe' in *Commentaire*, No. 73, Spring 1996, p. 208.

128. I am grateful to Radu Portocala for this quotation, which I have taken from his article 'Economies de l'Est: en avant vers le passé' in *La Libre Belgique*, 26 October 1994.

129. 'Russian president's press secretary comments on Russia–Belarus union', NTV, Moscow, 1600 GMT on 23 March 1996; see *BBC Summary of World Broadcasts*, op. cit.

130. *Newsweek*, 1 April 1996.

131. *Le Monde*, 31 March–1 April 1996.

132. *Frankfurter Allgemeine Zeitung*, 3 April 1996.

133. Interfax News Agency, Moscow, 0854 GMT on 24 March 1996; see *BBC Summary of World Broadcasts*, op. cit.

134. Ekho Moskvy News Agency, Moscow, 2130 GMT on 23 March 1996; see *BBC Summary of World Broadcasts*, op. cit.

135. *Frankfurter Allgemeine Zeitung*, 27 January 1996.

136. Gustav Molnar, 'Say "No" to Yeltsin's Monroe Doctrine' in the *Wall Street Journal Europe*, 17–18 May 1996.

137. *Frankfurter Allgemeine Zeitung*, 7 October 1997.

138. Daniel Vernet, *Le Monde*, 30 September 1997.

139. *Le Monde*, 24 September 1997.

140. Delegation of the Russian Federation, 'Regarding the Work on a Model of Universal and Comprehensive Security for Europe in the Twenty-first century': meeting of the Senior Council, 31 March 1995; quoted in 'Restructuring European Security' by Michael Mihalka, in *Transition*, Vol. 1, No. 11, 30 June 1995, p. 8.

141. Voice of Russia World Service, 28 March 1996.

142. Gorbachev, 'Plaidoyer pour une "Maison Commune"', op. cit., p. 108.

143. Op. cit., p. 109.
144. *Newsday*, BBC World Service, 25 April 1996.
145. *Le Monde*, 27 April 1996.
146. Speech by Prime Minister John Major to the WEU Parliamentary Assembly, Church House, London, 23 February 1996.
147. Voice of Russia World Service, 29 March 1996.
148. A. Prokhanov in *Den*, No. 28, 1992. In what follows, I am greatly indebted to Françoise Thom's article, 'Eurasisme et néo-eurasisme' in *Commentaire*, No. 66, Summer 1994, pp. 303–9, from which this quotation is taken.
149. *Elementy*, No. 4, 1993.
150. See Thom, op. cit., p. 305.
151. *Sovietskaya Rossiya*, 24 February 1994.
152. Ekho Moskvy News Agency, Moscow, 2130 GMT on 23 March 1996; see BBC *Summary of World Broadcasts*, op. cit.
153. *Elementy*, op. cit.
154. Sunley, op. cit., p. 10; see also his 'First Find Your Threatened Minority' in the *Spectator*, 26 March 1994.
155. Georges Charachidze, 'Pourquoi il faut soutenir les Tchétchènes' in *Le Monde*, 9 March 1996.
156. Roger W. Robinson, Jr., 'Why We Should Care About Caspian Oil' in the *Wall Street Journal Europe*, 14 November 1995.
157. See the following reports by the British Helsinki Human Rights Group: 'Democracy and Human Rights in Georgia' (1992); 'The Azerbaidjani Presidential Elections, 1993: Democracy and Human Rights' (1993); 'Georgia: Torture and Abuse of Due Process in Case No. 7493810' (1995); 'Armenia 1995: Democracy and Human Rights' (1995); 'Azerbaidjan 1995: Parliamentary Elections' (1995); 'Georgia: Parliamentary Elections' (1995); and 'Presidential and Parliamentary Elections in Georgia' (1995).
158. These two quotations, from Shevardnadze's book, *The Future Belongs to Freedom* (available in English translation by Catherine Fitzpatrick, The Free Press, New York, 1991) are taken from Françoise Thom, *Les Fins du communisme* (Criterion, Paris, 1994), p. 29.
159. Thom, *Les Fins du communisme*, op. cit.

160. Gorbachev, 'Plaidoyer pour une "maison commune"', op. cit., pp. 105–12.

161. Baranovsky and Spanger, op. cit., pp. vii–ix.

162. Gorbachev, 'Plaidoyer pour une "maison commune"', op. cit., p. 111.

163. Andrei Sakharov, *Progress, Co-existence and Intellectual Freedom* (W. W. Norton & Co., New York, 1968).

164. Ibid., quoted in Harrison E. Salisbury (ed.), *Sakharov Speaks* (Collins/Harvill, London, 1974), pp. 53, 65, 72.

165. Op. cit., pp. 93ff.

166. Baranovsky and Spanger, op. cit., p. 26.

167. 'Our Global Neighbourhood' report by the Commission on Global Convergence, Oxford, 1995, pp. 69–70; see also p. 337.

168. Op. cit., pp. 342–3.

169. Quoted in 'We are the World?' by Walter Berns, *National Review*, New York, 26 February 1996, p. 48.

170. *Die Welt*, 5 June 1996.

171. Gorbachev, 'Plaidoyer pour une "maison commune"', op. cit., pp. 105–12.

172. Budapest Decisions, op. cit., Chapter IV, I, 4, emphases added.

173. Kozyrev, op. cit., pp. 93–100.

174. Op. cit., p. 94.

175. Op. cit., p. 95.

176. Ibid.

177. Op. cit., p. 98.

178. László Kovács, speech in Helsinki, 1 August 1995, reprinted in *OSCE 1995: The Year in Print*, op. cit.

179. CSCE Budapest Document 1994, 'Towards a Genuine Partnership in a New Era', pp. 1, 2.

180. Budapest Decisions, Chapter IV, VI, 17, 18.

181. Hulburt, 'Russia, the OSCE and European Security Architecture' in *Helsinki Monitor*, Vol. 6, No. 2, pp. 9–10.

182. Kovács speech, op. cit.

183. For example Chapter X of the Decisions of the Rome Council Meeting of the CSCE, 1993.

184. 'Conference on Security and Co-operation in Europe: Report of the CSCE Meeting of Experts on National Minorities', 19 July 1991, 30 ILM 1692, Part II, Para. 3, at 1695–6.

185. Thomas Buergenthal, 'The CSCE Rights System' in the *George Washington Journal of International Law and Economics*, Vol. 25, No. 2, 1991, p. 380.

186. Ettore Greco, 'The OSCE After the Budapest Summit: The Need for Specialisation' in the *International Spectator*, Vol. XXX, No. 2, April/June 1995, p. 7. The article draws largely on a comprehensive analysis and assessment of the CSCE's activities during the Italian Chairmanship with the revealing title: *L'Europa senza muri: le sfide della pace fredda* (Europe Without Walls: The Challenges of the Cold Peace) edited by Greco (Franco Angeli, Milan, 1995).

187. Audrey Glover, 'National Minorities in Europe' in *Studia diplomatica*, Vol. XLVIII, No. 3, 1995, pp. 53–61. The quotation here is from page 60.

188. Budapest Decisions, Chapter IV, VII, 25.

189. Patrice van Ackere, *L'Union de l'Europe occidentale* (Presses Universitaires de France, Collection 'Que sais-je?', Paris, 1995), p. 120.

190. The military accord with Georgia was reported in the *Wall Street Journal Europe*, 2 April 1996.

191. Victor-Yves Ghebali, 'La Crise tchétchène devant l'OSCE' in *Défense Nationale*, Année 51, May 1995, p. 93.

192. *Izvestiya*, 31 January 1995.

193. Ghebali, op. cit.

194. 'The closer states are *intertwined* with one another, the more durable will be the *net* of their relationships': *Frankfurter Allgemeine Zeitung*, 8 January 1994, p. 2, emphases added.

195. Speech by Dr Wilhelm Höynck, Pilavesi, 3 September 1995, op. cit., p. 6.

Chapter VII: A Continent in Decline (pages 321 to 327)

1. Joint declaration by members of the French and German parliaments, published in the *Frankfurter Allgemeine Zeitung*, 11 October 1995, and *Le Monde*, 13 October 1995.

2. Horst Köhler, the chief German negotiator of Maastricht, interviewed in *Le Monde*, 6 February 1996.

3. *Izvestiya*, 20 July 1990.
4. Speech to the European Parliament, 23 August 1991; *The Times*, 24 August 1991.
5. The story was told by Arkady Volsky in the Romanian newspaper, *Curierul National*, 21 September 1994. I am indebted to Radu Portocala for drawing my attention to this quotation.

BIBLIOGRAPHY

Chapter II: Fascists and Federalists

Primary Sources

There is a massive amount of material on this subject. The following is a list of the references the author has been able to collect, but there are undoubtedly many more.

Germany

Abetz, Otto, *Histoire d'une politique franco-allemande 1930–1950. Mémoires d'un ambassadeur* (Librairie Stock, Paris, 1953)

Backe, Herbert, *Die Nährungsfreiheit Europas* (Wilhelm Goldmann Verlag, Leipzig, 1942)

Brech, John, 'Europa findet sich: Konturen einer Festlandwirtschaft' in *Das Reich*, 26 May 1940

——, 'Europa ohne Übersee' in *Das Reich*, 16 June 1940

Daitz, Werner, *Deutschland und die europäische Großraumwirtschaft* (Felix Meiner Verlag, Leipzig, 1939)

——, 'Die Neuordnung Europas aus Rasse und Raum' in *Nationalsozialistiche Monatshefte*, No. 126, 1940

——, 'Das neue Europa, seine Lebenseinheit und Rechtsordnung' in *Deutsches Recht*, with *Juristische Wochenschrift*, Issue A, No. 49, 1940

——, 'Das Reich als europäischer Ornungsgedanke' in No. 5/6 of the *Mitteilungsblatt der Gesellschaft für europäische Wirtschaftsplanung und Großraumwirtschaft i.V.*, 1941

——,'Lebensraum und Gerechte Weltordnung, Grundlagen einer Anti-Atlantikcharta' in *Ausgewählte Aufsätze von Werner Daitz* (De Amsterdamsche Keurkamer, Amsterdam, 1943)

——, *Wiedergeburt Europas durch Europäischen Sozialismus, Europa-Charta*, (Zentralforschungsinstitut für Nationale Wirtschafts-ordung und Großraumwirtschaft, De Amsterdamsche Keurkamer, Amsterdam, 1944)

Europa. Handbuch der politischen, wirtschaftlichen und kulturellen Enticklung des neuen Europa. Herausgegeben vom Deutschen Institut für Außenpolitische Forschung, mit einem Geleitwort von Joachim von Ribbentrop (Helingsche Verlagsanstalt, Leipzig, 1943). The articles in the book are as follows: Gesandter Professor Dr Friedrich Berber, 'Europa als Erbe und Aufgabe'; Gesandter Dr Paul Schmidt, 'Die Achse als Grundlage des neuen Europa'; Hermann Stein, 'Europäisches Bewußtsein'; Ministerialdirektor Dr Friedrich Stieve, 'Deutschland und Europa im Laufe der Jahrhunderte'; Botschafter z.V. Ulrich von Hassell, 'Lebensraum oder Imperialismus?'; Reichsstudentenführer Gauleiter Dr Gustav Adolf Scheel, 'Europäisches Studententum'; Exzellenz Professor Dr Balbino Giuliani, 'Der Beitrag Italiens zur europäischen Kultur'; Staatssekretär a. D. J. Benoist-Méchin, 'Frankreich im neuen Europa', Professor Dr Antonio de Luna, 'Europa – von Spanien gesehen'; Ministerpräsident a. D. László Bardossy, 'Ungarns europäische Sendung'; Professor Dr Lueben Dikoff, 'Bulgariens Weg zum Dreimächtepakt'; Professor Dr V. A. Koskenniemi, 'Finnland und die europäische Zukunft'; Ministerialdirektor Dr Angelo Piccioli, 'Die europäische Bedeutung der italienischen Afrikapolitik'; Reichswirtschaftsminister Dr Walther Funk, 'Der wirtschatfliche Aufbau Europas'; Professor Dr G. N. Leon, 'Der Südosten als europäischer Wirtschaftspartner'; Staatsrat Dr Roland Freisler, 'Das Rechtsdenken des jungen Europa'; Professor Dr Justus Wilhelm Hedemann, 'Das Recht als gestaltende Macht im europäischen Wirtschaftsleben'; Assessor Joachim Radler, 'Europäische Wirtschaft im Querschnitt' (Subtitle: 'Kann man heute schon von einer europäischen Wirtschaftsgemeinschaft

sprechen?'); Dr Hans Pflug, Deutschland – das Herz Europas';
Dozent Dr Theodor Wilhlem, 'Europa als Kulturgemeinschaft';
Dr Herbert Geirgk, 'Musik in Europa'; Generaldirektor Eitel
Momaco, 'Der europäische Film'; Dr Wilhelm Lotz, 'So baut
Europa'; Dr Carl Diem, 'Der europäische Sport'; Soprintendente
Dr Roberto Salvini, 'Die italienische Malerei der Gegenwart';
Jürgen von Kempinski, 'Das deutsche Buch und die europäische
Zukunft'.

Europäische Wirtschaftsgemeinschaft (Verein Berliner Kaufleute und
Industrieller und Wirtschafts-Hochschule, Berlin, 1942). The lec-
tures delivered in the colloquium were: Walther Funk, 'Das
Wirtschaftliche Gesicht des neuen Europa'; Horst Jecht, 'Die
Entwicklung zur europäischen Wirtschaftsgemeinschaft'; Emil
Woermann, 'Europäische Landwirtschaft'; Anthon Reithinger,
'Europäische Industriewirtschaft'; Phillip Beisiegel, 'Der Arbeits-
einsatz in Europa'; Gustav Königs, 'Europäische Verkehrsfragen';
Bernhard Benning, 'Europäische Währungsfragen'; Carl Clodius,
'Europäische Handels und Wirtschaftsverträge'; Heinrich Hunke,
'Die Grundfrage: Europa: ein geographischer Begriff oder eine poli-
tische Tatsache'.

Fahrenknog, Rolf (ed.), *Europas Geschichte als Rassenschicksal. Vom
Wesen und Wirken der Rassen im Europäischen Schicksalsraum. Mit
Beiträgen von Walter Gross, Werner Kulz, Bernard Pier, et al.* (Hesse
& Becker, Leipzig, 1937)

Fried, Ferdinand, *Les Problèmes sociaux dans l'Europe nouvelle* (Groupe
'Collaboration', Paris, 1941)

Funk, Walther, 'Die wirtschaftliche Neuordnung Europas': speech to
domestic and foreign press, 25 July 1940 (M. Müller & Sohn,
Berlin)

——, 'Der wirtschaftliche Aufbau Europas' in *EUROPA*, q.v.

Ganzer, Karl-Richard, 'Das Reich als europäische Ordnungsmacht' in
*Reich und Reichsfeinde. Schriften des Reichsinstituts für Geschichte des
neuen Deutschland* (Band 2, Hamburg, 1942)

Goebbels, Joseph, 'Das Europa der Zukunft' ('The Europe of the
Future'): speech to Czech intellectual workers and journalists,
11 September 1940, in *Die Zeit ohne Beispiel. Reden und Aufsätze
aud den Jahren 1939/40/41* (Zentralverlag der NSDAP, Munich,
1941)

——, 'Die Vision eines neuen Europa' in *Das Reich*, 6 December 1942

Grimm, Friedrich, Foreword to the German translation of Jules Romains' *Le Couple franco-allemand* (Batschari Verlag, Berlin, 1935)

——, *Hitler und Europa* (Albert Nauck & Cie, Zurich, 1936)

——, *Hitler et la France* (Paris, 1938)

——, *Allemagne et France: hier, aujourd'hui et demain* (Groupe 'Collaboration', Paris, 1941)

——, *Le Testament politique de Richelieu*, Preface by Fernand de Brinon (Flammarion, Paris, 1941; also published as *Das Testament Richelieus* by Schriftenreihe der NSDAP, Berlin, 1941)

Haushofer, Karl, 'Friedrich List. Ein Pionier des modernen Großraum-Gedankens,' in *Zeitschrift für Geopolitik*, 1942

——, 'Der Kontinentalblock. Mitteleuropa–Eurasien–Japan' in *Kriegsschriften der Reichsstudentenführung*, No. 7 (Zentralverlag der NSDAP, Munich, 1941)

Herre, Paul, *Deutschland und die europäische Ordnung* (Weltpolitische Bücherei, Deutscher Verlag, Berlin, 1941)

Hess, Rudolf, 'Europas Schicksalskampf im Osten. Ausstellung zum Reichsparteitag 1938 unter der Schirmherrschaft des Stellvertreter des Führers, Reichsministers Rudolf Hess': '4 Jahrtausende europäischer Geschichte in Funden, Kunstwerken, Karten, Urkunden und Schriften, veranstaltet von der Dienststelle des Beauftragten des Führers für die gesamte geistige und weltanschauliche Erziehung der NSDAP'

Hunke, Heinrich, *Reichsgedanke und europäische Wirtschaft* (Berlin, 1940)

Jahrreiß, Hermann, *Deutschland und das Reich* (Cologne, 1939)

Kapp, Rolf, *Europa – Erbkrieg oder Lebensgemeinschaft?* (Deutsche Verlagsanstalt, Stuttgart and Berlin, 1941)

Lipgens, Walter (ed.), *Documents on the History of European Integration*, especially Vol. I, 'Continental Plans for European Union 1939–45' (De Gruyter, Berlin and New York, 1985)

Muck, Otto, 'Der Großeuropäische Wolhfahrtstraum' in *Zeitschrift für Geopolitik*, 1943

Obst, Erich, *Die Großraumidee in der Vergangenheit und als tragender Gedanker unserer Zeit* (Wilh. Gottl. Korn, Breslau, 1941)

Oesterheld, Alfred, *Wirtschaftsraum Europas* (Gerhard Stalling Verlagsbuchhandlung, Oldenburg and Berlin, 1942)

Olivecrona, Karl, *England oder Deutschland* (Lübeck, 1941)

Pfeffer, Karl Heinz, *Die angelsächsische Neue Welt und Europa* (Junker und Dünnhaupt Verlag, Berlin, 1941)

Rein, Adolf, *Europa und das Reich. Betrachtungen zur Geschichte der europäischen Ordnung* (Essener Verlagsanstalt, Essen, 1943)

von Rheinbaben, Werner Graf, *Vers une nouvelle Europe* (Groupe 'Collaboration', Paris, 1941)

von Ribbentrop, Joachim, 'Der Freiheitskampf Europas': speech on 26 November 1941 in Berlin (pamphlet, no date or publisher)

Rosenberg, Alfred, 'Krisis und Neugeburt Europas' in *National-sozialistische Monatshefte*, No. 33, 1932

Ross, Colin, *L'Avènement d'une nouvelle Europe dans le cadre d'un nouvel ordre mondial* (Groupe 'Collaboration', Paris, 1941)

Schmitt, Carl, *Völkerrechtliche Großraumordnung mit Interventionsverbot für raumfremde Mächte. Ein Beitrag zum Reichsbegriff im Völkerrecht* (Berlin/Vienna/Leipzig, 1939)

Schmidt, W., Meissner, P., and Weber, C. A., *England und Europa* (W. Kohlhammer Verlag, Stuttgart and Berlin, 1941)

Sinclair, Upton, 'Vereinigte Staaten von Europa' in *Zeitschrift für Geopolitik*, 1929

Stieve, Friedrich, *Wendepunkte europäischer Geschichte vom Dreißigjährigen Krieg bis zur Gegenwart* (Phillip Reclam, Leipzig, 1940)

——, *Deutschlands europäische Sendung im Laufe der Jahrhunderte* (Aschendorffsche Verlagsbuchhandlung, Münster, 1942)

——, *L'Avenir de l'Europe* (Maison Internationale d'Edition, Brussels, 1943)

——, 'Deutschland und Europa im Laufe der Jahrhunderte' in *EUROPA*, q.v.

——, *Deutsche Tat für Europa: Von Armin bis Hitler* (Rütten & Loening Verlag, Potsdam, 1944)

Weingärtner, Arnold, 'Jenseits des Nationalismus' in *Nation und Staat*, hrsg. *Verband der deutschen Volksgruppen in Europa* by Werner Hasselblatt (Vienna, 1942–43)

Ziegfeld, A. Hillen, *Europas Erbfeind: England* (Edwin Runge Verlag, Berlin, 1941)

——, *Deutschland, Das Gewissen Europas* (Edwin Runge Verlag, Berlin, 1941)

France

Braibant, Marcel, *L'Europe: espace vital de l'agriculture française* (Groupe 'Collaboration', Paris, 1941)

de Châteaubriant, Alphonse, *La Gerbe des forces* (Bernard Grasset, Paris, 1937)

Delaisi, Francis, *Les deux Europes* (Payot, Paris, 1929)

——, *La Révolution européenne* (Editions de la Toison d'Or, Brussels, 1942)

Dupuis, René, and Marc, Alexandre, *Jeune Europe* (Plon, Paris, 1933)

Fabre-Luce, Alfred, *Anthologie de la nouvelle Europe* (Plon, Paris, 1942)

——, *Histoire de la Révolution européenne* (Domat, Paris, 1954)

La France contre l'Angleterre (Editions Européennes, Paris; Maison Internationale d'Edition, Brussels, 1940)

de Jouvenel, Bertrand, *Vers les états-unis de l'Europe* (Valois, Paris, 1930)

——, *Le Réveil de l'Europe* (Gallimard, Paris, 1938)

——, *Napoléon et l'économie dirigée: le blocus continental* (Editions de la Toison d'Or, Brussels and Paris, 1942)

de Lesdain, Jacques, *Notre Rôle européen* (Groupe 'Collaboration', Paris, 1941)

Perroux, François, *L'Europe sans rivages* (Presses Universitaires de France, Paris, 1954)

——, *L'Indépendance de l'économie nationale et l'interdépendence des nations* (Aubier-Montaigne, Paris, 1969)

Schweizer, Jacques, *La Jeunesse française est une jeunesse européenne* (Jeunesse de l'Europe Nouvelle, Paris, 1944)

Romains, Jules, *Le Couple franco-allemand* (Flammarion, Paris, 1935)

de Rougemont, Denis, *Penser avec les mains* (Gallimard, Paris, 1972)

Weiland, Jean, *Pourquoi nous croyons en la collaboration* (Groupe 'Collaboration', Paris, 1940)

Wintermayer, Edouard, *L'Europe en marche* (Editions du Livre Moderne, Paris, 1943)

Italy

Gangemi, L., *L'Europa nuova* (Ed. Italiane, Rome, 1941)

Gayda, V., *Profili delle nuova Europa. L'economia di domani* (Il Giornale d'Italia, Rome, 1941)

Pellizi, Camillo, 'L'idea dell'Europa' in *Civiltà Fascista*, December 1942

de Stefani, A., *Sopravivenze e programmi nell'ordine economico* (Ed. Italiane, Rome, 1942)

Great Britain

Mosley, Sir Oswald, *Europe: Faith and Plan – A Way Out from the Coming Crisis and an Introduction to Thinking as a European* (Washburn & Sons, London, 1958)

Belgium

Daye, Pierre, *Guerre et révolution. Lettres d'un Belge à un ami français* (Bernard Grasset, Paris, 1941)

——, *L'Europe aux Européens* (Nouvelle Société d'Editions, Brussels, 1942)

Journals

Dates of publication are provided where known.

Die Aktion. Kampfschrift für ein neues Europa

Cahiers franco-allemands / Deutsch-Französische Monatshefte (*Cahiers du Sohlberg* from 1933–35) [1935–]

Europäische Revue [1924–44]

The European [1953–59]

La France Européenne [1940–43]

Jeune Europe [1933–]; also published in German (*Junges Europa*), Italian (*Giovane Europa*); Finnish (*Nuori Euroopa*); Dutch (*Jong Europa*); Norwegian (*Det Unge Europa*); Spanish (*La Joven Europa*); Portuguese (*A Jovem Europa*); Hungarian (*Az Ifju Europa*); Romanian (*Europa Tanara*); and Bulgarian (*Mlada Evropa*)

Mitteilungsblatt der Gesellschaft für europäische Wirtschaftsplanung und Großraumwirtschaft i.V.

Das Neue Europa, Kampfschrift gegen das englisch-amerikanische Welt und Geschichtsbild. Pressedienst, hrsg. von Walter Körber [1941–42]

Das Reich [May 1940–March 1945]

Zeitschrift für Geopolitik [1924–68]

380 THE TAINTED SOURCE

Secondary Sources

Aron, Robert, *Histoire de Vichy 1940–1944* (Fayard, Paris, 1954)

Bergès, Michel, *Vichy contre Mounier. Les non-conformistes face aux années 40* (Economica, Paris, 1997)

Beyer, Henry, *Robert Schuman. L'Europe par la réconciliation franco-allemande* (Lausanne, 1986)

Bock, Hans Manfred, Meyer-Lakus, Reinhart, and Trebitsch, Michel (eds.), *Entre Locarno et Vichy: les relations culturelles franco-allemandes dans les années 1930* (CNRS Editions, Paris, 1993)

Chabrol, Claude, *L'Oeil de Vichy* (documentary film made in 1992 composed entirely of Vichy newsreels)

Chélini, Michel-Pierre, 'Robert Schuman et l'idée européenne (1886–1963)' in *France-Forum*, October–December 1996

Cofrancesco, D., 'Il mito europeo del fascismo (1939–45)' in *Storia contemporanea*, Vol. 14, 1983

——, 'Ideas of the Fascist Government and Party on Europe' in Lipgens, q.v.

Conway, Martin, *Collaboration in Belgium: Léon Degrelle and the Rexist Movement* (Yale University Press, New Haven and London, 1993)

le Crom, Jean-Pierre, *Syndicats, nous voilà! Vichy et le corporatisme* (Editions de l'Atelier, Paris, 1995)

Durand, Yves, *Le Nouvel Ordre européen Nazi, 1938–1945* (Editions Complexe, Brussels, 1990)

Freymond, Jean, *Le IIIe Reich et la réorganisation économique de l'Europe 1940–1942. Origines et Projets* (Sijthoff, Leiden, 1974)

Gervereau, Laurent, and Peschanski, Denis, *La Propagande sous Vichy 1940–1944* (Collection des Publications de la Bibliothèque de Documentation Internationale Comtemporaine, Paris, 1990)

Gordon, Bertram M., *Collaborationism in France During the Second World War* (Cornell University Press, Ithaca and London, 1980)

Hellman, John, *Emmanuel Mounier and the New Catholic Left 1930–1950* (University of Toronto Press, Toronto, 1981)

——, *The Knight Monks of Vichy France: Uriage 1940–1945* (McGill-Queen's University Press, Montreal, 1993)

Herzstein, Robert, *When Nazi Dreams Come True: The Horrifying Story of the Nazi Blueprint for Europe* (Abacus, London, 1982)

Judt, Tony, *Past Imperfect: French Intellectuals 1944–1956* (University of California Press, Berkeley and Los Angeles, 1992)

Keegan, John, 'From Albert Speer to Jacques Delors' in *The Question of Europe*, ed. Peter Gowan and Perry Anderson (Verso, London, 1997)

Kinsky, Ferdinand, and Knipping, Franz (eds.), *Le Fédéralisme personnaliste aux sources de l'Europe de demain. Hommage à Alexandre Marc* (Nomos Verlagsgesellschaft, Baden-Baden, 1996)

Kluke, Paul, 'Nationalsozialistische Europaideologie' in *Vierteljahresschrift für Zeitgeschichte*, No. 3, 1955

König, M., 'Europa marschiert gegen den Weltfeind. Bilder, Agenturen, Illustrierte. Deutsche Propaganda gegen die Sowjetunion und ihr Weg in die Schweiz 1941–1945' in *Neue Zürcher Zeitung*, No. 276/26, November 1988

Madire, Jean, *La Brigade Frankreich. La tragique aventure des SS français* (Fayard, Paris, 1973)

Militärgeschichtliches Forschungsamt, Stuttgart, 'Das deutsche Reich und der II Weltkrieg'; Band 2, 'Die Errichtung der Hegemonie auf dem europäischen Kontinent'

Milza, Pierre, *Fascisme français. Passé et présent* (Flammarion, Paris, 1987)

Neulen, H. W., *Eurofaschismus und der zweite Weltkrieg. Europas verratene Söhne* (Munich, 1980)

——, *Europa und das dritte Reich: Einigungsbestrebungen im deutschen Machtbereich 1939–1945* (Munich, 1987)

Paxton, Robert O., *Vichy France: Old Guard and New Order 1940–1944* (Columbia University Press, New York, 1972)

Le personnalisme d'Emmanuel Mounier, hier et demain (Seuil, Paris, 1985)

Poidevin, Raymond, *Robert Schuman, homme d'état* (Imprimerie Nationale, Paris, 1985)

Reveille, Thomas, *The Spoil of Europe: the Nazi Technique in Political and Economic Conquest* (W. W. Norton & Co., New York, 1941)

Rossignol, Dominique, *Histoire de la propagande en France de 1940 à 1944: l'utopie Pétain* (Presses Universitaires de France, Paris, 1991)

Smith, M. L., and Stirk, Peter M. R. (eds.), *Making the New Europe: European Unity and the Second World War* (Pinter, London and New York, 1990)

Spears, Major-General Sir Edward, *Two Men Who Saved France* (Stein & Day, New York, 1966)

Sternhell, Zeev, *Ni Droite, ni Gauche. L'Idéologie fasciste en France* (Editions Complexe, Brussels, 1987)

Tombs, Robert, 'The Dark Years' in the *Times Literary Supplement*, 28 January 1994

Winock, Michel, *Nationalisme, antisémitisme et fascisme en France* (Seuil, Paris, 1982)

Chapter III: Holding the Centre

Bainville, Jacques, *Les Conséquences politiques de la paix* (first published 1919, reprinted by Editions de l'Arsenal, Paris, 1995)

——, *Bismarck* (first published 1932, reprinted by Editions Godefroy de Bouillon, Paris, 1995)

——, *Histoire de deux peuples* (Fayard, Paris, 1933)

Berghahn, Volker, *Quest for Economic Empire: European Strategies of German Big Business in the 20th Century* (Berghahn Books, Providence, USA, and Oxford, England, 1996)

Chevènement, Jean-Pierre, *France–Allemagne. Parlons franc* (Plon, Paris, 1996)

Dehio, Ludwig, *Gleichgewicht oder Hegemonie* (Krefeld, Scherpe, 1948)

Desforges, Philippe Moreau, *Introduction à la géopolitique* (Seuil, Paris, 1994)

Duchêne, François, *Jean Monnet: The First Statesman of Interdependence* (W. W. Norton & Co., New York, 1994)

Dumont, Louis, *German Ideology: From France to Germany and Back* (University of Chicago Press, Chicago, 1994)

Ebeling, Frank, *Geopolitik. Karl Haushofer und seine Raumwissenschaft 1919–1945* (Akademie Verlag, Berlin, 1994)

Forsyth, Murray, *Unions of States: The Theory and Practice of Confederation* (New York, 1981)

Fuhrmann, Horst, 'Wer hat die deutschen zu Richtern über die Völker bestellt? Die deutschen als Ärgernis im Mittelalter': lecture by the President of the Bavarian Academy of Sciences in the Bavarian State Parliament on 23 January 1994, reprinted in *Matinee im Bayerischen Landtag* (Bayerischer Landtag, Munich, 1994)

Garton Ash, Timothy, *In Europe's Name: Germany and the Divided Continent* (Jonathan Cape, London, 1993)

de Habsbourg, Otto, *Europe: Champ de bataille ou grande puissance* (Hachette, Paris, 1966)

James, Harold, *A German Identity: 1770 to the Present Day* (Phoenix, London, 1994)

John of Salisbury, *Policraticus: Of the Frivolities of Courtiers and the Footprints of Philosophers*, edited and translated by Cary J. Nederman (CUP, Cambridge, 1990)

Kant, Immanuel, 'Zum Ewigen Frieden', see Band VI of the *Werke in 6 Bänden* (Insel Verlag, Frankfurt, 1964)

Kissinger, Henry, *Diplomacy* (Simon & Schuster, New York, 1994)

Korinman, Michel, *Quand l'Allemagne pensait le monde. Grandeur et décadence d'une géopolitique* (Fayard, Paris, 1990)

Mann, Thomas, *Betrachtungen eines Unpolitischen* (first published Berlin, 1918, reprinted by Fischer Verlag, Frankfurt, 1991)

Marienstras, Richard, *Le Proche et le Lointain; sur Shakespeare, le drame élisabéthain et l'idéologie anglaise au XVIe et XVIIe siècles* (Minuit, Paris, 1981)

Röhl, John C. G., *The Kaiser and his Court: Wilhelm II and the Government of Germany* (CUP, Cambridge, 1994)

Roussakis, Emmanuel N., *Friedrich List, the Zollverein and the Uniting of Europe* (College of Europe, Bruges, 1968)

Schöllgen, Gregor, *Die Macht in der Mitte Europas: Stationen deutscher Außenpolitik von Friedrich dem Groben bis zur Gegenwart* (C. H. Beck, Munich, 1992)

Schwarz, Hans-Peter, *Die Zentralmacht Europas: Deutschlands Rückkehr auf die Weltbühne* (Siedler Verlag, Berlin, 1994)

Sheehan, Michael, *The Balance of Power: History and Theory* (Routledge & Kegan Paul, London, 1996)

Soutou, Georges-Henri, *L'Or et le Sang: les buts économiques de la première guerre mondiale* (Fayard, Paris, 1989)

de Stael, Germaine, *De l'Allemagne* (1810)

Stern, Fritz, *Gold and Iron: Bismarck, Bleichröder, and the Building of the German Empire* (Alfred A. Knopf, New York, 1977)

Szporluk, Roman, *Communism and Nationalism: Karl Marx versus Friedrich List* (OUP, Oxford, 1988)

Taylor, A. J. P., *The Course of German History* (Hamish Hamilton, London, 1945)

Triepel, Heinrich, *Unitarismus und Föderalismus im Deutschen Reich* (Tübingen, 1906)

——, *Die Hegemonie: ein Buch von führenden Staaten* (W. Kohl-hammer Verlag, Stuttgart and Berlin, 1938)

Weidenfeld, Werner, *Der deutsche Weg* (Siedler Verlag, Berlin, 1990)

Wollenberg, Jörg, *Les Trois Richelieu. Servir Dieu, le Roi et la Raison* (François-Xavier de Guibert, Paris, 1995)

Chapter IV: The European Ideology

Arendt, Hannah, *The Human Condition* (University of Chicago Press, Chicago, 1958)

——, 'Lectures on Kant's Political Philosophy', edited by Ronald Beiner (University of Chicago Press, Chicago, 1982)

Aristotle, *Politics*, translated by Benjamin Jowett, with introduction, analysis and index by H. W. C. Davis (Clarendon Press, Oxford, impression of 1926, first edition 1905)

Saint Augustine, *City of God*, translated by Henry Bettenson (Penguin, Harmondsworth, 1984)

Burke, Edmund, *Reflections on the Revolution in France* (first published 1790, edited by Conor Cruise O'Brien and reprinted by Penguin, Harmondsworth, 1986)

Collins, Stephen, *From Divine Cosmos to Sovereign State: An Intellectual History of Consciousness and the Idea of Order in Renaissance England* (OUP, Oxford, 1989)

Constant, Benjamin, *De l'Esprit de conquête et de l'usurpation* (first published 1814, reprinted by Flammarion, Paris, 1986)

Copleston, F. C., *Aquinas* (Penguin, Harmondsworth, 1955)

Cotta, Alain, *Le Corporatisme* (Presses Universitaires de France, Collection 'Que sais-je?', Paris, 1984)

Daujat, Jean, *Y a-t-il une verité?* (Tequi, Paris, 1974)

Disraeli, Benjamin, 'A Vindication of the English Constitution in a letter to a learned and noble lord' (London, 1835)

The Federalist, or the New Constitution: papers by Alexander Hamilton, James Madison and John Jay (The Heritage Press, New York, 1945)

Freund, Julien, *Qu'est-ce que la politique?* (Editions Sirey, Paris, 1965)

Gierke, Otto, *Political Theories of the Modern Age*, translated and with an introduction by F. W. Maitland (CUP, Cambridge, 1900; reprinted by Beacon Paperbacks, Boston, 1958)

Girardet, Raoul, *Mythes et mythologies politiques* (Seuil, Paris, 1986)

Halévy, Elie, *L'Ère des tyrannies. Études sur le socialisme et la guerre* (Gallimard, Paris, 1938)

Hall, Stuart, and Jacques, Martin (eds.), *New Times: The Changing Face of Politics in the 1990s* (Lawrence & Wishart, in association with *Marxism Today*, London, 1989)

Hart, H. L. A., *The Concept of Law* (Clarendon Press, Oxford, second edition 1994)

von Hayek, Friedrich, *The Constitution of Liberty* (Routledge & Kegan Paul, London, 1960)

——, *Law, Legislation and Liberty* (Routledge & Kegan Paul, London, 1973)

——, *The Counter-Revolution of Science: Studies in the Abuse of Reason* (Liberty Press, Indianapolis, 1979)

——, *The Fatal Conceit: The Errors of Socialism* (Routledge & Kegan Paul, London, 1988)

Kantorowicz, Ernst, *The King's Two Bodies: A Study in Medieval Political Theology* (Princeton University Press, Princeton, 1957)

Kelsen, Hans, *Reine Rechtslehre. Einleitung in die rechtswissenschaftliche Problematik* (F. Deuticke, Leipzig, 1934)

Macpherson, C. B., *The Political Theory of Possessive Individualism: Hobbes to Locke* (OUP, Oxford, 1962)

Malcolm, Noel, *Sense on Sovereignty* (Centre for Policy Studies, London, 1991)

Mathieu, Jean-Luc, *L'Union européenne* (Presses Universitaires de France, Collection 'Que sais-je?', Paris, 1994)

von Mises, Ludwig, *Human Action* (Yale University Press, New Haven, 1949)

Oakeshott, Michael, *On Human Conduct* (OUP, Oxford, 1975)

Ohmae, Kenichi, *The End of the Nation-State* (The Free Press, New York, 1995)

Schmitt, Carl, *Politische Theologie. Vier Kapitel zur Lehre von der Souveränität* (first published 1922, reprinted by Duncker & Humblot, Berlin, 1990)

——, *Der Begriff des Politischen* (first published 1932, third edition 1963, reprinted by Duncker & Humblot, Berlin, 1991)

Scruton, Roger, *The Philosopher on Dover Beach* (Carcanet, London, 1990)

Slama, Alain-Gerard, *L'Angélisme exterminateur. Essai sur l'ordre moral contemporain* (Grasset, Paris, 1993)

Villey, Michel, *Le Droit et les droits de l'homme* (Presses Universitaires de France, Paris, 1983)

Chapter V: Money Matters

Aristotle, *Nicomachean Ethics*, translated by David Ross (OUP, Oxford, 1986)

Bartley, Robert L., *The Seven Fat Years and How to Do it Again* (The Free Press, New York, 1992)

Binswanger, Hans Christoph, *Geld und Magie. Deutung und Kritik der modernen Wirtschaft anhand von Goethes 'Faust'* (Weitbrecht, Stuttgart and Vienna, 1985)

Buchan, James, *Frozen Desire: An Enquiry into the Meaning of Money* (Picador, London, 1997)

Burke, Edmund, *Discours sur la monnoie de papier* (Paris, 1790)

——, *Reflections on the Revolution in France* (first published 1790, edited by Conor Cruise O'Brien and reprinted by Penguin, Harmondsworth, 1986)

Carlile, William Warrand, *The Evolution of Modern Money* (Burt Franklin, New York, 1901, reprinted 1967)

de Ceco, Marcello, 'The Gold Standard' in *The New Palgrave Dictionary of Money and Finance* (Macmillan, London, 1992)

Cherlonneix, Bernard, 'Les degrés de la convertibilité monétaire' (unpublished paper)

Connolly, Bernard, *The Rotten Heart of Europe: The Dirty War for Europe's Money* (Faber & Faber, London, 1995)

Coquelin, Charles, *Dictionnaire de l'économie politique* (Hachette, Paris, 1854)

van Dormael, Armand, *La Guerre des Monnaies* (Editions Racine, Brussels, 1995)

Friedman, Milton, *Money Mischief: Episodes in Monetary History* (Harcourt Brace & Co., San Diego, New York and London, 1994)

Gallarotti, Giulio, *The Anatomy of an International Monetary Regime: The Classical Gold Standard 1880–1914* (OUP, Oxford, 1995)

de Gaulle, Charles, *Discours et messages*, Vol. 4 (Plon, Paris, 1970)

Guénon, René, *Le Règne de la quantité et les signes des temps* (Gallimard, Paris, 1945, reprinted 1972)

——, *Autorité spirituelle et pouvoir temporel* (Guy Tredaniel, Paris, 1984)

Hobbes, Thomas, *Leviathan* (Collins, London, 1983)

Hoppe, Hans-Hermann, 'How is Fiat Money Possible? Or, The Devolution of Money and Credit' in *The Review of Austrian Economics*, Vol. 7, No. 2, 1994

Lindsey, David E., and Wallich, Henry C., 'Monetary Policy', in *The New Palgrave Dictionary of Money and Finance* (Macmillan, London, 1992)

von Mises, Ludwig, *Human Action: A Treatise on Economics* (Contemporary Books Inc., Chicago, 1949, revised edition 1963)

——, *The Theory of Money and Credit* (Liberty Press, Indianapolis, 1980)

Nataf, Philippe, 'An inquiry into the free banking movement in nineteenth-century France, with particular emphasis on Charles Coquelin's writings' (William Lyons University, San Diego, 1987)

Rothbard, Murray, *Economic Thought Before Adam Smith* (Edward Elgar, London, 1995)

——, *Classical Economics* (Edward Elgar, London, 1995)

——, 'The Case for a Hundred-percent Gold Dollar' (pamphlet, no date or publisher)

Rueff, Jacques, *L'Ordre social* (Sirey, Paris, 1945)

——, *Monnaie saine ou état totalitaire* (SEDTF, Paris, 1947)

——, *L'Age de l'inflation* (Payot, Paris, 1963)

——, (and Roche, Emile, Chalandon, Albin, and de Largentaye, Rioust), *La Réforme du système monétaire international* (Editions France-Empire, Paris, 1967)

——, *Le Péché monétaire de l'Occident* (Plon, Paris, 1971)

Salin, Pascal, *L'Union monétaire européenne, au profit de qui?*, with a Preface by F. A. Hayek (Economica, Paris, 1980)

——, *La Verité sur la monnaie* (Editions Odile Jacob, Paris, 1990)

Shelton, Judy, *Money Meltdown: Restoring Order to the Global Currency System* (The Free Press, New York, 1994)

Smith, Vera, *The Rationale of Central Banking and the Free Banking Alternative* (first published by P. S. King & Son, London, 1936, reprinted by Liberty Press, Indianapolis, 1990)

Stützel, Wolfgang, *Über unsere Währungsverfassung* (Walter Eucken Institut Vorträge und Aufsätze No. 56, J. C. B. Mohr [Paul Siebeck], Tübingen, 1975)

Theurl, Theresia, 'Sprengsatz war immer das Budget: Die Vorläufer der Europäischen Währungsunion scheiterten an der Etatfinanzierung souveräner Staaten. Die Geldbünde des 19. Jahrhunderts' in *Frankfurter Allgemeine Zeitung*, 12 August 1995

Weatherford, Jack, *The History of Money* (Crown, New York, 1997)

White, Lawrence, *Free Banking in Britain: Theory, Experience and Debate, 1800–1845* (Institute of Economic Affairs, London, second edition 1995)

Journals
Auszüge aus Presseartikeln (Deutsche Bundesbank, Frankfurt)

Chapter VI: The Third Rome

Baranovsky, Vladimir, and Spanger, Hans-Joachim (eds.), *In from the Cold: Germany, Russia and the Future of Europe*, with a Foreword by Eduard Shevardnadze (Westview Press, Boulder, Colorado, 1992)

Buergenthal, Thomas, 'The CSCE Rights System' in *The George Washington Journal of International Law and Economics*, Vol. 25, No. 2, 1991

Bukovsky, Vladimir, *Jugement à Moscou. Un dissident dans les archives du Kremlin* (Robert Laffont, Paris, 1995)

Commission on Global Convergence, *Our Global Neighbourhood* (Oxford, 1995)

Gorbachev, Mikhail, *Perestroika: New Thinking for Our Country and the World* (HarperCollins, London, 1987)

Lisiecki, Jerzy, 'Financial and Material Transfers Between East and West Germany' in *Soviet Studies*, Vol. 42, No. 3, July 1990

Malcolm, Neil (ed.), *Russia and Europe: An End to Confrontation?* (Pinter, London, 1994)

Malcolm, Noel, *Bosnia: A Short History* (Macmillan, London, 1994)

Neumann, Iver, *Russia and the Idea of Europe* (Routledge & Kegan Paul, London, 1996)

Sakharov, Andrei, *Progress, Co-existence and Intellectual Freedom* (W. W. Norton & Co., New York, 1968)

Salisbury, Harrison E. (ed.), *Sakharov Speaks* (Collins/Harvill, London, 1974)

Thom, Françoise, *Les Fins du communisme* (Criterion, Paris, 1994)

——, 'Eurasisme et néo-eurasisme' in *Commentaire*, No. 66, 1994

Verluise, Pierre, *Le Nouvel Emprunt russe* (Odilon Média, Paris, 1995)

Journals
BBC Summary of World Broadcasts
Frankfurter Allgemeine Zeitung
Le Monde
Neue Zürcher Zeitung
Wall Street Journal Europe

INDEX

Page numbers in **bold** denote major section devoted to subject.

394

INDEX

D-Mark, 141, 143, 144, 152, 245, 257,
 322; depreciation of, 229, 246;
 dominance of within EMS, 249–50
dollar, US, 212, 213–14, 216
Doriot, Jacques, 50
Drieu La Rochelle, Pierre, 14
du Page, René Pichard, 58
Duboin, Jacques, 43–4
Dumas, Roland, 285–6
Dupuis, René, 64–5

Ebeling, Frank, 127
EC *see* European Community
'Economic Council', 38
economic integration: and 'European
 Confederation', 32–5, 37–8, 38–9;
 and Nazi 'European Economic
 Community' conference, 30–2, 36,
 40, 42; and Nazi *Großraumwirtschaft*,
 26–30, 115; and *Zollverein* see
 Zollverein; *see also* EMU
Economic Security Council, 311, 312
economism, 159, 203; and democracy,
 163–7
ecu: change in name to Euro, 143
Editions de la Toison d'Or, Les, 68
EEC (European Economic Community),
 22, 75, 93, 268
EFTA (European Free Trade
 Association), 138
EMS (European Monetary System), 143,
 249–51
EMU (European Monetary Union), 6,
 139–44, 166, 167, 174, 206, 214;
 compared with German monetary
 union, 167; constitutional
 implications, **254–6**; disadvantages,
 257, 321–2; France and, 140;
 Germany and, 322; steps in
 consolidating German hegemony
 over, 141–4; undemocratic nature of,
 7–8, 166; *see also* single currency
England *see* Britain
enterprise association, 192, 198
ERM (Exchange Rate Mechanism), 226,
 236, 240, 249, 250, 251

Esprit, 62, 64, 65; in Belgium, 66, 71;
 and fascism, 65–6; and Nazism, 67;
 prospering of in France, 71–2
Esprit Nouveau, 66
ethnic conflict, 284–6
EU (European Union), 136, 142, 163,
 165, 262, 292, 314, 319, 327; and
 'concentric circles' proposal, 146; and
 sovereignty, **173–7**; and subsidiarity,
 172; and WEU, 262, 264, 317
Eurasianism, 300–3
Euro, 143–4, 144, 257
Europa, 13
Europe: decline, 324; map of according
 to Genscher, 154; view of divided,
 16, 59
European Central Bank, 7, 147, 165–6,
 213, 256; constitutional implications
 of, 254–5; and independence, 244;
 modelled on Bundesbank, 141–2,
 144, 255
European Coal and Steel Community
 (ECSC), 75, 88
European Commission, 7, 50, 75, 165,
 166, 256
European Communities Act (1972), 169
European Community (EC), 89, 106,
 138; institutions seen as
 undemocratic, 163; primacy of law
 over national, 142, 164, 169, 173–4
European Confederation, 32–5, 37–8,
 38–9
European Court of Human Rights, 319
European Court of Justice, 174
European Customs Union, 120
European Economic Community
 conference (1942), 30–2, 36, 40, 42
European Economic Community *see*
 EEC
European Federal Union, 120
European federalists *see* federalists,
 European
European integration: and abolition of
 borders, 200, 207, 300, 311–12, 314;
 attempts at after First World War,
 119–20; and centralisation of

multinational companies, 3, 160
Munich agreement, 75–6
Mussert, Anton Adriaan, 24
Mussolini, Benito, 19, 47, 48

Napoleon, 60, 112
nation-states, 168, 171; fascist contempt
    for, **14–23**, 48; German view of, 6,
    90; hostility towards, 3, 62, 159, 160;
    replacement of by region-state, 3,
    160; seen as encouraging war, 6, 18,
    161–2; and technological
    development, 23–4; *see also*
    sovereignty
national liberation movements, 101
national minorities: exploitation of by
    Russia, 303–7; and OSCE, 314–17
National Socialist Party, 13, 46
nationalism, 6, 11, 87; European
    ideology and myth of, **282–9**, 303;
    fascist view of, 20–1; OSCE and
    'aggressive', 315
NATO (North Atlantic Treaty
    Organisation), 312; agreement with
    Russia (1997), 270; enlargement
    proposal, 263, 264, 278; and France,
    264, 281; and national sovereignty,
    175, 176; Russian hostility towards,
    266, 267, 268, **275–8**, 280, 298, 299,
    300; Russian *volte-face* over, 281–2;
    summit (1996), 260, 281
Natural Justice, 184, 185
Natural Law, 184–5
Nazis, 301; and 'clearing' system, 40;
    economic policy, **44**; and European
    Economic Community conference,
    30–2, 36, 40, 42; and
    Großraumwirtschaft, **26–30**, 115;
    hatred of balance of power policy,
    128–33; hostility towards gold
    standard, **39–46**; ideology, 14;
    plans for European integration, 26,
    32–9, 128; propaganda on Germany
    as model for European integration,
    129–31; rejection of nation-state,
    15–19, 26; and sovereignty, 15–16,

19, 37–8; stress on harmonious
    European integration, 36, 37, 38;
    technological development and
    Europe, 24
neo-corporatism, 323
New Europe, The, 130
Nixon, Richard, 235, 267

Oakeshott, Michael, 190–1, 192, 198
Oesterheld, Alfred, 29–30
Ohmae, Kenichi, 160
one-worldism, **307–11**, 314
Order of the Templars, 217
Ordre Nouveau, 62, 63–4, 65, 72, 74
OSCE (Organisation for Security and
    Co-operation in Europe), 269–70,
    284, **312–20**; compliance over
    Chechen war, 316–19; mission sent
    to Russia, 272, 273; and national
    minorities, 314–17; neutralisation of
    Western Europe, 318; and Russia,
    269, 276, 280, 298–9, 312–13, 314,
    316–19; *see also* CSCE
Ostpolitik, 134–5, 265
Ouest, 70

Pact of Tashkent, 276
pan-European integration, **261–70**
Pan-European Union, 120
paper currencies (fiat), 221–2, 236,
    237–8, 239, **240–4**, 249, 257
Paxton, Robert, 51
Peel, Sir Robert, 256–7
Pellizi, Camillo, 21–2, 23
Perroux, François, 67, 72, 74
personalism, **62–6**, 71; *see also* Mounier,
    Emmanuel
personhood, 178, 179
Pétain, Marshal, 7, 45, 61, 76, 77, 78;
    and collaboration with Germany, 49,
    51, 54, 57–8, 253; on France's defeat,
    71–2
Peter the Great, 302
Pfeffer, Karl-Heinz, 15
Pflug, Dr Hans, 131
Philip the Fair, 217